MySQL™

Your visual blueprint™ to open source database management

by Michael Moncur

D1540662

Visual

From

maranGraphics®

&

Wiley Publishing, Inc.

MySQL™: Your visual blueprint™ to open source database management

Published by
Wiley Publishing, Inc.
909 Third Avenue
New York, NY 10022

Published simultaneously in Canada

Library of Congress Control Number: 2002110260

ISBN: 0-7645-1692-2

Manufactured in the United States of America

10 9 8 7 6 5 4 3 2 1

1V/SR/RQ/QS/IN

Trademark Acknowledgments

Important Numbers

For U.S. corporate orders, please call maranGraphics at 800-469-6616 or fax 905-890-9434.

For general information on our other products and services or to obtain technical support, please contact our Customer Care Department within the U.S. at 800-762-2974, outside the U.S. at 317-572-3993, or fax 317-572-4002.

Permissions

maranGraphics

Certain text and illustrations by maranGraphics, Inc., used with maranGraphics' permission.

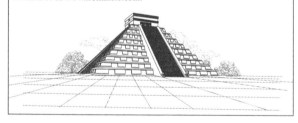

Was it a monument? A temple? Perhaps the giant Pyramid of Kukulkán, called El Castillo by Spanish visitors to the ancient Mayan city of Chichén-Itzá, was both, and more. Built with mathematical precision, it dominates the city from every direction, and is among the most recognized ancient landmarks. Explore the mysteries of Chichén-Itzá in *Frommer's Cancún, Cozumel and the Yucatán,* available wherever books are sold or at www.frommers.com.

Wiley Publishing, Inc. is a trademark of Wiley Publishing, Inc.

U.S. Corporate Sales	U.S. Trade Sales
Contact maranGraphics at (800) 469-6616 or fax (905) 890-9434.	Contact Wiley at (800) 762-2974 or fax (317) 572-4002.

MySQL™

Your visual blueprint™ to open source database management

maranGraphics is a family-run business located near Toronto, Canada.

At **maranGraphics**, we believe in producing great computer books — one book at a time.

maranGraphics has been producing high-technology products for over 25 years, which enables us to offer the computer book community a unique communication process.

Our computer books use an integrated communication process, which is very different from the approach used in other computer books. Each spread is, in essence, a flow chart — the text and screen shots are totally incorporated into the layout of the spread. Introductory text and helpful tips complete the learning experience.

maranGraphics' approach encourages the left and right sides of the brain to work together — resulting in faster orientation and greater memory retention.

Above all, we are very proud of the handcrafted nature of our books. Our carefully-chosen writers are experts in their fields, and spend countless hours researching and organizing the content for each topic. Our artists

rebuild every screen shot to provide the best clarity possible, making our screen shots the most precise and easiest to read in the industry. We strive for perfection, and believe that the time spent handcrafting each element results in the best computer books money can buy.

Thank you for purchasing this book. We hope you enjoy it!

Sincerely,

Robert Maran

President
maranGraphics
Rob@maran.com
www.maran.com

CREDITS

Acquisitions, Editorial, and Media Development

Project Editor
Sarah Hellert

Acquisitions Editor
Jen Dorsey

Product Development Supervisor
Lindsay Sandman

Copy Editor
Jill Mazurczyk

Technical Editor
Scott Hofmann

Editorial Manager
Rev Mengle

Permissions Editor
Carmen Krikorian

Media Development Specialist
Megan Decraene

Manufacturing
Allan Conley
Linda Cook
Paul Gilchrist
Jennifer Guynn

Production

Book Design
maranGraphics®

Production Coordinator
Nancee Reeves

Layout
Beth Brooks
Melanie DesJardins
Carrie Foster
LeAndra Johnson
Kristin McMullan
Heather Pope
Erin Zeltner

Screen Artists
Jill A. Proll

Cover Illustration
David E. Gregory

Proofreader
Laura L. Bowman

Quality Control
John Bitter
Dave Faust
John Greenough
Angel Perez
Dwight Ramsey

Indexer
Liz Cunningham

Special Help
Cricket A. Krengel

ACKNOWLEDGMENTS

Wiley Technology Publishing Group: Richard Swadley, Vice President and Executive Group Publisher; Bob Ipsen, Vice President and Executive Publisher; Barry Pruett, Vice President and Publisher; Joseph Wikert, Vice President and Publisher; Mary Bednarek, Editorial Director; Mary C. Corder, Editorial Director; Andy Cummings, Editorial Director.

Wiley Production for Branded Press: Debbie Stailey, Production Director

ABOUT THE AUTHOR

Michael Moncur is the author of many books on system administration and Web development topics. He has recently written books about JavaScript and DHTML. He works as an independent network consultant and Web programmer.

Michael also manages and maintains several popular Web sites. His oldest and most popular site, The Quotations Page, has been online since 1994. Most of the site's content is stored in a MySQL database, and presented using PHP. Michael lives with his wife, Laura, in a suburb of Salt Lake City, Utah.

AUTHOR'S ACKNOWLEDGMENTS

I am continually amazed at how complicated it is to write and publish a computer book. Fortunately, a great deal of this complexity was handled smoothly by the team at Wiley. This began with Jen Dorsey, the acquisitions editor, who was instrumental in getting the project started and keeping it running smoothly. The project editor, Sarah Hellert, communicated with me constantly, managed every detail of the production, and helped me figure out the intricacies of the visual format I have grown to love.

The copy editor, Jill Mazurczyk, saved me from many embarrassing errors and kept the style consistent. The technical editor, Scott Hofmann, painstakingly tested all of the examples, helped me avoid technical errors, and made some valuable suggestions about content and coverage. Thanks are also due to the many people in the graphics and production departments who handled the final details.

I'd also like to thank Neil Salkind at Studio B, for his help in getting this project lined up and keeping it going, and David and Sherry Rogelberg, Jessica Richards, and the rest of the team at Studio B. Finally, thanks to my wife, Laura, and the rest of my friends and family.

Dedicated to my wife, Laura, my parents, and everyone else
who sees less of me while I'm busy writing.

TABLE OF CONTENTS

MYSQL:
Your visual blueprint to open
source database management

3) MODIFY TABLES

4) ADD AND DELETE DATA

5) UPDATE DATA IN TABLES

TABLE OF CONTENTS

6) USING SELECT QUERIES

7) USING MYSQL FUNCTIONS

MYSQL:
Your visual blueprint to open
source database management

8) IMPORT AND EXPORT DATA

9) MANAGE THE MYSQL SERVER

10) OPTIMIZE AND TROUBLESHOOT MYSQL

TABLE OF CONTENTS

MYSQL:
Your visual blueprint to open
source database management

APPENDIX A

APPENDIX B

APPENDIX C

INDEX

MySQL: Your visual blueprint to open source database management uses simple, straightforward examples to teach you how to create powerful and dynamic programs.

To get the most out of this book, you should read each chapter in order, from beginning to end. Each chapter introduces new ideas and builds on the knowledge learned in previous chapters. When you become familiar with *MySQL: Your visual blueprint to open source database management*, you can use this book as an informative desktop reference.

Who This Book Is For

If you are interested in creating databases, applications, and data-driven Web sites using MySQL, *MySQL: Your visual blueprint to open source database management* is the book for you.

This book introduces you to the SQL language that forms the foundation of MySQL as well as the specific commands, utilities, and features unique to MySQL. It also covers the use of MySQL with the popular PHP and Perl languages for creating dynamic, database-backed Web pages.

Although this book requires no prior experience with databases or SQL, a basic familiarity with either Windows or UNIX servers is an asset.

What You Need to Use This Book

To perform the tasks in this book, you need a computer to run the MySQL server. This can be either a machine running Windows 98, ME, NT, 2000, or XP; or a machine running a UNIX-based operating system such as Linux.

The MySQL server software is available at no charge, and installing it on your system is detailed in Chapter 1.

The Conventions in This Book

A number of typographic and layout styles have been used throughout *MySQL: Your visual blueprint to open source database management* to distinguish different types of information.

Courier Font

Indicates the use of MySQL commands, command-line utilities, HTML tags and attributes, and commands in PHP or Perl.

Bold

Indicates information that you must type.

Italics

Indicates a new term.

Apply It

An Apply It section usually contains a segment of code that takes the lesson you just learned one step further. Apply It sections offer inside information and pointers that you can use to enhance the functionality of your code.

Extra

An Extra section provides additional information about the task you just accomplished. Extra sections often contain interesting tips and useful tricks to make working with MySQL easier and more efficient.

Please note that the majority of the tasks in this book are performed using the MySQL monitor. Chapter 1 explains how to start the MySQL monitor. The tasks in later chapters assume that the reader knows how to start the monitor or another MySQL client.

MYSQL:
Your visual blueprint to open
source database management

The Organization of this Book

MySQL: Your visual blueprint to open source database management contains 13 chapters and three appendices.

The first chapter, "Introducing MySQL," introduces the basics of MySQL and describes the components of a MySQL system. It shows you how to install MySQL's client and server software and to start client software, such as the MySQL monitor.

Chapter 2, "Manage Databases and Tables," introduces you to the MySQL commands for creating and deleting databases and tables. It describes the column types supported in MySQL tables and shows you how to create tables using them.

Chapter 3, "Modify Tables," introduces the MySQL commands for modifying tables and demonstrates various changes you can make to existing tables, as well as indexes and table options.

Chapter 4, "Add and Delete Data," introduces the commands you can use in MySQL to add data to tables and delete existing data. You are also shown how to use some special column types in MySQL tables.

Chapter 5, "Update Data in Tables," describes the MySQL commands for modifying data in existing tables. Tasks demonstrate a variety of common procedures for updating the data in a table.

Chapter 6, "Using SELECT Queries," explains how you can use SELECT commands to retrieve data from MySQL tables in a variety of ways. It begins with basic queries and proceeds to advanced options, such as multiple-table queries.

Chapter 7, "Using MySQL Functions," introduces you to the functions included with MySQL. You can use these with any MySQL command to process numeric and text data and to test conditions.

Chapter 8, "Import and Export Data," describes how to use MySQL commands to export data to text files and import data into a MySQL table. It also explains how to export data to MySQL from applications like Microsoft Access and Excel.

Chapter 9, "Manage the MySQL Server," describes the commands you can use to start and stop the server, and check version information and server status. It also introduces Windows-based utilities that provide a friendly administration interface.

Chapter 10, "Optimize and Troubleshoot MySQL," shows you how to optimize tables, check for errors and repair damaged tables, and check on and improve the performance of a MySQL server.

Chapter 11, "Configure MySQL Security," describes MySQL's security features and shows how you can use them to configure users, control privileges, and manage passwords.

Chapter 12, "Using MySQL with PHP," describes how you can use the PHP language with MySQL to create database-driven Web sites and other applications.

Chapter 13, "Using MySQL with Perl," shows how you can use the Perl language to connect to MySQL databases and create dynamic Web sites and applications.

Appendix A is a glossary of common MySQL and database terms, which you'll find useful as you work your way through this book.

Appendix B is a reference with detailed information about the most important MySQL commands and utilities.

Appendix C includes detailed information about the CD-ROM included with this book.

What's on the CD-ROM

The CD-ROM included in this book contains SQL files you can use to create the example tables used throughout this book. It also includes several open-source software applications, including MySQL itself. Finally, the PHP and Perl code used in Chapters 12 and 13 is included in its entirety. An e-version of the book and all the URLs mentioned in the book are also available on the disc.

UNDERSTANDING MYSQL

Whenever you need to store large amounts of data, whether for a corporate accounting system or a large Web site, a *database* provides many advantages. A database system allows you to store and work with many types of data, and a database server handles many of the data management tasks in an efficient way.

DATABASE BASICS

MySQL is a *relational database management system*, or *RDBMS*. This type of system stores one or more databases, each of which can contain tables of data of various types. Here is a simple example of a table with names and addresses:

This table includes three rows, or individual entries. Each one stores a person's name and address information. Each item of information, such as an address or name, is called a *column*, also known as a *field*.

NAME	ADDRESS	CITY	STATE
Henry J. Tillman	321 Elm St.	Sacramento	CA
John Smith	122 Oak St.	New York City	NY
Amy Johnson	333 Poplar Lane	Chicago	IL

Relational Databases

While it is quite useful to store data in simple tables like this, the strength of a relational database system is that you can link data between multiple tables. For example, you may have a separate table of names and phone numbers:

NAME	PHONE
Henry J. Tillman	713-555-2395
John Smith	212-555-9344
Amy Johnson	312-555-2904

Because this table uses the same names as the address table, you can easily find the address and phone number for a name by connecting information in the two tables. By looking at several different tables, the database server can manage complex systems of data easily.

Client-Server Systems

MySQL, like most RDBMS systems, is a *client-server* system. In this type of system, a server manages the actual data storage. One or more clients can connect to the server, send it data or request data, and obtain their results from the server.

Client-server systems are powerful because the server can focus on data management without worrying about the user interface or other issues. Different types of clients or multiple clients can connect to the server simultaneously.

The MySQL client sends a request, or *query*, to the server. This may be a request for a certain record or group of records from a database, a request to add data to the database, or any of several other types of requests. The server receives the query and sends a result back to the client.

HOW MYSQL WORKS

MySQL consists of client components and server components. The basic components of MySQL are described in the sections below.

Hardware

The MySQL server runs on many different types of hardware. PC systems running Linux or 32-bit Windows are the most common hardware used. The hardware required for the server depends on how busy the server will be with client requests.

Client Software

A simple MySQL client, the MySQL monitor, is included with the server software. You can also use any client that knows the correct protocols to communicate with the server. Another such client, MySQLGUI, is described later in this chapter.

Server Software

The MySQL server software is available from MySQL AB. You can find their Web page at www.mysql.com/. The MySQL server is available free of charge for non-commercial use under the open source Gnu Public License (GPL). You can download the software and install it on a Windows, Linux, or other machine.

Programming Languages

In addition to the existing MySQL clients, you can use programming languages such as PHP and Perl to create applications that can communicate with a MySQL server. This allows you to create custom client software for virtually any purpose.

MYSQL AND THE WEB

MySQL's most popular use is as a back-end system for Web sites. This is largely due to the fact that most of the systems that run the popular Apache Web server can also run the MySQL server. MySQL is also included with many Linux distributions, and can be installed as an option during the installation of Linux.

Simple Web Sites

A basic Web site uses simple, flat HTML (hypertext markup language) files and has no need for a database. While this is sufficient for a simple home page, if your site needs to display large amounts of data, the number of HTML files quickly becomes difficult to manage.

Web Languages

PHP is a popular language for use with MySQL. It uses a friendly syntax, has powerful features, and has support for all of MySQL's functions built in. Creating MySQL applications using PHP is simple, and is described in Chapter 12.

Perl is another popular Web language, and one of the oldest languages used on the Web. While its syntax is a bit more difficult to master, Perl is a powerful language. Like PHP, it supports all of the MySQL client functions. You can learn more about using Perl with MySQL in Chapter 13.

Database-Backed Web Sites

When you use a database to manage a Web site, all of the data is divided into convenient pieces and stored on the MySQL server. You can then use a language such as Perl or PHP to dynamically build the HTML pages for the site based on the data from the server.

This has several advantages over a simple Web site: first, the data is stored in a central location and is easy to back up, restore, or move to a different server. Second, the data can be dynamically assembled as needed — rather than static pages, you can easily create search engines and other interactive features. Third, rather than editing HTML files when you need to update the site, you can use a simple MySQL client to enter or modify data from a friendly interface.

Most importantly, a database allows you to separate the content of the site from the format it is displayed in. When you want to change the look of the site, you can make some simple changes to the program that displays the data, and the look of thousands of pages can be changed.

MYSQL TERMINOLOGY

Databases in general, and MySQL in particular, use a few terms you may be unfamiliar with. The following is an overview of some of the MySQL terms you will encounter throughout this book.

MySQL Server

The *MySQL server* is a software service that runs on a computer, typically a UNIX or Windows machine. The MySQL server accepts requests from clients and sends results back to them.

MySQL Client

A *MySQL client* is an application that sends requests to a MySQL server and works with the resulting data. A simple command-line client comes with the MySQL server software. Applications written in Web languages such as PHP and Perl can act as customized MySQL clients.

Database

A *database* is a file structure for organizing data, and consists of one or more tables. The MySQL server can store any number of databases, and clients can work with them concurrently.

Table

A *table* is a unit of data storage within a database. Each database can contain one or more tables. Tables are defined with a set number and type of columns, and can contain any number of rows.

Column (or Field)

The *columns*, or *fields*, define the types of data stored in a database table. For example, a table that stores a mailing list may include columns called Name, Address, City, and State. A table can have one or more columns. Each column is defined with the type of data it will store — for example, a number, a string of text, or a date.

Row (or Record)

Each entry in the database is a *row*, and each row includes a data item for each column. For example, in a mailing list table, each combination of name and address would form one row of the table. Rows can be added, removed, or modified at any time. When clients request data, it is returned in rows. Rows are also known as *records*.

Primary Key

In order to access a single record in a database table, the server needs a unique identifier for each row. The *primary key* is a column chosen to be this unique identifier. For example, the name would be an appropriate primary key for an address database. Each table can have one primary key consisting of one or more columns.

Index

The database server stores extra information about the values used in the primary key field in an index. This allows for faster searching by this field. You can also specify that other fields in a table be indexed if they will be searched on frequently. These indexes are known as secondary keys.

Query

Each request that a MySQL client sends to a server is called a *query*. Queries use SQL, or *Structured Query Language*. A query can request one or more rows of data, or request that an action be performed — for example, adding a new row or deleting an existing row.

SQL

SQL, or *Structured Query Language*, is the language used in MySQL queries. SQL is a standardized language that uses commands to perform various functions on the database server. Examples of SQL commands include `INSERT` to add a row to a table and `SELECT` to find one or more rows within a table.

OTHER DATABASE SYSTEMS

While this book focuses on MySQL, it is actually just one of several *database management systems*, also known as *DBMS*, that you may find useful. Many of these systems use similar languages and can be used interchangeably, and you can choose whichever server fits the needs of your application.

MySQL is neither the simplest nor the most sophisticated of database systems. The following are some of the other popular systems, ranging from simpler than MySQL to far more sophisticated.

Flat File Database

The most basic of databases does not use a DBMS at all. Applications can simply store data in one or more files. This is the traditional approach used by many simple applications such as spreadsheets. Languages such as Perl have features that allow you to use DBMS-like features to manage simple files. The advantage of this approach is that it can run on many platforms and does not require a database server, but it offers few of the advantages of a true database management system.

Microsoft Access

Microsoft Access is by far the most popular desktop database software and is available as part of the Microsoft Office suite. Access uses an internal DBMS that stores data in local files, and the ability to share files between networked computers is limited. Nevertheless, it is useful for simple applications and has a friendly user interface. Access can also work as a client for Microsoft SQL Server, and includes tools to simplify the migration of Access databases to SQL Server.

mSQL

Mini SQL from Hughes Technologies, known more popularly as mSQL, is another popular choice as the back end of Web sites. Similar to MySQL in language and functionality, mSQL's advantages are also similar to those of MySQL: Its server software is lightweight, can run on machines with limited resources, and is supported by many programming languages. mSQL is a commercial product, but free copies are available for educational users and nonprofit organizations.

PostgreSQL

PostgreSQL is another popular DBMS and an alternative to MySQL. It is free and open source software. PostgreSQL supports some features of the SQL language beyond what MySQL supports, and offers features like transaction support that may make it a better choice for high-end applications. PostgreSQL can be run on most Linux and UNIX systems.

Microsoft SQL Server

While Access is a simple desktop database, Microsoft SQL Server is a full-featured client-server DBMS. The server software runs exclusively on Windows NT, 2000, and XP systems. The advantages of SQL Server include its wide support in Windows-based applications and its reliability, which has led to its use by many corporations, banks, and even stock exchanges.

Oracle

Oracle is a high-end DBMS popular for use in corporate databases and in larger and more critical Web sites. It supports transactions and other features for high reliability, availability, and speed. Its server software runs under UNIX or Windows systems. Visit Oracle's Web site at www.oracle.com for more information.

DB2

IBM's DB2 is a DBMS with a long history in mainframe computing. The latest version, DB2 Universal Database, runs under AIX, Windows, and most UNIX systems. It is another popular choice for banks and other corporations with critical data storage needs, and includes features that make it work well with Web standards such as Java and XML.

STRUCTURED QUERY LANGUAGE (SQL)

S QL (Structured Query Language) was first developed by IBM and is now a standard maintained by the ANSI, or American National Standards Institute. Most current DBMS systems follow the SQL standard to some degree. MySQL's query language is based on this standard.

The following is an overview of some of the most important commands in MySQL. You can use these commands from any MySQL client, such as the MySQL Monitor introduced later in this chapter. Each of these commands is explained in detail with examples in later chapters.

CREATE DATABASE

The CREATE DATABASE command creates the file structure for a new database and assigns it the name you specify. This command does not by itself store any data, but you must create a database before you can use it.

Example:
```
CREATE DATABASE testdb;
```

DROP DATABASE

The DROP DATABASE command deletes an existing database. Do not expect a friendly warning when using this command: The database is deleted immediately, without confirmation, including all tables and rows. Use this command with extreme caution.

Example:
```
DROP DATABASE testdb;
```

USE

The USE command selects a database for use by other commands. The database you specify with USE must already exist. The commands that work with tables and rows of data will only work if you have selected a database using this command.

Example:
```
USE testdb;
```

SHOW DATABASES

The SHOW DATABASES command displays a list of the databases that have been created on the MySQL server. The SHOW command can also be used to display tables for a database and other categories of information.

Example:
```
SHOW DATABASES;
```

CREATE TABLE

The CREATE TABLE command creates a table within the currently selected database. To create a table, you specify the fields (columns) it will contain and a field type for each one. The CREATE TABLE command can optionally include information about the keys and indexes available in the table. This command often requires multiple lines.

Example:
```
CREATE TABLE address (
    name CHAR(100),
    address CHAR(120),
    phone CHAR(10) );
```

DROP TABLE

The DROP TABLE command deletes a table from the currently selected database. All of the data stored in the table is permanently deleted and, as with the DROP DATABASE command, this happens instantly and without confirmation. Use this command with caution.

Example:
```
DROP TABLE address;
```

SHOW TABLES

The SHOW TABLES command displays a list of tables available in the currently selected database. You can use this command when you are unsure of the exact name of a table within the database.

Example:
```
SHOW TABLES;
```

INSERT

The INSERT command inserts a new row of data into an existing table within the currently selected database. You can specify a list of fields in the INSERT command along with values for each field. The INSERT command is described in detail in Chapter 4.

Example:
```
INSERT INTO address(name, address, phone)
    VALUES ('John Smith','321 Elm Street',
    '804-555-1234');
```

UPDATE

The UPDATE command alters one or more existing rows of data within a table. The WHERE keyword can be used with this command to specify one or more rows to alter. The command specifies new values for one or more of the fields within each row. These values can be based on existing fields or constant values specified within the command.

If you do not specify a WHERE clause, this command will update all of the rows in the table. While you will sometimes want to update all of the rows, using UPDATE without a WHERE clause can cause loss of data if you are not careful. Update queries are described in detail in Chapter 5.

Example:
```
UPDATE address SET phone = '801-555-1234'
    WHERE name = 'John Smith';
```

DELETE

The DELETE command deletes one or more rows of data within an existing table. The WHERE clause should be used to specify the rows that will be deleted. Use this command with care: If you omit the WHERE clause, all rows of data within the table are deleted. See Chapter 4 for further information about the DELETE command.

Example:
```
DELETE FROM address WHERE name = 'John Smith';
```

SELECT

The SELECT command retrieves one or more rows from a database. You can specify the columns to be returned or use the wildcard * to return values for all columns in the order they appear in the table definition. You can use a WHERE clause to specify one or more conditions that rows must match in order to be returned. If you do not use a WHERE clause, the specified columns from all of the rows in the database are returned.

Example:
```
SELECT name, address, phone FROM address
    WHERE name like '%Smith';
```

DOWNLOAD MYSQL

Before you can use MySQL, you need a working MySQL server. If you do not already have access to one, you can download the MySQL software from the MySQL Web site, www.mysql.com/, and install it on a computer running UNIX, Windows, or another supported operating system. MySQL is freely available for non-commercial use.

To access the downloadable files, click the Download link from the MySQL Web site and then click the link for the version of MySQL to install. At this writing, the current stable release is MySQL 3.23. Under this site's Download page, several different versions of MySQL are available. The version you should download depends on your operating system. For Windows, the choice is simple — a ZIP file is available with everything you need for installation.

The download for Red Hat Linux and other versions that support RPM packages is also simple. MySQL is divided into several packages for its different components: server software, client software, shared libraries, development files, and benchmarking utilities. You can install these using the `rpm` command.

If you have a different version of Linux or UNIX, the next alternative is to download the binary distribution. These are stored as tar.gz files, one for each of the five components. The installation process for these is slightly more complex, but easier than installing from source code.

Binary packages are available for Linux running under Intel (PC) systems, DEC Alpha, IA64, Sun Sparc, and S/390. Additional binary versions are available for other operating systems. If one is not available for your operating system, you can download the source code and compile and install it.

DOWNLOAD MYSQL

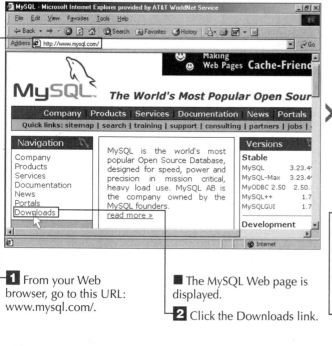

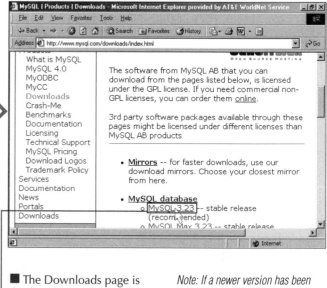

1 From your Web browser, go to this URL: www.mysql.com/.

■ The MySQL Web page is displayed.

2 Click the Downloads link.

■ The Downloads page is displayed.

3 Click the link for MySQL 3.23.

Note: If a newer version has been released, you can download the latest version instead.

Extra

Along with Windows and Linux, binary versions of the MySQL server are available for Solaris, FreeBSD, MacOS X, HP-UX, AIX, SCO, SGI Irix, DEC OSF, and BSDi UNIX. The tip in the next section describes the process of installing these binary distributions.

MySQL is actually available in multiple versions. The basic version, MySQL 3.23, should work for most purposes. The additional versions include MySQL-Max, which is the same version but includes support for additional types of tables and transactions.

Transactions are a feature used in mission-critical database systems, such as those at financial institutions. These systems allow you to begin a transaction, perform updates to the database, and then end the transaction. The server keeps track of the changes made during the transaction, allowing the server to roll back the entire transaction if it was not completed. This ensures that the database is not corrupted by partial transactions.

MySQL 4.0 is also under development at this writing. This release increases the speed of the MySQL server and clients and supports additional SQL statements.

Currently, unless you need the new features of MySQL-Max or MySQL 4.0, MySQL 3.23 is the safest choice.

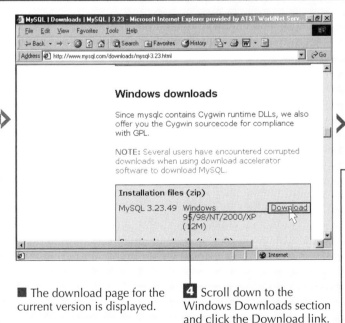

■ The download page for the current version is displayed.

4 Scroll down to the Windows Downloads section and click the Download link.

Note: For other operating systems, download the appropriate files instead.

■ A list of download locations is displayed.

5 Choose a download location near you and click the HTTP or FTP link.

■ You will be prompted for a location to save the downloaded file.

INSTALL MYSQL UNDER LINUX FROM A PACKAGE

I f you are using Linux, there is a good chance you can install MySQL from the package files in RPM format. This format was developed by Red Hat Linux, but is now supported by several other systems. Using packages is the simplest way to install the MySQL server. MySQL is distributed in several packages with different components.

The first package, `MySQL-version-i386.rpm`, contains the MySQL server software, and the second, `MySQL-client-version-i386.rpm`, contains the MySQL monitor and other client software. The third package, `MySQL-shared-version.i386.rpm`, contains shared files needed by the MySQL client software.

Two additional packages are available but not required: `MySQL-bench-version.i386.rpm` contains benchmarking and testing utilities, and `MySQL-devel-version.i386.rpm` contains development libraries and header files.

In most cases, installing all five packages is a good idea. If you have a limited amount of space, you can leave out the benchmarking package. You can also leave out the development files if you will not be using MySQL with programming languages such as Perl.

As with other MySQL distributions, you can download the package files from the Download section of the MySQL Web page at www.mysql.com/. Download all five of the RPM files, or only the files you will be installing, before beginning the installation process.

You install RPM packages using the package manager utility, `rpm`. This allows you to install complex software like MySQL with a minimum of user interaction. The disadvantage of this approach is that the software will be installed in the default location and with the default compilation settings. If you require different installation settings, you can install MySQL from the source packages, as described in the next task.

INSTALL MYSQL UNDER LINUX FROM A PACKAGE

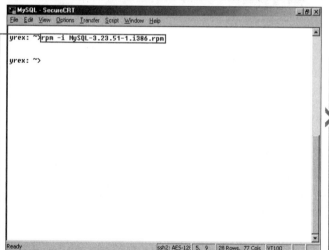

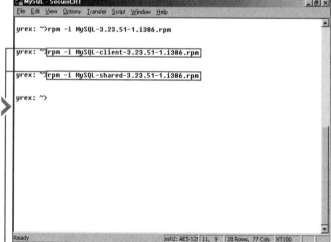

1 From the Linux command prompt, type **rpm -i MySQL-version.i386.rpm**, replacing *version* with the version number of the downloaded package, and press Enter.

Note: You should be logged on as the root user to install MySQL.

■ The software is installed. This may take several minutes to complete.

Note: The package manager automatically starts the MySQL server after the installation of this package.

2 Type **rpm -i MySQL-client-version.i386.rpm**, replacing *version* with the version number, and press Enter.

3 Type **rpm -i MySQL-shared-version.i386.rpm**, replacing *version* with the version number, and press Enter.

Note: You can stop here for a minimal installation of MySQL, or continue to install the other packages.

Extra If your particular operating system does not support RPM files, there is an alternative to installing from source code. Pre-compiled binaries for a variety of operating systems are available from the Download section at www.mysql.com. These are archived in the tar (tape archive) format and compressed with gzip, and typically have an extension of .tar.gz.

Binary files have the advantage of being much easier to install. The potential disadvantages are that you cannot customize the way MySQL is compiled, and that binary packages are available only for some operating systems and may not be as up to date as the source code version.

After you have downloaded the correct binary distribution for your operating system and hardware, you can use the following sequence of commands to install MySQL. This example assumes that you have the .tar.gz file stored in the /usr/local directory.

Example:
```
cd /usr/local
tar zxfv mysql-version-OS.tar.gz
ln -s mysql-version-OS mysql
cd mysql
scripts/mysql_install_db
```

This example stores the MySQL files in the /usr/local/mysql directory. The MySQL server is not yet running; you can start it by running /usr/local/mysql/bin/safe_ mysqld or following the instructions in the section "Start the MySQL Server," later in this chapter.

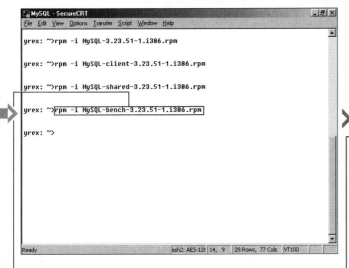

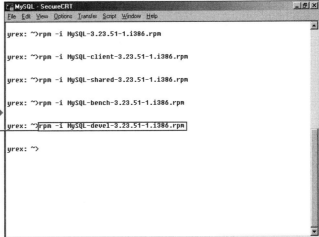

4 Type **rpm -i MySQL-bench-version.i386.rpm**, replacing *version* with the version number, and press Enter.

■ The benchmark files are now installed.

5 Type **rpm -i MySQL-devel-version.i386.rpm**, replacing *version* with the version number, and press Enter.

■ The development files are now installed. This completes the MySQL installation.

INSTALL MYSQL UNDER UNIX FROM SOURCE

I f you need to change MySQL's installation location or other options, or if there is no binary distribution of MySQL for your operating system or hardware, you can download the MySQL source code and install it from source. This process is mostly automated and is not much more difficult than installing a binary version.

The source code is distributed in a .tar.gz archive, and you can download it from the Download section of the MySQL Web page at www.mysql.com/. Before you begin the process of installing from source, copy this archive to your server at your choice of location. The instructions in this section assume your source archive is in the /usr/local/src directory.

Note that while Windows source code is also available, these instructions are for Linux and other UNIX-like systems. Compiling from source code in Windows is a more complex process — in most cases, the easiest thing to do is to use

the regular Windows installation files. The only reason to install from source is if there is no easier way to get MySQL running in your particular environment.

To install MySQL from source, first unpack the archive of source files. Next, use the `configure` program within the distribution to set up the correct options for your operating system. After this completes, use the `make` command to compile the source code, and the `make install` command to install the files.

This procedure compiles and installs all of the files you need to run the MySQL server, the client software, benchmarking and testing utilities, and to connect with programming languages such as Perl. The installation does not start the MySQL server; you will need to start it following the instructions presented in the section "Start the MySQL Server," later in this chapter.

INSTALL MYSQL UNDER UNIX FROM SOURCE

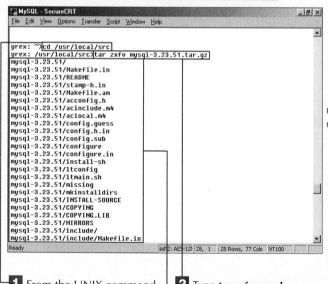

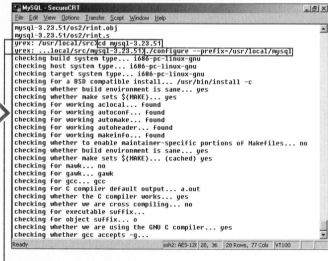

1 From the UNIX command prompt, type **cd /usr/local/src** to switch to the source directory, and press Enter.

2 Type **tar zxfv mysql-version.tar.gz**, replacing *version* with the correct version number, and press Enter.

■ The source files are uncompressed into a new directory.

3 Type **cd mysql-version**, replacing *version* with the correct version number, and press Enter.

4 Type **./configure --prefix=/usr/local/mysql** and press Enter.

■ MySQL is configured for your operating system and hardware.

Note: You may need additional configure options to compile MySQL. See the Extra section.

Extra

The `configure` script actually has a wide variety of options. If you have trouble compiling MySQL or need to change installation locations or other settings, you will need to use one or more of these options. You can type `configure --help` from the source distribution directory to view a list of these options. The table below shows some of the most useful options for `configure`:

OPTION	PURPOSE
`--help`	Display complete option list
`--without-server`	Install the MySQL client only, no server
`--prefix=path`	Use *path* as the installation directory
`--with-charset=CHAR`	Use CHAR instead of the standard (US English) character set

If you are installing MySQL from an operating system that supports RPM packages but still want to compile from source, you can use the source RPM distribution. Use this command to build a binary RPM from the source; you can then install the binary RPM in the normal way.

Example:

```
rpm --rebuild MySQL-version.src.rpm
```

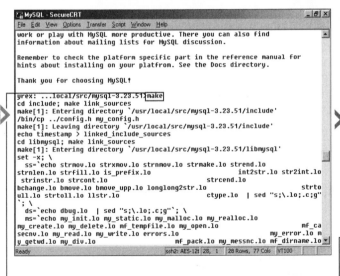

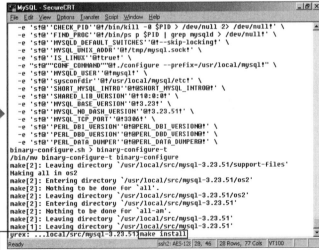

5 Type **make** and press Enter.

■ The MySQL files are now compiled. This may take several minutes. Watch for any compilation errors.

6 Type **make install** and press Enter.

■ The compiled MySQL program files are now installed.

Note: You need to be logged on as the root user on most systems to complete this last step.

INSTALL MYSQL UNDER WINDOWS

While Linux is the most common platform for MySQL, a Windows version is also available. You can install the MySQL server under any 32-bit version of Windows. Windows 2000, Windows XP, and the older Windows NT are the best platforms for the MySQL server because they are true multitasking systems and can run MySQL as a service.

The Windows version of MySQL requires that you have the TCP/IP protocol installed. This is installed by default on Windows 98, 2000, and XP. If you currently do not have this protocol installed, you can add it from the Network control panel. You will also need to upgrade to the latest Winsock drivers if you are running an early version of Windows 95.

One limitation of the MySQL server on some versions of Windows is that the FAT file system does not allow files larger than 4GB, and thus the tables in your databases will

be limited to this size. If you need to use larger tables, you can use the NTFS file system under Windows NT, 2000, or XP to overcome this limitation.

You can download the Windows version of MySQL from the Download section of the MySQL Web site at www.mysql.com/. Before installing MySQL, you need to expand the contents of the ZIP file into a folder. Be sure no other programs are running while you perform the installation.

After the ZIP file is expanded, you can run the installation program, `setup.exe`, to begin the installation. The installation provides three options: Typical, which installs the standard client and server files; Compact, which installs only the minimum files needed to run the server; and Custom, which allows you to choose which components to install.

INSTALL MYSQL UNDER WINDOWS

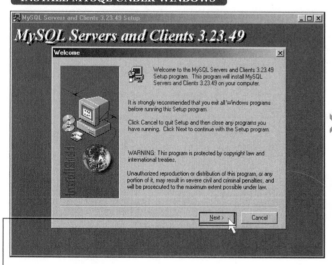

1 A Welcome dialog box is displayed. Click Next to continue with the installation.

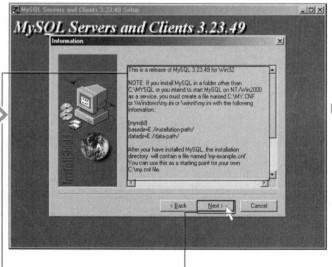

■ The release notes for this version of MySQL are displayed.

2 Click Next to continue.

Extra

The installation process places all of the files for MySQL in the c:\mysql directory by default. Within this directory, the following subdirectories are available:

DIRECTORY	PURPOSE
c:\mysql\bin	The server and client EXE files
c:\mysql\data	The database data storage area
c:\mysql\Docs	The MySQL documentation in HTML format
c:\mysql\bench	Benchmarking and testing utilities

Within the mysql\bin directory, two utilities unique to the Windows version are included. The first, `winmysqladmin.exe`, is a graphical utility that allows you to create users and passwords, edit MySQL server settings, and monitor the MySQL server's status.

The second utility, `MySqlManager.exe`, allows you to monitor one or more servers and to browse the data structure of the databases stored on the servers.

The configuration settings for the MySQL server are stored in the my.ini file, which the server looks for in c:\mysql by default. You can create this file using a text editor or the editor built into the `winmysqladmin.exe` utility.

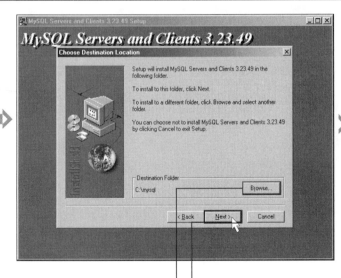

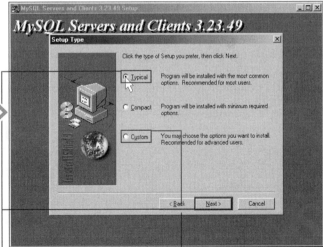

■ The Choose Destination Location dialog box is displayed.

3 Click Next to continue and install the components into the c:\mysql directory.

■ Click Browse if you need to choose a different directory.

■ The Setup Type dialog box is displayed.

4 Choose Typical for a standard installation and click Next.

■ Choose Custom if you want to select the components to install.

■ The MySQL server and client software is now installed. This may take a moment to complete.

START THE MYSQL SERVER

After you have installed the MySQL Server software, you can start the server. The server software is a *daemon*, a program that runs in the background and usually does not have a window or output of its own. The process of starting the MySQL server depends on your operating system.

Under Windows, the simplest way to start the server is to run the `c:\mysql\bin\mysqld-max` program from a DOS prompt. You can also use the `winmysqladmin` utility to set up the MySQL server to run as a service and start automatically when the computer is booted.

Under Linux or UNIX, you can start the server by executing the `safe_mysqld` program in the bin directory under the MySQL installation directory. You should log on using a user specifically created to run the MySQL server before starting MySQL. Depending on the installation method you used, a user account may have been created automatically.

The Linux installation of MySQL includes a script, `mysql.server`, in the share/mysql directory. This script can be used to start or stop the server. The following are the start and stop commands:

```
mysql.server start
mysql.server stop
```

You can use this script to automatically start the MySQL server. How to do this depends on the operating system you are using. In most versions of Linux, you can add the command to start the server to the /etc/rc.d/rc.local file to start MySQL when Linux starts.

If you are using the MySQL server for experimentation rather than for a production server, you can simply type `/bin/safe_mysqld &` from the command prompt. The `&` character indicates that the program will be run in the background. See Chapter 9 for more details about starting and stopping the MySQL server.

START THE MYSQL SERVER

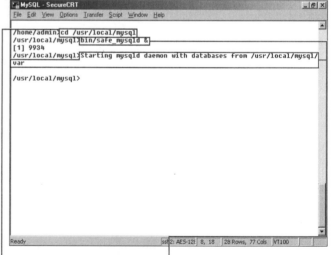

STARTING MYSQL UNDER WINDOWS

1 From a DOS prompt, type **c:\mysql\bin\mysqld-max** and press Enter.

■ The server starts in the background and returns you to the DOS prompt. It may take a moment to initialize.

Note: If you used a directory other than c:\mysql when installing, substitute the correct directory.

STARTING MYSQL UNDER LINUX

1 From the command prompt, type **cd /usr/local/mysql** to change to the directory where MySQL is installed.

Note: If you installed MySQL into a different directory, substitute its name here.

2 Type **bin/safe_mysqld &** and press Enter.

■ The MySQL server starts in the background.

TEST THE MYSQL INSTALLATION

After you have installed the MySQL server, you should test it to be sure it is running correctly. Because the MySQL server software runs in the background and does not provide any obvious evidence that it is running, you will need to use the utilities included with MySQL to communicate with the server and check on it.

The `mysqladmin` program in the bin directory of the installation can perform a wide variety of administration tasks, most of which will be introduced in Chapter 9. To check whether the server is running correctly, you can use two simple options, `mysqladmin status` and `mysqladmin variables`.

The `status` command in `mysqladmin` displays a summary of the server's current status, including the amount of time it has been running. Its output under Linux typically looks something like this example:

```
Uptime: 2938036   Threads: 3
Questions: 35941287
```

```
Slow queries: 5   Opens: 60462
Flush tables: 1
Open tables: 53
Queries per second avg: 12.233
```

You can also display this information using the MySQL monitor utility. You will learn how to do this in the next section.

The `variables` command displays the values of a number of MySQL settings. The variables themselves are not important for this test — if you see a list of variables at all, then `mysqladmin` has successfully communicated with the MySQL server, and you are ready to begin using the server to work with data.

The `mysqladmin` command works identically in Windows and Linux. In both systems, it is located in the bin directory under the directory where you installed MySQL. The steps below are shown using Linux; notes are included where the Windows version differs.

TEST THE MYSQL INSTALLATION

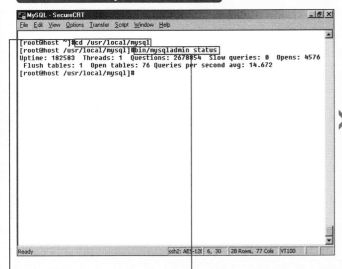

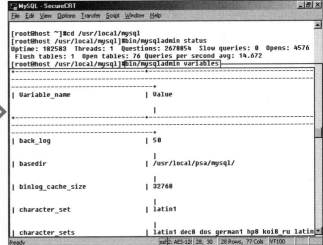

1 From the Linux command prompt, type **cd /usr/local/ mysql** to switch to the MySQL installation directory.

Note: In Windows, switch to the c:\mysql directory.

2 Type **bin/mysqladmin status** and press Enter.

Note: In Windows, type c:\mysql\bin\mysqladmin status.

■ The server's current status is displayed.

Note: If an Uptime value is not displayed, the server is either not running or you are not communicating with it.

3 Type **bin/mysqladmin variables** to display the variable values.

Note: In Windows, type c:\mysql\bin\mysqladmin variables.

■ The values are displayed.

USING THE MYSQL MONITOR

The *MySQL Monitor* is a command-line interface to MySQL and was installed when you installed the MySQL server. You can use the monitor to experiment with SQL commands, and you will use it throughout this book to work with MySQL databases.

MySQL uses a client-server architecture: the server interacts with one or more client applications, either on the same machine or different machines. The server deals with the actual data for the database, and the client makes requests and receives data from the server. The MySQL Monitor is a simple client for the MySQL server.

To start the monitor, use the `mysql` command from your operating system's command prompt. By default, the monitor will try to connect to a server on the local computer, using the current user's username and no password. If you need to access a server on a different computer or using a specific username or password, you will need to specify one or more options to the `mysql` command.

The options you will commonly use include `-uUSERNAME` to specify a username, `-pPASSWORD` to specify a password, and `-hHOST` to specify an address for the MySQL server.

When you are in the MySQL Monitor, the commands you can use include monitor commands and SQL queries. The results of your command or query are shown on the monitor screen.

You can type monitor commands, such as `EXIT` and `HELP`, directly. SQL queries can be long and can extend across multiple lines, so the monitor requires that you end each query with a semicolon (;). If you type a query and press Enter without including the semicolon, you are prompted for another line to add to the command.

USING THE MYSQL MONITOR

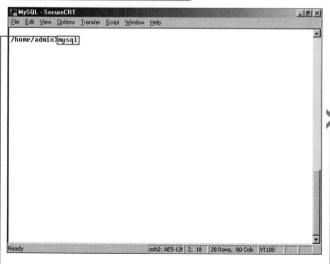

1 From the UNIX or DOS command prompt, type **mysql** to start the monitor.

Note: You may need to add a username, password, and host name to this command, depending on your server.

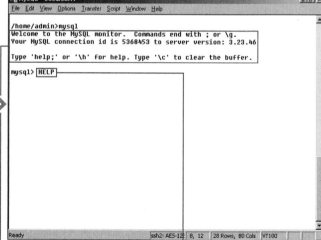

■ The MySQL Monitor displays a welcome message.

2 Type **HELP** at the monitor prompt to display a list of commands.

Extra

If an error message is displayed when you try to start the monitor, be sure you have correctly specified the username, password, and host name for the MySQL server. The following table lists some of the most useful options for the `mysql` command:

COMMAND	DESCRIPTION
-?	Display a complete list of options
-D	Select a database to use
-h	Specify the host (server name or IP address)
-p	Specify the password to access the server
-P	Specify the TCP/IP port number for the server
-u	Specify a username for the server
-V	Display the server version number

If your MySQL server is on the local machine, and you have created a username and password to access it, you only need to specify the username and password to start the MySQL Monitor.

Example:
```
mysql -uFRED -pPASSWORD
```

While monitor commands and SQL queries are typically shown in uppercase, such as EXIT and SHOW DATABASES, the commands are not case-sensitive, and you can type them in lowercase if you prefer.

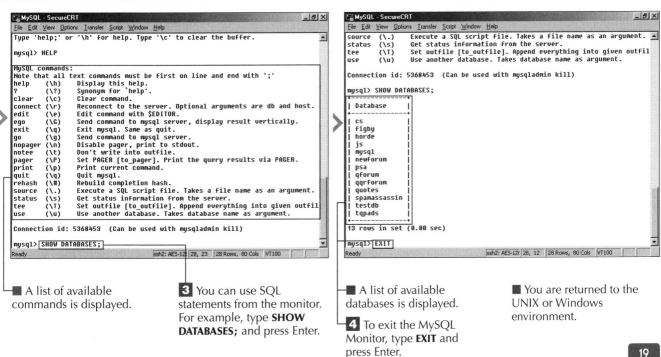

■ A list of available commands is displayed.

3 You can use SQL statements from the monitor. For example, type **SHOW DATABASES;** and press Enter.

■ A list of available databases is displayed.

4 To exit the MySQL Monitor, type **EXIT** and press Enter.

■ You are returned to the UNIX or Windows environment.

VIEW THE SERVER STATUS

You can use the STATUS command in the MySQL Monitor to view the current status of the MySQL server. This displays a table of basic status information for the server. This command is useful to verify that the server is running and to view details about your current client session.

The first section of the status display contains version information for the MySQL server. It displays the username and hostname you are currently using, the currently selected database, if any, and the length of time the server has been running since the last time it was started.

The last two lines of the status display provide a snapshot of the current performance of the server. *Threads* is the number of processes currently communicating with clients, *Questions* is the number of queries that have been processed since the server was started, and *Slow queries* is

the number of queries that have taken more than a typical amount of time to complete.

Opens is the number of times databases have been opened by clients, which increases as the server continues to run. *Open tables* is the number of tables currently in use by queries, a rough measure of how busy the server is. The last value, *Queries per second*, is a measure of the server's average speed in responding to queries from clients.

While this information can let you know at a glance whether the MySQL server is running and whether it is keeping up with its workload, you can also use the data displayed here to optimize the server's performance and detect potential errors and slowdowns before they become serious. You will learn more about this status information in Chapter 10.

VIEW THE SERVER STATUS

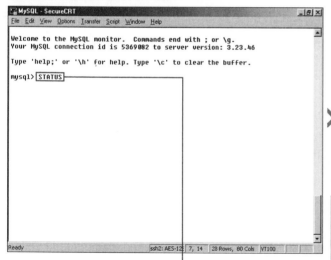

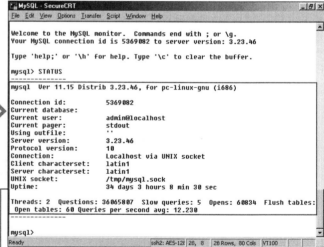

1 Start the MySQL Monitor by typing **mysql** at the command prompt.

2 Type **STATUS** and press Enter to display the server's current status.

■ The status information is displayed on the monitor screen.

TRY AN SQL QUERY

While you can use the MySQL Monitor to view status and other information about the server, you will find it most useful for testing MySQL queries and for using queries to work with data in databases.

A MySQL query begins with an SQL command, such as CREATE, INSERT, or SELECT. The remainder of the query specifies the parameters of the command. You must end each MySQL query with the ; (semicolon) character.

You can use a MySQL query at any time from the MySQL Monitor prompt. Some query commands, such as SELECT and INSERT, require that you first specify a database using the USE command. This command is explained in Chapter 2.

When you enter a query into the MySQL monitor, it is executed immediately by the MySQL server. The monitor displays the results of your query. For queries such as

SELECT, it will display the data you requested. For queries that affect the database, such as DELETE and INSERT, it will display a message informing you how many rows were affected by the query.

While the MySQL monitor is a great way to test MySQL queries and perform simple tasks, it is not the most efficient interface for complex database management. If you need to use a large number of queries, you can do so using a database client such as phpMyAdmin, introduced in Chapter 12. You can also write your own programs in a language such as PHP or Perl to work with the data in your database.

In this example, you will enter a simple query at the MySQL Monitor prompt to create a database. The database you create here, testdb, will be used in subsequent examples, so keep it available on the server.

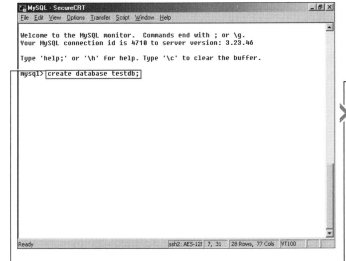

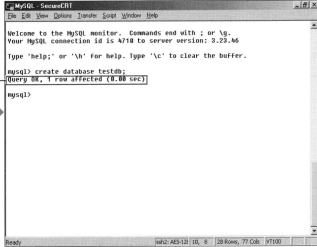

1 From the MySQL Monitor, type **create database testdb;** and press Enter.

■ A message is displayed indicating that the database was created successfully.

Note: If the message Query OK was not displayed, the server may not be running, or you may not have the correct permissions to create a database. See Chapter 10 for troubleshooting tips.

CONFIGURE A MYSQL USER

MySQL has its own access control system using usernames and passwords. To work with data on a MySQL server, you will need a valid MySQL username and password. MySQL usernames are completely separate from UNIX or Windows usernames.

When you install MySQL, it creates the root user by default. This user has access to all databases on the server, and can create and manage additional users. You should not use the root user to work with the MySQL server unless absolutely necessary. Instead, use a username and password that has been given access to the database you are working with.

You will use the testdb database for examples throughout this book. Rather than use the root user for these tests, you can create a username specifically for this purpose. To create the user, you will need to be connected to the MySQL monitor as the root user. Use the following command to create the new user:

```
GRANT ALL ON testdb.* TO testuser
   IDENTIFIED BY 'testpw';
```

This GRANT command creates a new user, testuser, and grants the user access to all tables in the testdb database. The IDENTIFIED BY section specifies a password for the user. You should choose your own password rather than using the value given here.

After you have created the testuser username, you can use it to access the MySQL monitor. The following command starts the MySQL monitor with this username. You may need to specify a hostname or other options, as described in the section "Using the MySQL Monitor," earlier in this chapter.

```
mysql -utestuser -ptestpw
```

MySQL security is a complex topic. You can create any number of users with different levels of access to databases, tables, and even specific columns. See Chapter 11 for more information about MySQL security.

CONFIGURE A MYSQL USER

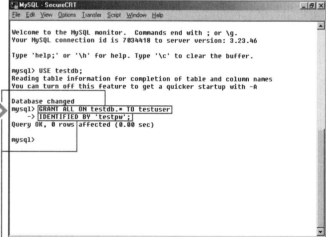

1 From the MySQL monitor, type **USE testdb;** and press Enter.

■ This selects the database.

Note: Be sure you have started the MySQL monitor using the root user.

2 Type **GRANT ALL ON testdb.* TO testuser** and press Enter.

3 Type **IDENTIFIED BY 'testpw';** and press Enter.

■ This creates the testuser account.

Note: Choose your own password rather than using the one shown here.

Extra

When MySQL is installed, the root user has a default password of mysql. Because this is common knowledge, you should change the password for the root user as soon as possible to secure the server. To change the password, start the MySQL monitor as the root user and use the following command.

Example:

```
set password = password('newpass');
```

Replace newpass with the password of your choice, and be sure to choose a password that is not easy for others to guess. See Chapter 11 for detailed information about changing passwords for MySQL users.

Because you will be using the testdb database throughout this book, you may find it useful to make the MySQL monitor automatically use the testuser user by default. This can easily be done on UNIX systems. Create a file in your home directory with the filename .my.cnf and add the following lines to the file:

Example:
```
[client]
user=testuser
password=testpw
```

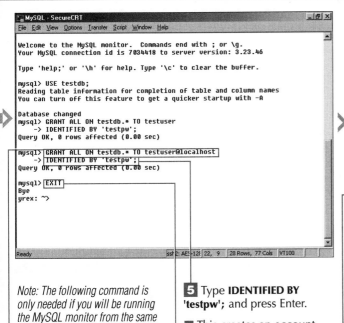

Note: The following command is only needed if you will be running the MySQL monitor from the same machine as the MySQL server.

4 Type **GRANT ALL ON testdb.* TO testuser@localhost** and press Enter.

5 Type **IDENTIFIED BY 'testpw';** and press Enter.

■ This creates an account for use from the local host.

6 Type **EXIT** to exit the MySQL monitor.

■ You are returned to the command prompt.

7 Type **mysql -utestuser -ptestpw** to start the MySQL monitor.

■ You are now connected to MySQL as the new user.

Note: Use the same password you specified when creating the user.

SPECIFY A MULTIPLE-LINE QUERY

While simple SQL queries fit on a single line, some query commands require several lines. You can enter a multiple-line query in the MySQL monitor by pressing Enter after each section of a command.

Because you must use the semicolon character at the end of a query, the MySQL monitor does not act on the query until you end a line with a semicolon. You can enter any number of lines, in order, and use a semicolon at the end of the last line to indicate the end of the query.

After you have entered a line, you can press the up-arrow key to return to that line and edit it further. Press Enter again to continue to the next line. The MySQL monitor also supports a special command, \c (clear). If you type \c as the first characters in a line, the monitor clears the command you have entered so far, and you can start a new command on the next line. This is useful if you have made a mistake.

As an example of using a multiple-line query, you can try the CREATE TABLE command below:

```
CREATE TABLE address   (

    name CHAR(100) NOT NULL,

    address CHAR(120),

    city CHAR(50),

    state CHAR(2) );
```

This example will use the testdb database you created earlier in this chapter. If you have not already created the testdb database, you can create it before beginning using this command:

```
CREATE DATABASE testdb;
```

SPECIFY A MULTIPLE-LINE QUERY

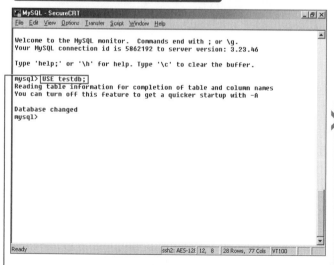

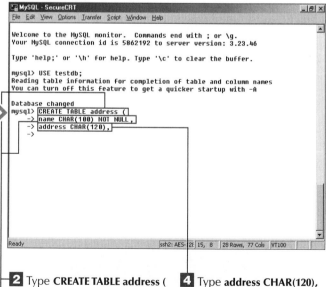

1 From the MySQL monitor, type **USE testdb;** and press Enter.

■ The test database is now selected.

2 Type **CREATE TABLE address (** and press Enter.

3 Type **name CHAR(100) NOT NULL,** and press Enter.

4 Type **address CHAR(120),** and press Enter.

Extra

Along with \c to clear the command, the MySQL monitor supports a number of other commands. Most of the commands have a short version beginning with the backslash character as well as a single-word version. The following table summarizes some of the most useful commands.

SHORT	LONG	DESCRIPTION
\c	CLEAR	Clears the current command
\e	EDIT	Edits the command in a text editor
\g	GO	Executes the current command
\G	EGO	Executes the current command and displays a vertical result
\h	HELP	Displays a list of commands and their descriptions
\p	PRINT	Displays the current command
\P	PAGER	Specifies a program to use to create paged output
\q	EXIT	Exits the MySQL monitor
\r	CONNECT	Attempts to reconnect to the server
\s	STATUS	Displays MySQL status information
\u	USE	Selects the database for subsequent commands
\	SOURCE	Executes MySQL commands from a specified file

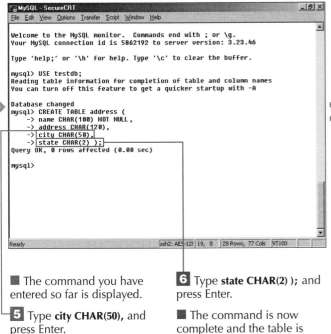

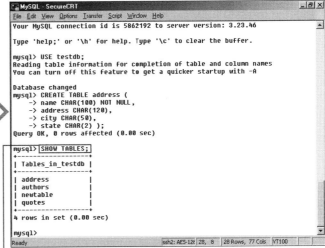

■ The command you have entered so far is displayed.

5 Type **city CHAR(50),** and press Enter.

6 Type **state CHAR(2));** and press Enter.

■ The command is now complete and the table is created.

7 Type **SHOW TABLES;** and press Enter.

■ The monitor displays the list of tables, including your new table.

EDIT A LONG COMMAND

While it allows you to split a long query into multiple lines, the MySQL monitor interface is unforgiving — if you made an error on the first line, you cannot correct it without entering the entire command again. Fortunately, the MySQL monitor provides an alternative.

You can use the \e command at the beginning of any line to edit the current command. This opens a text editor and allows you to use it to edit (or enter) the command. When you are finished, you save the command and exit the editor, and the full command is stored in the MySQL monitor buffer.

You can use \e as the first line in a command to enter the entire command in the editor and avoid using the regular MySQL monitor interface. You can also enter the \e command at any time, and the command you have entered so far will be transferred to the editor.

This feature is not included in the Windows version of the MySQL monitor. In the Linux version, it uses the text editor you have defined using the $EDITOR environmental variable. To set this variable, use a command like this from the command prompt:

```
export EDITOR=pico
```

This command may vary depending on your shell and operating system. This example uses pico, a simple editor included with most versions of Linux. You can use the editor of your choice instead.

When you finish editing, be sure to use the editor's Save command to save the file. If you do not save the file, the command will be lost. After you have edited a command, you will be returned to the MySQL monitor. You can then use the \g (go) command to execute the command.

EDIT A LONG COMMAND

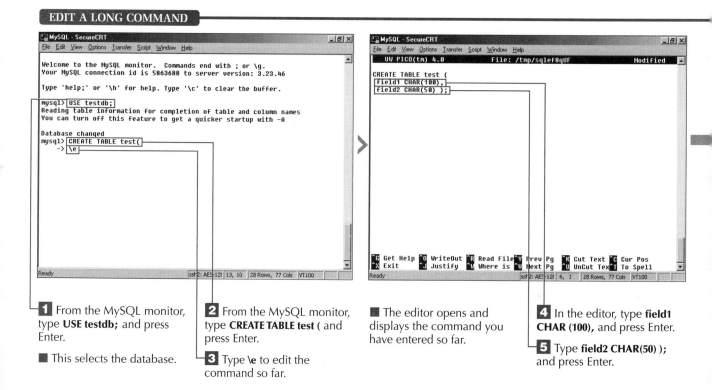

1 From the MySQL monitor, type **USE testdb;** and press Enter.

■ This selects the database.

2 From the MySQL monitor, type **CREATE TABLE test (** and press Enter.

3 Type **\e** to edit the command so far.

■ The editor opens and displays the command you have entered so far.

4 In the editor, type **field1 CHAR (100),** and press Enter.

5 Type **field2 CHAR(50));** and press Enter.

Extra

The Windows version of the MySQL monitor does not support the \e command. There are several alternative ways to deal with long MySQL commands if you are using a Windows system. The first is to type the command in a text editor, such as Notepad, select it, and use the Copy command to copy it to the clipboard, and then paste it into the MySQL monitor window.

Another alternative is to use the MySQLGUI utility, a graphical interface to MySQL, described in the next section. This utility includes a text box that you can use to enter a command of any length, and then submit it to the server. It also saves the most recent queries you have performed and allows you to easily repeat them.

The Windows version of the MySQL monitor can be used to connect to a MySQL server running on a UNIX system, and the UNIX version can connect to a Windows-based server. While there are slight differences in the client programs, they use the same protocols to communicate with the MySQL server.

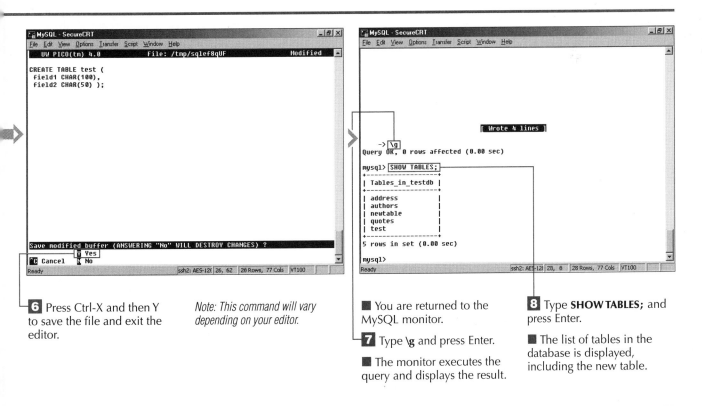

6 Press Ctrl-X and then Y to save the file and exit the editor.

Note: This command will vary depending on your editor.

■ You are returned to the MySQL monitor.

7 Type **\g** and press Enter.

■ The monitor executes the query and displays the result.

8 Type **SHOW TABLES;** and press Enter.

■ The list of tables in the database is displayed, including the new table.

CONFIGURE MYSQLGUI

The MySQL monitor is only one of the clients you can use with a MySQL server. You can use MySQLGUI, a graphical MySQL client, as an alternative interface to MySQL. This utility can do most of the same things as the MySQL monitor.

MySQLGUI was developed by the developers of MySQL, and is available from the Downloads section of the MySQL Web page at www.mysql.com/. Binary versions of this utility are available for Windows and Linux systems.

For Windows systems, MySQLGUI is distributed as a ZIP file. You will need to use a program such as WinZip to extract the files from the archive. WinZip is available from the following URL: www.winzip.com/.

To install MySQLGUI, simply copy the files from the ZIP archive to a directory on your computer. You can use it from any machine that can reach your MySQL server across

the network; it does not have to be installed on the same machine as the MySQL server software.

After you have installed the files, open the directory and double-click the mysqlgui.exe file. MySQLGUI prompts you for a password for the root user. After you specify this once, you can click the Options button to specify a different username for future sessions.

The MySQLGUI utility is also available for Linux and several other systems, and the source code is available. See the MySQL Web site for complete instructions for installing or compiling MySQLGUI on your system.

MySQLGUI allows you to send queries to the MySQL server, display the server status, and perform other tasks. See Chapter 6 for information about using MySQLGUI to perform a query, and see Chapter 9 for information about server management using MySQLGUI.

CONFIGURE MYSQLGUI

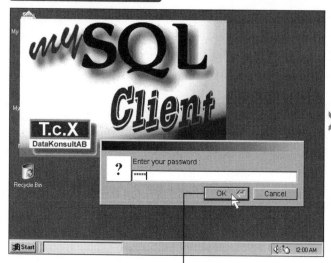

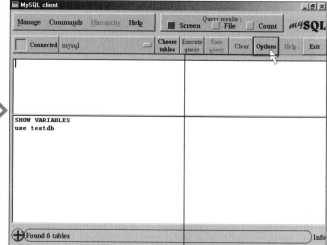

■ When you start MySQLGUI, you are prompted for a password. The root user is used by default.

1 Enter the password and click OK.

■ The main MySQLGUI window is displayed.

2 Click the Options button to configure MySQLGUI.

Extra

After you have configured `MySQLGUI`, you can use it to work with the MySQL server. The main window includes a drop-down menu that allows you to select a database to work with, similar to the `USE` command in the MySQL monitor. There is also an indicator that is green in color if you have a valid connection to the MySQL server.

The main part of the window is divided into two sections. The top area allows you to specify a MySQL query with one or more lines. You can edit the query as needed. Do not use a semicolon to end queries you enter into `MySQLGUI`. When the query is finished, click the Execute query button to send it to the MySQL server. `MySQLGUI` opens a new window to display the results of the query.

The bottom portion of the window displays a list of your most recent queries for the selected database. You can click an entry in this list to copy the query to the top window, and use the Execute query button to send the query to the MySQL server again.

To exit `MySQLGUI`, click the Exit button on the toolbar or close its window. The list of recent queries is saved and displayed again the next time you run the utility.

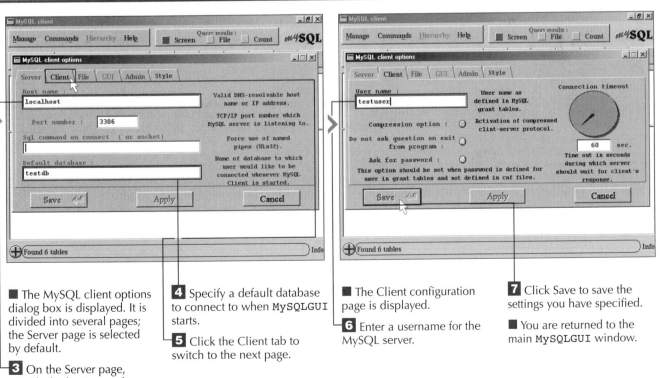

■ The MySQL client options dialog box is displayed. It is divided into several pages; the Server page is selected by default.

3 On the Server page, specify the host name for the MySQL server.

4 Specify a default database to connect to when `MySQLGUI` starts.

5 Click the Client tab to switch to the next page.

■ The Client configuration page is displayed.

6 Enter a username for the MySQL server.

7 Click Save to save the settings you have specified.

■ You are returned to the main `MySQLGUI` window.

DESIGN A DATABASE

C reating a database and one or more tables is easy. The complex part of the process is designing the database: determining the data you need to store, how it should be divided into tables and fields, and the type of tables to use.

DATABASE DESIGN BASICS

The process of database design includes choosing tables, the columns that will make up the tables, and the keys, indexes, and relationships among tables.

Plan Tables

The first step in designing the database is to list all of the data you need to store and decide how it can be divided into tables. Often separate tables are more practical than one large table, but avoid duplicating information between tables. If you will be using applications to work with the tables, plan accordingly so that each application only needs to access a minimum number of tables.

Plan Columns

After deciding on a list of tables to include in the database, list the fields, or columns, to include in each table and the type of data to be stored in each column. You can add columns at a later time, but your list of columns should be as complete as possible when you create the tables. Keep the list of columns short and to the point; do not include unnecessary data, duplicates of data available in another table, or fields that can be calculated from existing fields.

Keys and Indexes

Each table will need a *primary key*: a unique index that you can use to single out any record, or row, from the table. Along with the primary key, you may want to create additional indexes, also known as *secondary keys*, to make it easier for the server to find data within columns that are frequently searched.

Relationships

Often you will need to consider the relationship between two tables. For example, you may have an address book table and a phone list table. Each would include a name field, and you could relate data between the two tables using this field. To ensure that table relationships can be taken advantage of, be sure any fields that can be used to link tables are the same type and are set up as keys to the tables.

Security

Some data requires more security than other data. You may need a more secure type of table to store certain data, and you may want to separate the non-critical data and the critical data. In addition to security, your design should take reliability into account. You may need to use multiple database servers to make data reliably available, and use regular backups to keep the data safe.

Plan for the Future

Along with your current needs, you should take any plans for the future into account when designing the database. If you will be adding additional tables at a later time, plan the current tables to use similar columns and make relationships between tables easier.

One important way of preparing for future changes is to use a standard naming convention for the columns in your tables. If two tables have a column that stores the same data, be sure they both use the same column name and store the data in the same format.

MYSQL TABLE TYPES

MySQL supports a variety of different table types. Each database on a MySQL server can contain tables of any of these types. While the default type is sufficient for most purposes, you should be familiar with the different types available and know when there may be a more appropriate choice.

You can choose the table type to use with the `TYPE` keyword within a `CREATE TABLE` query in MySQL. You can convert a table to a different type later if needed.

MyISAM

MyISAM is the default MySQL table type. This type of table is based on the *ISAM*, or Indexed Sequential Access Method, standard. The main disadvantage of MyISAM tables is that they are not transaction safe. Transactions are used with critical data storage, such as that used by financial institutions, to ensure that only complete transactions are recorded in the database. Incomplete transactions can be rolled back to prevent corruption of the data.

Because using transactions is not necessary for most Web database applications or for many non-critical business uses, MyISAM tables are useful. If you create a table on the MySQL server without specifying a table type, the MyISAM type is used by default.

ISAM

ISAM is the standard table type that MyISAM tables are based on. Because MyISAM tables are smaller and more efficient, use of ISAM tables is discouraged by the MySQL developers, and this type may not be supported by future versions of MySQL. You should use it only if you need compatibility with data already in the ISAM format.

Heap

Heap tables are specialized. They use a hashed index, which uses a mathematical formula to quickly find the location of data for a key. Heap tables are stored in RAM rather than on disk. This makes a Heap table extremely fast, but not reliable for permanent storage. Heap tables are a perfect choice when you need to create a temporary table.

BDB

BDB, short for Berkeley DB, is a new table type supported by MySQL 3.23.34 and later. This table type is not supported by default when you install MySQL unless you use the MySQL-Max distribution. You can compile the regular MySQL distribution to optionally include support for BDB tables.

The main advantage of BDB tables is that they support transactions. You can begin a transaction, submit data, and use the `COMMIT` command to commit the data to the database. If the application is interrupted before the data is complete, you can use the `ROLLBACK` command to remove the partial transaction and keep the database stable. BDB is also designed for high performance when working with large amounts of data and many concurrent users.

BDB is developed by Sleepycat Software. You can find out more about this database system at the developer's Web site, www.sleepycat.com.

InnoDB

InnoDB is an industrial-strength database system that is supported by MySQL 3.23.34a and later. Like BDB, InnoDB is not supported by default; you need to compile MySQL with InnoDB support or use the MySQL-Max distribution.

Like DBD, InnoDB supports transactions, committing, and rollbacks. InnoDB provides greater performance than basic MyISAM tables, especially when you are working with large amounts of data. You can find out more about InnoDB at www.innodb.com.

CREATE AND DROP DATABASES

Databases are the largest unit of data on a MySQL server. Each MySQL server can store any number of databases. Each table of data is stored in one of these databases.

USING CREATE DATABASE

You can create a new database with the CREATE DATABASE command in MySQL. To use this command, simply specify a name for the new database.

Example:
```
CREATE DATABASE newdb;
```

Database Internals

When you create a database, the MySQL server creates a directory on the server's file system. When you install MySQL, you can choose the location for these directories. Within each database's directory, the MySQL server creates files for each of the tables you create in the database.

Existing Databases

If you attempt to create a database using CREATE DATABASE, but a database with the name you specify already exists on the server, an error message is returned. To avoid this error, you can use the IF NOT EXISTS keywords with the CREATE command. If this is specified and the database already exists, no error is returned, no new database is created, and the existing database is unchanged.

Example:
```
CREATE DATABASE IF NOT EXISTS newdb;
```

USING DROP DATABASE

The DROP DATABASE command in SQL allows you to delete an existing database. This command immediately deletes the database. You are not asked to confirm this action. All tables within the database and the data they contain are deleted.

Normally, using DROP DATABASE will return an error if the database does not exist. You can avoid this error by adding the phrase IF EXISTS to the DROP DATABASE query.

Example:
```
DROP DATABASE newdb;
```

Show Database Contents

Because the DROP DATABASE command is drastic, use it carefully. One way to be sure you are deleting the correct database is to use the SHOW TABLES command to display a list of tables in the database. Be sure none of the tables listed contains important data.

The SHOW TABLE STATUS command displays a more detailed list of tables, including the number of rows stored in each table. Use this command to be sure you are going to delete the right tables.

Example:
```
SHOW TABLES FROM newdb;
SHOW TABLE STATUS FROM newdb;
```

Data Security and Backups

Because DROP DATABASE and other commands can cause drastic and immediate loss of data if not used carefully, it is always a good idea to maintain backups of important data and to make a backup before using the DROP command. Chapter 8 explains how to back up data on the MySQL server.

CREATE A DATABASE

B efore you can store data in tables within a MySQL database, you must first create the database. You can do this using the CREATE DATABASE command in SQL. The basic form of this command simply specifies a database name:

CREATE DATABASE newdb;

When you create a database, no tables or data are stored in the database. The MySQL server stores each database as a directory on the server. When you create a new database, a directory is created to store its tables. When you later create one or more tables, they are stored as files within this directory.

If you attempt to create the newdb database and a database with that name already exists, an error message is displayed. To avoid this error, you can specify IF NOT EXISTS. This

tells the server to create the database only if it does not exist, and no error is returned:

CREATE DATABASE IF NOT EXISTS newdb;

Because the database name is used as a directory name on the server, you can use any valid name as a directory on your system. Two characters that are explicitly disallowed in database names are period (.) and slash (/). On most systems, safe characters to use in directory names include letters, numbers, and the underscore (_). Spaces are not allowed in names in some systems.

The opposite of CREATE DATABASE is the DROP DATABASE command. This command deletes the directory structure for a database, including all tables. Because it does not warn you that data will be lost, DROP DATABASE should be used carefully.

CREATE A DATABASE

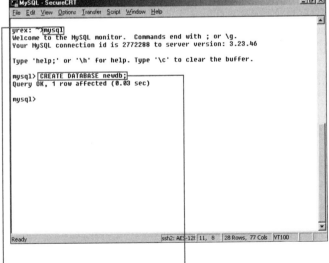

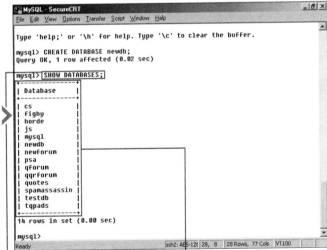

1 From the command prompt, type **mysql** and press Enter to start the MySQL monitor.

Note: You may need to specify a username and password when starting the monitor. See Chapter 1 for details.

2 From the MySQL monitor, type **CREATE DATABASE newdb;** and press Enter.

■ The server creates the database.

3 Type **SHOW DATABASES;** and press Enter.

■ The complete list of databases on the server is displayed, including your new database.

SHOW AVAILABLE DATABASES

Y ou can use the SHOW DATABASES command from within the MySQL monitor to list all of the databases available on the server. The basic command is simple:

```
SHOW DATABASES;
```

You can also use the LIKE keyword to show only databases whose names match a pattern. The following shows a list of all databases that begin with the letter t:

```
SHOW DATABASES LIKE 't%';
```

The LIKE clause supports wildcard characters. These are useful when you are unsure of the exact name of the database you are looking for, or when you need to list all of the databases that match a certain keyword. The first wildcard, underscore (_), matches any character. This command would list the testdb database and any others that contain testd followed by one letter:

```
SHOW DATABASES LIKE 'testd_';
```

The second wildcard is the percent (%) character. This matches any string of characters, or no characters. The following command would list the testdb database along with any other with a name containing 'test':

```
SHOW DATABASES LIKE '%test%';
```

Because this command includes wildcards at the beginning and end of the database name, it looks for the characters test at any location. This example would match databases named testdata, datatest, or newtest23.

Rather than using the MySQL monitor, you can also use the mysqlshow utility, which is included with the MySQL server, to list the databases. Use mysqlshow with no parameters to list all of the databases on the server. You can also specify a database name to display the tables included in the database. The following mysqlshow command displays the tables within the testdb database:

```
mysqlshow testdb
```

SHOW AVAILABLE DATABASES

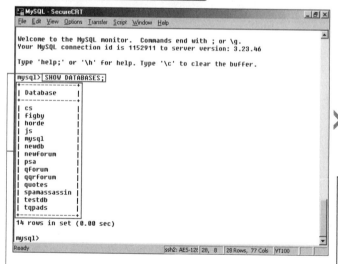

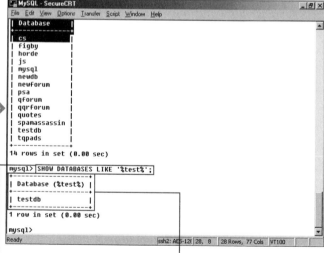

1 From the MySQL monitor, type **SHOW DATABASES;** and press Enter.

■ The complete list of databases on the server is displayed.

Note: Depending on the databases you have created, your list will vary from the results shown here.

2 Type **SHOW DATABASES LIKE '%test%';** and press Enter.

■ All databases containing the word 'test' are displayed. If you created the testdb database in Chapter 1, it will be listed here.

SELECT A DATABASE

ater in this chapter you will work with tables. Before you can work with the tables in a database, you must first select the database. You can do this with the USE command. To use this command, type USE followed by the database name and a semicolon to end the statement. For example, the following command selects the testdb database:

```
USE testdb;
```

After you have selected a database with the USE command, it is used as the default database for any queries you make. If you refer to a table in a subsequent query, the MySQL server looks for that table in the database you previously selected.

In order to select a database, you must be logged in to the MySQL server using the MySQL monitor, or another client,

and the username you have specified must have permission to access the database you select. You can use the SHOW DATABASES command, described in the previous section, to determine a database name to select.

As an alternative to the USE command, you can also specify a database name and table name when you perform a query that involves a table. You do this by separating the database name from the table name using a period. For example, testdb.address refers to the address table within the testdb database.

After you have selected a database with the USE command, you can use commands like CREATE TABLE or SELECT to work with the current database. This database remains as the default until you specify another database with USE or until you exit from the MySQL monitor or other MySQL client.

SELECT A DATABASE

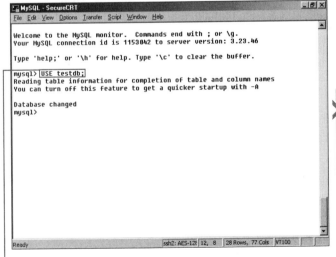

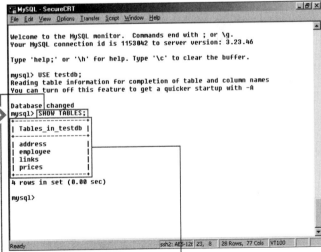

1 From the MySQL monitor, type **USE testdb;** and press Enter.

■ The database is selected.

Note: This command will only work if you have created the testdb database. Follow the instructions in Chapter 1 if you need to create it.

2 Type **SHOW TABLES;** and press Enter.

■ The list of tables in the current database is displayed.

CREATE AND DROP TABLES

After creating a database on the MySQL server, you can create one or more tables to store data. Each database can contain any number of tables.

CREATE TABLES

You can use the CREATE TABLE command to create a table. As with the CREATE DATABASE command, this command normally returns an error if the table already exists. If you use the optional keywords IF NOT EXISTS, this error is suppressed.

Specify Columns

The list of columns, or fields, for the table is included in parentheses in the CREATE TABLE command. Column types such as CHAR and DECIMAL can have parameters in parentheses; include these within the column list. Commas separate the column names.

Example:
```
CREATE TABLE test (
   Column1 INTEGER,
   Column2 CHAR(50) );
```

Specify Column Attributes

You can specify one or more optional attributes for a column after its column type. For example, the NULL or NOT NULL attribute indicates whether the column can store NULL values. NULL is a special value that indicates that nothing has been stored in the column.

The DEFAULT attribute specifies a default value for a column. For columns that allow NULL values, NULL is the default; otherwise the default is zero for numeric columns and a blank value for text columns. If you specify a value for the DEFAULT attribute it overrides this default.

Example:
```
CREATE TABLE test2 (
   Column1 CHAR(10) NOT NULL,
   Column2 INT DEFAULT 10 );
```

Create Indexes

When you index a table, the server stores a list of values and pointers into the database to make it easier to search for values in the indexed columns. You can create a simple index with the INDEX keyword. You can specify an optional name for the index and one or more columns to index in parentheses.

Create a Unique Index or Primary Key

You can use the keyword UNIQUE to create a *unique index*, also known as a *key*. A unique index is similar to a standard index, but each row's value for the indexed column must be unique.

As with INDEX, you can specify an optional name for the index and one or more columns to be indexed. When you index more than one column, only the combination of values of the columns needs to be unique. A table can have any number of unique indexes.

A *primary key* is similar to a unique index, but each table can have only one primary key. Additionally, the primary key must have the NOT NULL attribute. The primary key is used to uniquely identify each row of the table.

You can assign the primary key using the PRIMARY KEY keywords, similar to INDEX. Alternately, you can specify the PRIMARY KEY attribute for one of the columns.

Example:
```
CREATE TABLE phonelist (
   name VARCHAR(20) NOT NULL,
   phone VARCHAR(12),
   UNIQUE phoneindex (phone),
   PRIMARY KEY (name) );
```

Example:
```
CREATE TABLE clients (
   name VARCHAR(20),
   city VARCHAR(30),
   INDEX index1 (name,city) );
```

CREATE TABLES (CONTINUED)

Specify Table Type

You can include the TYPE keyword within the CREATE TABLE command to specify one of MySQL's supported table types. The basic table types include ISAM, MyISAM, and Heap. Depending on your installation of the MySQL server, other table types may be available. MyISAM tables are used by default.

Example:
```
CREATE TABLE test (
   field1 INT ) TYPE = ISAM;
```

Table Options

You can also specify one or more options when creating a table. These are summarized in the following table.

OPTION	PURPOSE
AUTO_INCREMENT	Specify the next value for an AUTO_INCREMENT column.
AVG_ROW_LENGTH	An estimate of the row length when variable-length columns are used.
CHECKSUM	Specify 1 to create checksums, which slows down the server but prevents some errors.
COMMENT	An optional description of the table, up to 60 characters long.
MAX_ROWS	The maximum number of rows you will store in the table.
MIN_ROWS	The minimum number of rows you will store in the table.

To specify an option, include it at the end of the column specifications for the table followed by an = sign and its value. Separate multiple options with spaces. Use quotation marks around text options such as COMMENT. Note that table types, such as ISAM, should not be quoted.

Example:
```
CREATE TABLE students (
   name VARCHAR(100) )
   COMMENT='student names';
```

Using Temporary Tables

You can optionally specify the TEMPORARY keyword to create a temporary table. The table will be automatically deleted when you close your connection with the server. Temporary tables are guaranteed to be unique; if you create a temporary table with the same name as an existing table, it is assigned a unique name and is visible only to your current connection. Because of this, temporary tables are not shown in the list when you use the SHOW TABLES command.

Example:
```
CREATE TEMPORARY TABLE temptable (
   Name CHAR(50),
   Address CHAR(200) );
```

Copy Fields from Another Table

You can optionally use the SELECT keyword when you create a table to copy one or more columns from an existing table. MySQL will automatically create fields in the new table that match the fields of the existing table.

Example:
```
CREATE TABLE phone2
   SELECT name, phone from phonelist;
```

DELETE TABLES

You can use the DROP TABLE command in MySQL to delete an existing table. This immediately deletes the table, whether it currently contains any data or not. Because it deletes without confirmation, use this command with caution.

The DROP TABLE command will return an error if the table you attempt to delete does not exist. You can avoid this error by adding the IF EXISTS phrase to the DROP TABLE command.

Example:
```
DROP TABLE temptable;
```

CREATE A SIMPLE TABLE

You can use the CREATE TABLE command from the MySQL monitor or other client to create a new table. To create a table, you specify the columns, or fields, the table will use and their types. The following command creates a simple table with one column:

```
CREATE TABLE test ( field1 char(10) );
```

Because you will usually be specifying more than one column for the table, a CREATE TABLE statement often takes more than one line. For this example, you will create a table that can be used to store a price list. The fields include an alphanumeric item number, a price, and a minimum quantity. The following is the complete command to create this table:

```
CREATE TABLE prices (
    itemno CHAR(10),
    price DECIMAL(9,2),
    quantity TINYINT UNSIGNED );
```

This specifies that the itemno column can store up to ten characters. Because the CHAR type is used for this column, each row of the table will be the same length. The price column stores a decimal number that can have up to nine digits, including two digits after the decimal. The quantity column stores an integer. The TINYINT type can store numbers from 0 to 255. You learn more about these field types in the section "Numeric Column Types."

Tables are physically stored on the MySQL server as files within the directory for the database. You can use any character in a table name that is allowed in a filename on your operating system. The period (.) and slash (/) characters are not allowed. You need to choose a unique name for each table within a database, but separate databases can have tables with the same name.

CREATE A SIMPLE TABLE

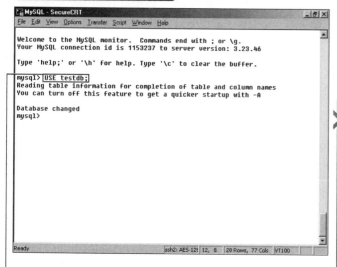

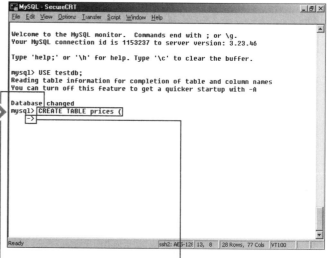

1 From the MySQL monitor, type **USE testdb;** and press Enter.

■ This selects the database in which you will create the table.

Note: If you have not created the testdb database in Chapter 1, you need to create it before creating this table.

2 Type **CREATE TABLE prices (** and press Enter.

■ The MySQL monitor prompts for the next line.

Apply It

As another example, you can create a table for an employee list. This table will include columns for the employee's first and last names, salary, date hired, and department number. The following is the CREATE TABLE command for this table:

Example:
```
CREATE TABLE employee (
    FirstName VARCHAR(50),
    LastName VARCHAR(50),
    Salary DECIMAL(8,2),
    HireDate DATE,
    Department INT );
```

This command uses the VARCHAR type for the FirstName and LastName fields. Because this type is used, each row of the table will have a variable length. This can conserve space if the full size of the columns is not always used.

The Salary field stores decimal numbers with up to eight digits including two digits after the decimal point. The HireDate field is a DATE field. The Department field is an integer. These column types are described in detail later in this chapter, starting with the section "Numeric Column Types."

Because this is a long command, you may find it useful to use the \e command in the MySQL monitor, as described in Chapter 1. This allows you to use a text editor to enter the complete command.

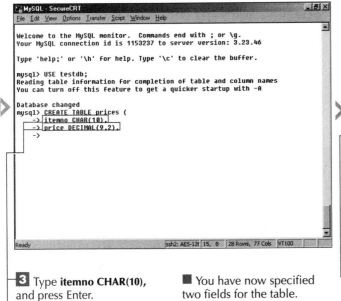

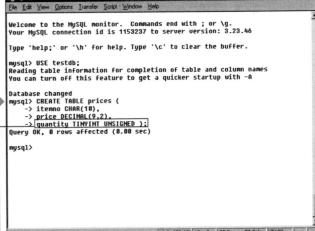

3 Type **itemno CHAR(10),** and press Enter.

4 Type **price DECIMAL(9,2),** and press Enter.

■ You have now specified two fields for the table.

5 Type **quantity TINYINT UNSIGNED);** and press Enter.

■ You have specified the last field, and the closing) character ends the command. The table is now created.

SHOW TABLE INFORMATION

You can use several SHOW commands from a MySQL client to find out information about the tables in the current database. The first command, SHOW TABLES, lists all of the tables in the currently selected database.

You can optionally use the LIKE keyword to show only tables matching a string. Like the SHOW DATABASES command, you can use the wildcard _ for one character and % for any number of characters. The following example lists all tables that have names beginning with the letter A:

SHOW TABLES LIKE 'a%';

The SHOW TABLE STATUS command also displays information about the tables in the current database. Rather than simply listing the tables, this command displays specific information about each table: its name, type, row format, number of rows, average length of rows, the times the table was created and last updated, and other details. As with SHOW TABLES, you can use the LIKE keyword to display only selected tables.

The SHOW COLUMNS command lists the columns for a table with detailed information about each. To use this command, you specify a table name with the FROM keyword:

SHOW COLUMNS FROM address;

You can also use the LIKE keyword with SHOW COLUMNS. In this case, LIKE allows you to display only the column names that match the string you specify. You can use wildcards to specify a partial column name. The following command lists any columns of the address table that begin with the letter n:

SHOW COLUMNS FROM address LIKE 'n%';

A final command is SHOW INDEX. This command displays information about the indexes and keys used with the table you specify with the FROM keyword. Here is a simple example of this command:

SHOW INDEX FROM address;

SHOW TABLE INFORMATION

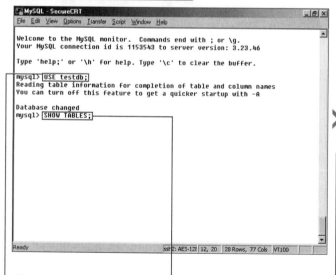

1 From the MySQL monitor, type **USE testdb;** and press Enter.

■ The database is selected.

Note: This example requires the testdb database and the address table. Create these using the instructions in Chapter 1 or on the CD-ROM.

2 Type **SHOW TABLES;** and press Enter.

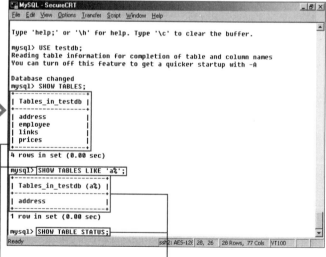

■ The list of tables for the database is displayed.

3 Type **SHOW TABLES LIKE 'a%';** and press Enter.

■ Only tables beginning with the letter A are displayed.

4 Type **SHOW TABLE STATUS;** and press Enter.

Extra

The SHOW TABLE STATUS command includes a list of details for each table in the database. Here is an explanation of the fields in this list:

ITEM	DESCRIPTION
Name	The table name
Type	The table type, typically MyISAM
Row_format	Whether the rows are fixed or variable length
Rows	Total number of rows
Avg_row_length	Average row length
Data_length	Total length of the table's data file
Max_data_length	Maximum size of the data file
Index_length	Length of the table's index file
Data_free	Amount of unused space in the table
Auto_increment	Next value for an autoincrement column
Create_time	The time the table was created
Update_time	The time the table was last modified
Check_time	The time the table was last checked for errors
Create_options	The options used when creating the table
Comment	An optional comment specified when the table was created

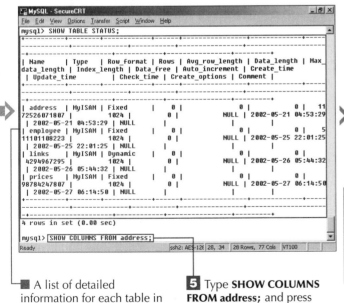

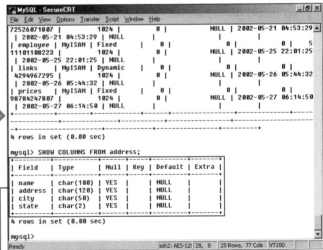

■ A list of detailed information for each table in the database is displayed.

5 Type **SHOW COLUMNS FROM address;** and press Enter.

■ A list of detailed information for each column in the address table is displayed.

NUMERIC COLUMN TYPES

S ome of the most important data you can store in a database is in the form of numbers: monetary figures, quantities, sequence numbers, and so on. MySQL includes a variety of standard column types for the storage of numeric values.

DETAILS OF NUMERIC TYPES

When choosing a numeric column type, you should consider the type of numbers you need to store: integers, numbers with a fixed decimal as used in currency, or floating-point numbers with longer decimal values. Your choice of type also depends on the maximum value the column can store.

INTEGER

An INTEGER column stores an *integer* — a round number with no decimal portion. An INTEGER column can store values from –2,147,483,648 to 2,147,483,647. You can optionally specify the UNSIGNED attribute for integers, which doubles the range of positive numbers allowed and disallows negative numbers.

The numeric range of a column type depends on the number of bytes MySQL uses to store the column's data. *Bytes* are a basic unit of memory or disk storage. Each byte consists of eight binary digits, or *bits*, and can store 256 unique values. Multiple bytes allow exponentially larger numbers. MySQL uses four bytes for each row of an INTEGER column.

You can optionally specify a display length for an INTEGER column in parentheses. This length will be used to pad small values with spaces. If you specify the ZEROFILL attribute, zeroes are used instead of spaces. For example, a column with a length of 3 and ZEROFILL will return a value of 7 as 007. You can use INT as a shorter form of INTEGER.

Example:
```
CREATE TABLE inventory (
  item INTEGER,
  quantity INTEGER(3) ZEROFILL );
```

TINYINT

The TINYINT column type is a smaller version of INTEGER. This type stores each value using a single byte, so it is limited to –128 to 127. If you specify the UNSIGNED keyword, values can range from 0 to 255. As with INT, you can specify a display size in parentheses.

SMALLINT

SMALLINT is another version of INTEGER. This type stores each value using two bytes, so the range of values is –32,768 to 32,767. The UNSIGNED range is 0 to 65,535. As with INT, you can specify a display size in parentheses.

MEDIUMINT

MEDIUMINT is another version of INTEGER. This type stores each value using three bytes, so the range of values is –8,388,608 to 8,388,607. The unsigned range is 0 to 16,777,216. As with INT, you can specify a display size in parentheses.

BIGINT

The largest integer column type is BIGINT. This type is similar to INTEGER, but stores each of its values using eight bytes. This allows numbers an order of magnitude larger than INTEGER can store. As with INT, you can specify a display size in parentheses.

In general, be sure to use whichever type is closest to the range of numbers you need to store in the column without going over. Using larger types than you need is an unnecessary waste of space.

Example:
```
CREATE TABLE numbers (
  Smallnum TINYINT(3),
  bignum BIGINT(20) UNSIGNED );
```

FLOAT

The FLOAT type allows you to store floating-point numbers. The MySQL server normally uses four bytes to store these numbers, and the precision depends on the size of the numbers. You can store numbers as large as 39 digits long in a FLOAT column. As with integer types, you can specify UNSIGNED to double the range and limit values to positive numbers.

You can specify two parameters in parentheses when defining a FLOAT column: the first is the number of bits used to store the number, up to 53. When you use a number of bits larger than 24, MySQL uses eight bytes to store the values. The second parameter is the number of digits that should follow the decimal point. Both parameters are optional.

Example:
```
CREATE TABLE stats (
  distance FLOAT,
  velocity FLOAT(24,4) );
```

REAL or DOUBLE

You can use REAL columns to store an eight-byte floating-point number with a larger range than FLOAT. The types DOUBLE and DOUBLE PRECISION are equivalent to REAL. Unlike FLOAT, you cannot specify the precision when you create a column.

DECIMAL

DECIMAL columns are used to store numbers with a fixed decimal position. When you create a DECIMAL column, you specify two values in parentheses: the total number of digits, and the number of digits after the decimal point.

Unlike floating-point numbers, DECIMAL values are stored as text: the number 39,400, for example, would be stored in five bytes of text, one for each digit. These values are not rounded, so you can expect them to be accurate.

COLUMN ATTRIBUTES

All of the numeric column types can have one or more optional attributes. These specify how the column stores numbers, how the numbers retrieved from the column will be displayed, and the default value for the column for new rows.

UNSIGNED

You can specify the UNSIGNED attribute for any numeric column. This allows only positive numbers to be stored in the column and doubles the largest number you can store.

ZEROFILL

If you specify a display width for an integer column, you can also specify the optional ZEROFILL attribute. This uses zeroes rather than spaces to pad the values that are smaller than the width you have specified.

Auto-Increment Columns

You can optionally use the AUTO_INCREMENT attribute with an integer column. MySQL automatically uses a new value for this column each time a row is added, starting with one. If you insert a value of zero or a null value into this column, the next number in the sequence is used.

Using Null Values

You can specify NULL or NOT NULL for numeric columns. If specified, the column can contain null values, and the null value is used as the default unless you specify a different default. The null value is not the same as zero, but means "no value." NULL is the default.

DEFAULT

If you specify the DEFAULT keyword in a column definition, you can set a default value. This value will be used whenever a row is added and a value for the column is not explicitly set. The default is zero for numeric columns if you do not specify a default.

Example:
```
CREATE TABLE stock (
  item INTEGER UNSIGNED,
  price DECIMAL(5,2),
  quantity INTEGER(3) DEFAULT 1);
```

TEXT AND DATE COLUMN TYPES

While data is often in the form of numbers, MySQL also includes a variety of column types for storing non-numeric data. This includes text columns that store a length of text, also known as a string, and several column types devoted to the storage of dates and times.

TEXT COLUMN TYPES

When choosing a text column type, you should consider the amount of text you need to store, whether fixed or variable-length columns are appropriate, and whether certain values are used repeatedly.

CHAR

CHAR is the basic text column type. A CHAR column can store up to 255 characters of text. You can specify the number of characters allowed in parentheses. CHAR columns have a fixed length; if you define a column as CHAR (50), 50 bytes are required to store any entry in the column, even if the actual value is shorter than 50 characters.

VARCHAR

A VARCHAR column can also store up to 255 characters of text, and you can specify the maximum length of values in parentheses. Unlike CHAR, VARCHAR columns have a variable length. Shorter values will use less space in the table than longer values. The disadvantage of variable-length columns is that they are harder for the MySQL server to work with, and consequently slower.

You must use fixed or variable length consistently in all of the columns of a table. If you use one VARCHAR column, all CHAR columns will be converted to VARCHAR because the table's rows will have variable lengths.

TEXT

A TEXT column allows you to store a larger amount of text. You do not need to specify a maximum length, and each item can range from zero to 65,535 characters in length. Because TEXT columns have a variable length, longer values will use more space.

Along with the basic TEXT column type, MySQL allows several variations with different sizes. TINYTEXT columns can store up to 255 characters, similar to VARCHAR. MEDIUMTEXT columns can store up to 16MB of text. LONGTEXT columns can store up to 4GB of text. In practice, MEDIUMTEXT and LONGTEXT columns will be limited to smaller values because MySQL clients and servers limit the size of communication packets.

Example:
```
CREATE TABLE applicants (
    firstname VARCHAR(50),
    lastname VARCHAR(50),
    resume TEXT);
```

BLOB

BLOB column types are fundamentally the same as TEXT, but can store binary data. You can use these columns to store images, data files, or anything that is not simple text. BLOB is shorthand for Binary Large Object. The basic BLOB column type can store up to 65,535 bytes of data.

As with TEXT, a number of variations on BLOB have different size limitations. TINYBLOB columns can store up to 255 bytes, MEDIUMBLOB columns can store up to 16MB, and LONGBLOB columns can store up to 4GB.

TEXT COLUMN TYPES (CONTINUED)

ENUM

You can use an ENUM, or enumerated, column when you need to use a set number of text values as possible values in the column. For example, you could define an ENUM column for an address table to store a contact type: personal, business, or other.

```
ContactType
ENUM("personal","business","other")
```

You specify the allowable values when you create the table. When you add a row, it can assign either an empty string or one of the values you specify. MySQL stores these values as a number, starting with zero for the first possible value.

SET

The SET column type is similar to ENUM, but each row can contain one or more of the string values you specified when creating the table. If you defined a contact type column as a SET, it could contain combinations of values, such as personal and business.

```
ContactType
SET("personal","business","other")
```

DATE COLUMN TYPES

Dates are another type of data you can store in a MySQL table. MySQL includes column types that can store a date and time, a simple date, or a timestamp that can be updated automatically.

DATETIME

You can use a DATETIME column to store a date and time. This stores the year, month, day of month, hours, minutes, and seconds. You can set it using a string like "2005-10-22 06:30:00" or using the numeric equivalent, 20051022063000.

DATE

A DATE column is similar to DATETIME, but stores only a year, month, and day of month. The dates in DATE and DATETIME columns can range from January 1st, 1000 to December 31, 9999.

TIME

A TIME column is similar to DATETIME, but stores only the time of day in hours, minutes, and seconds.

YEAR

The YEAR column type simply stores a year. Its values can range from 1900 to 2155.

TIMESTAMP

A TIMESTAMP column is a special type that stores a date and time, similar to DATETIME, but can be updated automatically. The first TIMESTAMP column in a table is automatically updated to the current date and time whenever you insert or modify a row, unless you explicitly set the TIMESTAMP column to another value. You can also force any TIMESTAMP column to update to the current time by storing zero or NULL in the column.

TIMESTAMP columns can store any date and time from the beginning of 1970 to the end of 2037, with a different unique value for each second. You can specify a display width up to 14 characters when you create the table. This does not affect the values the column can store.

Example:
```
CREATE TABLE names (
   Name VARCHAR(30),
   LastUpdate TIMESTAMP(14) );
```

USING TEXT COLUMNS

MySQL's various types of text columns are useful whenever you need to store non-numeric data. For example, you can create a table to store links to Web sites. The links table includes text columns for the title of a Web page, the URL, and a description.

When choosing which text column type to use, the first factor you should consider is the length of the text that will be stored in the column. For the links table, a title will rarely be more than 100 characters, so CHAR(100) or VARCHAR (100) will work for the title column. URLs are almost always under 255 characters, so CHAR(255) or VARCHAR (255) is ideal.

A description may be longer than 255 characters, the limit of the CHAR and VARCHAR types, so a TEXT column is needed. You do not need to specify the length of TEXT columns. The limit for this type is 65,535 characters, but smaller descriptions will save space in the table.

The second factor to consider is whether to use fixed-length columns with CHAR or variable-length columns with

VARCHAR. If you use any variable-length columns, the table's rows will be variable length. This may save disk space, but fixed-length rows are faster for the server to index or search.

All of the columns of a table should be consistently fixed or variable length. If you specify a combination of fixed and variable-length columns in a CREATE TABLE statement, MySQL will automatically convert any CHAR columns to VARCHAR, and the table will have variable-length rows.

In this example, because the TEXT column used for the description has a variable length, you must use VARCHAR for the other text fields. Here is the complete CREATE TABLE command for the links table:

```
CREATE TABLE links (
    title VARCHAR(100),
    url VARCHAR(255),
    description TEXT );
```

USING TEXT COLUMNS

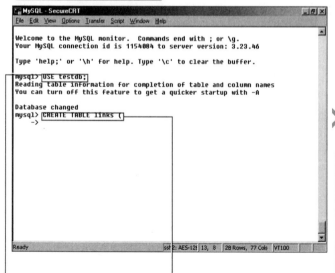

1 From the MySQL monitor, type **USE testdb;** and press Enter.

■ The database is now selected.

Note: See Chapter 1 to create the testdb database.

2 Next, type **CREATE TABLE links (** and press Enter.

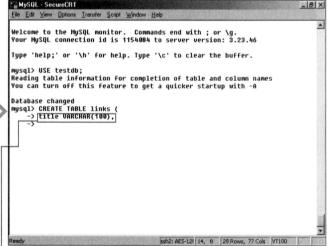

■ The MySQL monitor prompts for the next line.

3 Type **title VARCHAR(100),** and press Enter.

Note: Do not forget the comma after each line except the last one.

Extra

If you are not sure what length to use for a CHAR or VARCHAR column, specify a value large enough to store a typical value. You can always change the length later. You can also change VARCHAR columns to TEXT columns without losing data. This is explained in Chapter 3.

The MySQL server may automatically change the type of some of your columns if there is a conflict between them. In particular, if you use fixed-length CHAR columns and at least one variable-length VARCHAR or TEXT column, the entire row must be variable length, so your CHAR columns are converted to VARCHAR.

In addition, the server automatically changes VARCHAR columns with a length of one to three characters to CHAR columns, because it is not practical to use variable length when the column is this small.

While it is important to choose the correct column types when you create a table, after you have created it, you can work with VARCHAR and CHAR columns in exactly the same ways. TEXT columns also work in most of the same ways, except that you cannot use the entire body of a TEXT field as an index.

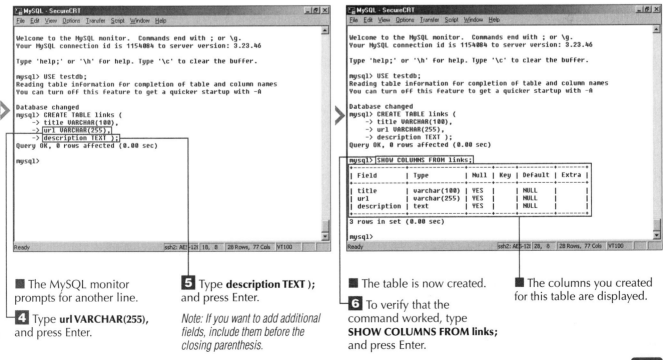

■ The MySQL monitor prompts for another line.

4 Type **url VARCHAR(255),** and press Enter.

5 Type **description TEXT);** and press Enter.

Note: If you want to add additional fields, include them before the closing parenthesis.

■ The table is now created.

6 To verify that the command worked, type **SHOW COLUMNS FROM links;** and press Enter.

■ The columns you created for this table are displayed.

USING SETS AND ENUMERATIONS

Sets and enumerations are different from normal text columns in that they are limited to a specific list of values. You can use these columns whenever you need to assign categories to the items in a table. For example, suppose you were using a database table to catalog music recordings. You could use a SET column to store the category of music that each recording contains:

```
category SET("rock", "pop", "blues",
"country", "dance")
```

The one potential disadvantage of a SET column is that each item can have only one value. Anything that fits more than one category could only be listed in one. This is where ENUM columns are useful.

With an ENUM column, each item can be assigned any number of values from the list you specify when you create

the table. You can look at an ENUM column as a list of flags, each of which can be assigned or not assigned to an item. In the music catalog example, an ENUM column would be ideal to store the media the music is available on:

```
media ENUM("CD","DVD","LP","Cassette")
```

Although you could use separate columns to achieve the same effect, ENUM columns are convenient because they can be assigned values as a single unit. They are also stored on the server in a highly efficient way, using only one bit per item, and are thus especially useful when you are storing many rows of data in a table.

Because ENUM and SET columns can have a large number of possible values, you may need to split the column specification into two or more lines when you create the table.

USING SETS AND ENUMERATIONS

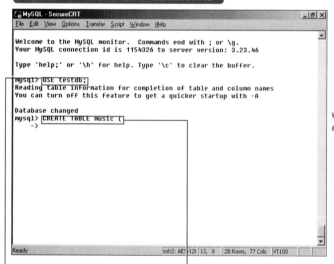

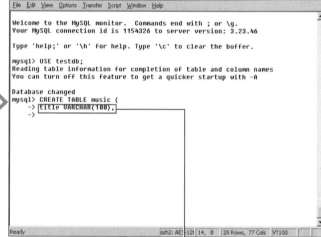

1 From the MySQL monitor, type **USE testdb;** and press Enter.

■ The database is now selected.

Note: If you did not create the testdb database in Chapter 1, you need to create it first.

2 Type **CREATE TABLE music (** and press Enter.

■ This starts the table definition.

■ The MySQL monitor prompts for the next line.

3 Type **title VARCHAR(100),** and press Enter.

Extra

The values for an ENUM column are actually stored as integers. A value of 1 represents the first possible value, 2 represents the second possible value, and so on. ENUM columns can have a maximum of 65,535 total values available. ENUM values use one byte of storage if there are less than 256 possible values and two bytes if there are 256 or more.

The values for a SET column are stored using individual bits. This means that one byte, or eight bits, of storage is required for every eight members of the set. A SET column can have a maximum of 64 members, which requires eight bytes of storage.

You can change the definition for a SET or ENUM column using the ALTER TABLE query in MySQL, described in Chapter 3. However, changing the definition does not change the values stored for existing data. If you add a value at the beginning of the list, the numeric values for the entire list will change. You can safely add values at the end of the list, but the best strategy is to determine the possible values in advance and include them when you first create the table.

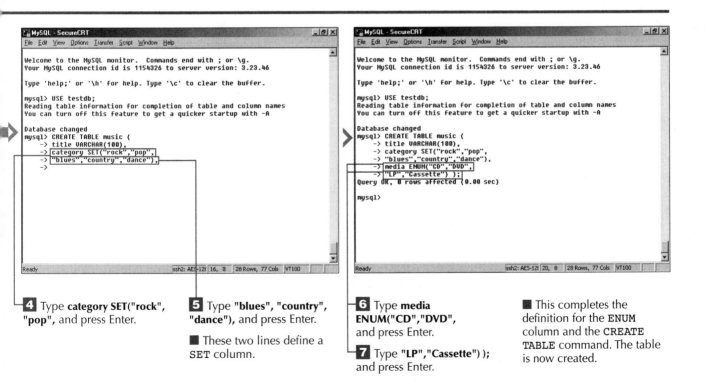

4 Type **category SET("rock", "pop"**, and press Enter.

5 Type **"blues", "country", "dance")**, and press Enter.

■ These two lines define a SET column.

6 Type **media ENUM("CD","DVD")**, and press Enter.

7 Type **"LP","Cassette"))**; and press Enter.

■ This completes the definition for the ENUM column and the CREATE TABLE command. The table is now created.

CREATE AN INDEXED TABLE

Along with the various columns the table will contain, you can specify a primary key and one or more indexed columns. In general, you will want to have at least a primary key for any table. If there is no primary key, there may be no way to uniquely identify a single record. This makes it impossible to edit or delete a single row without affecting other rows in the table.

For the primary key, you should choose a column that will have a unique value for each row of the table. For example, for a table that stores a list of names and mailing addresses, the name field is usually a good primary key, assuming that the list is small enough that duplicate names is not a concern.

You can define the primary key by including the keywords PRIMARY KEY with one of the column definitions when you create the table, or with a separate PRIMARY KEY definition that specifies a column for the key in parentheses. In this case, you can also use multiple fields as a primary key.

The following CREATE TABLE query creates a MailList table with columns for the name, address, city, state, and postal code. The name column is defined as the primary key.

```
CREATE TABLE MailList (
    name VARCHAR(80) PRIMARY KEY,
    address VARCHAR(120),
    city VARCHAR(50),
    state VARCHAR(2),
    postal VARCHAR(5) );
```

CREATE AN INDEXED TABLE

■1 From the MySQL monitor, type **USE testdb;** and press Enter.

■ This selects the testdb database.

■2 Type **CREATE TABLE MailList (** and press Enter.

■ The MySQL monitor prompts for the next line.

■3 Type **name VARCHAR(80) PRIMARY KEY,** and press Enter.

■ This defines the name field as the primary key.

Apply It

Along with the primary key, one or more additional indexes are often useful. You should only define an index on an additional column if you frequently need to search for values in that column. You can add an index with the INDEX keyword, and optionally specify the UNIQUE keyword to require a unique value for each row.

The following example shows an expanded mailing list table with an index on the postal code field. In this case, the UNIQUE keyword is not used because multiple records can have the same code.

Example:
```
CREATE TABLE MailList2 (
    name VARCHAR(80) PRIMARY KEY,
    address VARCHAR(120),
    city VARCHAR(50),
    state VARCHAR(2),
        postal VARCHAR(5),
        INDEX (postal) );
```

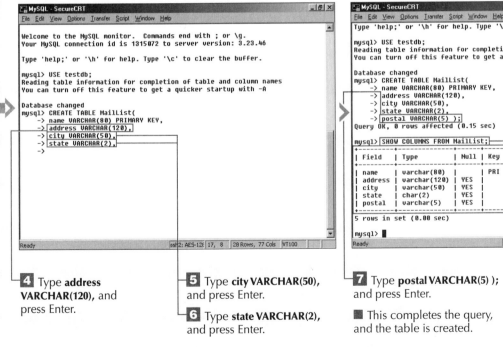

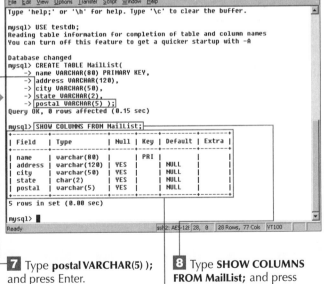

■ **4** Type **address VARCHAR(120),** and press Enter.

■ **5** Type **city VARCHAR(50),** and press Enter.

■ **6** Type **state VARCHAR(2),** and press Enter.

■ **7** Type **postal VARCHAR(5));** and press Enter.

■ This completes the query, and the table is created.

■ **8** Type **SHOW COLUMNS FROM MailList;** and press Enter.

■ The columns for the table you created are displayed.

DELETE TABLES AND DATABASES

If you no longer have any use for a table, you can delete it using the DROP TABLE command. This command immediately deletes the table, including all data. You can specify more than one table to drop with DROP TABLE, separated by commas. The following command deletes the prices table:

```
DROP TABLE prices;
```

When you attempt to drop a table that does not exist, MySQL returns an error. You can optionally specify the IF EXISTS keywords to prevent the error. The following example deletes the test1 table only if it exists:

```
DROP TABLE IF EXISTS test1;
```

If you want to delete an entire database, you can use the DROP DATABASE command. This command deletes the entire database including all tables and data. As with DROP TABLE, you can use the IF EXISTS keyword to prevent an error if the database does not exist. The following command deletes a database called newdb:

```
DROP DATABASE newdb;
```

The DROP command does not prompt you for confirmation, whether you are deleting a table or an entire database. After you have issued the DROP command, there is no way to recover the data unless you have a backup copy. Be sure that you have a backup before you use the DROP command.

In order to drop a database or table, the MySQL username you are using must have the correct privileges. Only the root user is allowed to delete databases by default. See Chapter 11 for more information about MySQL security.

In this example you delete the prices table and the newdb database, which you created in the sections "Create a Database" and "Create a Simple Table," earlier in this chapter. Be sure you specify the names correctly to avoid deleting the wrong data.

DELETE A TABLE

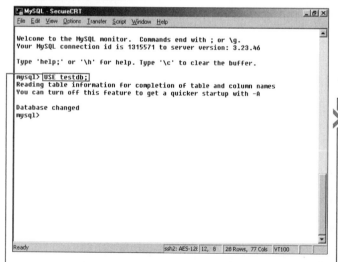

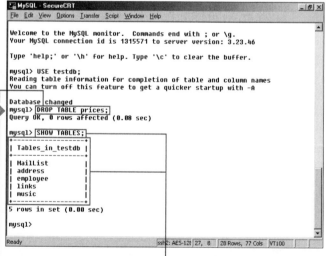

1 From the MySQL monitor, type **USE testdb;** and press Enter.

■ This selects the database.

Note: This task uses the prices table created earlier in this chapter.

2 Type **DROP TABLE prices;** and press Enter.

■ The table is deleted.

3 Type **SHOW TABLES;** and press Enter.

└■ Verify that the deleted table is not listed.

Extra

The DROP TABLE command deletes the disk files that MySQL uses to store a table's data. There are typically three separate files for each table. The DROP DATABASE command deletes the files for each table in the database and additionally deletes the directory for the database. If non-MySQL files are also in this directory, it may prevent the directory from being entirely deleted.

Because the DROP command is drastic, be sure you have a backup of all data before deleting a table or database. You will learn more about backing up MySQL databases in Chapter 8.

If you are unsure whether to delete a table, you can use the SHOW COLUMNS command to display the columns of the table.

Example:

```
SHOW COLUMNS FROM tablename;
```

You can also use a SELECT query to display the data in the table before deleting it. The following command displays all of the rows of a table.

Example:

```
SELECT * FROM tablename;
```

DELETE A DATABASE

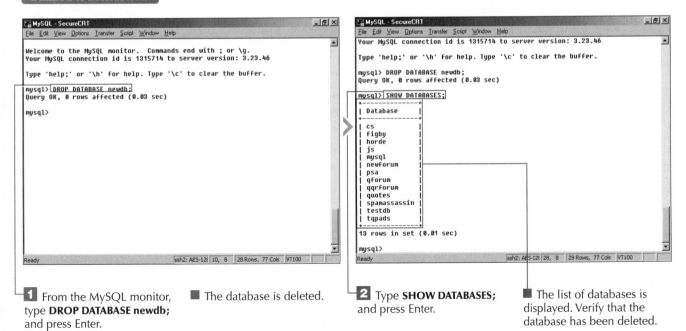

1 From the MySQL monitor, type **DROP DATABASE newdb;** and press Enter.

■ The database is deleted.

2 Type **SHOW DATABASES;** and press Enter.

■ The list of databases is displayed. Verify that the database has been deleted.

USING ALTER TABLE QUERIES

When you create a table with the CREATE TABLE command in MySQL, you specify the column definitions and other options. If you later decide to change any aspect of the table's definition, you can do so using the ALTER TABLE command. This command allows you to change column names, column types, and other aspects of a table's definition.

Basic ALTER TABLE Syntax

You can make any number of changes with a single ALTER TABLE command. You can use a variety of commands within ALTER TABLE to add columns, remove columns, and make other changes. If you use multiple keywords to make changes, separate them with commas.

```
Example:
ALTER TABLE address
    ADD COLUMN lastvisit DATE,
    DROP COLUMN postal;
```

ADD COLUMN

Use the ADD COLUMN command to add a column to the table. Specify the new column name, the column type, and any attributes. You can use the same syntax as you use when creating a table, as described in Chapter 2.

You can optionally specify the keyword FIRST after ADD COLUMN to add the column at the beginning of the table, or the AFTER keyword and a column name to add it after an existing column. If you do not specify either of these, the column is added at the end of the table.

DROP COLUMN

The DROP COLUMN command enables you to delete an existing table column. Use this command with caution, because it deletes all of the data stored in that column in existing table rows without asking for confirmation. To use DROP COLUMN, simply specify the column name.

CHANGE

The CHANGE command changes the definition of an existing column. To use this command, specify the old column name followed by the new name, the column type, and any options such as DEFAULT or NULL. Specify the old name twice if you are not renaming the column.

The MySQL server attempts to convert any existing data in the column to the new column type. However, in some cases, such as when you change the length of a VARCHAR column to a smaller amount, the data in the column will be truncated and cannot be restored.

```
Example:
ALTER TABLE address
    CHANGE name name CHAR(120) NOT NULL;
```

MODIFY

The MODIFY command changes the definition for a column without changing its name. To use this command, specify the column name, the new column type, and any options. As with CHANGE, the data is converted wherever possible to the new format.

```
Example:
ALTER TABLE address
    MODIFY name CHAR(120) NOT NULL;
```

ADD INDEX

Use the `ADD INDEX` command to add an index to the table for an existing column. To use this command, specify an optional index name followed by the column or columns to index in parentheses. If you use `ADD UNIQUE` instead of `ADD INDEX`, a unique index is created. Before adding a unique index, be sure the existing rows of the table have unique values for the column or columns you plan to index.

Example:
```
ALTER TABLE address
   ADD INDEX postindex (postal);
```

DROP INDEX

The `DROP INDEX` command deletes an existing index. To use this command, specify the index name. The index name is the column name by default, or the name you specified when creating the index.

Example:
```
ALTER TABLE address
   DROP INDEX postindex;
```

ADD PRIMARY KEY

The `ADD PRIMARY KEY` command adds a primary key. This can only be used if the table does not have an existing primary key. To use this command, specify one or more columns to act as the primary key. Each existing row of the table must have a unique value for the column or columns specified. The column you specify must also have the `NOT NULL` attribute. You can alter the column to add this attribute if necessary, as described earlier in this section.

Example:
```
ALTER TABLE address
   ADD PRIMARY KEY (name, address);
```

DROP PRIMARY KEY

The `DROP PRIMARY KEY` command removes an existing primary key. This only removes the indexing information, not the column or columns that act as the key. This command does not require any parameters.

Example:
```
ALTER TABLE address
   DROP PRIMARY KEY;
```

RENAME

The `RENAME` command renames an existing table. To use this command, specify the existing table name and the new name. You can use `RENAME TO` as a synonym for `RENAME`.

Example:
```
ALTER TABLE temp
   RENAME TO temp2;
```

Table Options

You can change table options using an `ALTER TABLE` command. These options include `TYPE`, the table type, `COMMENT`, the optional comment field, and other options. The complete list of options is in Chapter 2. To change options, specify each option followed by an equal sign and the new value.

Example:
```
ALTER TABLE temp
   TYPE=Heap,
   COMMENT="I changed the table type.";
```

ORDER BY

The `ORDER BY` command sorts the existing data in a table by the value of a specified column. While you can retrieve the rows of the table in any order, this command is useful to make the order permanent when the table is rarely changed and usually retrieved in a particular order.

Example:
```
ALTER TABLE address
   ORDER BY name;
```

ADD A COLUMN TO A TABLE

I f you have created a few tables in MySQL, you learned that there are many decisions to be made — the columns to include, their types, and other aspects of the table. Fortunately, you can change most of these after the table is created with the ALTER TABLE command.

You can use ALTER TABLE ADD COLUMN to add a column to an existing table. The basic query syntax specifies the table, the name of the new column, and its column type:

```
ALTER TABLE address ADD COLUMN
    country VARCHAR(10);
```

You can optionally specify where the new column should be added. Either specify the keyword FIRST to insert the new column as the first column in the table's definition, or specify the AFTER keyword followed by the name of an existing column. The following example adds a country column to the address table after the existing state column:

```
ALTER TABLE address ADD COLUMN
    country VARCHAR(10) AFTER state;
```

When you add a column, you can specify the same attributes that you use when creating a table, as described in Chapter 2. You can specify the column's type and display width, select a default value for the column, and specify whether null values are allowed.

You cannot specify values for the data in the table's rows for the new column. The default value of the column will be used for all rows of the table until you change the data.

Be sure the new column's name does not conflict with other columns in the table. The column must also be compatible with the existing columns: In particular, if there are existing variable-length text columns, such as VARCHAR or TEXT, you cannot add a fixed-length CHAR column.

ADD A COLUMN TO A TABLE

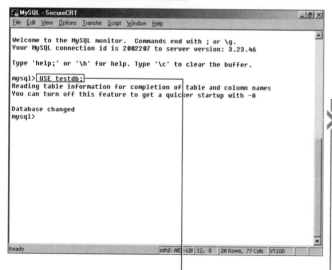

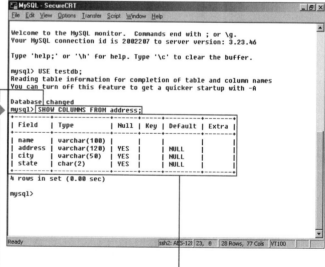

Note: This example uses the testdb database and the address table. If you have not created these, follow the instructions in Chapter 1 or on the CD-ROM.

1 From the MySQL monitor, type **USE testdb;** and press Enter.

■ The database is now selected.

2 Type **SHOW COLUMNS FROM address;** and press Enter.

■ The current list of columns is displayed.

Extra

You can add multiple columns within the same ALTER TABLE command by separating them with commas and enclosing the entire list of new columns in parentheses. For example, the following command adds three new columns to the address table:

Example:
```
ALTER TABLE address ADD COLUMN (
    country VARCHAR(10),
    unit VARCHAR(5),
    notes TEXT );
```

The parentheses shown in this example are not necessary unless you are adding more than one column. When you use this form of the command to add multiple columns, the columns are always added at the end of the table; you cannot use the AFTER or FIRST keywords to control the position of the new columns. You can combine the ADD COLUMN option with other ALTER QUERY commands, described later in this chapter. To include multiple commands, separate them with commas.

Although it makes the ALTER TABLE query easier to read, the word COLUMN is actually optional. If you use ADD by itself, MySQL assumes you are adding one or more columns.

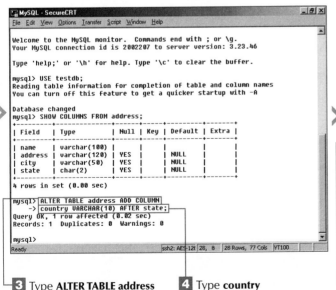

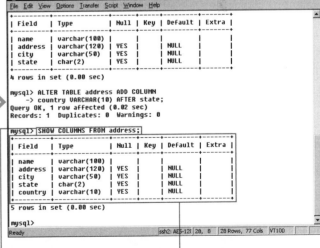

3 Type **ALTER TABLE address ADD COLUMN** and press Enter.

■ The MySQL monitor prompts for the next line.

4 Type **country VARCHAR(10) AFTER state;** and press Enter.

■ The column is now added to the table.

5 Type **SHOW COLUMNS FROM address;** and press Enter.

■ The list of columns is displayed, including the new country column.

ADD AN INDEX

A s you work with a table in MySQL, you may find that an index on an additional field would improve performance. You can use the ALTER TABLE command to add an index to an existing table. To add an index, you specify the ADD INDEX keywords, an optional name for the index, and the existing column or columns to be indexed.

For example, the following ALTER TABLE query adds an index called stateindex to the address table, as an index for the existing state column:

```
ALTER TABLE address ADD INDEX
    stateindex (state);
```

Because the ADD INDEX command adds a simple index rather than a primary key, it is unaffected by existing indexes in the table's definition. When you use this command to add an index, the MySQL server immediately begins scanning the table and building the index file.

You can optionally specify more than one column for the index, separated by commas. In this case, the index will be

based on the combination of values in all of the columns you list. This example adds an index that uses both the state and country columns:

```
ALTER TABLE address ADD INDEX
    location (state,country);
```

If you are adding a column to the table with ADD COLUMN, you can use ADD INDEX within the same ALTER TABLE command to add an index based on the new column, as long as you specify the index after the column definition:

```
ALTER TABLE address
    ADD COLUMN custnum INT UNSIGNED,
    ADD INDEX (custnum);
```

Keep in mind that adding an index does not always improve performance. In fact, extra indexes on fields that are not frequently used for searching can slow down access to the table. See Chapter 10 for information on determining whether an added index will be beneficial.

ADD AN INDEX

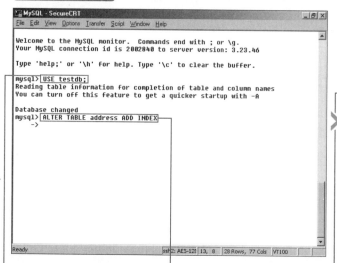

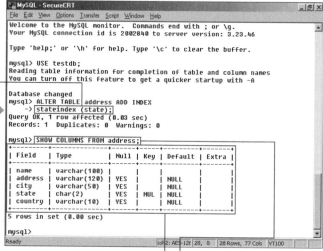

Note: This example uses the testdb database and the address table. The instructions for creating these are in Chapter 1 and on the CD-ROM.

■ The database is now selected.

2 Type **ALTER TABLE address ADD INDEX** and press Enter.

■ The MySQL monitor prompts for the next line.

3 Type **stateindex (state);** and press Enter.

■ The index is now created.

4 Type **SHOW COLUMNS FROM address;** and press Enter.

■ The list of columns is displayed. The value NULL in the Key field shows the new index on the state column.

1 Type **USE testdb;** and press Enter.

Extra

MySQL version 3.22 and later supports an alternate command for adding indexes to tables. You can use the `CREATE INDEX` command to add a regular index, a unique index, or a full-text index to an existing column.

To add a simple index with `CREATE INDEX`, specify a name for the new index, the `ON` keyword, and the table name. This should be followed by one or more column names in parentheses. The following command adds an index on the state column of the address table:

```
CREATE INDEX stateindex ON address (state);
```

You can optionally specify the keyword `UNIQUE` after `CREATE` to make the new index a unique index, or `FULLTEXT` to make it a full-text index. Full-text indexes index the entire text of a `VARCHAR` or `TEXT` column. If you add a regular index on a `TEXT` column, you must specify the length of the column to index in parentheses. This example adds an index on only the first ten characters of the name column:

```
CREATE INDEX first10 ON address (name(10));
```

Functionally, `CREATE INDEX` is equivalent to the `ADD INDEX` and `ADD UNIQUE` commands with `ALTER TABLE`, described in this section and the next section. You cannot add a primary key using `CREATE INDEX`.

ADD A NEW INDEXED COLUMN

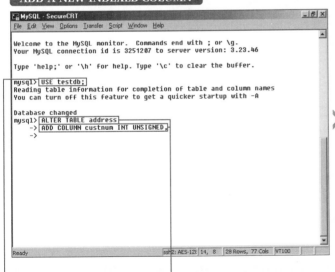

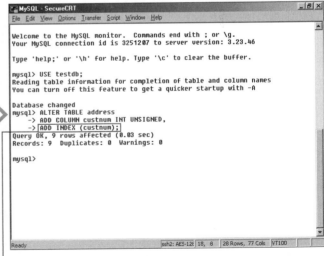

Note: This example uses the testdb database and the address table. The instructions for creating these are in Chapter 1 and on the CD-ROM.

1 From the MySQL Monitor, type **USE testdb;** and press Enter.

■ This selects the database.

2 Type **ALTER TABLE address** and press Enter.

3 Type **ADD COLUMN custnum INT UNSIGNED,** and press Enter.

4 Type **ADD INDEX (custnum);** and press Enter.

■ This adds the custnum column and creates an index on that column.

ADD A PRIMARY KEY OR UNIQUE INDEX

You can also use the ALTER TABLE command in MySQL to add a unique index or a primary key to an existing table. Unique indexes require a unique value for each row of the table. The primary key is a special type of unique index that is used as the primary identifier for each row. Each table can have any number of unique indexes but only one primary key.

To add a primary key, use ADD PRIMARY KEY with ALTER TABLE. You can only add a primary key if the table does not have an existing primary key. The following example adds a primary key on the name field of the address table:

```
ALTER TABLE address ADD PRIMARY KEY (name);
```

To add a unique index, you use the ADD UNIQUE keywords with the ALTER TABLE command. This example adds a unique index called key1 to the address table, indexing the address and city columns:

```
ALTER TABLE address ADD UNIQUE key1
(address, city);
```

While adding an ordinary index to a table is simple, you must consider any data in the table when adding a unique index or primary key. Because these indexes require a unique value for each row, MySQL will return an error if there are duplicate values for the column you are indexing. To successfully add the index, you will need to ensure that the rows have unique values for the column that you are making into a key.

If you are adding a column that will act as the new primary key, you can specify PRIMARY KEY as part of its column definition. However, this will only work on an empty table, because existing rows need unique values for the primary key.

ADD A PRIMARY KEY

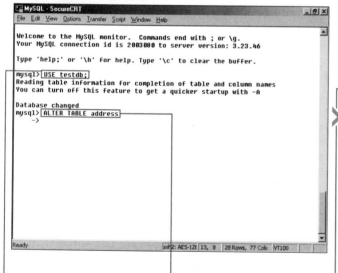

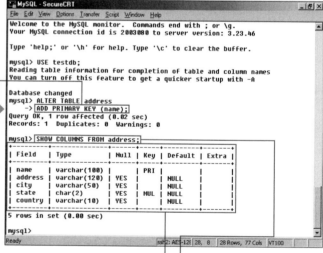

Note: This example uses the testdb database and the address table. To create them, see Chapter 1 or the CD-ROM.

■ **1** From the MySQL monitor, type **USE testdb;** and press Enter.

■ The database is selected.

■ **2** Type **ALTER TABLE address** and press Enter.

■ The MySQL monitor prompts for the next line.

■ **3** Type **ADD PRIMARY KEY (name);** and press Enter.

■ The primary key is now added.

■ **4** Type **SHOW COLUMNS FROM address;** and press Enter.

■ The list of columns is displayed. The value PRI in the Key column indicates that the name field is a primary key.

Extra

While you can add any type of index or primary key to a table using ALTER TABLE, you can also define them when the table is created with the CREATE TABLE command. This is often the better way to add an index, because it ensures that you define the index before any rows are added to the table, and eliminates problems with non-unique rows.

For example, the following CREATE TABLE statement creates an addressindex table. This is identical to the address table, but has the primary key on the name field and the unique index on the address field already defined.

Example:
```
CREATE TABLE addressindex (
  name VARCHAR(100) PRIMARY KEY,
  address VARCHAR(120),
  city VARCHAR(50),
  state CHAR(2),
  UNIQUE key1 (address) );
```

This example uses the PRIMARY KEY keyword with the name column to define the primary key. It uses the UNIQUE keyword in the last line to define a unique index named key1 on the address column.

ADD A UNIQUE INDEX

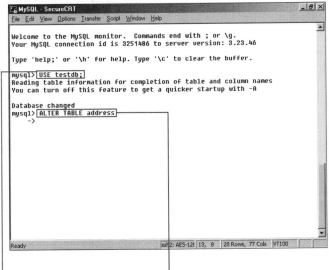

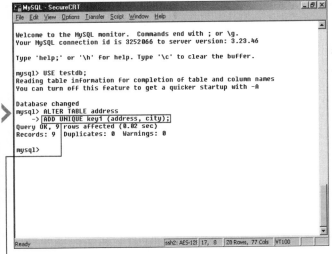

Note: This example uses the testdb database and the address table. To create them, see Chapter 1 or the CD-ROM.

1 From the MySQL monitor, type **USE testdb;** and press Enter.

■ This selects the database.

2 Type **ALTER TABLE address** and press Enter.

3 Type **ADD UNIQUE key1 (address, city);** and press Enter.

■ The unique index is now added on the address and city columns.

ADD A TIMESTAMP COLUMN

Timestamp columns are useful for keeping track of when a row of the table has been updated. Each time you modify or insert a row, the first timestamp column in the table's definition is automatically set to the current date and time.

As with other column types, you can add a timestamp column to an existing table using the ALTER TABLE command in MySQL. For example, the following command adds a timestamp column called updatetime with a display width of 14 characters to the address table:

```
ALTER TABLE address
  ADD COLUMN updatetime TIMESTAMP(14);
```

When you add a new timestamp column to an existing table, it is filled with the default value for each existing row.

Because the default value for the first timestamp column is the current date and time, all rows will be set to the current date and time when you add the column.

If you add a second timestamp column to a table, it is not updated automatically. The default value for the second timestamp column will be zero. You can set this column to the current time and date manually when you add a row.

You can use a timestamp column as an index or primary key. However, if data already exists in the table, you cannot make a new timestamp column the primary key when you add it to the table, because all of the rows will have the current date and time as the value and the rows will be non-unique. You must assign unique values before adding a unique index.

ADD A TIMESTAMP COLUMN

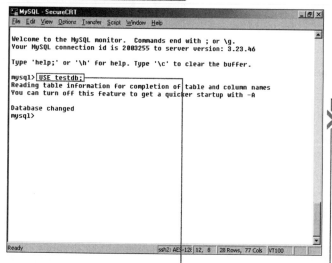

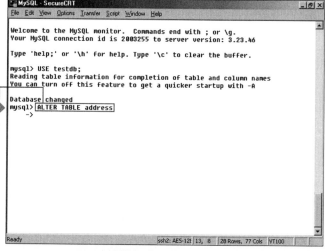

Note: This example uses the testdb database and the address table. See Chapter 1 or the CD-ROM to create them.

1 From the MySQL monitor, type **USE testdb;** and press Enter.

■ The database is now selected.

2 Type **ALTER TABLE address** and press Enter.

■ The MySQL monitor prompts for the next line.

Extra

A timestamp column's display width can be up to 14 digits. When 14 digits are used, the column displays the year, month, date, hour, minute, and second values. For example, a `TIMESTAMP(14)` column set to January 3rd, 2005 at midnight would return the value 20050103000000.

Smaller values for the display width display only a partial date, as shown in the table below. The display width does not affect the actual value. Timestamps always store a value down to the second.

DISPLAY WIDTH	FORMAT
14	YYYYMMDDHHMMSS
12	YYMMDDHHMMSS
10	YYMMDDHHMM
8	YYYYMMDD
6	YYMMDD

Because MySQL stores years as four digits, you should always specify all four digits of the year when assigning a value to a timestamp or date field. If you only specify two digits, MySQL assumes that values from 70 to 99 are in the 1900's, and values from 0 to 69 are in the 2000's.

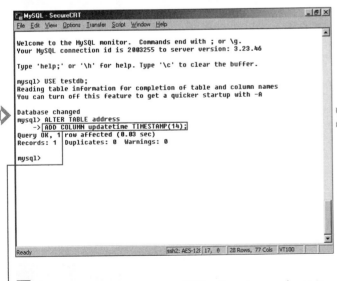

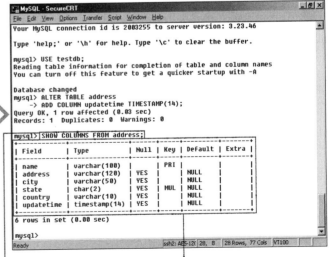

3 Type **ADD COLUMN updatetime TIMESTAMP(14);** and press Enter.

■ The timestamp column is now added to the table.

4 Type **SHOW COLUMNS FROM address;** and press Enter.

■ The list of columns is displayed, including the column you added.

ADD AN AUTO-INCREMENT COLUMN

While some tables have an obvious choice for a primary key, such as a name column, some tables have no value that is guaranteed to be unique for each row. In this case, you can use an auto-increment column as a key. When you specify the AUTO_INCREMENT attribute for a column, each row you add is automatically assigned a new unique value for that column.

As with other column types, you can use ALTER TABLE to add an auto-increment column to an existing table. For example, this command adds a new auto-increment column called num to the links table:

```
ALTER TABLE links ADD COLUMN
   num INTEGER UNSIGNED NOT NULL
   AUTO_INCREMENT PRIMARY KEY;
```

Any column you use as an auto-increment column must have the NOT NULL attribute. If you insert a NULL value

into an auto-increment column, the next sequence number for the field is inserted instead. Auto-increment columns should also have the UNSIGNED attribute because negative numbers can cause conflicts.

You can use any of MySQL's integer types for an auto-increment column. However, be sure to use a type that can store a wide enough range of values to account for the maximum amount of rows you will be adding to the table. You can change the column type later if you need a larger range, as explained in the section "Change a Column Type," later in this chapter.

Auto-increment columns are ideal for use as primary keys or unique indexes, and in fact MySQL requires that any auto-increment column be defined as a unique index. You can use only one auto-increment column per table.

ADD AN AUTO-INCREMENT COLUMN

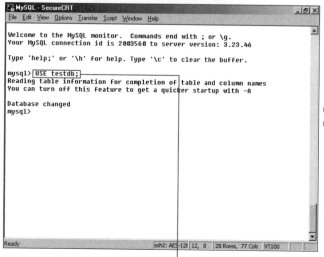

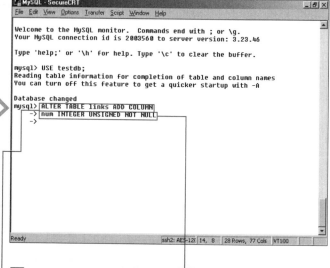

Note: This example uses the testdb database and the links table. The instructions to create them are in Chapter 1 and on the CD-ROM.

1 From the MySQL monitor, type **USE testdb;** and press Enter.

■ The database is now selected.

2 Type **ALTER TABLE links ADD COLUMN** and press Enter.

■ The MySQL monitor prompts for the next line.

3 Type **num INTEGER UNSIGNED NOT NULL** and press Enter.

Extra

When you add an auto-increment column to a table with existing data, the rows of the table are assigned values for the column automatically, counting up from one. This allows you to use a new auto-increment column as a primary key or unique index, because the values are guaranteed to be unique.

When you delete a row from a table with an auto-increment column, the sequence number on that row is usually not re-used. Thus, you should not assume that every number in a certain range will be used for one of the rows of the table — the only thing you are guaranteed is that every row has a unique value for the auto-increment column. If you delete all of the rows of the table, the auto-increment numbers start over at one.

You can specify the first number to be used when assigning values to an auto-increment column when you create the table with the AUTO_INCREMENT parameter. You can also use this when adding a new auto-increment column to a table.

When you insert a new row in an auto-increment column, it is assigned the number after the largest number used by a current row of the table.

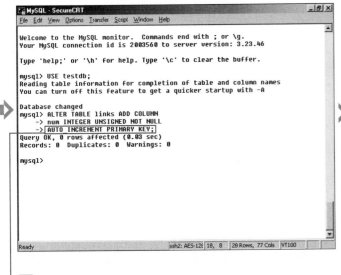

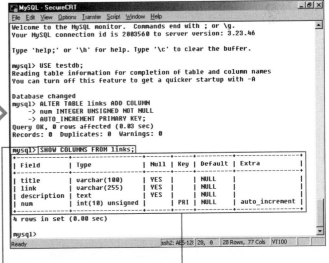

4 Type **AUTO_INCREMENT PRIMARY KEY;** and press Enter.

■ The new column is added to the table.

5 Type **SHOW COLUMNS FROM links;** and press Enter.

■ The list of columns is displayed, including the new auto-increment column.

RENAME A COLUMN

You can use the ALTER TABLE command in MySQL to change the name of an existing column. To change a column's name, use the CHANGE keyword. For example, this command changes the name of the url column in the links table to link:

```
ALTER TABLE links
    CHANGE url link VARCHAR(255);
```

To use CHANGE with ALTER TABLE, you specify the current name of the column, followed by the new name, the column's type, and any attributes such as DEFAULT or UNSIGNED. If you do not want to change the type of the column, specify the same information you used when creating the column.

If you are unsure of the column's current type and attributes, you can use the SHOW COLUMNS command to find out the details of the column, and repeat them with a new name. The rules for the new column name are the

same as when creating a table, but you cannot use a name that is already used in the table.

Keep in mind that when you rename a column, any applications that refer to the column by name will need to be modified to use the new name. You will also need to refer to the new name in any further references to the column.

In MySQL 4.0 and later, you can use the optional keyword FIRST after the column definition to move the column to the beginning of the column list for the table, or the AFTER keyword followed by a column name to move the column to a new position after the specified column. Changing the order of columns does not affect existing data or applications.

If you specify a different column type or attributes with the CHANGE keyword, the column's definition will be modified. This is explained in the next section.

RENAME A COLUMN

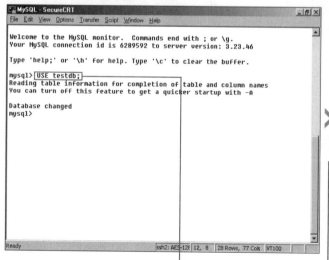

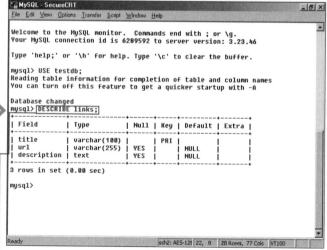

Note: This example uses the testdb database and the links table. See Chapter 1 or the CD-ROM for information on creating them.

1 From the MySQL monitor, type **USE testdb;** and press Enter.

■ The database is now selected.

2 Type **DESCRIBE links;** and press Enter.

■ This displays the current column list for the links table.

Extra

If you change the column order using ALTER TABLE, it may create potential problems with applications that were built to work with the table. For example, suppose an application used the following command to add a record to a table:

Example:
```
INSERT INTO links
  VALUES("Netscape",
  "http://www.netscape.com/",
  "Netscape Corp.");
```

This command adds a row to the table, specifying values for each of the three columns. While this command will work with the current version of the links table, it does not specify the columns for the insert and thus relies on the current column order. If you have changed the column order using the CHANGE or ADD COLUMN features of ALTER TABLE, the INSERT command will fail, or worse, may insert incorrect data into the table.

Applications that retrieve data without using column names can run into the same problem. While the best practice is to specify column names in all queries, you can avoid these potential issues if you avoid changing the order of table columns.

If your applications do use column names, of course, a renamed column could cause an error. Keep both of these issues in mind any time you modify a working table.

See Chapter 4 for more information about the INSERT command in MySQL.

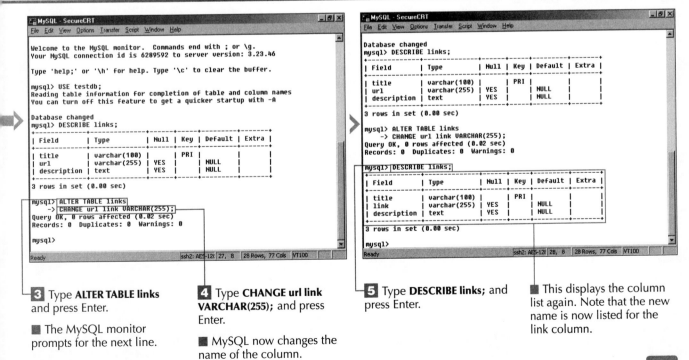

-3 Type **ALTER TABLE links** and press Enter.

■ The MySQL monitor prompts for the next line.

-4 Type **CHANGE url link VARCHAR(255);** and press Enter.

■ MySQL now changes the name of the column.

-5 Type **DESCRIBE links;** and press Enter.

■ This displays the column list again. Note that the new name is now listed for the link column.

CHANGE A COLUMN TYPE

While it is important to choose each column's type and attributes carefully when creating a table, you can change a column's type using ALTER TABLE. The basic syntax for this is similar to renaming a table, using the CHANGE keyword. For example, the following command changes the description field in the links table to a VARCHAR(200) column:

```
ALTER TABLE links CHANGE
    description description VARCHAR(200);
```

To avoid renaming the table when using CHANGE, specify the same name for the old and new names. You can also specify any attributes of the column you want to change with the CHANGE keyword. For example, you can specify the NULL or NOT NULL attributes or specify a default value using the DEFAULT keyword. Include these items after the column definition.

You can alternately use the MODIFY keyword, which allows changing a column type but not renaming it. The MODIFY

keyword is supported only in MySQL 3.22 and later. The following example makes another change to the description column using MODIFY:

```
ALTER TABLE links
    MODIFY description VARCHAR(150);
```

When you change a column's type, MySQL makes an effort to preserve the data in existing rows as much as possible and convert it to the new type. If you change a table's type to a type that stores less data — for example, changing a TEXT column to a VARCHAR column — the values will be truncated to fit in the new size. Changing the column's type back to its original type will not restore the data.

As when creating a table or adding a column, the MySQL server may not allow some changes. If the table currently has one or more variable-length fields, you cannot change a column's type to a fixed-length CHAR field. Conversely, if the existing fields are fixed-length, you cannot change one to a variable-length field unless you make the same change to all columns.

CHANGE A COLUMN TYPE

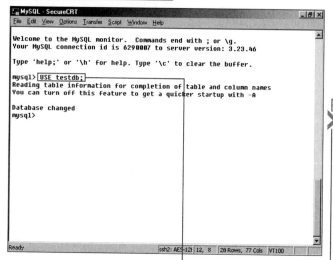

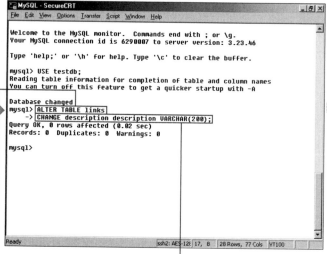

Note: This example uses the testdb database and the links table. See Chapter 1 or the CD-ROM if you have not created them.

1 From the MySQL monitor, type **USE testdb;** and press Enter.

■ The database is now selected.

2 Type **ALTER TABLE links** and press Enter.

■ The MySQL monitor prompts for the next line.

3 Type **CHANGE description description VARCHAR(200);** and press Enter.

■ The column's type is now changed.

Apply It

When you want to make one change to a column in a table, often you will find that other changes are required. For example, suppose you want to make the title field of the links table into a primary key. The following ALTER TABLE command tries to add the primary key:

Example:
```
ALTER TABLE links
   ADD PRIMARY KEY (title);
```

If you attempt to use this command, however, MySQL will display an error message because you cannot make a column a primary key unless it has the NOT NULL attribute. To add the primary key, you must first use CHANGE or MODIFY to add this attribute to the column's definition.

You can change the attributes and add the primary key within the same ALTER TABLE statement, as long as the ADD PRIMARY KEY command appears last, after the NOT NULL attribute has been set. The following example correctly adds the primary key:

Example:
```
ALTER TABLE links
   CHANGE title title VARCHAR(100) NOT NULL,
   ADD PRIMARY KEY(title);
```

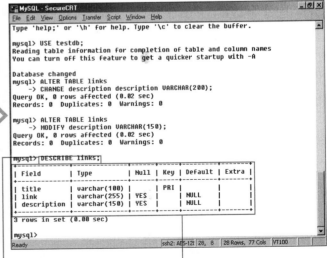

4 Type **ALTER TABLE links** and press Enter.

5 Type **MODIFY description VARCHAR(150);** and press Enter.

■ This changes the column type again.

Note: If MODIFY does not work, you may be using a version of MySQL prior to version 3.22.

6 Type **DESCRIBE links;** and press Enter.

■ The column list for the table is displayed, including the modified description column.

DELETE A COLUMN

If you no longer need a column in a table, you can use ALTER TABLE with the DROP COLUMN keywords to delete the column from the table. For example, the following command deletes the country column from the address table:

```
ALTER TABLE address DROP COLUMN country;
```

This command removes the column from the table definition, and removes any data stored in the column in the existing rows of the table. As with other DROP commands, there is no warning or confirmation before the data is lost, so be sure you do not inadvertently delete a column that contains important data.

The word COLUMN is optional. You can simply use DROP and the column name to drop a column. You can combine DROP with other ALTER TABLE commands within the same

query by separating the commands with commas. For example, this command drops the country column and adds a test column:

```
ALTER TABLE address DROP COLUMN country,
    ADD COLUMN test INTEGER(5);
```

If you drop a column that is used as an index or a primary key on the table, the indexing information is also deleted. If the index is based on multiple columns, it is not deleted until all of the columns associated with the index have been dropped from the table.

If you attempt to drop a column and the table only has one column, MySQL will return an error because a table must have at least one column. You can delete the table entirely using the DROP TABLE command, explained in Chapter 2.

DELETE A COLUMN

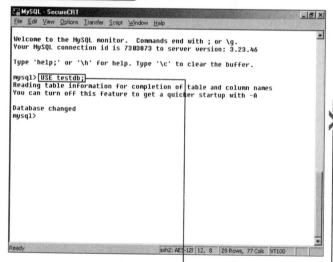

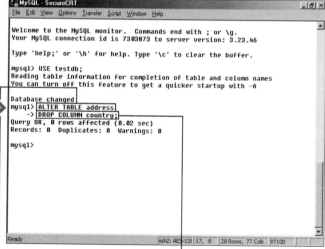

Note: This example uses the address table in the testdb database, created in Chapter 1. The country column was added in the section "Add a Column to a Table," earlier in this chapter.

1 From the MySQL monitor, type **USE testdb;** and press Enter.

■ The database is now selected.

2 Type **ALTER TABLE address** and press Enter.

■ The MySQL monitor prompts for the next line.

3 Type **DROP COLUMN country;** and press Enter.

■ The column is now deleted from the table.

Extra

When you use most variations of the ALTER TABLE command, the MySQL server actually performs the alterations in several steps. It first creates a new table with a copy of the existing table's data. Next, the changes you specified in your query are made to the new table. Finally, the original table is deleted and the new one is renamed to the old name.

Clients are able to read data from the table during the alteration process, but no data can be written to the table until the process is completed. Because alterations may take a while on large tables and consume a large amount of the server's CPU and memory resources, it is best to alter tables while few clients are using them.

Because ALTER TABLE copies the table, you can use it to sort a table's data. To do this, use the ORDER BY keywords:

Example:
```
ALTER TABLE address ORDER BY name;
```

While you usually do not need to manually sort a table in this way, it can improve performance with a large table that will not be modified frequently. The sorting process can take a long time on a large table.

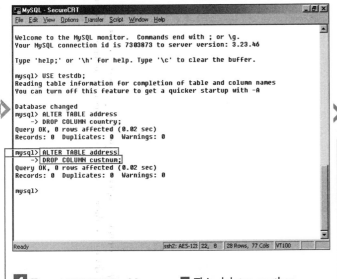

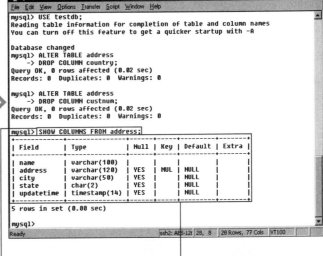

■ **4** Type **ALTER TABLE address** and press Enter.

■ **5** Type **DROP COLUMN custnum;** and press Enter.

■ This deletes another column.

Note: The country and custnum columns were added earlier in this chapter.

■ **6** Type **SHOW COLUMNS FROM address;** and press Enter.

■ The list of columns is displayed, without the dropped column.

DELETE AN INDEX OR PRIMARY KEY

Y ou can remove an index or a primary key from a table with the ALTER TABLE command. This may be useful if you are adding a new key, or if you no longer require an index — if you do not frequently search on a column, having an index on the column may decrease rather than increase the MySQL server's speed.

To remove an index or a unique index, use the DROP INDEX keywords and specify the name of the index to delete. While the index name, by default, is the same as the column name it indexes, you may have specified a different name for the index when it was created. For example, the following command removes the stateindex index you added earlier in this chapter from the address table:

ALTER TABLE address DROP INDEX stateindex;

Because this command requires the index name rather than the column name, you can use the SHOW INDEX command to determine the name of the index if you are not sure. If

you did not specify an index name when the index was created, it will have the same name as the column it indexes. The following command lists the indexes for the address table:

SHOW INDEX FROM address;

When you drop an index, only the indexing information is deleted. No data in any column is affected, and you can re-create the index using another ALTER TABLE command at any time.

You can also delete a primary key using ALTER TABLE. To do this, use the DROP PRIMARY KEY keywords. Because there can be only one primary key, an index name is not required. This command removes the primary key from the address table:

ALTER TABLE address DROP PRIMARY KEY;

DELETE AN INDEX

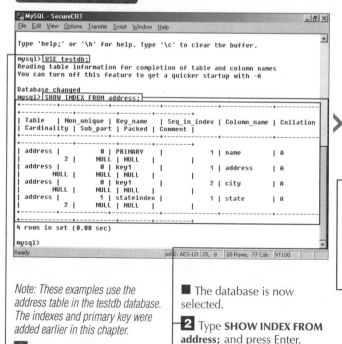

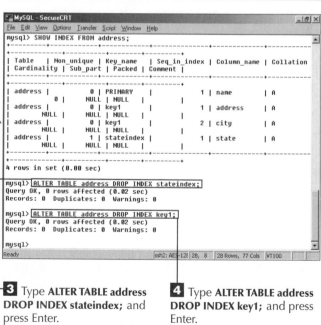

Note: These examples use the address table in the testdb database. The indexes and primary key were added earlier in this chapter.

1 From the MySQL monitor, type **USE testdb;** and press Enter.

■ The database is now selected.

2 Type **SHOW INDEX FROM address;** and press Enter.

■ The list of indexes is displayed.

3 Type **ALTER TABLE address DROP INDEX stateindex;** and press Enter.

■ The index is deleted.

4 Type **ALTER TABLE address DROP INDEX key1;** and press Enter.

■ This deletes the unique index.

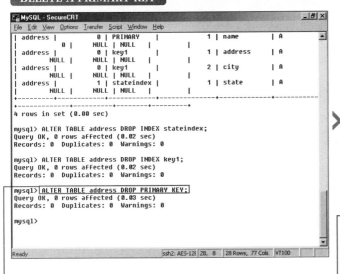

Apply It

If you are removing an index or primary key, you often need to add a new index or primary key. You can perform both of these actions with a single `ALTER TABLE` command. The following example removes the index and primary key from the address table and then adds a new auto-increment column and sets it as the new primary key.

Example:
```
ALTER TABLE address
    DROP INDEX stateindex,
    DROP PRIMARY KEY,
    ADD COLUMN num INT UNSIGNED AUTO_INCREMENT,
    ADD PRIMARY KEY (num);
```

When you use multiple operations with `ALTER TABLE`, they are performed in order. This example will only work if the existing primary key is dropped before the last line of the command where the new one is added.

You can combine any of the available clauses for `ALTER TABLE` in this way. However, it is often more practical to use separate statements. If you make the changes in separate statements, you can check the table and verify that the operation worked before continuing with further changes.

DELETE A PRIMARY KEY

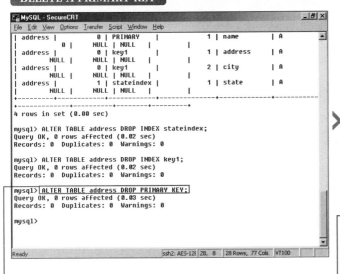

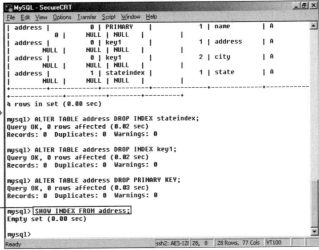

Note: The testdb database should already be selected.

◼ The primary key is removed.

1 Type **ALTER TABLE address DROP PRIMARY KEY;** and press Enter.

2 Type **SHOW INDEX FROM address;** and press Enter.

◼ Because the index and primary key have been removed, the list is now empty.

RENAME A TABLE

You can use the ALTER TABLE command in MySQL to rename an existing table. To rename a table, specify the old name and the new name with the RENAME TO keywords. For example, the following command renames the MailList table to simply mail:

```
ALTER TABLE MailList
    RENAME TO mail;
```

When choosing a new name for the table, follow the same rules you follow when you create a table. Be sure that the new table name does not conflict with an existing table in the same database.

Renaming a table is virtually instantaneous. Once the table has been renamed, you need to use the new name whenever you refer to it, and any applications that use the table should be updated to use the new name.

Unlike other ALTER TABLE queries, the MySQL server does not create a temporary copy of the table when renaming a table. Instead, the data files for the table in the file system are simply renamed. This is much faster than copying the table, and is unaffected by the amount of data stored in the table.

MySQL 3.23 and later also support the RENAME TABLE command for the same purpose. The following example renames the MailList table to mail using RENAME TABLE:

```
RENAME TABLE MailList TO mail;
```

There is no difference in the way a table is renamed using RENAME TABLE or ALTER TABLE, so you can use the command of your choice if your MySQL server supports both. If you are unsure which version of MySQL you are using, simply use ALTER TABLE.

RENAME A TABLE

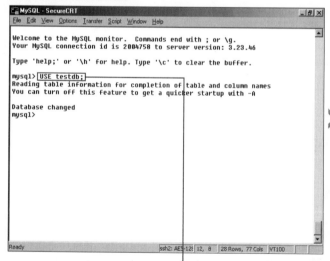

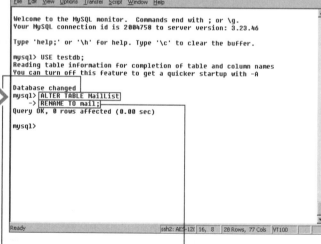

Note: The instructions for creating the MailList table are in Chapter 2 and on the CD-ROM.

1 From the MySQL monitor, type **USE testdb;** and press Enter.

■ The database is now selected.

2 Type **ALTER TABLE MailList** and press Enter.

■ The MySQL monitor prompts for the next line.

3 Type **RENAME TO mail;** and press Enter.

■ The table is now renamed.

CHANGE A TABLE TYPE

You can use ALTER TABLE to change the options used when the table was created, including the table type. If you do not specify a type when a table is created, MySQL uses the default type, MyISAM.

Along with MyISAM, MySQL supports several alternate table types. These include ISAM, the older format used to support legacy data; Heap tables, which are stored in memory and use a hashed index; and BDB and InnoDB tables, high-performance types that support transactions for increased reliability. Chapter 2 explains these table types in more detail.

To change a table type, use ALTER TABLE with the TYPE= option. You do not need to know the original table type to do this. For example, the following command changes the type of a table called temp to Heap:

```
ALTER TABLE temp TYPE=Heap;
```

You can change a table's type to any of the types supported by your particular MySQL server installation. Keep in mind that the BDB and InnoDB table types are only supported if you have installed the MySQL-Max package or explicitly included them when compiling MySQL from source.

You can also use ALTER TABLE with other table options. Table options allow you to specify various settings for the table, such as MAX_ROWS and MIN_ROWS to define the expected maximum and minimum numbers of rows, AUTO_INCREMENT to set the next value to be used in an auto-increment column, and COMMENT to specify a comment or description of the table. The various table options are listed in Chapter 2.

You can change table options with ALTER TABLE using the same keywords you use when creating a table. For example, you can use the COMMENT keyword to add a comment to a table, replacing any comment specified when the table was created:

```
ALTER TABLE temp COMMENT="This is the new comment.";
```

CHANGE A TABLE TYPE

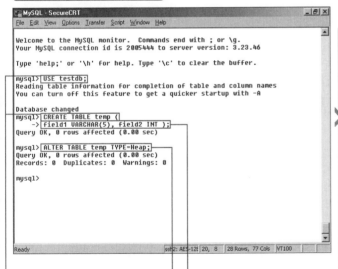

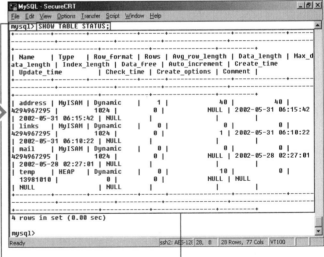

Note: This example uses the testdb database. Instructions for creating it are in Chapter 1 and on the CD-ROM.

1 Type **USE testdb;** and press Enter.

■ The database is now selected.

2 Type **CREATE TABLE temp (** and press Enter.

3 Type **field1 VARCHAR(5), field2 INT);** and press Enter.

■ This creates the temp table as a default MyISAM table.

4 Type **ALTER TABLE temp TYPE=Heap;** and press Enter.

■ The table is converted to a Heap table.

5 Type **SHOW TABLE STATUS;** and press Enter.

■ The list of tables and details is displayed, verifying that the table type has changed.

USING INSERT AND DELETE QUERIES

After you create a database and one or more tables to store data, you can use the INSERT and REPLACE commands in MySQL to add rows of data to the table. After a table contains data, you can use the DELETE command to delete a row, a group of rows, or the entire table.

REPLACE DATA WITH REPLACE

The REPLACE command is identical to INSERT with the exception that if you add a row that duplicates the value of an existing row in a unique index or primary key column, the existing row is deleted and replaced with the new row.

Example:
```
REPLACE INTO mail (name, address)
  VALUES ("John Doe", "33 Birch Street");
```

ADD DATA WITH INSERT

The INSERT command in MySQL adds one or more records to an existing table. To insert data, use INSERT INTO *tablename* and specify the values for each column of the table. The keyword INTO is optional.

Example:
```
INSERT INTO address
    VALUES ("John Smith", "321 Elm Street",
    "Chicago", "IL", 0
```

Specify Column Names

You can optionally specify one or more column names and provide values for those columns only. If you do not specify column names, you must provide values for all columns in the correct order.

Example:
```
INSERT INTO address (name, state)
   VALUES ("Jane Doe", "CA");
```

Using LOW_PRIORITY

You can optionally specify the LOW_PRIORITY keyword with INSERT. If this is specified, MySQL will wait until no clients are reading from the table before inserting the record. This prevents other clients from being delayed when the table is locked. The MySQL client waits until the INSERT has completed before returning.

Using DELAYED

The DELAYED option is similar to LOW_PRIORITY. When you specify this keyword, the MySQL client returns immediately, but the server holds the row and inserts it when no clients are reading from the table.

Copy Data Between Tables

You can use SELECT with INSERT to select one or more columns of data in one or more rows of an existing table to copy to the destination table. The SELECT clause can specify column names and the table to take data from. You can also use an optional WHERE clause to specify one or more conditions that each row must match in order to be copied.

Example:
```
INSERT INTO mail (name, address)
   SELECT name, address FROM address;
```

DELETE DATA FROM TABLES

You can use the DELETE command in MySQL to delete one or more rows of data from a table. The simplest version of a DELETE query deletes all of the rows from a table. Be cautious because this command erases the entire table.

Example:
```
DELETE FROM address;
```

Using the WHERE Clause

You can add the WHERE clause to a DELETE query to select a single row or group of rows to be deleted. WHERE can be followed by a condition that matches a value in any of the fields of the table.

MySQL displays the number of deleted rows after a DELETE query when the WHERE clause is completed. This is the only way to determine whether rows were successfully deleted. MySQL does not display an error message if the WHERE clause matches no rows.

Using LIMIT

You can optionally use the LIMIT clause with a DELETE query to limit the number of rows to be deleted. This serves two purposes: first, if you are unsure how many rows will be matched by a WHERE clause, using a LIMIT clause will ensure that a large number of rows cannot be deleted by mistake.

Second, it limits the amount of time a table is locked during the DELETE process. You can minimize the slowdown caused by a DELETE query by using a LIMIT clause and repeating the DELETE command until all of the desired rows have been deleted.

Example:
```
DELETE FROM address
   WHERE state = "CA" LIMIT 10;
```

Using ORDER BY

In MySQL 4.0 and later, you can use the ORDER BY clause along with LIMIT in a DELETE query. This allows you to control not only how many rows are deleted, but which rows are chosen. Rows are deleted in alphabetical or numeric order based on the value of the column you select.

You can optionally follow the ORDER BY clause with the keyword ASC to delete rows in ascending order, the default, or DESC to delete in descending order.

Example:
```
DELETE FROM address
   ORDER BY name ASC LIMIT 10;
```

Using TRUNCATE

The TRUNCATE query is identical to DELETE except that it does not allow a WHERE clause. It deletes all of the table's records without confirmation. When you delete all rows using TRUNCATE or DELETE, MySQL actually deletes the entire table and then creates a new, empty table. This improves speed, but there is no way to determine the number of rows that were deleted by the query.

Example:
```
TRUNCATE TABLE address;
```

ADD A ROW TO A TABLE

After you create a table in a MySQL database, you can begin adding data to the table. The primary way to add rows of data to a table is with the INSERT query. To add a row, you specify the values for all of the row's columns:

```
INSERT INTO address
    VALUES ("John Smith", "321 Elm Street",
    "Chicago", "IL", 0);
```

Within the VALUES section of the INSERT query, you specify a value for each of the columns of the table. Values for text fields should be enclosed within single or double quotes. Values for numeric fields can simply be included as a number. The entire list of values should be enclosed within parentheses.

With this form of the INSERT query, you need to specify the values for each of the fields in the order they are

defined in the table's definition. If you are unsure of the order, you can use one of these two equivalent commands to list the fields:

```
DESCRIBE tablename;
SHOW COLUMNS FROM tablename;
```

As with other SQL queries that work with tables, you should first use the USE command to select the database that contains the table you will be working with. You can insert one row into the table with each INSERT query.

You can add data with INSERT from the MySQL monitor's command line or from an application that works with MySQL. One common solution for data entry is to use a Web form linked to a program written in PHP, Perl, or another language to validate and insert the data.

ADD A ROW TO A TABLE

Note: This example uses the address table in the testdb database. See Chapter 1 or the CD-ROM to create them if necessary.

1 From the MySQL monitor, type **USE testdb;** and press Enter.

■ The database is now selected.

2 Type **INSERT INTO address** and press Enter.

■ The MySQL monitor prompts for the next line.

3 Type **VALUES ("John Smith", "321 Elm Street",** and press Enter.

■ The MySQL monitor prompts for the next line.

Apply It

As another example of the INSERT query in MySQL, you can add a row of data to the employee table you created in Chapter 2. The fields of this table are defined with the following CREATE TABLE query:

Example:
```
CREATE TABLE employee (
    FirstName CHAR(50),
    LastName CHAR(50),
    Salary DECIMAL(8,2),
    HireDate DATE,
    Department INT );
```

To add a row to this table, you can specify values for the fields in the same order they were specified when the table was created. When using this type of INSERT command, be sure to specify a value for every column of the table.

Example:
```
INSERT INTO employee VALUES (
    "Sue", "Johnson", "30000",
    "2002/05/11", 21);
```

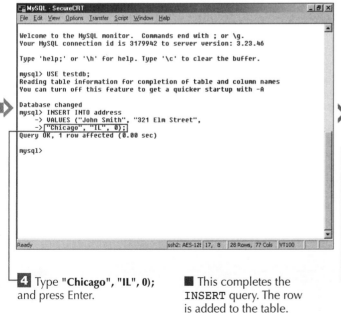

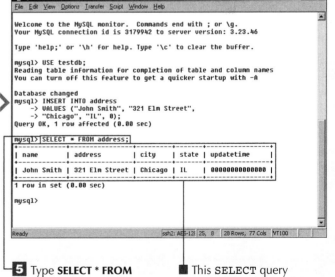

4 Type **"Chicago", "IL", 0);** and press Enter.

■ This completes the INSERT query. The row is added to the table.

5 Type **SELECT * FROM address;** and press Enter.

■ This SELECT query displays the contents of the table. Verify that the new row was added.

SPECIFY COLUMNS FOR A NEW ROW

In a table with a large number of fields, you may find it cumbersome to specify values for each of the columns in order. Fortunately, you can use an alternate INSERT query syntax to insert a row and specify values for whichever columns you choose, in the order you specify.

To insert a row and specify the columns to add, list the column names in parentheses before the list of values. For example, this query inserts a row into the address table and specifies values for the name and address columns only:

```
INSERT INTO address
   (name, address)
   VALUES ("John Doe", "1445 West 10th Ave.");
```

In this form of the INSERT query, you need to use the correct column names to match the table's definition, but you do not need to specify values for all columns or in any particular order. The row added to the table will contain the columns and values you specified. It will also include default values for any columns your INSERT query did not include.

This type of INSERT query has the advantage of being simpler when you are not specifying values for all fields. Another advantage is that if you later change the definition of the table and add columns or change the column order, the same INSERT query will still work as long as the columns you include in the query have not changed.

If you specify a column name that is not defined in the table, MySQL will return an Unknown column error message. If you are unsure of the exact column names, use DESCRIBE tablename to display a list.

SPECIFY COLUMNS FOR A NEW ROW

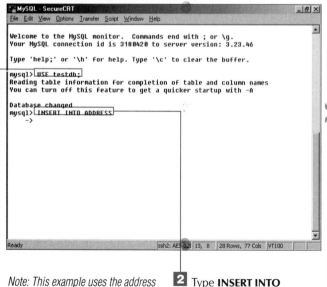

Note: This example uses the address table in the testdb database.

1 From the MySQL monitor, type **USE testdb;** and press Enter.

■ The database is now selected.

2 Type **INSERT INTO ADDRESS** and press Enter.

■ The MySQL monitor prompts for the next line.

3 Type **(name, address)** and press Enter.

■ You are prompted for the next line.

4 Type **VALUES ("John Doe", "1445 West 10th Ave.");** and press Enter.

■ This completes the INSERT query. The row is added to the table.

SPECIFY INSERT PRIORITY

With some MySQL table types, an `INSERT` query that adds data to the table will lock the table, and the table cannot be read by other clients during the processing of `INSERT`. You can optionally specify the `LOW_PRIORITY` keyword in an `INSERT` query to allow clients to continue to read the table:

```
INSERT LOW_PRIORITY INTO address
   VALUES ("Jane Smith", "321 Elm Street",
   "Chicago", "IL", 0);
```

When you specify `LOW_PRIORITY`, your client waits until no clients are reading from the table before inserting the row. In a busy table, this may take some time.

A similar option is provided with the `DELAYED` keyword. When you specify `DELAYED`, your client returns immediately as if the insert were successful. The server then holds the request until no clients are reading from the table, and then

inserts the row. This provides a faster alternative, but there is no immediate way to confirm that the insert was successful.

```
INSERT DELAYED INTO address (name, address)
   VALUES("Susan Jones", "112 West 5th");
```

The `LOW_PRIORITY` and `DELAYED` options perform similar functions and cannot both be used in the same `INSERT` query. By default, neither option is enabled.

With MySQL's default MyISAM table type, `LOW_PRIORITY` and `DELAYED` are usually unnecessary because this table type supports concurrent inserts: You can insert a row while other clients are reading data from the table. These options are mostly useful for tables using the older ISAM format. Because an `INSERT` operation is usually fast on a table with few users, these options are unnecessary in this case and may slow down the process of inserting rows.

SPECIFY INSERT PRIORITY

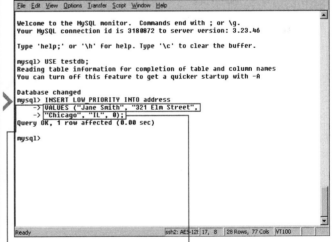

Note: This example uses the address table in the testdb database.

1 From the MySQL monitor, type **USE testdb;** and press Enter.

■ The database is now selected.

2 Type **INSERT LOW_PRIORITY INTO address** and press Enter.

■ The MySQL monitor prompts for the next line.

3 Type **VALUES ("Jane Smith", "321 Elm Street",** and press Enter.

■ You are prompted for the next line.

4 Type **"Chicago", "IL", 0);** and press Enter.

■ This completes the `INSERT` query. The client waits until the table is free before inserting the data.

USING AUTO-INCREMENT COLUMNS

As another usage of INSERT queries, you can use INSERT to work with a table that includes an auto-increment column. Auto-increment columns are integer columns created with the AUTO_INCREMENT attribute. They are automatically filled with a unique numeric value when you create a row.

To insert a row in a table with an auto-increment column, simply use a zero or NULL as the value for that column. For example, this INSERT query adds a row to the links table you created in Chapter 2. It includes values for the title and link fields as well as the auto-increment num field.

```
INSERT INTO links (title, link, num)
  VALUES ("Yahoo", "http://www.yahoo.com/",
  NULL);
```

Because NULL is specified as the value for the num column, a new value is stored in the column. The MySQL server keeps track of the largest number used in the column so far, and adds one to that number to create the value for a new row.

Because the default value for an auto-increment column is the next numeric value, you can also specify no value for the column. It will still be assigned a unique value.

If you specify an integer value greater than zero for the auto-increment column, this value will be used instead of the next value in order. However, because an auto-increment column must be defined as a unique index or primary key, the INSERT query does not work if you specify a value that already exists in the table. If the INSERT is successful, the value you specified is used as the new starting point for the automatic numbering.

USING AUTO-INCREMENT COLUMNS

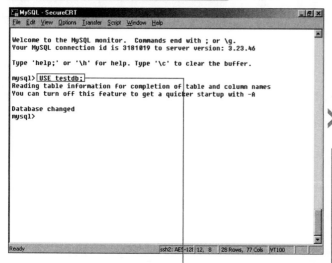

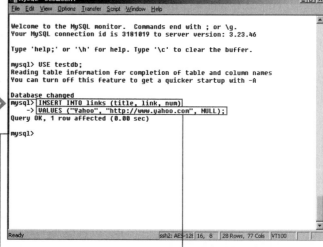

Note: This example uses the links table in the testdb database. See the Extra section if you have not created this table.

1 From the MySQL monitor, type **USE testdb;** and press Enter.

■ The database is now selected.

2 Type **INSERT INTO links (title, link, num)** and press Enter.

■ The MySQL monitor prompts for the next line.

3 Type **VALUES ("Yahoo", "http://www.yahoo.com/", NULL);** and press Enter.

■ This completes the INSERT query. The row is added to the table.

Extra

The links table was created in Chapter 2, and the num field was added in Chapter 3. If you have not created this table, you can use the following MySQL command to create it now, including the auto-increment num field.

Example:
```
CREATE TABLE links (
    title VARCHAR(100),
    url VARCHAR(255),
    description TEXT,
    num INT AUTO_INCREMENT PRIMARY KEY);
```

You can find out the next value for a table's auto-increment column with the SHOW TABLE STATUS command in the MySQL monitor. This command lists all of the tables in the current database and various details about each table. The auto-increment column lists the next auto-increment value for each table.

While sequential numbers are used for the auto-increment column when you add rows to the table, the values of all of the existing rows are not necessarily continuous. If you delete rows, MySQL does not re-use the auto-increment values from the deleted rows. Thus, do not assume that the next auto-increment value indicates the number of existing rows.

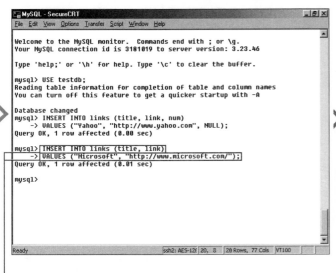

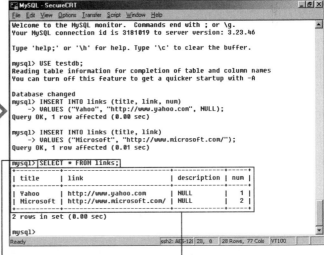

4 Type **INSERT INTO links (title, link)** and press Enter.

■ You are prompted for the next line.

5 Type **VALUES ("Microsoft", "http://www.microsoft.com/");** and press Enter.

■ This completes another INSERT query. A row is added to the table.

Note: Although no value was specified for the num column this time, it is still filled with the next auto-increment value.

6 Type **SELECT * FROM links;** and press Enter.

■ This displays the data in the links table, including the two rows you added.

USING TIMESTAMP COLUMNS

Timestamp columns store a date and time to the exact second. If a table includes a timestamp column, it will usually be updated with the current time and date when you add a row using INSERT. Only the first timestamp column in a table is automatically updated.

To add a row and ensure that the timestamp column is updated, specify the NULL value for the timestamp column. This example inserts a row into the address table and updates the timestamp in the updatetime column:

```
INSERT INTO address (name, updatetime)
   VALUES ("Albert Einstein", NULL);
```

The NULL value updates the timestamp column with the current date and time. Unlike auto-increment columns, you cannot use zero to force an update. Timestamp columns can actually contain a zero value, so use NULL when you want to update the timestamp.

Because the first timestamp column is updated by default, you do not need to specify a value at all. The following example will also add a row to the address table and update the timestamp:

```
INSERT INTO address (name, address)
   VALUES ("Mae West", "333 Cedar St.");
```

If you are updating a timestamp column other than the first one in a table, you must explicitly set it to NULL to store the current date and time. If for some reason you want to use a different value in a timestamp, you can override it by specifying a date and time value:

```
INSERT INTO address (name, updatetime)
   VALUES ("Mark Twain", "20050510123000");
```

As with other columns that store dates and times, the value you assign to a timestamp column should include the year, month, date, hours, minutes, and seconds values in order. You can also specify a date without a time, and zero values will be used for the time portion of the timestamp.

USING TIMESTAMP COLUMNS

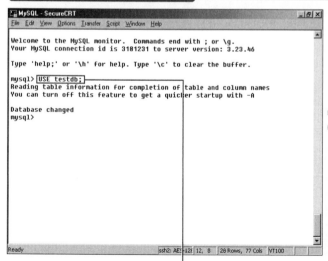

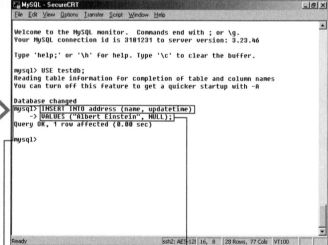

Note: This example uses the address table in the testdb database. See Chapter 1 or the CD-ROM to create them.

1 From the MySQL monitor, type **USE testdb;** and press Enter.

■ The database is now selected.

2 Type **INSERT INTO address (name, updatetime)** and press Enter.

■ You are prompted for the next line.

3 Type **VALUES ("Albert Einstein", NULL);** and press Enter.

■ This completes the INSERT query. The row is added to the table.

Extra

The UPDATE query in MySQL, discussed further in Chapter 5, updates one or more rows of a table with new information. When you update a row, MySQL automatically sets the first timestamp column of the row to the current date and time, even if you did not specify a value for that column. For example, this command updates a row with a new address:

Example:
```
UPDATE address
   SET address="123 Oak Street"
   WHERE name = "Albert Einstein";
```

When this command is executed, the updatetime field for that row will be set to the current date and time. While this is usually a useful feature, there are times when you will want to update a row without changing the timestamp column. To do this, you can specify that the column should keep its old value by specifying the column name as the value.

Example:
```
UPDATE address
   SET address="123 Oak Street",
   updatetime=updatetime
   WHERE name = "Albert Einstein";
```

As with new table rows, if you want to update a timestamp column that is not the first one in the table, you need to explicitly assign the NULL value to the column.

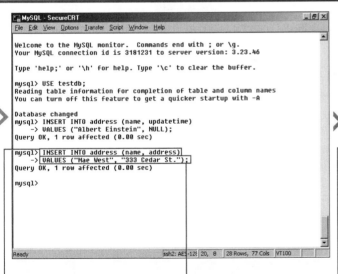

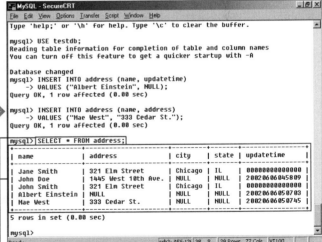

4 Type **INSERT INTO address (name, address)** and press Enter.

■ You are prompted for the next line.

5 Type **VALUES ("Mae West", "333 Cedar St.");** and press Enter.

■ This completes the INSERT query to add a second row to the table.

6 Type **SELECT * FROM address;** and press Enter.

■ This displays all of the table's rows, including the two you added.

Note: Both rows should show the date and time when you typed the INSERT commands in the timestamp field.

REPLACE AN EXISTING ROW

A long with INSERT, MySQL also includes a REPLACE command. Like INSERT, REPLACE adds a new row to a table. The difference is that when you add a row with INSERT that has the same value as an existing row for a unique index or primary key column, an error is returned. If you add a row with REPLACE, it replaces the existing row. If there is no existing row, REPLACE works just like INSERT.

For example, the following query adds a new row to the mail table using REPLACE:

```
REPLACE INTO mail (name, address)
  VALUES ("Samuel Johnson", "3394 Willow
  Ave.");
```

In this example, the name field is the table's primary key. If the table has an existing row with the same name specified

here, the existing row will be deleted before the new row is added.

Do not be tempted to use REPLACE when you want to update information in a row. While the command above will replace the old record with the new one, it does not specify values for all of the table's columns. Any existing data in the unspecified columns will be lost, because the old row is deleted entirely before the new one is inserted. You can use the UPDATE command, discussed in Chapter 5, to update one or more columns of a row without erasing existing data.

When you execute a REPLACE query using the MySQL monitor, it displays the number of rows affected by the query. This number will be one if the new row did not replace an existing row, or two if the old row was deleted and the new row was added.

REPLACE AN EXISTING ROW

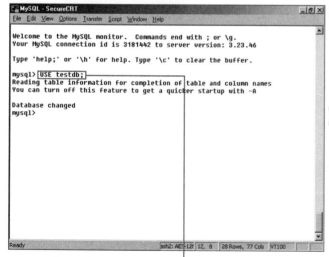

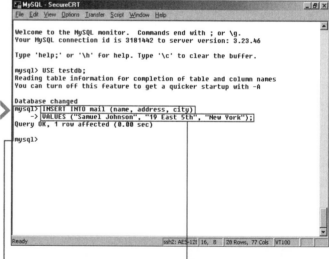

Note: This example uses the mail table in the testdb database. If you have not created this table, see the instructions in the Extra section.

1 From the MySQL monitor, type **USE testdb;** and press Enter.

■ This selects the database.

2 Type **INSERT INTO mail (name, address, city)** and press Enter.

■ You are prompted for the next line.

3 Type **VALUES ("Samuel Johnson", "19 East 5th", "New York");** and press Enter.

■ This completes the INSERT query. The row is added to the table.

Extra

The mail table was created in Chapter 2 and modified in Chapter 3. If you have not created this table and its primary key, you can simply use this CREATE TABLE statement to create the table:

Example:
```
CREATE TABLE mail (
    name VARCHAR(80) PRIMARY KEY,
    address VARCHAR(120),
    city VARCHAR(50),
    state CHAR(2),
    postal VARCHAR(5) );
```

This command creates the mail table and specifies its five columns. The name column is defined as the primary key. Because the primary key always requires unique values, the REPLACE command will replace any existing row with the same value in the name field as the row you are adding.

If you use REPLACE on a table that does not include a primary key or unique index, no rows are ever replaced because the table allows duplicate values for any of its columns. In this case, the REPLACE command is equivalent to INSERT.

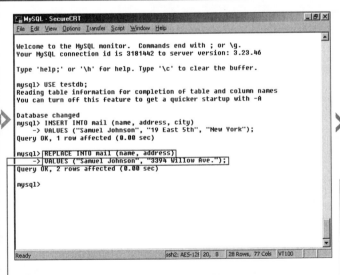

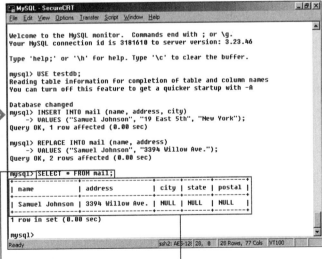

━ **4** Type **REPLACE INTO mail (name, address)** and press Enter.

━ **5** Type **VALUES ("Samuel Johnson", "3394 Willow Ave.");** and press Enter.

■ This completes the REPLACE query.

Note: Because the row you added with REPLACE has the same name as the previous one, it replaces the other row you added.

━ **6** Type **SELECT * FROM mail;** and press Enter.

■ The rows of the table are displayed. Because the row was replaced, only one row is present.

INSERT ROWS FROM ANOTHER TABLE

Often, the data you want to add to a table is already listed in another table. You can use the SELECT keyword with INSERT to copy one or more rows from one table to another. For example, the following query copies data from the address table to the mail table:

```
INSERT INTO mail (name, address)
   SELECT name, address FROM address;
```

In this example, all of the rows of the address table are copied. The name and address fields are copied to their corresponding fields for each row. In this case the field names are the same, but any fields can be used. If the field names for two tables are the same, you can use a wildcard to copy all of the fields:

```
INSERT INTO mail SELECT * FROM address;
```

With this syntax, all of the columns will be copied if there is a column with the same name in the destination table. If a column does not exist in the destination table, the other columns are still copied and a warning message is displayed.

If the source and destination tables have a column of different types, MySQL will convert the data wherever possible. Some column values may be truncated when you copy them to a column with a smaller field length.

If any of the selected rows in the source table have the same value for a primary key or unique index as an existing row in the destination table, MySQL will return an error. You can specify the IGNORE option to ignore this error and continue copying. In this case, only the rows that are not present in the destination table are copied.

INSERT ROWS FROM ANOTHER TABLE

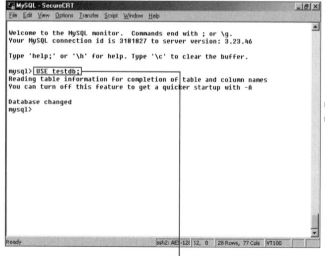

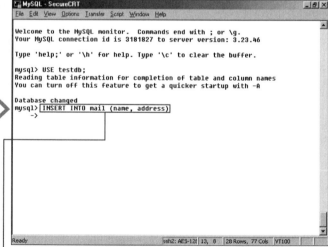

Note: This example uses the mail and address tables in the testdb database.

1 From the MySQL monitor, type **USE testdb;** and press Enter.

■ The database is now selected.

2 Type **INSERT INTO mail (name, address)** and press Enter.

■ The MySQL monitor prompts for the next line.

Extra

You can use a SELECT query without INSERT to display one or more rows of data from a table. The simplest SELECT statement displays all of the columns and rows of a table:

Example:
```
SELECT * FROM tablename;
```

If you specify one or more column names instead of the wildcard (*) character, only the values of those columns will be displayed for each row. The following query displays a list of names and addresses from the address table:

Example:
```
SELECT name, address
  FROM address;
```

You can add the WHERE clause to single out one or more rows from the table. For example, this query displays all of the rows of the address table with the value 'CA' in the state field:

Example:
```
SELECT * FROM address WHERE state = "CA";
```

Many other options are available for SELECT to control the rows displayed, their order, and other aspects. The SELECT statement and the WHERE clause are described in detail in Chapter 6.

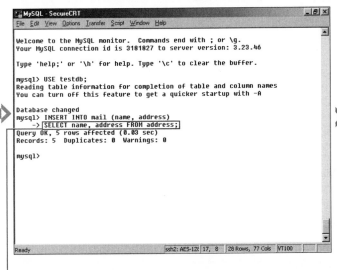

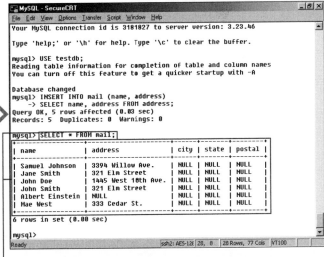

3 Type **SELECT name, address FROM address;** and press Enter.

■ This completes the INSERT query. All of the rows of the address table are copied to the mail table.

4 Type **SELECT * FROM mail;** and press Enter.

■ The rows of the mail table are displayed.

Note: Because the postal field does not exist in the address table, the default value was used for this column in the rows that were copied.

DELETE A SPECIFIC ROW

f you need to remove one or more rows of data from a table, you can use a DELETE query in MySQL. The following is a simple DELETE query:

```
DELETE FROM address
   WHERE name="John Smith";
```

To use DELETE, you specify the table to delete rows from. You can use the WHERE clause to specify one or more records to delete. To delete a single row, be sure the condition you specify in the WHERE clause applies to only one row — this is always the case if you use a primary key or unique index as the column to check.

Be careful not to use a WHERE clause that matches more rows than expected, because all of the matching rows will be lost. If you omit the WHERE clause entirely, all of the rows of the table are deleted without confirmation.

You can specify the LOW_PRIORITY option with DELETE to minimize the operation's impact on other users. If this is specified, the MySQL server will wait until no clients are reading from the table before deleting the rows, and your client will not return until the rows have been successfully deleted.

To delete more than one row, specify a WHERE condition that matches several rows. For example, the following DELETE query deletes all rows from the address table where the state column has the value of 'CA':

```
DELETE FROM address
   WHERE state = "CA";
```

You can use a second DELETE option, QUICK, to speed up deletion. When the QUICK option is specified, the server does not update index files when it deletes the rows. If you are deleting a large number of records, this will speed up the operation.

DELETE A SPECIFIC ROW

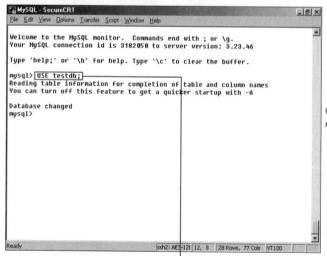

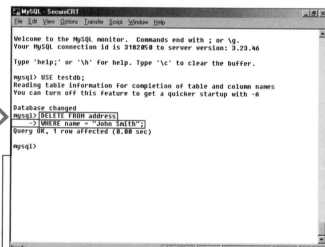

Note: This example uses the address table in the testdb database.

1 From the MySQL monitor, type **USE testdb;** and press Enter.

■ The database is now selected.

2 Type **DELETE FROM address** and press Enter.

■ The MySQL monitor prompts for the next line.

3 Type **WHERE name = "John Smith";** and press Enter.

■ This completes the DELETE query and the row is deleted.

Note: This row was added to the table earlier in this chapter. No records will be deleted if this row is not present in the table.

Extra

When you delete a row in MySQL's standard MyISAM table format, the row is not actually removed from the table at all. Instead, MySQL stores a list of the records that have been marked as deleted, and these records are ignored in queries. When you later insert a row, MySQL finds the first deleted record in the list and replaces it with the new row.

The advantage of this system is that `DELETE` and `INSERT` operations are fast, and in a table where records are frequently added and removed, the table remains efficient. However, when you delete a large number of records, the space they used remains in the table and uses disk space.

To reclaim the space used by deleted records, you can use the `OPTIMIZE TABLE` command in the MySQL monitor. For example, this command optimizes the address table:

Example:
```
OPTIMIZE TABLE address;
```

This command compresses the table and permanently removes the deleted records. Keep in mind that this may take a while on a large table, and the table is unavailable to other users during the optimization process.

The `OPTIMIZE TABLE` command and similar commands for managing MySQL tables are described in Chapter 10.

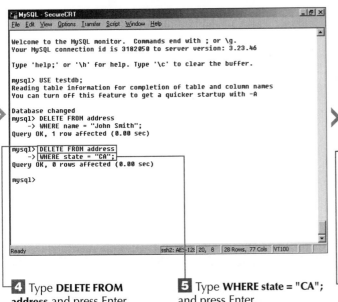

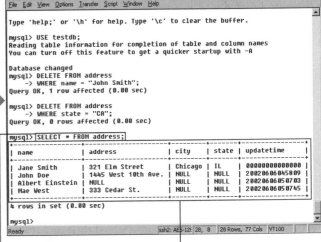

4 Type **DELETE FROM address** and press Enter.

■ You are prompted for the next line.

5 Type **WHERE state = "CA";** and press Enter.

■ This deletes any records with 'CA' in the state field.

6 Type **SELECT * FROM address;** and press Enter.

■ This displays the contents of the table. Verify that the record was deleted.

DELETE ALL TABLE ROWS

I f you use a DELETE query without the WHERE clause, all rows of the table will be deleted. For example, this command deletes all of the rows in the address table:

```
DELETE FROM address;
```

This command immediately deletes all of the rows of the table. Because it is easy to delete an entire table by simply leaving out the WHERE clause, be careful when using DELETE queries, and be sure you have a backup of critical table data before using DELETE.

When you use DELETE to delete all rows, the MySQL server does not individually delete each row. Instead, it deletes the original table and creates a new, empty table with the same name and specifications. The advantage of this approach is that it is much faster.

Because deleting all rows is optimized this way, MySQL will usually not return the number of rows that were deleted when you delete all rows. Instead, it will report that zero

rows were affected. If you need to count the number of deleted rows, you can add a WHERE clause that always matches. This slows down the DELETE process, but the deleted rows are counted. The following example uses a WHERE clause that compares two numbers. This will match all rows and ensure that the correct number of deleted rows is displayed.

```
DELETE FROM address
  WHERE 1 > 0;
```

The TRUNCATE command works the same way as DELETE but does not accept a WHERE clause and always deletes all rows. The following command deletes all rows from the address table:

```
TRUNCATE TABLE address;
```

When you use DELETE or TRUNCATE, the MySQL server will wait until no clients are reading or writing to the table before deleting the records.

DELETE ALL TABLE ROWS

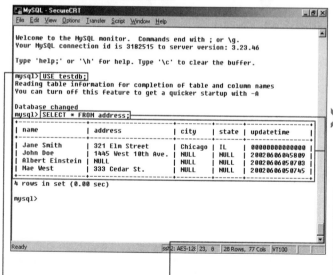

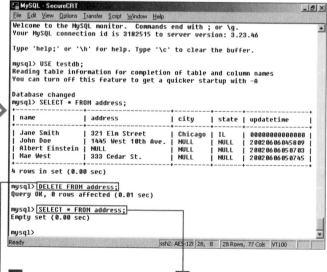

Note: This example uses the testdb database and the mail table. You added records to this table earlier in this chapter.

1 From the MySQL monitor, type **USE testdb;** and press Enter.

■ The database is now selected.

2 Type **SELECT * FROM address;** and press Enter.

■ This displays the existing rows of the table.

3 Type **DELETE FROM address;** and press Enter.

■ All rows of the table are deleted.

4 Type **SELECT * FROM address;** and press Enter.

■ No rows are displayed because the table is empty.

LIMIT THE NUMBER OF DELETED ROWS

When you use DELETE without a WHERE clause, all of the records will be deleted. Even when you use a WHERE clause, more rows may match the clause than you expected. To minimize the damage by overreaching DELETE queries, you can add the LIMIT clause. The following command deletes only one row from the mail table:

DELETE FROM mail LIMIT 1;

When you use the LIMIT clause, the MySQL server ensures that only the number of rows you specified will be deleted. This has two advantages: first, it prevents you from deleting more rows than expected. Second, when you intend to delete a large number of rows, you can use the LIMIT clause to delete a portion of the rows at a time, and repeat the command until all of the rows are deleted. This allows

you to minimize the slowdown for other clients caused by deleting the records.

In MySQL 4.0 and later, you can also use the ORDER BY clause to control the order in which rows will be deleted. This only makes sense when you use it with LIMIT. Using ORDER BY allows you to delete the oldest row in the table or order by a different field. For example, this command deletes the five oldest rows from the address table:

DELETE FROM address
   ORDER BY updatetime LIMIT 5;

You can use any field in the ORDER BY clause. You can also optionally follow it with the keyword ASC for an ascending sort, the default, or DESC for a descending sort.

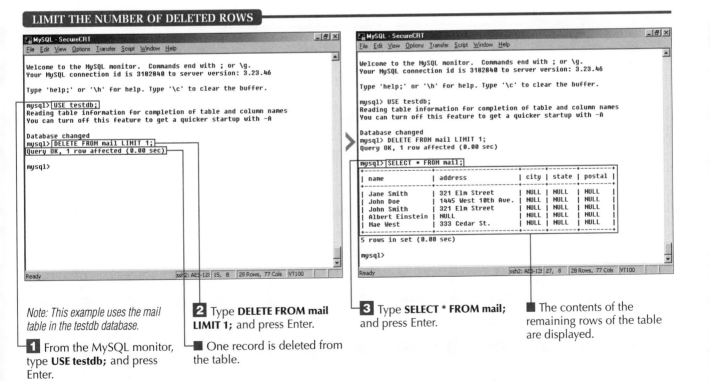

LIMIT THE NUMBER OF DELETED ROWS

Note: This example uses the mail table in the testdb database.

1 From the MySQL monitor, type **USE testdb;** and press Enter.

■ The database is now selected.

2 Type **DELETE FROM mail LIMIT 1;** and press Enter.

■ One record is deleted from the table.

3 Type **SELECT * FROM mail;** and press Enter.

■ The contents of the remaining rows of the table are displayed.

DELETE DATA BY DATE

When you include a timestamp field in a table, it is automatically updated with the current date and time when each row is added to the table. If you are using a table to store data that becomes less useful as it gets older, you can use a timestamp field with a DELETE query to delete all of the rows that were created or updated before a certain date.

For example, the address table has a timestamp column called updatetime. You can use a WHERE clause with a DELETE query to delete older data from the table. The following example deletes all rows that were created or updated before January 1st, 2001:

```
DELETE FROM address
   WHERE updatetime < 20010101000000;
```

The WHERE clause in this command compares the updatetime column with the numeric date value for January 1st, 2001. Any value less than this number indicates that the row has not been updated since that date and can thus be deleted.

This type of DELETE command is especially useful with tables that are used to log events. For example, you may be using a table to log an entry for each user that visits a Web page. On a busy site, this table will quickly become large and unwieldy. You can use a DELETE query regularly to delete all of the rows that are older than you need.

If you use this technique, be sure that the timestamp field is being updated whenever you insert or update a row. This is only done automatically with the first timestamp column for each table. With other timestamp columns, you need to explicitly assign the NULL value to update the timestamp, as described earlier in this chapter.

DELETE DATA BY DATE

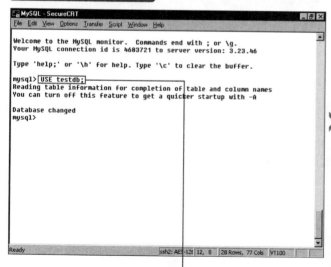

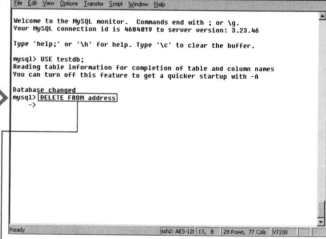

Note: This example uses the address table and the testdb database. You can create these using the instructions in Chapter 1 or on the CD-ROM.

1 From the MySQL monitor, type **USE testdb;** and press Enter.

■ The database is now selected.

2 Type **DELETE FROM address** and press Enter.

■ You are prompted for the next line.

Extra

In some cases, you may need to delete the older rows from a table to make room, but avoid losing the data in those rows entirely. You can use an INSERT and SELECT statement, as described in the section "Insert Rows from Another Table," earlier in this chapter, to copy the older rows to a separate table before deleting them.

The following CREATE TABLE statement creates an archive table that includes the same fields as the address table:

Example:
```
CREATE TABLE archive (
  name VARCHAR(100),
  address VARCHAR(120),
  city VARCHAR(50),
  state CHAR(2),
    updatetime TIMESTAMP );
```

Using this table, you can use an INSERT query with the SELECT clause to copy the older data, and then delete the older data.

Example:
```
INSERT INTO archive SELECT * FROM address
    WHERE updatetime < 20010101000000;
DELETE FROM address
  WHERE updatetime < 20010101000000
```

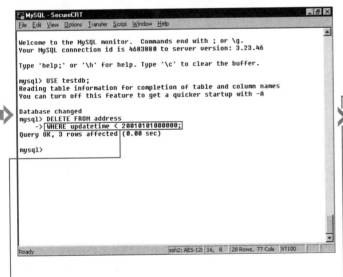

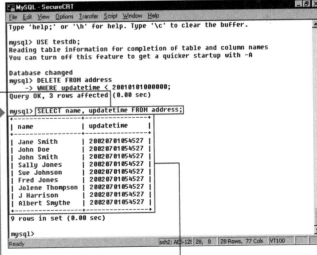

3 Type **WHERE updatetime < 20010101000000;** and press Enter.

■ This completes the query. Rows older than the specified date are deleted.

Note: You may need to specify a different date for rows to be affected.

4 Type **SELECT name, updatetime FROM address;** and press Enter.

■ The remaining rows of the table are displayed.

USING UPDATE QUERIES

While INSERT allows you to add a new row to a table, the UPDATE query provides another useful function. Using UPDATE, you can make changes to one or more rows of the table. The UPDATE query can change the value of one column or several, and can work with existing column values for each row.

USING UPDATE

The basic UPDATE query updates all of the rows of the table. You can use the SET keyword to specify a column name and its new value. When MySQL executes the UPDATE query, it returns the number of rows that were affected by the update.

Note that unlike ALTER TABLE or CREATE TABLE, an UPDATE query does not use the TABLE keyword. Using TABLE with UPDATE will cause a syntax error.

Example:
```
UPDATE address SET city = "New York City";
```

The WHERE Clause

If you want to update a single row or group of rows, you can specify a WHERE clause with one or more conditions that test the columns of each row. Only the rows that match the WHERE clause will be modified in the UPDATE query.

The syntax of the WHERE clause is identical to that used with DELETE and SELECT queries.

Example:
```
UPDATE address SET state="NY"
  WHERE city = "New York City";
```

Update a Limited Number of Rows

You can optionally specify the LIMIT keyword and a number to limit the number of rows the MySQL server will modify in an UPDATE query. You cannot specify the order of the update, so this feature does not control which rows will be updated. It is useful for limiting the potential damage done by an incorrect query.

Example:
```
UPDATE address SET city="Chicago" LIMIT 5;
```

Specify Update Priority

You can optionally specify the LOW_PRIORITY keyword with an UPDATE query. If this keyword is specified, the MySQL server waits until no clients are reading from the table before performing the update. This can minimize the slowdown experienced by other users of the table, but increases the time spent performing the update.

Example:
```
UPDATE LOW_PRIORITY address
  SET city="New Orleans";
```

Along with basic updates, you can perform more complex operations with an UPDATE query. You can update multiple rows and multiple columns, and you can calculate values based on existing data.

Update Key Values

If you use an UPDATE query to modify the value of a column that is defined as a primary key or unique index, MySQL will return an error if any of the updated rows would duplicate the value of an existing row for the key. When this happens, the update is aborted.

If you specify the IGNORE keyword within the UPDATE query, any duplicate keys are skipped. The update is not aborted, and the update is performed for all rows that do not create a duplicate key value.

Example:
```
UPDATE IGNORE address
   SET city="Santa Fe";
```

Update Multiple Columns

You can specify more than one column to update after the SET keyword within an UPDATE query. Separate the column and value pairs with commas.

The MySQL server executes the UPDATE query from left to right. If you assign two different values to a column, the last one in the query is the value used.

Example:
```
UPDATE address
   SET city = "Santa Fe", state = "NM"
   WHERE name="John Smith";
```

Update Timestamp Columns

Timestamp columns are a special case in MySQL. When your UPDATE query updates a row in a table that contains a timestamp column, the column is automatically updated with the current date and time, whether it was included in the UPDATE query or not.

While automatic updates of timestamps are usually a useful practice, you may need to preserve the existing

Using Current Values

You can use the current value of any column in an UPDATE query. You can assign the value to another column or use it within a function or calculation to reach a value.

Because MySQL interprets the UPDATE query from left to right, if you change the value of a column and use it in an assignment, the order of the statements controls whether the new value or the old value is used.

Example:
```
UPDATE address
   SET city = state;
```

Using MySQL Functions

You can use MySQL functions to calculate a value assigned in an UPDATE query. MySQL includes a wide variety of functions, such as UPPER to return the uppercase equivalent of a text value or ROUND to round a numeric value. You can also use arithmetic operations, such as + (add), − (subtract), * (multiply), and / (divide). The functions and operators supported by MySQL are explained in detail in Chapter 7.

Example:
```
UPDATE address
   SET name = UPPER(name);
```

value of the timestamp column. You can do this by explicitly assigning the column to its existing value along with the other assignments within the UPDATE query.

Example:
```
UPDATE address
   SET name = UPPER(name),
   updatetime = updatetime;
```

MODIFY A SINGLE ROW

Often, you will need to modify the data in a row of a MySQL database table. While you can delete the row and insert a replacement, it is often easier to update the row in place. You can use the UPDATE query in MySQL to modify the values of one or more columns in one or more rows of data.

For a basic UPDATE query, you simply specify the table name to update and use the SET keyword to name one or more columns to modify and their new values. For example, this query sets the city column to a new value in the mail table:

```
UPDATE mail SET city="Salt Lake City";
```

As with other MySQL queries, UPDATE will affect all of the table's rows unless you specify otherwise — so unless all of

the members of the database are really in the same city, the above query would change more records than you intended and potentially cause the loss of data. Thus, like DELETE and DROP, use this command with caution.

To specify one or more rows to modify, you add the WHERE clause to the UPDATE query. For example, this query limits the update to a single row of the mail table:

```
UPDATE mail SET city="Salt Lake City"
   WHERE name="John Smith";
```

Because the name column is a primary key and must have a unique value for each row, this ensures that only a single row is updated. If you specify a WHERE clause that matches more than one row, any rows that match will be changed.

MODIFY A SINGLE ROW

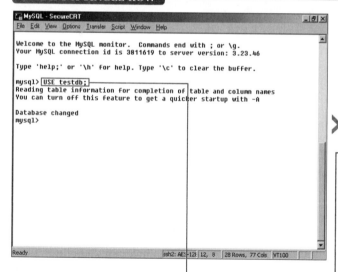

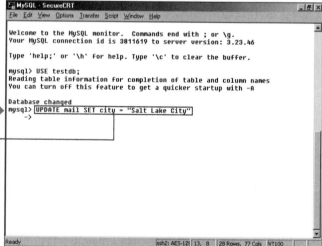

Note: This example uses the mail table in the testdb database. If you have not created this database or added data to it, follow the instructions in the Extra section.

■1 From the MySQL monitor, type **USE testdb;** and press Enter.

■ The database is now selected.

■2 Type **UPDATE mail SET city="Salt Lake City"** and press Enter.

■ The MySQL monitor prompts you for the next line of the query.

Extra

If you have not created the mail table or added records to it, you can use the following MySQL queries to prepare the table for this example:

Example:
```
CREATE TABLE mail (
  name VARCHAR(80) PRIMARY KEY,
  address VARCHAR(120),
  city VARCHAR(50),
  state CHAR(2),
  postal VARCHAR(5) );
INSERT INTO mail (name, address, city)
  VALUES ("John Smith", "321 Elm Street", "Chicago");
INSERT INTO MAIL (name, address, city)
  VALUES ("John Jones", "1141 Oak Lane", "Kalamazoo");
INSERT INTO MAIL (name, address, city)
  VALUES ("Jane Smith", "321 Elm Street", "Chicago");
```

The CREATE TABLE query creates the mail table and defines its fields. The name field is the primary key. The INSERT queries create three example rows within the new table.

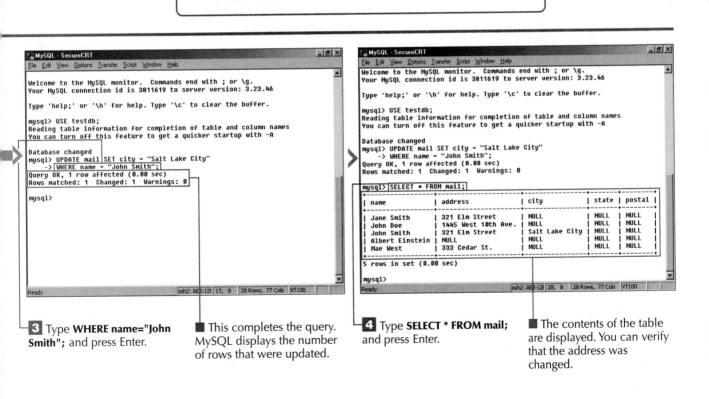

3 Type **WHERE name="John Smith";** and press Enter.

■ This completes the query. MySQL displays the number of rows that were updated.

4 Type **SELECT * FROM mail;** and press Enter.

■ The contents of the table are displayed. You can verify that the address was changed.

MODIFY MULTIPLE ROWS

I f you specify a WHERE clause that matches more than one row in an UPDATE query, all of the matching rows will be modified. This is useful when you need to make a global change to a group of rows in a table.

For example, the following query updates the mail table. It looks for a NULL value in the city column and assigns the value "Unknown" to the column instead.

```
UPDATE mail SET city="Unknown"
  WHERE city IS NULL;
```

Note that you cannot use the standard = sign to check for a NULL value, because the NULL value really means that the value is not defined at all. Instead, MySQL provides the IS NULL keywords, which allow you to test for a NULL value.

You can use any column name in the WHERE clause. You can also use the AND and OR keywords to combine multiple WHERE conditions. These keywords are explained in detail in Chapter 6. The following query checks for a NULL value or a blank value and updates either one:

```
UPDATE mail SET city="Unknown"
  WHERE city IS NULL OR city = "";
```

After you perform an UPDATE query that affects one or more rows, MySQL displays the number of rows that were affected. If no rows were affected, it does not mean your query was incorrect, just that no rows matched the WHERE clause.

Because an UPDATE query that affects a large number of rows can take a long time, you can use the LOW_PRIORITY option with UPDATE. If this option is specified, the MySQL server will wait until no clients are accessing the table before performing the update. This reduces the impact of the query on other users, but will increase the length of time the update takes when the table is busy.

For example, the following query uses the LOW_PRIORITY keyword and updates the city column as in the previous example:

```
UPDATE LOW_PRIORITY mail SET city="Unknown"
  WHERE city IS NULL;
```

MODIFY MULTIPLE ROWS

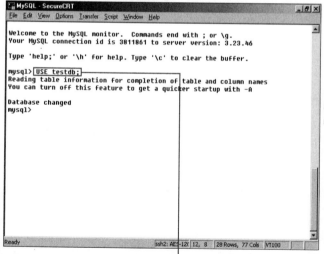

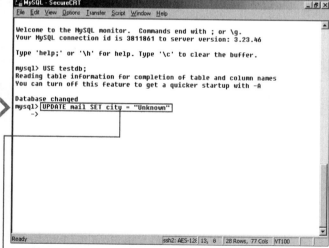

Note: This example uses the mail table in the testdb database. If you have not created this table, see the instructions in the Extra section of "Modify a Single Row," earlier in this chapter.

1 From the MySQL monitor, type **USE testdb;** and press Enter.

■ The database is now selected.

2 Type **UPDATE mail SET city="Unknown"** and press Enter.

■ The MySQL monitor prompts you for the next line.

Extra

When you specify an UPDATE query with a WHERE clause that can affect multiple rows, there is a potential for errors if one of the columns you are updating is a primary key or unique index. If the UPDATE query changes one of these columns to a value that duplicates an existing row's value, the query will abort because there cannot be duplicate values for a key.

If you add the IGNORE option to your UPDATE query, instead of aborting when a duplicate key is created, the MySQL server will instead skip that row and continue with the remaining rows to be updated. When the query is completed, the status report will display a number of warnings if one or more duplicate keys have been skipped.

Example:
```
UPDATE IGNORE mail SET name="John Smith"
    WHERE name LIKE '%Smith%';
```

This example looks for names that contain "Smith" and attempts to change them. Any duplicate keys will be ignored, and a warning message will be displayed.

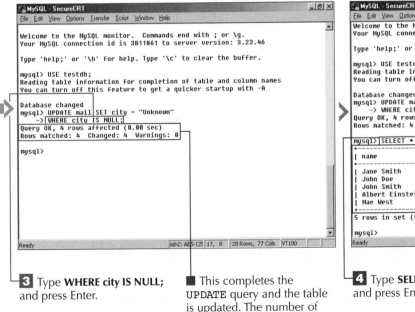

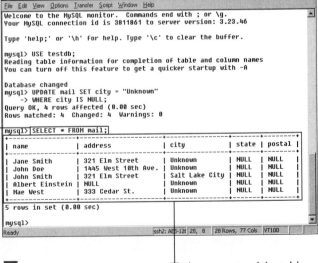

3 Type **WHERE city IS NULL;** and press Enter.

■ This completes the UPDATE query and the table is updated. The number of updated records is displayed.

4 Type **SELECT * FROM mail;** and press Enter.

■ The contents of the table are displayed. You can verify that the update was performed correctly.

UPDATE ALL TABLE ROWS

I f you omit the WHERE clause from an UPDATE query, it will affect all of the rows of the table. For example, this query sets the address field of the mail table to a single value for all rows:

```
UPDATE mail
   SET address="32 South E Street";
```

In a simple example like this, the UPDATE query replaces all values for the column with the new value. This causes the loss of some unique data and is only useful in rare cases. For example, you may find it useful if you are adding a new field to the table or deciding on a new purpose for an existing field, and want to start with a default value for all rows.

An UPDATE query without the WHERE clause becomes more useful when you combine it with one or more MySQL functions. For example, the UPPER function changes all of the letters of a text string to uppercase. You can use this function to change the data in a column to all uppercase:

```
UPDATE mail
   SET address=UPPER(address);
```

Rather than setting every address field to the same value, this version of the query performs a useful purpose. It runs each address through the UPPER function to convert it to uppercase and stores the new value in the address field. This technique is useful for making a formatting change to a field throughout a table's rows. You will learn more about UPPER and other MySQL functions in Chapter 7.

UPDATE ALL TABLE ROWS

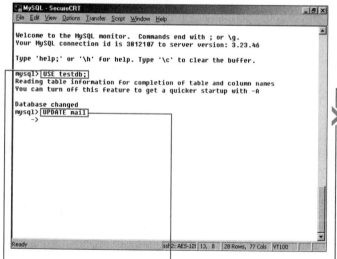

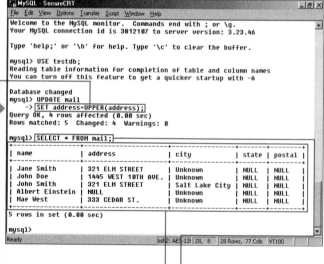

Note: This example uses the mail table in the testdb database. If you have not created this table, see the instructions in the Extra section of "Modify a Single Row," earlier in this chapter.

■ 1 From the MySQL monitor, type **USE testdb;** and press Enter.

■ The database is now selected.

■ 2 Type **UPDATE mail** and press Enter.

■ You are prompted for the next line.

■ 3 Type **SET address=UPPER(address);** and press Enter.

■ This completes the query, and the update is performed.

■ 4 Type **SELECT * FROM mail;** and press Enter.

■ The contents of the table are displayed. All words in the address fields are now uppercase.

LIMIT THE NUMBER OF ROWS TO UPDATE

You can add the LIMIT clause to an UPDATE query to limit the number of rows that can be updated. For example, this query updates only three rows:

```
UPDATE mail
  SET postal="33422" LIMIT 3;
```

Although this example does not include a WHERE clause to control the rows to be updated, the LIMIT clause specifies that only a maximum of three rows will be updated. You cannot specify the order of the UPDATE query, so you cannot control which rows will be updated.

The LIMIT clause is useful for two purposes. First, you can use it as a safeguard either with or without the WHERE clause to prevent an incorrect query from damaging data. If your WHERE clause unexpectedly matches more records than you

expected, this can prevent the loss of too much existing data. The following example uses LIMIT with a WHERE clause:

```
UPDATE mail SET postal="33422"
  WHERE postal IS NULL LIMIT 1;
```

The second use for the LIMIT clause is to minimize the slowdown of the MySQL server. If you are performing a complicated UPDATE query on a large table, it can slow down the table for other clients, and may take minutes or even hours depending on the size of the table and the speed of the server.

If you specify a number in the LIMIT clause, you can perform only part of the update and test the server's response or repeat the same query later to update more rows of the table.

LIMIT THE NUMBER OF ROWS TO UPDATE

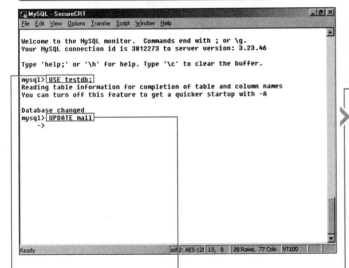

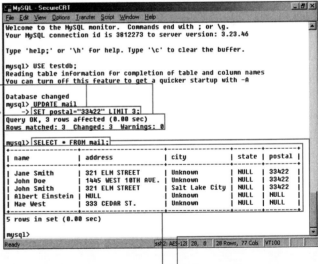

Note: This example uses the mail table in the testdb database. If you have not created this table, see the instructions in the Extra section of "Modify a Single Row," earlier in this chapter.

1 From the MySQL monitor, type **USE testdb;** and press Enter.

■ The database is now selected.

2 Type **UPDATE mail** and press Enter.

■ You are prompted for the next line of the query.

3 Type **SET postal="33422" LIMIT 3;** and press Enter.

■ The server now performs the UPDATE query. Because you specified the LIMIT clause, only three rows of the table are changed.

4 Type **SELECT * FROM mail;** and press Enter.

■ The contents of the table are displayed. Note that three rows have been changed.

UPDATE MULTIPLE COLUMNS

You can use multiple assignment statements after the SET keyword within an UPDATE query to update multiple columns for each row being updated. To update multiple columns, simply separate the assignments with a comma.

For example, suppose you are working with the mailing list in the mail table again. For any listing that does not have a value in the postal code column, you want to change the address, city, and state columns to blanks. You can do this with the following UPDATE query:

```
UPDATE mail
   SET address="", city=", state=""
   WHERE postal IS NULL;
```

This example includes three assignments after the SET keyword, assigning blank values to the address, city, and

state columns. The WHERE clause looks for any row that has a NULL value in the postal column.

When you specify multiple assignments, the MySQL server evaluates them from left to right for each row. While this makes no difference in the example above, it can affect some queries. For example, if you assign two different values to the same column in the UPDATE query, the one you specify last will be the final value of the column.

Because a query like this can cause data loss, be careful when entering it and verify the syntax before you execute the query. For example, if you inadvertently added a semicolon at the end of the second line of this query, it would execute immediately without the WHERE clause, erasing the address, city, and state of all rows in the entire table.

UPDATE MULTIPLE COLUMNS

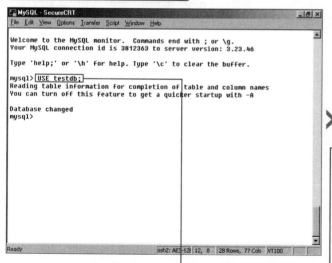

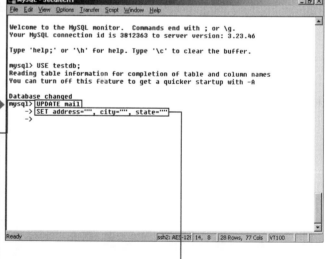

Note: This example uses the mail table in the testdb database. If you have not created this table, see the instructions in the Extra section of "Modify a Single Row," earlier in this chapter.

1 From the MySQL monitor, type **USE testdb;** and press Enter.

■ The database is now selected.

2 Type **UPDATE mail** and press Enter.

■ The MySQL monitor prompts you for the next line of the query.

3 Type **SET address="", city="", state=""** and press Enter.

■ You are prompted for the next line.

Apply It

In the real world, the example here may update fewer rows than necessary. Some rows may have a valid postal code but may be missing a value in the address, city, or state columns, any of which would result in an invalid address. You can extend the query to check for NULL values in any of these columns and assign blank values.

Example:
```
UPDATE mail
  SET address="", city="",
  state="", postal=""
  WHERE postal IS NULL
  OR address IS NULL
  OR city IS NULL
  OR state IS NULL;
```

This example looks for NULL values in the postal, address, city, or state fields by using the OR keyword. If any of them are null, all of the fields are replaced with blank values.

The OR keyword is used to combine multiple conditions in a WHERE clause so that rows that match any of the conditions will be updated. You can also use the AND keyword to combine conditions. When you use AND, only rows that match all of the conditions are updated.

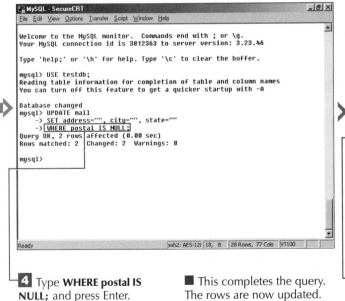

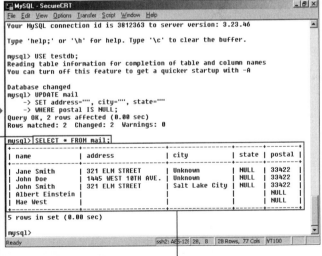

4 Type **WHERE postal IS NULL;** and press Enter.

■ This completes the query. The rows are now updated.

5 Type **SELECT * FROM mail;** and press Enter.

■ This displays the contents of the table. Verify that the correct columns were updated.

UPDATE DEPENDING ON COLUMN VALUES

You can use the value of any existing column of the table within an UPDATE query. This allows you to update one column based on the value of one or more other columns.

For example, suppose you were to add columns for a second address to the mail table. Using an UPDATE query, you could copy the current address columns for each row to use as the default value of each of the second address columns. The following ALTER TABLE query adds the new columns to the table:

```
ALTER TABLE mail ADD COLUMN
   (address2 VARCHAR(120), city2 VARCHAR(50),
   state2 CHAR(2), postal2 VARCHAR(5) );
```

After the new columns have been added to the table, you can use an UPDATE query to copy the corresponding fields from the first address to the second:

```
UPDATE mail SET address2=address,
   city2=city, state2=state, postal2=postal;
```

This query uses the existing values in the address, city, state, and postal columns as the values of the new address columns. Because no WHERE clause is specified, this query affects all of the rows of the table. You can also use a WHERE clause to update only certain rows. The following example updates only rows where the state field has the value 'CA':

```
UPDATE mail SET address2=address,
   city2=city, state2=state, postal2=postal
   WHERE state='CA';
```

You can use any of the existing values from the table's columns in this way in an UPDATE query. You can also use a variety of MySQL functions to modify or combine the values of one or more columns to form the value of a column. See Chapter 7 for a detailed explanation of the many available MySQL functions.

UPDATE DEPENDING ON COLUMN VALUES

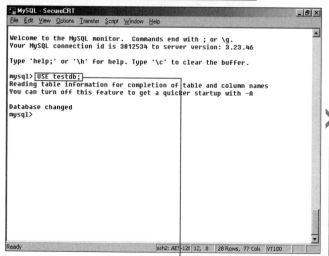

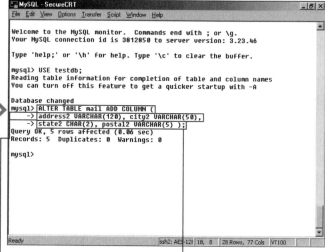

Note: This example uses the mail table in the testdb database. If you have not created this table, see the instructions in the Extra section of "Modify a Single Row," earlier in this chapter.

1 From the MySQL monitor, type **USE testdb;** and press Enter.

■ The database is now selected.

2 Type **ALTER TABLE mail ADD COLUMN (** and press Enter.

■ You are prompted for the next line.

3 Type **address2 VARCHAR(120), city2 VARCHAR(50),** and press Enter.

4 Type **state2 CHAR(2), postal2 VARCHAR(5));** and press Enter.

■ This completes the ALTER TABLE query. The new fields are added to the table.

Extra

If you are working with a table that has a timestamp column, this column is automatically updated with the current date and time in each row modified by any UPDATE query. If you want to update a row and preserve the current value of the timestamp column, you must explicitly set the column to its original value.

For example, if you were to add a second address to the address table and perform a similar update, you may want to avoid updating the timestamp in the updatetime column. The following query accomplishes this:

Example:
```
UPDATE address SET address2=address,
  city2=city, state2=state,
  updatetime=updatetime;
```

While setting a column to its own value normally has no effect, in a timestamp column this prevents the MySQL server from automatically updating the field. You can also set the timestamp column explicitly to a different value. For example, the following UPDATE query sets all rows to a specified updatetime value:

Example:
```
UPDATE address SET address2=address,
  city2=city, state2=state,
  updatetime="20030101120000";
```

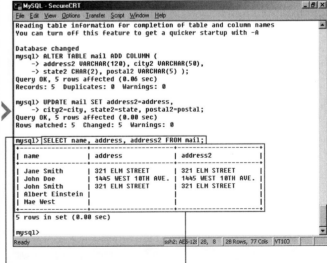

5 Type **UPDATE mail SET address2=address,** and press Enter.

■ You are prompted for the next line.

6 Type **city2=city, state2=state, postal2=postal;** and press Enter.

■ This completes the UPDATE query. All of the rows of the table are updated.

7 Type **SELECT name, address, address2 FROM mail;** and press Enter.

■ The values of the columns you specified are displayed for all rows. Verify that the address values were copied.

INCREMENT A COLUMN VALUE

O ften, you will find it useful to update a column's value based on its existing value. The simplest example of this is to increment a numeric column's value. This is easy to do in an UPDATE query by referring to the column's current value.

For example, suppose you created a table to store exam statistics for students. The following CREATE TABLE query creates this simple table:

```
CREATE TABLE exams (name VARCHAR(80),
   numtests INT, totalscore INT, avgscore
   TINYINT);
```

This creates a table called exams with four columns: name for the student name, numtests for the number of tests the student has taken, totalscore for the total of all test scores, and avgscore for an average.

When a new test is administered to students, you may want to increment the numtests column for all of the rows in the database. You can use a simple UPDATE query to accomplish this:

```
UPDATE exams
   SET numtests = numtests + 1;
```

This query adds one to the current value of the numtests column for each row and stores the resulting value in that row's numtests column, replacing the original value. The net effect is to increment the numtests column for every student.

As with other UPDATE queries, you could optionally add a WHERE clause. Specifying a WHERE clause may be useful to increment the number of tests for only a single student or group of students. You can use a wide variety of arithmetic operations on MySQL column values; these are listed in Chapter 7.

INCREMENT A COLUMN VALUE

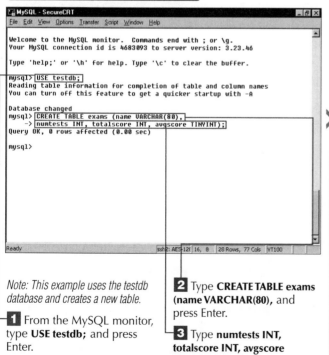

Note: This example uses the testdb database and creates a new table.

1 From the MySQL monitor, type **USE testdb;** and press Enter.

■ The database is now selected.

2 Type **CREATE TABLE exams (name VARCHAR(80),** and press Enter.

3 Type **numtests INT, totalscore INT, avgscore TINYINT);** and press Enter.

■ The table is created.

4 Type **INSERT INTO exams (name, numtests, totalscore)** and press Enter.

■ You are prompted for the next line.

5 Type **VALUES ("Sam", 5, 350),** and press Enter.

6 Type **("Ted",3, 220),("Sue",6, 510);** and press Enter.

■ This completes the INSERT query and adds three sample rows to the table.

Apply It

You can use math in UPDATE statements to do more than simply increment columns. For example, you could use an UPDATE query to automatically set the avgscore column for each student to be an average calculated by dividing totalscore by numtests.

Example:
```
UPDATE exams
    SET avgscore = totalscore / numtests;
```

This example uses the / (division) operator to calculate the average. Because there is no WHERE clause, this operation will be performed on all rows of the table.

Because UPDATE can modify multiple columns at once, you could combine this example with the previous example to increment the number of tests and calculate the average at the same time.

Example:
```
UPDATE exams
    SET numtests = numtests + 1,
    avgscore = totalscore / numtests;
```

Because MySQL processes the UPDATE query from left to right, the numtests column will be incremented for each row first, after which the new value will be used in the calculation of the average.

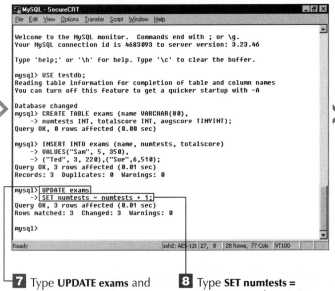

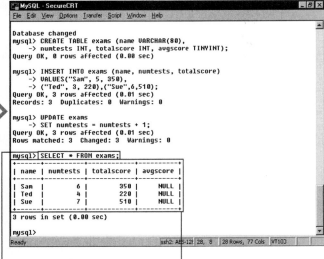

7 Type **UPDATE exams** and press Enter.

■ You are prompted for the next line.

8 Type **SET numtests = numtests + 1;** and press Enter.

■ This completes the UPDATE query. The column is incremented in all rows.

9 Type **SELECT * FROM exams;** and press Enter.

■ The contents of the table are displayed. The number of tests has been incremented for each row.

USING SELECT QUERIES

SELECT is one of the most powerful MySQL query commands, and one you will use frequently. A SELECT query returns one or more rows from one or more tables. You can use SELECT from the MySQL monitor to display data or from an application to retrieve data.

BASIC SELECT SYNTAX

The SELECT query has a specific syntax. The various clauses and keywords are optional, but must be specified in this order. Many of the clauses require that you specify a table with FROM.

```
SELECT columns or expressions
    FROM table or tables WHERE
    conditions
    GROUP BY columns ORDER BY
    columns
    LIMIT number;
```

Specify Columns

You can specify one or more column names in the SELECT query. The columns you specify will be displayed for each row returned by the query. You can use commas to separate multiple columns or use * to return all columns.

Example:
```
SELECT name, city FROM address;
```

Specify Tables

You use the FROM keyword in SELECT to specify one or more tables from which to retrieve rows. In most cases, a single table name is used.

THE LIMIT CLAUSE

The LIMIT clause allows you to limit the number of rows the SELECT query can return. If you specify a single number with LIMIT, only that number of rows will be returned. This clause can be combined with a WHERE clause to display a limited number of rows that match the condition.

If you specify two numbers in the LIMIT clause, the first is the number of the first result row to be returned. Rows are numbered starting with zero. The second number is the limit. You can use this to display pages of data from a query.

Example:
```
SELECT * FROM address LIMIT 10;
```

USING JOIN TO COMBINE TABLES

If you specify more than one table name in the FROM clause, the SELECT query will return data from multiple tables. This is known as a JOIN query, and requires a WHERE clause to match a column from each table with corresponding items in other tables.

You can also use the JOIN keyword to combine tables. When you use INNER JOIN or simply specify multiple tables, only rows that match between tables are displayed. When you use LEFT JOIN, all of the rows in the left table are displayed. If no corresponding values exist for the right table, NULL values are returned.

Example:
```
SELECT * FROM address, mail
    WHERE address.name = mail.name;
```

THE WHERE CLAUSE

You can use the WHERE clause to select only the rows that match a condition. You can use any of MySQL's available functions and comparison operators to form a WHERE condition.

Example:
```
SELECT * FROM address
    WHERE name LIKE "%Smith%";
```

Compare Numeric Values

MySQL includes a number of comparison operators you can use with numeric values:

OPERATOR	DESCRIPTION
=	Is equal to
>	Is greater than
<	Is less than
>=	Is greater than or equal to
<=	Is less than or equal to
<> or !=	Is not equal to

Work with NULL Values

The following comparison operators work with NULL values in columns:

OPERATOR	DESCRIPTION
IS NULL	Is the NULL value
IS NOT NULL	Is not the NULL value
<=>	Is equal to (allows NULL values)

Compare Text Strings

You can compare text values using the standard equal, greater-than, and less-than operators. Additionally, you can use LIKE or NOT LIKE to compare text strings. These operators allow the wildcard values % for any characters or no characters, and _ for one character.

Combine Conditions

You can use the AND keyword to combine two conditions in a WHERE clause. Only the rows that match both conditions will be returned. The OR keyword also combines conditions. In this case, any row that matches one condition or the other is returned. The NOT keyword negates one or more conditions.

You can use AND, OR, and NOT to combine any number of conditions for a WHERE clause. You can use parentheses to indicate the conditions that should be evaluated first.

Example:
```
SELECT * FROM address
    WHERE (state="CA" OR state="AZ")
    AND name LIKE "%Smith%";
```

THE GROUP BY CLAUSE

The GROUP BY clause is similar to ORDER BY, but all of the rows for each value of the group column are combined into a single row. You can use functions such as COUNT to perform calculations on the combined data.

Example:
```
SELECT state, COUNT(*) FROM address
GROUP BY state;
```

THE ORDER BY CLAUSE

The ORDER BY clause specifies one or more columns by which to sort the results of the SELECT query. You can specify a single column name or multiple columns separated by commas. You can optionally specify the keyword ASC (ascending) or DESC (descending) for each column. An ascending sort is the default.

Example:
```
SELECT * FROM address ORDER BY name;
```

DISPLAY DATA WITH SELECT

The SELECT query is one of the most powerful options available in MySQL. Using SELECT, you can display data from a table or retrieve data into an application. A basic SELECT query specifies the fields to display followed by the FROM keyword and the table to draw them from:

```
SELECT name, address FROM mail;
```

This example displays all of the rows of the mail table. For each row, the name and address columns are displayed. The columns for each row are displayed in the order you specified in the SELECT statement. You can also use a wildcard character (*) to select all of the table's columns:

```
SELECT * FROM mail;
```

This example displays all of the rows of the table. Each row includes the value of all columns. The columns are displayed in the order they were defined when the table was created.

You can also use SELECT without the FROM keyword to test MySQL functions and expressions. When you do not specify a table to select data from, MySQL will evaluate the expression in the SELECT statement and display the result. For example, this query displays the sum of several numbers:

```
SELECT 3 + 12 + 33;
```

When you include the FROM keyword to specify a table, you can also combine the table's fields into functions and expressions. For example, this SELECT query displays the name and address of each row in the mail table, converting all text to uppercase:

```
SELECT UPPER(name), UPPER(address) FROM
mail;
```

DISPLAY DATA WITH SELECT

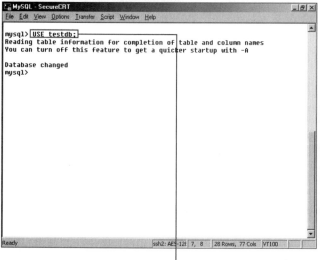

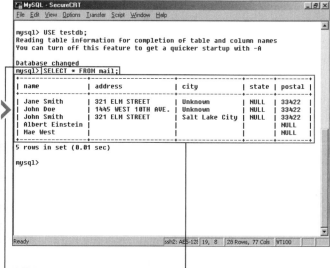

Note: This example uses the testdb database and the mail table. See Chapter 5 or the CD-ROM for instructions to create this table.

1 From the MySQL monitor, type **USE testdb;** and press Enter.

■ You are prompted for the next line.

2 Type **SELECT * FROM mail;** and press Enter.

■ All columns and rows of the table are displayed.

Extra

Sometimes, when you perform a function or calculation on one or more fields of a table in a `SELECT` query, you want to view the result as well as the original fields. You can do this by assigning a name, or *alias*, to the calculated value. For example, the following query displays the name field followed by its uppercase equivalent:

Example:
```
SELECT name, UPPER(name) AS name2 FROM mail;
```

The `AS` keyword is used to indicate an alias name for the calculated value. This name is displayed in the results when you use a query from the MySQL monitor. When you are using MySQL with a language such as PHP or Perl, the alias is available to your program as well as the columns you name directly in the `SELECT` query.

As another example, the `CONCAT` function in MySQL combines multiple text values into a single string. This example returns the name and an addr alias that combines the address, city, and state columns.

Example:
```
SELECT name, CONCAT(address, "/", city, "/", state) AS addr
  FROM mail;
```

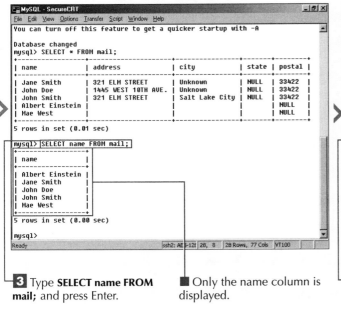

3 Type **SELECT name FROM mail;** and press Enter.

■ Only the name column is displayed.

4 Type **SELECT city, address, name FROM mail;** and press Enter.

■ The city, address, and name columns are displayed in order.

113

USING THE WHERE CLAUSE

By default, when you use a SELECT query, all of the rows of the table are returned. You can add a WHERE clause to your SELECT queries to select one or more specific rows. You can select rows by performing comparisons with one or more of the table's fields. The following is a simple example of a SELECT query with a WHERE clause:

```
SELECT * FROM mail
  WHERE name = "John Smith";
```

This example looks for a specific value within the name field of the mail table and displays the rows that match. Because the name field is the primary key in this case, only one row will be displayed.

MySQL uses case-insensitive matching with text fields. Aside from differences in case, the = operator will only match if the name is exactly as specified. You can also use other operators, such as less than (<) and greater than (>). Numbers are compared numerically, and text values are

compared alphabetically. If the values you are comparing are different types, MySQL converts them to a compatible type if possible.

With text fields, you can use the LIKE keyword to find partial matches. LIKE allows you to use wildcard characters. The first wildcard, _, matches a single character. The following example finds "John Smith", "John Smitt", or a name with any other final character:

```
SELECT * FROM mail
  WHERE name = "John Smit_";
```

The other wildcard, %, can represent any number of characters or no characters. You can use this at the beginning and ending of a word to find the word anywhere in the column. The example below will find the name "John Smith" as well as any other name containing "Smith":

```
SELECT * FROM mail
  WHERE name LIKE "%Smith%";
```

USING THE WHERE CLAUSE

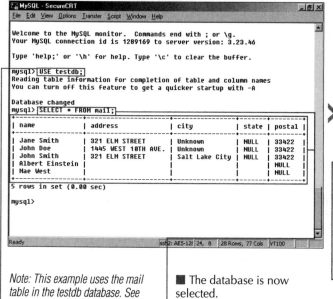

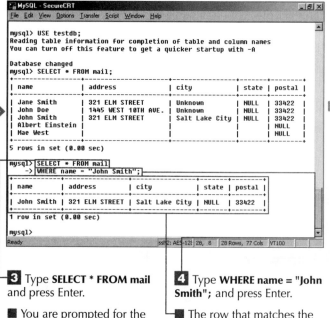

Note: This example uses the mail table in the testdb database. See Chapter 5 or the CD-ROM if you need to create this table.

1 From the MySQL monitor, type **USE testdb;** and press Enter.

■ The database is now selected.

2 Type **SELECT * FROM mail;** and press Enter.

■ All rows of the table are displayed.

3 Type **SELECT * FROM mail** and press Enter.

■ You are prompted for the next line of the query.

4 Type **WHERE name = "John Smith";** and press Enter.

■ The row that matches the WHERE clause is displayed.

Extra

MySQL supports a variety of operators for comparing numeric or text values. The table below lists each operator and its purpose.

OPERATOR	DESCRIPTION
=	Is equal to
>	Is greater than
<	Is less than
>=	Is greater than or equal to
<=	Is less than or equal to
<> or !=	Is not equal to
IS NULL	Is the NULL value
IS NOT NULL	Is not the NULL value
<=>	Is equal to (allows NULL values)
LIKE	Match text strings with wildcards
NOT LIKE	Text strings do not match

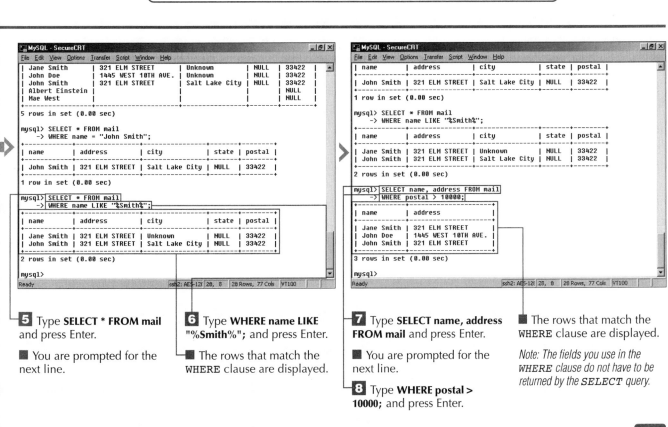

5 Type **SELECT * FROM mail** and press Enter.

■ You are prompted for the next line.

6 Type **WHERE name LIKE "%Smith%";** and press Enter.

■ The rows that match the WHERE clause are displayed.

7 Type **SELECT name, address FROM mail** and press Enter.

■ You are prompted for the next line.

8 Type **WHERE postal > 10000;** and press Enter.

■ The rows that match the WHERE clause are displayed.

Note: The fields you use in the WHERE clause do not have to be returned by the SELECT query.

SPECIFY MULTIPLE WHERE CONDITIONS

Often, in a large database, specifying a single condition would still return a huge number of rows. You can combine several conditions in a WHERE clause to make your search more specific. The logical operators AND, OR, and NOT are used to combine conditions.

The OR operator allows you to make a search more general. The following example displays records from the mail table that contain the names Smith or West:

```
SELECT * FROM mail WHERE
   name LIKE "%Smith%" OR name LIKE "%West%";
```

The AND operator allows you to make a search more specific. The following example displays only the records with a name column containing "Smith" and a value of "CA" in the state column:

```
SELECT * FROM mail WHERE
   name LIKE "%Smith%" AND state = "CA";
```

If you have not used AND and OR with computer languages before, they may be confusing. Remember that using OR will allow more rows to match the query, and using AND will allow less rows to match.

Finally, the NOT operator inverts a condition. If you use NOT LIKE or != (not equal), rows that do not match the condition are returned. You can use NOT to make any existing condition into its opposite.

You can combine any number of conditions with AND, OR, and NOT to create complex conditions. When you use AND and OR together, often the meaning is ambiguous. You can enclose conditions in parentheses to ensure that they are considered first, before combining the result with the other conditions.

SPECIFY MULTIPLE WHERE CONDITIONS

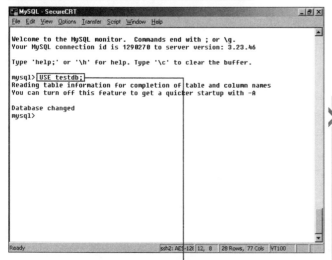

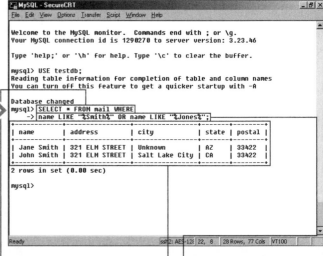

Note: This example uses the mail table in the testdb database. See Chapter 5 or the CD-ROM if you need to create this table.

1 From the MySQL monitor, type **USE testdb;** and press Enter.

■ The database is now selected.

2 Type **SELECT * FROM mail WHERE** and press Enter.

■ You are prompted for the next line.

3 Type **name LIKE "%Smith%" OR name LIKE "%Jones%";** and press Enter.

■ This completes the query. Rows that match either condition are displayed.

Apply It

You can create very complex WHERE conditions using AND, OR, NOT, and parentheses to combine multiple conditions. For example, here is a complex query using the mail table:

Example:
```
SELECT * FROM mail WHERE
 (name LIKE "%Smith%" OR name LIKE "%Jones%")
 AND NOT (state = "UT" or state = "AZ");
```

This query will return all of the rows that have a name column containing either "Smith" or "Jones", except for those with values of "UT" or "AZ" in the state column.

These operators can even be useful when working with a single field:

Example:
```
SELECT * FROM mail WHERE
 name LIKE "%Smith%"
 AND name NOT LIKE "%John%";
```

This example returns all rows that contain "Smith" in the name column, except for those that contain "John".

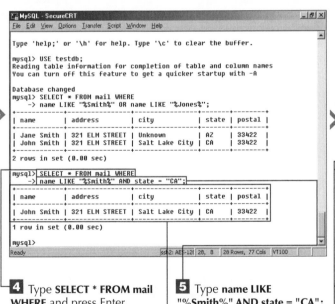

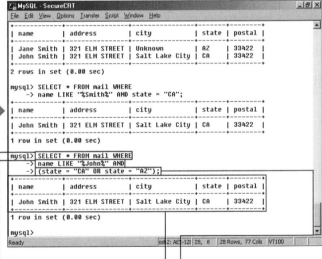

4 Type **SELECT * FROM mail WHERE** and press Enter.

■ You are prompted for the next line.

5 Type **name LIKE "%Smith%" AND state = "CA";** and press Enter.

■ This completes the query. Only the rows that match both conditions are displayed.

6 Type **SELECT * FROM mail WHERE** and press Enter.

■ You are prompted for the second line.

7 Type **name LIKE "%John%" AND** and press Enter.

■ You are prompted for the third line.

8 Type **(state = "CA" OR state = "AZ");** and press Enter.

■ This completes the query. Only the rows that match the first condition and either of the second or third are displayed.

USING THE LIMIT CLAUSE

I n a large database, a SELECT query can return a large number of rows. You can add the LIMIT clause to request that only a specified number of rows should be returned. In a basic LIMIT clause, you simply specify the number of rows. The following example displays the first ten rows of the mail table:

```
SELECT * FROM mail LIMIT 10;
```

If the table contains less than ten rows, all of the rows will be returned. You can optionally specify an offset for the first row to be included, followed by a comma and the limit. Rows are numbered starting with zero. If you do not specify an offset, zero is used by default.

As an example, the following queries will display the first three groups of ten rows in the table:

```
SELECT * FROM mail LIMIT 0, 10;
```

```
SELECT * FROM mail LIMIT 10, 10;
```

```
SELECT * FROM mail LIMIT 20, 10;
```

You can use LIMIT offsets like this to display data one page at a time. LIMIT in general is also useful if you simply want to control the number of rows that will be displayed. Exactly which rows are displayed depends on the order of the primary key, or the order you specify in an ORDER BY clause, described in the next section.

You can combine LIMIT with a WHERE clause to display a subset of the number of rows that match the condition of the WHERE clause. LIMIT can also be combined with the other SELECT options described in this chapter.

USING THE LIMIT CLAUSE

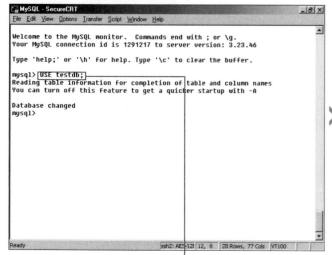

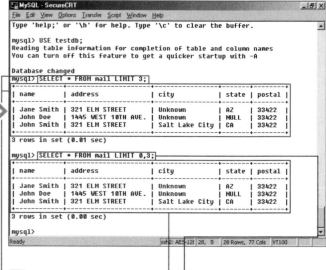

Note: This example uses the mail table. This book's CD-ROM includes a version of this table with a large number of rows that you can import into your MySQL server.

1 From the MySQL monitor, type **USE testdb;** and press Enter.

■ The database is now selected.

2 Type **SELECT * FROM mail LIMIT 3;** and press Enter.

■ The first three rows of the table are displayed.

3 Type **SELECT * FROM mail LIMIT 0,3;** and press Enter.

■ This also displays the first three rows.

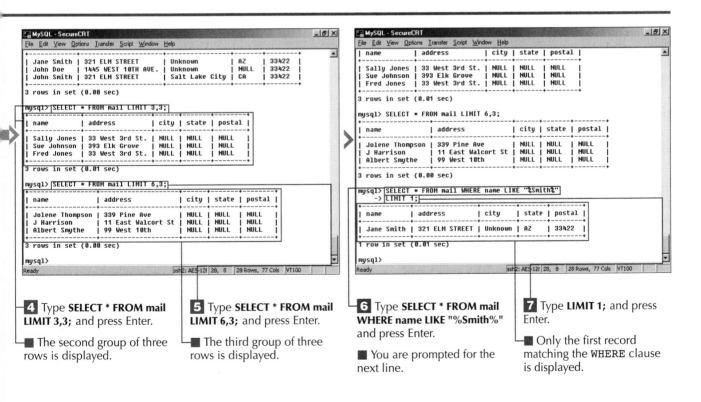

Apply It

You can use `LIMIT` to display data in pages. To do this, you use the same maximum value and a different offset for each query. If you know the number of the page you want to display and the number of rows per page, you can calculate the offset using this formula:

*offset = (page -1) * rows*

In this formula, *page* is the page number, starting with page 1, and *rows* is the number of rows per page. You can use this formula within a Web application in a language such as Perl or PHP to easily display one page of data at a time.

When you are displaying paged data, the rows returned for each page may not always be consistent. This can happen if rows are added to or deleted from the database between your `SELECT` queries. The pages will also be inconsistent if you use a different `ORDER BY` clause in subsequent `SELECT` queries.

4 Type **SELECT * FROM mail LIMIT 3,3;** and press Enter.

■ The second group of three rows is displayed.

5 Type **SELECT * FROM mail LIMIT 6,3;** and press Enter.

■ The third group of three rows is displayed.

6 Type **SELECT * FROM mail WHERE name LIKE "%Smith%"** and press Enter.

■ You are prompted for the next line.

7 Type **LIMIT 1;** and press Enter.

■ Only the first record matching the WHERE clause is displayed.

SORT DATA WITH THE ORDER BY CLAUSE

One of the most powerful features of a database management system like MySQL is the ability to sort large amounts of data by different fields. You can use the ORDER BY clause in a SELECT statement to control the order of the rows returned.

For example, suppose you defined a table to store famous quotations. This table would include text fields for the quotation, named quotes, and the author, named author, and an auto-increment column called num to act as a primary key. You could use a simple ORDER BY clause to list the quotations sorted by the author's name:

```
SELECT * FROM quotes ORDER BY author;
```

You can optionally follow an ORDER BY column with the keyword DESC for descending order, or ASC, the default, for ascending.

If you specify more than one column name in the ORDER BY clause, the table will first be sorted by the first column,

and then the second column, and so on. The following example would return a list of quotations sorted by author and then by the num field:

```
SELECT * FROM quotes ORDER BY author, num;
```

The second column to sort by will only be effective if there are multiple rows for some values of the author column. If all of the values in this column are unique, the other columns in ORDER BY have no effect.

If you specify one or more columns with SELECT, you can use numbers as shorthand in ORDER BY to refer to the columns being selected. This example orders by the author column:

```
SELECT quote, author FROM quotes ORDER BY 2;
```

SORT DATA WITH THE ORDER BY CLAUSE

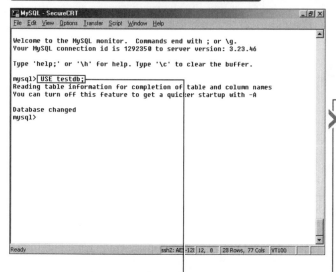

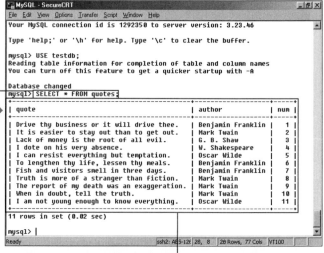

Note: This example uses the quotes table. See the Extra section for details.

1 From the MySQL monitor, type **USE testdb;** and press Enter.

2 Type **SELECT * FROM quotes;** and press Enter.

■ The rows of the table are displayed in the default order.

Extra

Rather than a column name or list of columns, you can also use a MySQL function in the ORDER BY clause. This allows you to customize the order in a number of ways. For example, the RAND function is useful for displaying results in random order.

Example:
```
SELECT * FROM quotes
    ORDER BY RAND();
```

When you use ORDER BY RAND(), MySQL automatically retrieves the row for your query in random order. While the order is random, each row will still only be returned once. If you use this clause with a WHERE clause, the rows that match the WHERE condition will be returned in random order.

You can create the quotes table for this example by importing it from the SQL file on the CD-ROM or with the following CREATE TABLE query. The version on the CD-ROM includes a number of example rows to work with.

Example:
```
CREATE TABLE quotes (
    quote VARCHAR(100),
    author VARCHAR(50),
    num INT(11) AUTO_INCREMENT PRIMARY KEY);
```

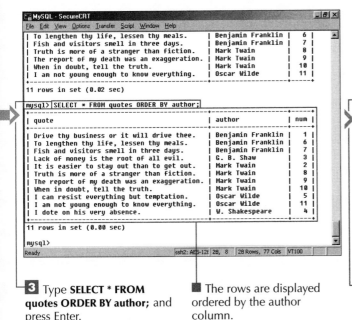

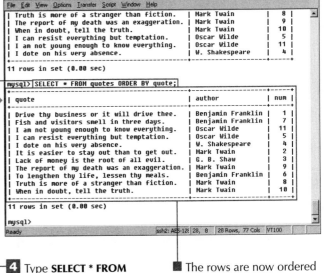

3 Type **SELECT * FROM quotes ORDER BY author;** and press Enter.

■ The rows are displayed ordered by the author column.

4 Type **SELECT * FROM quotes ORDER BY quote;** and press Enter.

■ The rows are now ordered by the quote column.

USING THE GROUP BY CLAUSE

Sometimes you want to look at groups of rows rather than single rows to extract data. You can use the GROUP BY clause in a SELECT query to combine all of the rows for a particular value into a single row. For example, this query displays a list of author names from the quotes table:

```
SELECT author FROM quotes GROUP BY author;
```

The GROUP BY clause is similar to ORDER BY, but it only returns a single row for each unique value of the grouping field. In this case, because you are displaying only the author field, it will display a list of authors. Even if the same author name is included in several rows of the database, it will be listed only once in the query with GROUP BY.

If you include fields in the SELECT query that you are not grouping by, only a single value will be displayed even though many rows have been grouped together. The following query will display a single quotation for each author, regardless of how many times the author appears in the database:

```
SELECT quote, author FROM quotes
   GROUP BY author;
```

You can optionally use an ORDER BY clause after the GROUP BY clause. This will control the order in which the rows are pulled from the database before they are grouped together as specified in the GROUP BY clause.

While GROUP BY in its simple form is useful for listing the unique values of a column in a MySQL table, you can actually gather statistics on each group using several MySQL functions. These are described later in this chapter, in the section "Calculate Totals and Averages."

USING THE GROUP BY CLAUSE

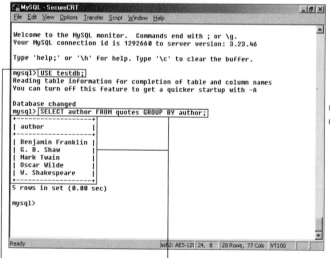

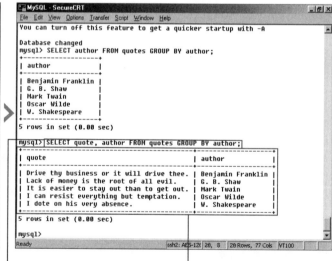

Note: This example uses the quotes table in the testdb database. See the CD-ROM for an importable SQL file to create this table.

■ 1 From the MySQL monitor, type **USE testdb;** and press Enter.

■ The database is now selected.

2 Type **SELECT author FROM quotes GROUP BY author;** and press Enter.

■ A list of unique author names in the table is displayed.

3 Type **SELECT quote, author FROM quotes GROUP BY author;** and press Enter.

■ One row for each unique author name is displayed.

USING MULTIPLE CLAUSES WITH SELECT

You can make a SELECT query as simple or as complex as necessary. The simplest version of SELECT is used to test a function or calculation, and does not even require a table name. This example multiplies two numbers and displays the result:

```
SELECT 17 * 34;
```

In a more complex SELECT query, you must use the various clauses in the correct order, or MySQL will return an error. The following is the basic syntax and order for a SELECT query in MySQL:

```
SELECT columns or expressions
   FROM table or tables WHERE conditions
   GROUP BY columns ORDER BY columns
   LIMIT number;
```

The WHERE, GROUP BY, ORDER BY, or LIMIT clauses are optional. Whichever ones you do include must be specified in the order shown. If you include any of these clauses, you must also include the FROM keyword to specify a table. For

example, the following query includes WHERE, ORDER BY, and LIMIT clauses:

```
SELECT * FROM quotes WHERE author LIKE
"%Franklin%"
   ORDER BY num LIMIT 2;
```

Several of the clauses in a SELECT statement allow multiple items. The FROM TABLE clause can list multiple tables — this is described in the section "Display Data from Multiple Tables," later in this chapter. You can use AND and OR to combine WHERE conditions, as described earlier in this chapter. The ORDER BY and GROUP BY clauses can include a list of column names, separated by commas.

Because a SELECT query that uses several complex clauses can be quite long, it is difficult to enter it into the MySQL monitor without an error. You can use the \e (edit) option in the MySQL monitor to edit the query in a text editor and then execute it with the \g (go) option. These options are described in detail in Chapter 1.

USING MULTIPLE CLAUSES WITH SELECT

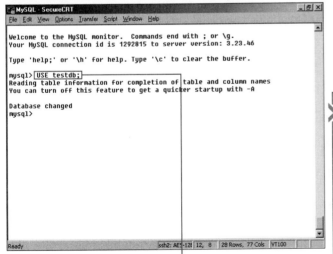

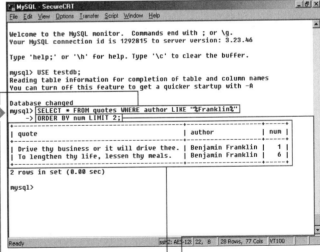

Note: This example uses the quotes table in the testdb database. See the CD-ROM for information on importing this table onto your server.

1 From the MySQL monitor, type **USE testdb;** and press Enter.

■ The database is now selected.

2 Type **SELECT * FROM quotes WHERE author LIKE "%Franklin%"** and press Enter.

■ You are prompted for the next line.

3 Type **ORDER BY num LIMIT 2;** and press Enter.

■ The query is now complete, and the results are displayed.

COUNT DATABASE ROWS

The SELECT queries you have used so far return all of the data that matches the WHERE criteria. Rather than the rows themselves, you can use SELECT to obtain a count of the rows in a table or the rows that match a condition. This is especially useful in applications that use MySQL, because the database server can return a count to the application rather than requiring your application to count all of the rows it receives.

To count the number of rows in a table, you use the COUNT function. This function accepts a column name as a parameter or the wildcard *. The following query displays a count of all of the rows in the quotes table:

```
SELECT COUNT(*) FROM quotes;
```

If you specify a column name rather than the wildcard, only the rows that have a non-NULL value for that column will be counted. The following query counts the rows that have a non-NULL value in the author column:

```
SELECT COUNT(author) FROM quotes;
```

If you specify a WHERE clause with COUNT, MySQL counts the rows that match the WHERE condition. The following query returns a count of the number of rows that have a specific value in the author column:

```
SELECT COUNT(*) FROM quotes
  WHERE author="Mark Twain";
```

Because the COUNT function returns a single-row result with the count, you cannot retrieve a count and a regular column value using the same SELECT query. You can, however, count values for multiple columns. The following example displays a count of rows that have a non-NULL value in the quote column, followed by a count of non-NULL values in the author column:

```
SELECT COUNT(quote), COUNT(author)
  FROM quotes;
```

If you are not interested in the values of a particular column and only want a count of rows, always use COUNT(*). The MySQL server can count the rows faster if a column is not specified, because it does not have to examine values in each row it counts.

COUNT DATABASE ROWS

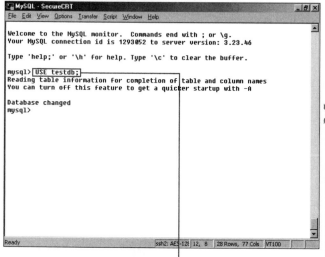

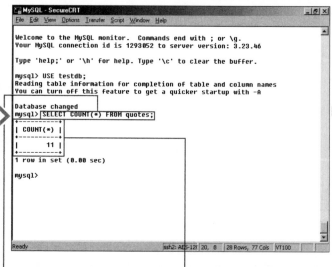

Note: This example uses the quotes table in the testdb database. This table is included on the CD-ROM.

1 From the MySQL monitor, type **USE testdb;** and press Enter.

■ The database is now selected.

2 Type **SELECT COUNT(*) FROM quotes;** and press Enter.

■ The count of all rows in the table is displayed.

Extra

You can use the DISTINCT keyword with COUNT to count the unique values of a column. For example, the following query counts the number of unique values for the author column in the quotes table. If the same value is included in the column for several different rows, it is only counted once.

Example:
```
SELECT COUNT(DISTINCT author) FROM quotes;
```

When using DISTINCT, you can list multiple columns. In this case, the count will be the number of rows that have a unique combination of values in the two columns. The following query counts unique combinations of values in the author and quote columns:

Example:
```
SELECT COUNT(DISTINCT author, quote) FROM quotes;
```

You can also use DISTINCT in a regular SELECT query to display the list of unique values. The result is similar to using the GROUP BY clause. The following example displays a list of unique values of the author column in the quotes table:

Example:
```
SELECT DISTINCT author FROM quotes;
```

If you specify any columns with DISTINCT that are primary keys or unique indexes, the result is the same as if you had not used DISTINCT, because these columns have a unique value for each row of the table.

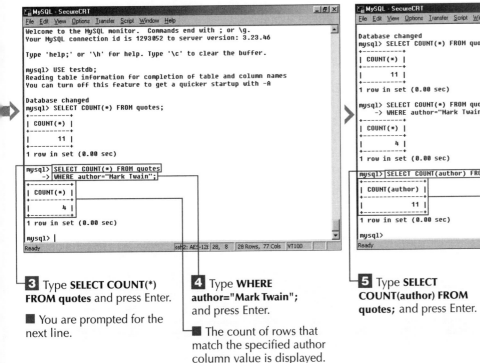

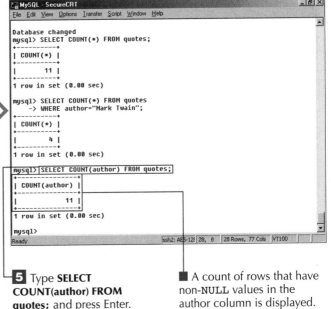

3 Type **SELECT COUNT(*) FROM quotes** and press Enter.

■ You are prompted for the next line.

4 Type **WHERE author="Mark Twain";** and press Enter.

■ The count of rows that match the specified author column value is displayed.

5 Type **SELECT COUNT(author) FROM quotes;** and press Enter.

■ A count of rows that have non-NULL values in the author column is displayed.

125

CALCULATE TOTALS AND AVERAGES

While the COUNT function is useful for counting the entire contents of a table, it becomes even more useful when you use it with the GROUP BY clause. You can use this combination to display detailed statistics about a table's contents. For example, the following query displays a list of author names from the quotes table, and for each one, a count of the number of rows it appears in:

```
SELECT author, COUNT(*) FROM quotes
   GROUP BY author;
```

Along with COUNT, MySQL includes several other functions that you can use to display statistics on grouped data from a table. The AVG function calculates the average of the values for a column in a group. The MIN function determines the smallest of a set of values, and MAX determines the largest value of a group.

For example, suppose you create a table to store student names and test scores. The scores table includes two simple

columns — name and score. After a number of rows are stored in this table, you can use this query to display the average, minimum, and maximum scores for each student:

```
SELECT name, AVG(score),
   MIN(score), MAX(score)
   FROM scores GROUP BY name;
```

You can also use the AVG, MIN, and MAX functions without GROUP BY to calculate statistics on the entire table. Other functions available include SUM for the sum of values and STD for the standard deviation. The following example displays the average score and total score for the entire scores table:

```
SELECT AVG(score), SUM(score)
   FROM scores;
```

Because the SELECT query returns a single-row result for the entire table when you use these functions, you cannot retrieve column values using the same SELECT query.

CALCULATE TOTALS AND AVERAGES

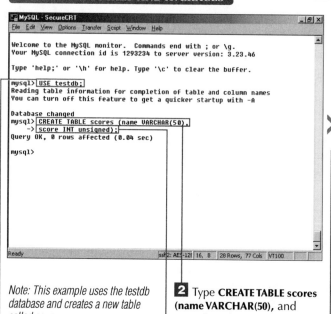

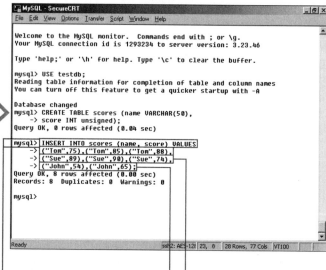

Note: This example uses the testdb database and creates a new table called scores.

1 Type **USE testdb;** and press Enter.

■ The database is now selected.

2 Type **CREATE TABLE scores (name VARCHAR(50),** and press Enter.

■ You are prompted for the next line.

3 Type **score INT UNSIGNED);** and press Enter.

■ This creates the scores table.

4 Type **INSERT INTO scores (name, score) VALUES** and press Enter.

5 Type **("Tom",75), ("Tom",85), ("Tom",88),** and press Enter.

6 Type **("Sue",89), ("Sue",90), ("Sue",74),** and press Enter.

7 Type **("John",54), ("John",65);** and press Enter.

■ This inserts some sample data into the table.

Extra

When you use GROUP BY, you can select any number of columns as well as functions such as COUNT and AVG that aggregate the data from the grouped rows. When you are not using GROUP BY, and you use a function like COUNT or AVG, you cannot select any normal column values in the same query. The following table describes the available functions in MySQL for use with GROUP BY clauses.

FUNCTION	DESCRIPTION
COUNT	Number of rows
AVG	Average value
SUM	Total value
MIN	Minimum value
MAX	Maximum value
STD	Standard deviation
BIT_OR	Bitwise OR
BIT_AND	Bitwise AND

This example uses a simple new table, scores. The CREATE TABLE command for this table only needs to specify two columns.

Example:
```
CREATE TABLE scores (
    name VARCHAR(50),
    score INT UNSIGNED);
```

Although this is a very basic table, you can achieve impressive results by storing multiple scores for each name and using the various MySQL grouping functions.

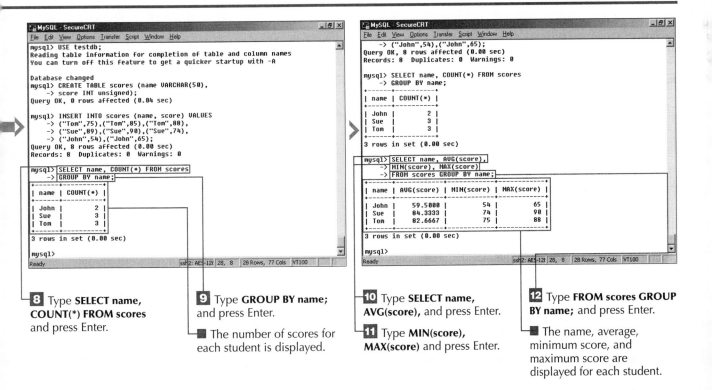

8 Type **SELECT name, COUNT(*) FROM scores** and press Enter.

9 Type **GROUP BY name;** and press Enter.

■ The number of scores for each student is displayed.

10 Type **SELECT name, AVG(score),** and press Enter.

11 Type **MIN(score), MAX(score)** and press Enter.

12 Type **FROM scores GROUP BY name;** and press Enter.

■ The name, average, minimum score, and maximum score are displayed for each student.

DISPLAY DATA FROM MULTIPLE TABLES

MySQL is known as a relational database system, and one of the most important features of a relational database is the ability to work with relationships between different tables. You can use SELECT to retrieve related data from multiple tables.

For example, the quotes table stores quotations and their corresponding authors. If you had a separate table, named authors, that stored birth and death dates for a list of authors, you could combine the two in a single SELECT query:

```
SELECT * FROM quotes, authors
   WHERE quotes.author = authors.author;
```

This query combines, or joins, data from the two tables. Each row in the result includes a combination of the columns from the quotes table and the columns of the authors table. A row is returned for each row that matches between the tables.

The WHERE clause is required when working with multiple tables. The first WHERE condition should identify the

relationship between the two tables. In the example above, the WHERE condition indicates that rows should be matched when the author columns from both tables are equal.

To refer to columns when working with multiple tables, you must specify the table name for each column. Separate the table and column names with a period. The column you match between the tables does not have to be included in the results. The following SELECT query displays only the quote field from the quotes table and the corresponding born field from the authors table:

```
SELECT quotes.quote, authors.born
   FROM quotes, authors
   WHERE quotes.author = authors.author;
```

Although the columns that match across the two tables in this example are both named author, the names do not need to be similar. However, they should contain the same type of data, such as a number or a string of text. MySQL will attempt to compare the columns even if they have different formats, but the results may not be consistent.

DISPLAY DATA FROM MULTIPLE TABLES

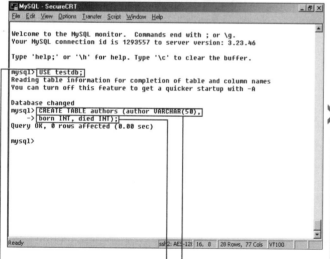

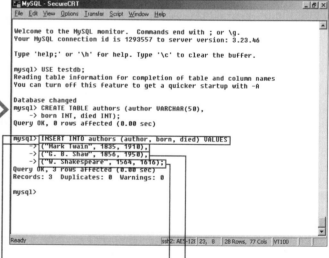

Note: This example uses the quotes table, which you can import from the CD-ROM, and creates a new authors table.

1 From the MySQL monitor, type **USE testdb;** and press Enter to select the database.

2 Type **CREATE TABLE authors (author VARCHAR(50),** and press Enter.

3 Type **born INT, died INT);** and press Enter.

■ This creates the authors table.

4 Type **INSERT INTO authors (author, born, died) VALUES** and press Enter.

5 Type **("Mark Twain", 1835, 1910),** and press Enter.

6 Type **("G. B. Shaw", 1856, 1950),** and press Enter.

7 Type **("W. Shakespeare", 1564,1616);** and press Enter.

■ This inserts three rows into the authors table.

Extra

You can use aliases to assign shorter names to the tables in a SELECT query. This is especially useful when you are retrieving data from multiple tables, because you must refer to a table name with each column name. To use an alias, include the AS keyword and the alias name after a table name. For example, the following query displays data from the quotes and authors tables using aliases:

Example:
```
SELECT * FROM quotes AS q, authors AS a
  WHERE q.author = a.author;
```

This statement assigns the aliases q and a to the two tables. This technique is most useful when you are working with tables with long names. Even when the tables have short names, aliases can be useful if you are retrieving several column values using SELECT, as in the next example.

Example:
```
SELECT q.quote, q.author, a.born, a.died
  FROM quotes AS q, authors AS a
  WHERE q.author = a.author;
```

When you define an alias in this manner, you can refer to columns throughout the query using either the alias name or the full column name.

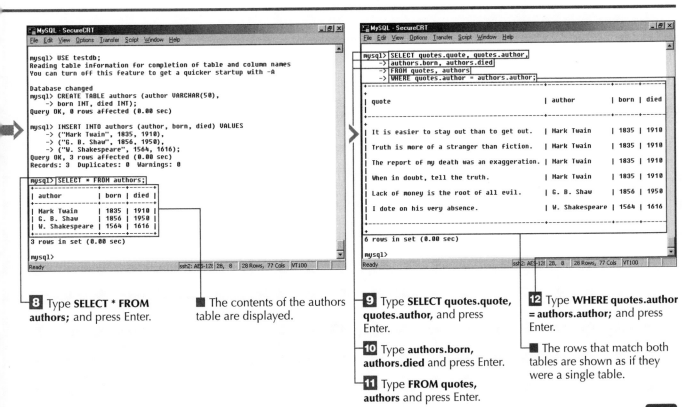

8 Type **SELECT * FROM authors;** and press Enter.

■ The contents of the authors table are displayed.

9 Type **SELECT quotes.quote, quotes.author,** and press Enter.

10 Type **authors.born, authors.died** and press Enter.

11 Type **FROM quotes, authors** and press Enter.

12 Type **WHERE quotes.author = authors.author;** and press Enter.

■ The rows that match both tables are shown as if they were a single table.

USING JOIN OPTIONS

In database terminology, a query that returns data from multiple tables is called a *join*. MySQL includes a JOIN keyword that you can use as an alternate syntax for combining data from tables. In addition, you can use various keywords with JOIN to request different combinations of data from the tables.

The basic type of join uses the INNER JOIN keyword. This is also the type used when you simply specify multiple table names with commas, as in the previous section. In an inner join, the only rows returned will be those that contain a matching, non-NULL value in both tables. The following example uses the quotes and authors tables with an inner join:

```
SELECT * FROM quotes INNER JOIN authors
   ON quotes.author = authors.author;
```

The ON keyword is used to specify the condition that links the two tables. In this example, if an author entry in the quotes table does not have a corresponding listing in the authors table, the row is not included in the result. Similarly,

if an entry in the authors table is not used in any rows of the quotes table, it is not included in the result.

If you use the NATURAL JOIN keywords, MySQL automatically joins the tables on any column names that match between the tables. Because the author column has the same name in both tables, the following query returns the same results as the previous one:

```
SELECT * FROM quotes NATURAL JOIN authors;
```

You can use the LEFT JOIN keywords to combine tables differently. In a left join, all of the rows of the first (left) table you specify are included in the result, whether or not there is a corresponding row in the second table. The following query displays every row of the quotes table, and includes information from the authors table when available. Otherwise, it includes NULL values for the fields of the author table.

```
SELECT * FROM quotes LEFT JOIN authors
   ON quotes.author = authors.author;
```

USING JOIN OPTIONS

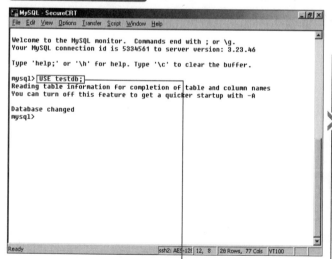

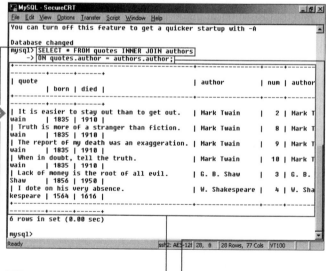

Note: This example uses the testdb database and the quotes and authors tables. See the CD-ROM if you have not yet created one of these.

1 From the MySQL monitor, type **USE testdb;** and press Enter.

■ The database is now selected.

2 Type **SELECT * FROM quotes INNER JOIN authors** and press Enter.

3 Type **ON quotes.author = authors.author;** and press Enter.

■ This displays matching rows from both tables.

Extra

You can use the NATURAL LEFT JOIN keywords to return the same result as LEFT JOIN, except that MySQL automatically matches identically-named columns between the two tables. The following query lists all rows of the quotes table and includes the corresponding information, if any, from the authors table:

Example:
```
SELECT * FROM quotes NATURAL LEFT JOIN authors;
```

Another variation, RIGHT JOIN, is similar to LEFT JOIN but includes all of the rows of the second (right) table rather than the first. The following query lists all of the quotations for all of the authors listed in the authors table. If an author is not listed in the quotes table, a single row is returned with NULL values for the fields of the quotes table.

Example:
```
SELECT * FROM quotes RIGHT JOIN authors
  ON quotes.author = authors.author;
```

The conditions you specify using the ON keyword will be used to match rows between the tables. If you want to include only certain rows, you can add a WHERE clause. The following example uses RIGHT JOIN to list all of the rows of the quotes table for each author in the authors table, but only includes the rows for a single author:

Example:
```
SELECT * FROM quotes RIGHT JOIN authors
  ON quotes.author = authors.author
  WHERE authors.author="Mark Twain";
```

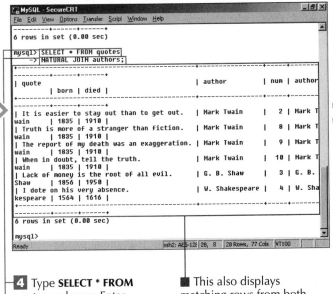

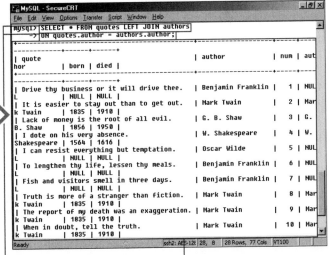

■ **4** Type **SELECT * FROM quotes** and press Enter.

■ **5** Type **NATURAL JOIN authors;** and press Enter.

■ This also displays matching rows from both tables.

■ **6** Type **SELECT * FROM quotes LEFT JOIN authors** and press Enter.

■ **7** Type **ON quotes.author = authors.author;** and press Enter.

■ This query displays all rows from the quotes table, regardless of whether the author was found in the authors table.

DISPLAY DATA WITH MYSQLGUI

The MySQLGUI utility, available from the MySQL Web site at www.mysql.com, provides a friendly graphical interface to a MySQL server. You can use MySQLGUI to perform most of the same tasks you use the MySQL monitor for, including displaying the results of queries. See Chapter 1 for information on installing and running MySQLGUI.

When you run MySQLGUI, you are prompted for a password for the MySQL server. The root user is used by default. If you need to specify a different username, see Chapter 1 for information on configuring MySQLGUI. After the password is entered correctly, the MySQLGUI dialog box is displayed. You can select a database to work with using a drop-down list.

To perform a SELECT query using MySQLGUI, first be sure you have selected the database. Next, enter the query into the text box. Unlike the MySQL Monitor, you should not end queries with a semicolon. After your query is complete, click the Execute Query button to send the query to the

MySQL server. When the server returns the query result, it is displayed on a separate screen.

The following is a simple query using the quotes table that you can test using MySQLGUI:

```
SELECT quote, author FROM quotes
```

This returns two columns of data. You can also use MySQLGUI to try any of the other queries presented in this chapter.

MySQLGUI keeps track of the most recent successful queries and displays them in the lower portion of the window. You can click a query in this list to copy it to the query field, and then click the Execute Query button to execute the query again.

MySQLGUI also includes an option to save the results of a query to a disk file after it has been processed. This is useful for backing up data in MySQL tables or exporting it to other applications.

DISPLAY DATA WITH MYSQLGUI

1 MySQLGUI prompts you for a password. Enter the correct password and click OK.

Note: See Chapter 1 for information on configuring this utility to use a specific username or server.

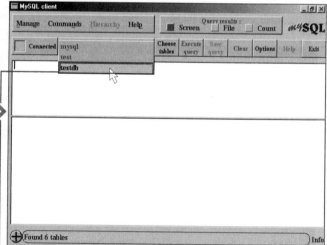

■ The main MySQLGUI screen is displayed.

2 Click the database drop-down menu and select the testdb database.

Note: This example uses the testdb database and the quotes table. See the CD-ROM for instructions on creating them.

Extra

The query results screen in `MySQLGUI` includes a Save to file button. To save your query results to a file on the local computer, click this button. A file selection dialog box is displayed, and you can select an existing file or enter the name for a new file. The file will be an ASCII text file with the .res extension. If you do not select another path, it will be saved in the same directory as the `MySQLGUI` program.

By default, if you select an existing file, the query results are appended to the file. You can choose the Append or Create options from the file selection dialog box to control whether to append or replace an existing file.

The files created by this utility are comma-delimited files. Each text field value is enclosed in single quotes. A comment at the top of the file indicates the query that was used to retrieve the results and the column names that are included.

This is a convenient way to export data from a `SELECT` query to a text file. MySQL includes a variety of other methods of exporting and backing up data from tables or databases. For details on these methods, see Chapter 8.

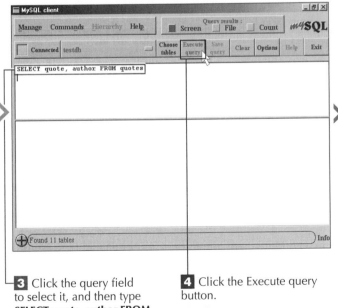

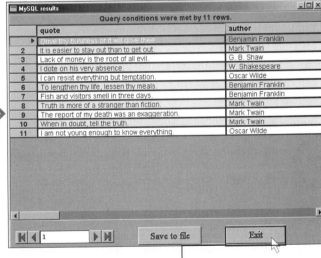

3 Click the query field to select it, and then type **SELECT quote, author FROM quotes** and press Enter.

4 Click the Execute query button.

■ The query is now sent to the MySQL server.

■ The results of your query are displayed.

5 Click the Exit button to return to the main `MySQLGUI` screen.

MATH FUNCTIONS

MySQL includes a wide variety of functions and operators for working with numeric values. All of these functions will work with integer values, such as INTEGER or TINYINT columns, or decimal values, such as FLOAT or DOUBLE columns.

Arithmetic Operators

MySQL supports the standard arithmetic operators for adding, subtracting, multiplication, and division. These are described in the table below.

OPERATOR	DESCRIPTION	EXAMPLE
+	Addition	a + 3
–	Subtraction	a - 1
*	Multiplication	a * 2
/	Division	a / 2
%	Modulo (remainder)	a % 2

The modulo (%) operator returns the remainder for a division operation. For example, the result of a % 2 is the remainder when the value of a is divided by 2.

Random Numbers

The RAND function returns a random floating-point number between zero and one. You can optionally specify a *seed*, or starting point for the calculation, for the random number generator. Any time you obtain random numbers using the same seed, the same numbers will be returned. The following example displays a random number:

```
SELECT RAND();
```

You can also use RAND() within an ORDER BY clause to make a SELECT statement return the records in random order. The following query displays the rows of the quotes table in random order:

```
SELECT * FROM quotes ORDER BY RAND();
```

Positive and Negative Numbers

MySQL can work with negative numbers. You can specify a negative number with a hyphen, as in -3. You can also use a hyphen to convert a value into its opposite with the - operator. For example, this query would convert the score value to a negative number if positive, and to a positive number if negative:

```
SELECT - score FROM table;
```

You can use the ABS (absolute value) function to convert a number to its positive form: the absolute value of 31 is 31, and the absolute value of –5 is 5. This example returns the absolute value of the score column:

```
SELECT ABS(score) FROM table;
```

The SIGN function is used to determine the sign of a value. It returns 1 for positive numbers, –1 for negative numbers, or zero for zero. This example returns the sign of the score column:

```
SELECT SIGN(score) FROM table;
```

Comparison Functions

Two MySQL functions allow you to compare a list of numbers. The LEAST function accepts two or more arguments and returns the smallest value from the list. The GREATEST function is similar, but returns the largest value from the list. The following statements would both return the number 17:

```
SELECT LEAST(97, 17, 22, 43, 23);
```

```
SELECT GREATEST(2, 3, 17, 9, 4);
```

Round Numbers

MySQL includes a variety of functions for rounding decimal numbers to integers. The FLOOR function rounds a number down to the nearest integer. The following example returns a rounded version of a column called average using FLOOR:

```
SELECT FLOOR(average) FROM table;
```

The CEILING function is similar, but rounds up instead of down: 3.1, 3.6, and 3.9 would all be rounded to 4. The ROUND function is more intelligent, rounding to the nearest integer: 3.1 to 3.49 would be rounded down to 3, and 3.5 to 3.9 would be rounded up to 4.

You can optionally specify the number of decimal places for the rounded number. If you do not specify this value, ROUND rounds the number to the nearest integer. The following example displays a rounded version of the average column with two decimal places:

```
SELECT ROUND(average,2) FROM table;
```

The TRUNCATE function is similar to ROUND, but simply removes the decimal digits beyond the specified number of places. This is similar to FLOOR, but not limited to integers. The following example uses TRUNCATE to return the average column's value with only one decimal place:

```
SELECT TRUNCATE(average,1) FROM table;
```

Exponential Functions

The POWER function returns a number raised to the power you specify. You can abbreviate this function as POW. The following statement displays the value of 2 raised to the 7th power:

```
SELECT POWER(2,7);
```

The SQRT function returns the square root of a number you specify. The following SELECT statement displays the square root of 36:

```
SELECT SQRT(36);
```

Logarithmic Functions

MySQL includes several functions for working with logarithms. The EXP function returns the value of e (the logarithmic constant, approximately 2.71) raised to the power you specify. The following SELECT statement displays the value of e raised to the 7th power:

```
SELECT EXP(7);
```

The LOG function returns the natural logarithm (base e logarithm) of the number you specify. The following SELECT statement displays the natural logarithm of 20:

```
SELECT LOG(20);
```

Finally, the LOG10 function returns the base-10 logarithm of the number you specify. The following SELECT statement displays the base-10 logarithm of 20:

```
SELECT LOG10(20);
```

Geometry and Trigonometry Functions

MySQL includes a wide variety of functions useful for geometry and trigonometry. The following table lists these functions and their uses:

FUNCTION	DESCRIPTION
PI	The value of PI (approximately 3.14)
SIN	Returns the sine of the argument
COS	Returns the cosine of the argument
TAN	Returns the tangent of the argument
ATAN	Returns the arc tangent of the argument
ASIN	Returns the arc sine of the argument
ACOS	Returns the arc cosine of the argument
COT	Returns the cotangent of the result
DEGREES	Converts from radians to degrees
RADIANS	Converts from degrees to radians

USING MATH FUNCTIONS

MySQL includes a wide variety of mathematical functions and operators. You can test any of these functions with a simple SELECT statement. For example, this statement displays the result of a mathematical expression:

```
SELECT 17 * 3 + 2;
```

You can combine any number of mathematical operators and functions to produce a result. The following example displays the value of 17 divided by 3, rounded to two decimal places:

```
SELECT ROUND(17/3, 2);
```

These functions can also be used within a SELECT statement that works with a table. The following statement displays the rows of the scores table. For each row, it displays the name column, the score column, and the value of 10 times the score column:

```
SELECT name, score, 10*score
  FROM scores;
```

You can use any MySQL column name or names in an expression like this, along with numeric constants and the results of MySQL functions. This allows you to calculate a result on the fly rather than storing unnecessary data in the table.

Some functions can also be used within the ORDER BY clause of a SELECT statement. For example, the following query displays five rows of the quotes table in random order, using the RAND function:

```
SELECT * FROM quotes
  ORDER BY RAND() LIMIT 5;
```

You can also use column names, operators, and MySQL functions in the ORDER BY clause. This allows you to modify a column's value or combine the values of two columns, and use the result to order the table.

USING MATH FUNCTIONS

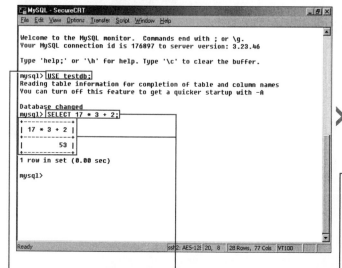

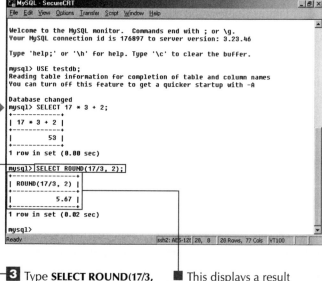

Note: This example uses the testdb database and the quotes and scores tables. These are available on the CD-ROM.

■ **1** From the MySQL monitor, type **USE testdb;** and press Enter.

■ The database is now selected.

■ **2** Type **SELECT 17 * 3 + 2;** and press Enter.

■ MySQL computes and displays the result.

■ **3** Type **SELECT ROUND(17/3, 2);** and press Enter.

■ This displays a result rounded to two decimal places.

Extra

The following example of a `SELECT` statement using MySQL's mathematical operators was included in this section:

Example:
```
SELECT 17 * 3 + 2;
```

If you work out this expression using a calculator, you will find there are two different results, depending on the order you evaluate the operators. If you first multiply 17 by 3, and then add 2, the result is 53. If you first add 3 and 2, and then multiply by 17, the result is 85. MySQL, like other computer languages, solves this dilemma by using a standard set of rules for *operator precedence*.

In MySQL's rules of precedence, multiplication and division are always evaluated before addition and subtraction, so either 2 + 17 * 3 or 17 * 3 + 2 would return the answer 53. You can also use parentheses to enforce your own rules of precedence. The following example performs the addition before the multiplication:

Example:
```
SELECT 17 * (3 + 2);
```

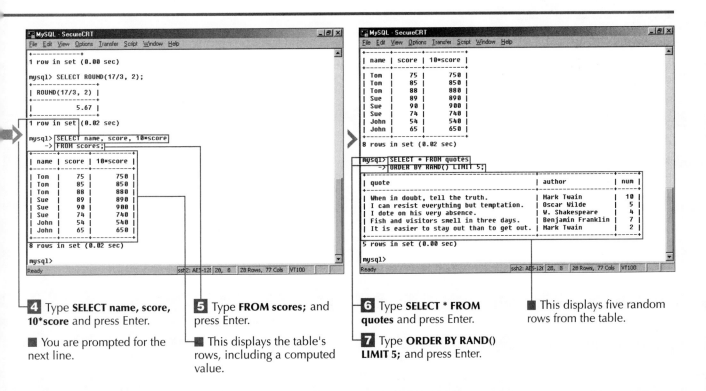

4 Type **SELECT name, score, 10*score** and press Enter.

■ You are prompted for the next line.

5 Type **FROM scores;** and press Enter.

■ This displays the table's rows, including a computed value.

6 Type **SELECT * FROM quotes** and press Enter.

7 Type **ORDER BY RAND() LIMIT 5;** and press Enter.

■ This displays five random rows from the table.

COMPARE NUMERIC VALUES

long with the standard arithmetic operators, MySQL includes a variety of functions that you can use to compare numeric values. The most basic of these is the = operator, which indicates whether two values are equal. MySQL also includes < (less than) and > (greater than) operators. The following simple SELECT statement indicates whether one number is greater than another:

```
SELECT 17 > 33;
```

If you use a comparison operator in a SELECT statement like this, it is evaluated to one if true and zero if false. Thus, because 17 is less than 33, this statement will display a zero result.

You can also use <= (less than or equal) and >= (greater than or equal) in comparisons. The <> or != operators mean not equal, and return the opposite of the value returned by the = operator.

You can use MySQL's comparison operators anywhere a number is expected. The most common use for them is in a WHERE clause to return records that match one or more criteria. This SELECT statement uses a numeric comparison in a WHERE clause:

```
SELECT * FROM scores
  WHERE score > 80;
```

MySQL also includes the GREATEST function, which accepts two or more values and returns the greatest value from the list. The LEAST function is similar but returns the lowest value. These provide an easy way to compare several constants or column values at once. The following statement displays the largest value from a list:

```
SELECT GREATEST(27, 2, 33, 31, 55, 10);
```

COMPARE NUMERIC VALUES

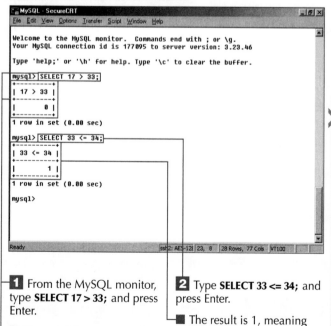

1 From the MySQL monitor, type **SELECT 17 > 33;** and press Enter.

■ The result is zero, meaning false.

2 Type **SELECT 33 <= 34;** and press Enter.

■ The result is 1, meaning true.

3 Type **SELECT GREATEST(27, 2, 33, 31, 55, 10);** and press Enter.

■ The largest number from the list is displayed.

4 Type **SELECT LEAST(27, 2, 33, 31, 55, 10);** and press Enter.

■ The smallest number from the list is displayed.

Apply It

MySQL allows you to compare text values using many of the same operators and functions that work with numeric values. Strings of text are compared in alphabetical order, with strings that would be ordered earlier treated as lesser, and strings that would be ordered later treated as greater. The following query indicates whether one string is greater than another:

```
SELECT "abalone" > "xylophone";
```

You can also use the GREATEST and LEAST functions to work with text. The following example displays the string that occurs last in alphabetical order from the specified list:

```
SELECT GREATEST("abalone", "xylophone", "breeze", "garden");
```

While functions such as GREATEST and LEAST work with either numeric or text values, most of MySQL's functions for working with numeric values do not apply to text strings. If you use a function such as ABS or SQRT with a string value, MySQL will first convert the string to a number if it contains a numeric value. Otherwise, a value of zero is used.

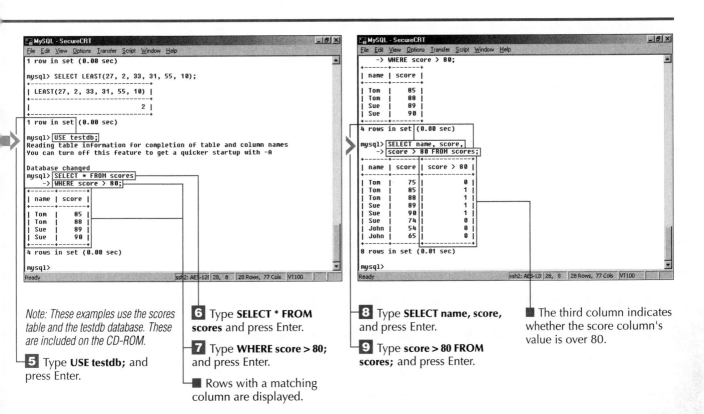

Note: These examples use the scores table and the testdb database. These are included on the CD-ROM.

5 Type **USE testdb;** and press Enter.

6 Type **SELECT * FROM scores** and press Enter.

7 Type **WHERE score > 80;** and press Enter.

■ Rows with a matching column are displayed.

8 Type **SELECT name, score,** and press Enter.

9 Type **score > 80 FROM scores;** and press Enter.

■ The third column indicates whether the score column's value is over 80.

UNDERSTANDING STRING FUNCTIONS

MySQL includes many functions for working with *strings*, or text values. You can use these functions with quoted strings or with the values of text columns such as CHAR, VARCHAR, and TEXT columns.

BASIC STRING FUNCTIONS

The functions in this section perform simple but useful functions, such as combining the values of strings.

CONCAT

The CONCAT function accepts two or more string values as arguments and returns a string that combines, or *concatenates*, the strings into a single string. You can specify numeric values as arguments, and they will be converted automatically into strings.

CONCAT_WS

The CONCAT_WS, or concatenate with separator, function is similar to CONCAT. This function accepts a separator string as the first argument, and uses this as a separator between each of the combined strings.

LENGTH

The LENGTH function returns the length of a string value, or the number of characters it contains. MySQL includes two alternate functions, CHAR_LENGTH and CHARACTER_LENGTH, that serve the same purpose.

WORK WITH SUBSTRINGS

MySQL also includes several functions that allow you to work with *substrings*, or portions of string values.

LEFT

The LEFT function accepts a string as its first parameter and a number as the second parameter. It returns the specified number of characters from the beginning of the string. The example displays the first five characters of a string.

Example:
```
SELECT LEFT("abcdefghij",5);
```

RIGHT

The RIGHT function is similar to LEFT, but returns a specified number of characters starting at the end of a string. The example displays the last five characters of a string.

Example:
```
SELECT RIGHT("qrstuvwxyz",5);
```

MID and SUBSTRING

The MID or SUBSTRING function accepts three arguments: a string value, a position to start from, and a length. It returns the specified number of characters beginning at the specified position. If you omit the last argument, the substring continues to the end of the string. The example displays five characters starting at the third position.

Example:
```
SELECT MID("abcdefghijk", 3, 5);
```

MySQL includes a variety of functions that allow you to work with space characters, such as removing extra spaces from a string.

LTRIM

The LTRIM function removes any spaces from the beginning of a string and returns the result. This is useful for removing unnecessary spaces from user input.

RTRIM

The RTRIM function removes any spaces from the end of a string and returns the result.

TRIM

The TRIM function is a generalized version of LTRIM and RTRIM. If you use TRIM with only a string as an argument, it trims any spaces from the beginning and end of the string and returns the result. You can also specify the keywords LEADING, TRAILING, or BOTH to indicate which ends of the string should be trimmed, and an optional character to remove instead of a space. The example removes any periods from the beginning or end of the string.

Example:
```
SELECT TRIM(BOTH "." FROM "...abcdef...");
```

MySQL includes a number of functions that convert strings in one fashion or another.

FUNCTION	DESCRIPTION
UPPER(string)	Converts all letters in a string to uppercase
LOWER(string)	Converts all letters in a string to lowercase
REPEAT (string, num)	Repeats a string the specified number of times
SPACE(num)	Returns a string containing the specified number of spaces
REVERSE string)	Reverses the order of the characters in a string
ASCII(string)	Returns the ASCII code value for the first character in a string
CHAR(num)	Returns a string converted from the specified ASCII codes

MySQL includes several functions that allow you to search for a substring within a larger string, or to insert or replace portions of a string value.

LOCATE

The LOCATE function searches for a substring within a larger string. It returns the position of the substring as an integer, or zero if the substring was not found. To use LOCATE, specify the substring followed by the larger string. You can optionally specify an index as a third argument. If this is specified, LOCATE begins the search at the position you specify.

Example:
```
SELECT LOCATE("def", "abcdefghi");
```

INSTR

The INSTR function is similar to LOCATE, but with the arguments in reverse order. To search for a substring using INSTR, specify the large string and then the substring.

Example:
```
SELECT INSTR("abcdefghi", "def");
```

REPLACE

The REPLACE function finds occurrences of a substring within a larger string and replaces them with the string you specify. To use REPLACE, specify the string, the substring to search for, and then the replacement string. The example replaces the string "xx" with "def".

Example:
```
SELECT REPLACE("abcxxghijkl", "xx", "def");
```

INSERT

The INSERT function replaces a substring with a specified string. To use INSERT, you specify the string to work with, the position to start replacing, the number of characters to replace, and a replacement string. The example replaces two characters, starting at the fourth position, with the new string "def".

Example:
```
SELECT INSERT("abcxxghijkl", 4, 2, "def");
```

COMPARE STRING VALUES

MySQL allows you to compare string values as easily as numbers. The basic string comparison uses the = operator. This SELECT statement indicates whether two strings are equal:

```
SELECT "apple" = "orange";
```

String comparisons can be used anywhere MySQL expects a value, but are most useful within WHERE clauses. The following SELECT query displays data from a table using a string comparison:

```
SELECT * FROM scores WHERE name="Tom";
```

For a more sophisticated string comparison, you can use the STRCMP function. This function returns a value of 0 if the two strings you specify are equal, –1 if the first string is smaller than the second when compared alphabetically, and 1 if the second string is smaller. For example, the following SELECT statement will display all of the names that start with a letter before N from the scores table:

```
SELECT * FROM scores
  WHERE STRCMP(name,"N") = -1;
```

You can also use the LIKE operator to compare strings, as described in Chapter 6. This is similar to the = operator, but allows the use of the wildcard characters % (zero or more characters) and _ (one character). The NOT LIKE operator is the opposite of LIKE, and returns a value of 1 if the strings do not match.

MySQL also includes an operator, REGEXP or RLIKE, which is similar to LIKE but supports a standard regular expression syntax instead of simple wildcards. For example, the following SELECT query uses a regular expression to find names beginning with "T" and at least three letters long:

```
SELECT * FROM scores
  WHERE name REGEXP "T.{2}";
```

COMPARE STRING VALUES

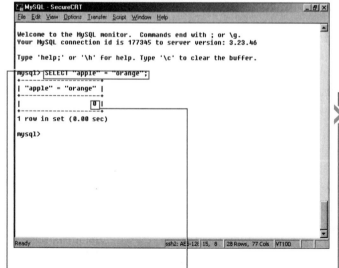

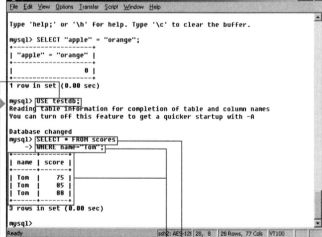

1 From the MySQL monitor, type **SELECT "apple" = "orange";** and press Enter.

■ The result is zero, because the strings are not equal.

Note: The remaining examples use the scores table in the testdb database, available on the CD-ROM.

2 Type **USE testdb;** and press Enter.

3 Type **SELECT * FROM scores** and press Enter.

4 Type **WHERE name="Tom";** and press Enter.

■ The matching rows are displayed.

Extra

The syntax used in MySQL's RLIKE and REGEXP operators follows the extended POSIX regular expression standard. The following table lists some of the special characters supported in MySQL regular expressions.

CHARACTER	DESCRIPTION
.	Matches any character
[abc]	Matches any of the characters in brackets
^	Anchors the match to the beginning of the string
$	Anchors the match to the end of the string
|	Matches the previous characters or the following ones
*	Repeats the previous character zero or more times
+	Repeats the previous character one or more times
?	Repeats the previous character zero or one times
{3}	Matches the previous character exactly 3 times
{2,5}	Matches the previous character between 2 and 5 times

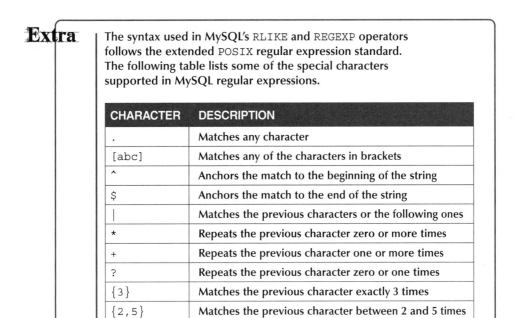

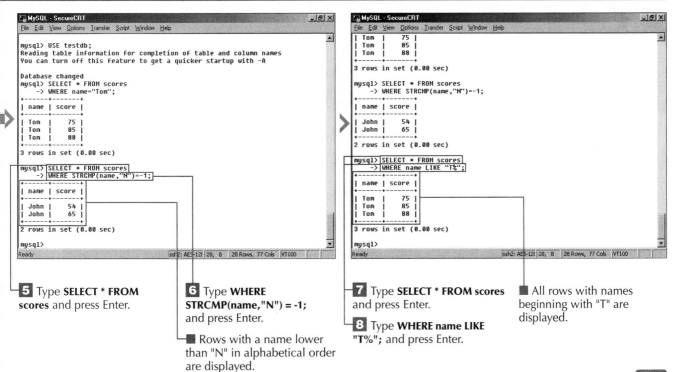

5 Type **SELECT * FROM scores** and press Enter.

6 Type **WHERE STRCMP(name,"N") = -1;** and press Enter.

■ Rows with a name lower than "N" in alphabetical order are displayed.

7 Type **SELECT * FROM scores** and press Enter.

8 Type **WHERE name LIKE "T%";** and press Enter.

■ All rows with names beginning with "T" are displayed.

USING STRING FUNCTIONS

You can use MySQL's string functions to work with data from a table in a SELECT statement. One reason you may want to use functions is to convert the data from the table columns into a more useful format. For example, you could use the CONCAT function to combine two fields into a single string:

```
SELECT CONCAT(name, " ", score)
  FROM scores;
```

As another example, you can use the UPPER function to convert a column to uppercase before displaying its value. The following query displays the quote and author fields of the quotes table in uppercase form:

```
SELECT UPPER(quote), UPPER(author)
  FROM quotes;
```

MySQL functions are also useful in the WHERE clause of a SELECT statement. While this is most often used with comparison functions, you can also convert a column's value before comparing it with a known value.

The UPDATE query in MySQL is often used with one or more functions. For example, the REPLACE function replaces part of a string with another string. You can use this function with UPDATE to replace a string in all of a table's rows. For example, this query changes any occurrence of "G." to "George" within the author field of the quotes table:

```
UPDATE quotes SET
  author = REPLACE(author, "G.", "George");
```

You can use any combination of column values from the table, constants, and MySQL functions and operators within an UPDATE query. You can also use a WHERE clause, if desired, to make sure that the update affects only the rows you want to update.

USING STRING FUNCTIONS

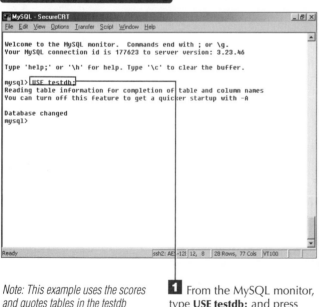

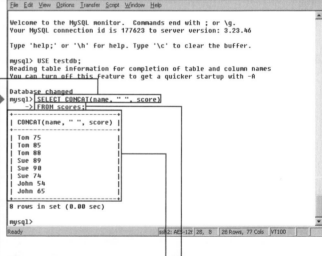

Note: This example uses the scores and quotes tables in the testdb database, available on the CD-ROM.

1 From the MySQL monitor, type **USE testdb;** and press Enter.

■ The database is now selected.

2 Type **SELECT CONCAT(name, " ", score)** and press Enter.

■ You are prompted for the next line.

3 Type **FROM scores;** and press Enter.

■ The calculated value is displayed for each row of the table.

Extra

When you use a MySQL function or other calculation within a `SELECT` query to return a value, you can optionally assign an *alias* to the calculated value. This is useful to give a shorthand name to the result. More importantly, if you are retrieving the data from the query using a program, using an alias allows the program to access the calculated value.

To assign an alias, you use the `AS` keyword and assign a name, which should follow the same rules as a valid column name. For example, this query concatenates the name and score fields from the scores table and returns the result as the alias nscore, along with the normal column values.

Example:
```
SELECT name, score,
   CONCAT(name, " ", score) AS nscore
   FROM scores;
```

You can use any number of aliases and calculated fields within a `SELECT` query. This allows you to avoid calculations outside of the MySQL server.

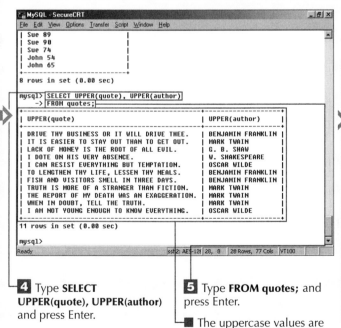

4 Type **SELECT UPPER(quote), UPPER(author)** and press Enter.

5 Type **FROM quotes;** and press Enter.

■ The uppercase values are displayed for each row.

6 Type **UPDATE quotes SET** and press Enter.

7 Type **author = REPLACE(author, "G.", "George");** and press Enter.

■ The replacement is performed on all matching rows.

8 Type **SELECT * FROM quotes;** and press Enter.

■ The updated contents of the table are displayed.

WORK WITH SUBSTRINGS

MySQL includes a number of functions that allow you to divide a text string into smaller pieces, or *substrings*. You can use these functions when you need to extract a portion of a text column's value.

The first substring function, LEFT, returns the number of characters you specify starting at the beginning of the string. For example, the following query uses this function to display the first ten characters of the quote field for each row of the quotes table:

```
SELECT author, LEFT(quote,10)
   FROM quotes;
```

The RIGHT function is similar, but returns the specified number of characters starting at the end of the string. The following example displays the last ten characters of the quote column for each row of the quotes table:

```
SELECT author, RIGHT(quote, 10)
   FROM quotes;
```

The third substring function is MID. You can use this function to find a number of characters anywhere in a text value. The first numeric parameter is the starting position, and the second is the number of characters. The starting position can range from one to the length of the string. The following example returns ten characters from the quote column, starting with the fifth character:

```
SELECT author, MID(quote, 5, 10)
   FROM quotes;
```

MySQL also includes a SUBSTRING function that is identical to MID. You can use the two interchangeably. If you do not specify the number of characters to return, these functions return the substring that starts at the specified index and ends at the end of the string. The following query displays the portion of the quote column's value from the fifth character to the end:

```
SELECT author, SUBSTRING(quote, 5)
   FROM quotes;
```

WORK WITH SUBSTRINGS

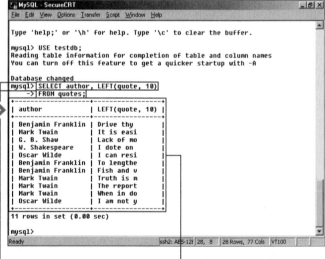

Note: This example uses the quotes table in the testdb database. If you have not created them, see the CD-ROM for instructions.

1 From the MySQL monitor, type **USE testdb;** and press Enter.

■ The database is now selected.

2 Type **SELECT author, LEFT(quote, 10)** and press Enter.

3 Type **FROM quotes;** and press Enter.

■ This displays the author column and the first ten characters of the quote column for each row.

Extra

MySQL also includes functions that allow you to search a string for a particular substring. The first of these, LOCATE, searches a text value for a string you specify. If the string is found within the larger string, it returns a number indicating the character position where it starts. If the string is not found, LOCATE returns zero. The following query searches the values of the quote column in the quotes table for the string "every" and displays the results:

Example:
```
SELECT LOCATE("every", quote)
  FROM quotes;
```

The LOCATE function also accepts a third optional parameter. If you specify a number after the two strings, MySQL will only search for the substring starting with the character index you specify. This is useful when you want to find the second or third occurrence of a string.

MySQL also supports the INSTR function for compatibility with other database systems. This function is similar to LOCATE, but the parameters are in the opposite order: you first specify the larger string, and then the substring to search for. Unlike LOCATE, INSTR does not support a starting position for the search.

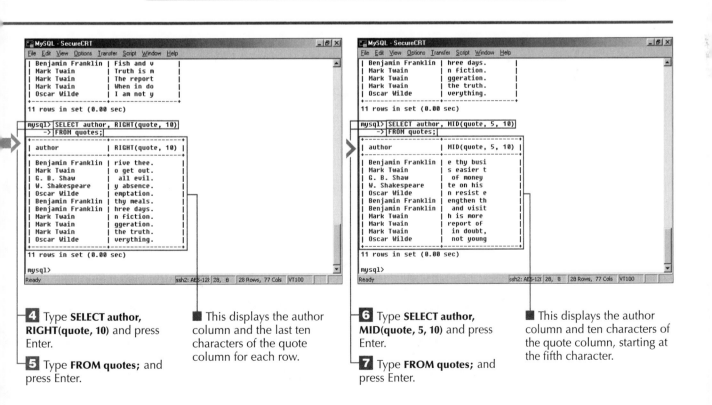

4 Type **SELECT author, RIGHT(quote, 10)** and press Enter.

5 Type **FROM quotes;** and press Enter.

■ This displays the author column and the last ten characters of the quote column for each row.

6 Type **SELECT author, MID(quote, 5, 10)** and press Enter.

7 Type **FROM quotes;** and press Enter.

■ This displays the author column and ten characters of the quote column, starting at the fifth character.

UNDERSTANDING DATE AND TIME FUNCTIONS

M ySQL allows you to store a date or date/time combination in several column types, including DATE, TIME, DATETIME, and TIMESTAMP.

MySQL also includes a number of functions that allow you to work with dates and times and convert them into different formats.

GET THE CURRENT DATE

If you need to know the current date within a MySQL query, you can use the NOW function. This function returns the current date and time. If you use this function as a string value, it will return a string with the year, month, date, hour, minute, and second with punctuation in between. If you use the result as a numeric value, it will contain no punctuation.

The NOW function does not require any parameters. The SYSDATE and CURRENT_TIMESTAMP functions are synonyms for NOW.

The CURRENT_DATE function returns the current date only. This function can be abbreviated CURDATE. The CURRENT_TIME and CURTIME functions are similar but return only the hours, minutes, and seconds values for the current time.

WORK WITH DATE COMPONENTS

MySQL includes a variety of functions for extracting components, such as the day of the week or the week of the year, from a date value. The following table describes these functions.

The HOUR, MINUTE, and SECOND functions work only with values that include a time, such as TIMESTAMP or TIME columns. The other functions work only with values that include a date.

FUNCTION	DESCRIPTION
DAYOFWEEK	Numeric day of week (1-7 for Sunday-Saturday)
WEEKDAY	Numeric day of week (0-6 for Monday-Sunday)
DAYNAME	Name of day of week
DAYOFMONTH	Day of month (1-31)
DAYOFYEAR	Day of year (1-366)
MONTH	Numeric month (1-12)
MONTHNAME	Name of month
QUARTER	Numeric quarter (1-4)
WEEK	Week of year (0-53)
YEAR	Numeric year (4 digits)
YEARWEEK	Year and week number (6 digits)
HOUR	Hour of day (0-23)
MINUTE	Minute of hour (0-59)
SECOND	Second (0-59)

ADD AND SUBTRACT

The DATE_ADD function adds an interval to a date value. To use this function, you specify the date to work with as an expression or column name, the keyword INTERVAL, a number specifying the amount of time to add, and a keyword indicating the type of interval. The basic intervals are SECOND, MINUTE, HOUR, DAY, MONTH, and YEAR.

The DATE_SUB function is similar, but subtracts the specified interval from the date. You can use ADDDATE and SUBDATE as synonyms for DATE_ADD and DATE_SUB. The example below subtracts two months from a date in the updatetime column.

Example:
```
SELECT DATE_SUB(updatetime, INTERVAL 2
MONTH) FROM address;
```

In addition to the basic intervals, you can use various keywords to specify multiple parts of a date, such as a year and month. The table below lists these keywords with an example of the syntax for each one.

KEYWORD	DESCRIPTION	EXAMPLE
MINUTE_SECOND	Minutes and seconds	"03:22"
HOUR_MINUTE	Hours and minutes	"12:03"
HOUR_SECOND	Hours, minutes, and seconds	"12:03:22"
DAY_HOUR	Days and hours	"2 12"
YEAR_MONTH	Years and months	"2-1"
DAY_MINUTE	Days, hours, and minutes	"2 12:03"
DAY_SECOND	Days, hours, minutes, and seconds	"2 12:03:22"

FORMAT DATES

The DATE_FORMAT function allows you to display a date with the format you specify. The first parameter should be a date value, and the second is a string with one or more codes for components of the date and time. The following codes display components of the date.

DATE_FORMAT FUNCTIONS	
CODE	**MEANING**
%d	Day of month (01, 02, 03, and so on)
%e	Day of month (1, 2, 3, and so on)
%D	Day of month (1st, 2nd, 3rd, and so on)
%m	Numeric month (01, 02, 03, and so on)
%c	Numeric month (1, 2, 3, and so on)
%M	Month name
%W	Name of day of week
%a	Name of day of week (abbreviated)
%Y	Year (4 digits)
%y	Year (2 digits)

The following codes can be used within the DATE_FORMAT function to display the components of the time. An additional function, TIME_FORMAT, is similar to DATE_FORMAT but only allows the following codes.

TIME_FORMAT FUNCTIONS	
CODE	**MEANING**
%H	Hour (24 hours, 2 digits)
%k	Hour (24 hours, 1-2 digits)
%h	Hour (12 hours, 2 digits)
%i	Minute (2 digits)
%S	Second (2 digits)
%p	AM or PM
%T	Complete 24-hour time
%t	Complete 12-hour time with AM or PM

WORK WITH DATES AND TIMES

You can use MySQL's date and time functions on dates you specify within a query, or dates and times stored in DATE, TIME, DATETIME, or TIMESTAMP columns. If you specify a date, you can use one of two formats: a number that combines the year, month, date, hour, minute, and second values, or a string with punctuation. The following two dates are equivalent:

```
2004-12-31 12:33:00
```

```
20041231123300
```

For TIME columns or functions that require only a time, you can simply specify the hours, minutes, and seconds as a number or string. Similarly, you can specify the year, month, and date for DATE columns or functions that work with dates.

For example, the address table defined earlier in this book has a TIMESTAMP column called updatetime. You can use

the MONTH and YEAR functions, which extract the corresponding components from a date, to display only the month and year for each row's TIMESTAMP:

```
SELECT MONTH(updatetime), YEAR(updatetime)
  FROM address;
```

When you use functions like this and are returning the data to an application, you may find it useful to use the AS keyword to assign an alias to the evaluated values.

You can compare dates using the = operator, as with other data types. You can also use functions like YEAR within a WHERE clause to compare just part of the date. The following SELECT query displays all of the rows with an updatetime column with the year 2002:

```
SELECT * FROM address
  WHERE YEAR(updatetime) = 2002;
```

WORK WITH DATES AND TIMES

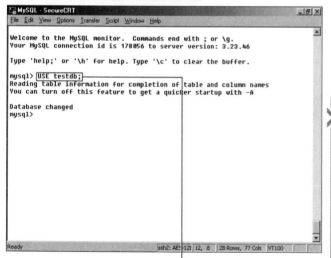

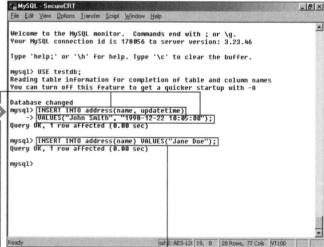

Note: This example uses the address table in the testdb database. You can import this table from the CD-ROM.

1 From the MySQL monitor, type **USE testdb;** and press Enter.

■ The database is now selected.

2 Type **INSERT INTO address (name, updatetime)** and press Enter.

3 Type **VALUES ("John Smith", "1998-12-22 10:05:00");** and press Enter.

■ This adds a record with a specified date.

4 Type **INSERT INTO address (name) VALUES ("Jane Doe");** and press Enter.

■ This record is assigned the current date and time.

Extra

MySQL includes several functions for converting date values to different formats. The following functions convert MySQL date and time values:

FUNCTION	DESCRIPTION
TO_DAYS	Converts to number of days since year zero
UNIX_TIMESTAMP	Converts to a UNIX timestamp (number of seconds since 1/1/1970)
TIME_TO_SEC	Converts a time value to a number of seconds

Conversely, the following functions convert from various formats back to a MySQL date or time value:

FUNCTION	DESCRIPTION
FROM_DAYS	Converts from number of days since year zero
FROM_UNIXTIME	Converts from UNIX timestamp
SEC_TO_TIME	Converts number of seconds to time (hours, minutes, seconds)

If you need to convert a date to a format not listed here, you can use the individual functions such as MONTH, DATE, and YEAR, or the DATE_FORMAT function, described in the next section.

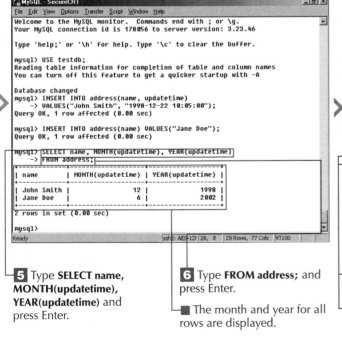

5 Type **SELECT name, MONTH(updatetime), YEAR(updatetime)** and press Enter.

6 Type **FROM address;** and press Enter.

■ The month and year for all rows are displayed.

7 Type **SELECT * FROM address** and press Enter.

8 Type **WHERE YEAR(updatetime) = 1998;** and press Enter.

■ Rows that match the specified year are displayed.

DISPLAY FORMATTED DATES

Often, you will need to display a date in a specific format. You can use the DATE_FORMAT function to do this in MySQL. This function is particularly useful to format a date before displaying it or returning it to an application.

To use DATE_FORMAT, you specify the date value, which can be a specified date or a column name, and a format string with one or more codes for date and time components. The following example displays the rows of the address table with a date such as "February 20th, 2004":

```
SELECT name,
  DATE_FORMAT(updatetime, "%M %D, %Y")
  FROM address;
```

As with other calculated values, you can use the AS keyword to assign an alias to the formatted date. This is particularly useful if you are passing the date to an application.

The format string you use with DATE_FORMAT can contain punctuation and text to accompany the date. Any text that is not a code beginning with the % symbol is passed through to the output. The following example obtains the current date using the NOW function and formats it with a text message:

```
SELECT DATE_FORMAT(NOW(), "The date is
%m/%d/%Y.");
```

If you are only working with the time for a date value, you can use the TIME_FORMAT function. This function is similar to DATE_FORMAT, but accepts only the codes that represent the components of the time. The following example displays the current time using this function:

```
SELECT TIME_FORMAT(NOW(), "%h:%i:%s");
```

The codes you can use with the DATE_FORMAT and TIME_FORMAT functions are listed in the section "Understanding Date and Time Functions," earlier in this chapter.

DISPLAY FORMATTED DATES

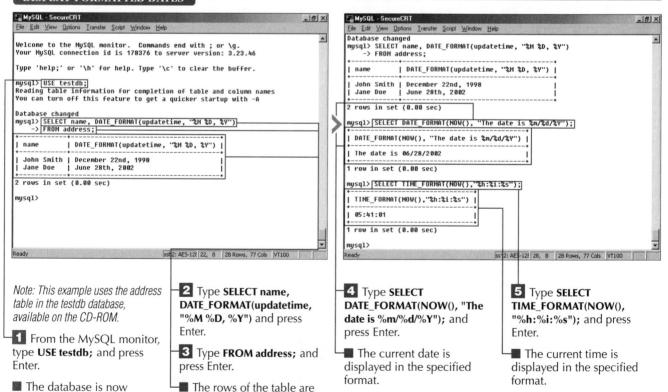

Note: This example uses the address table in the testdb database, available on the CD-ROM.

1 From the MySQL monitor, type **USE testdb;** and press Enter.

■ The database is now selected.

2 Type **SELECT name, DATE_FORMAT(updatetime, "%M %D, %Y")** and press Enter.

3 Type **FROM address;** and press Enter.

■ The rows of the table are listed with formatted dates.

4 Type **SELECT DATE_FORMAT(NOW(), "The date is %m/%d/%Y");** and press Enter.

■ The current date is displayed in the specified format.

5 Type **SELECT TIME_FORMAT(NOW(), "%h:%i:%s");** and press Enter.

■ The current time is displayed in the specified format.

ADD AND SUBTRACT DATES AND TIMES

You can use the MySQL functions DATE_ADD and DATE_SUB to add and subtract values from a date. This is useful when you need to calculate a future or past date, and is also useful when testing date values.

To add an interval to a date value, use DATE_ADD and specify the date, the keyword INTERVAL, the number to add, and the unit for the number, such as MONTH or DAY. For example, the following SELECT statement displays the date three months from the current date:

```
SELECT DATE_ADD(NOW(), INTERVAL 3 MONTH);
```

In MySQL version 3.23 and later, you can use the + and - operators as shorthand for DATE_ADD and DATE_SUB. To use these, simply specify the same INTERVAL keyword and unit type. The following example adds two years to the current date and displays the result:

```
SELECT NOW() + INTERVAL 2 YEAR;
```

While you can use date addition and subtraction to modify existing date values, they can also be useful in a WHERE clause. For example, the following SELECT query displays the rows from the address table where the updatetime column has a value within the last 30 days:

```
SELECT * FROM address WHERE
    updatetime > (NOW() - INTERVAL 30 DAY);
```

This example subtracts an interval of 30 days from the NOW function to obtain the date 30 days ago and then tests whether the updatetime column's value is after that date.

Be sure to use singular values such as DAY, MONTH, and YEAR in the INTERVAL clause. Plural values, such as YEARS, will result in an error.

ADD AND SUBTRACT DATES AND TIMES

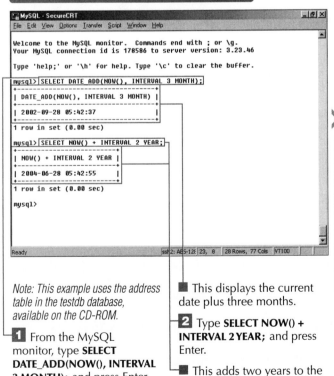

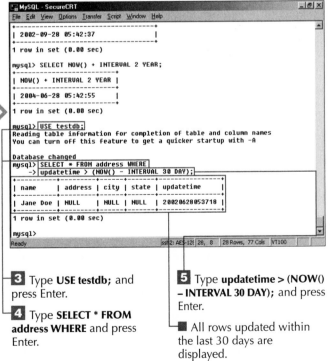

Note: This example uses the address table in the testdb database, available on the CD-ROM.

1 From the MySQL monitor, type **SELECT DATE_ADD(NOW(), INTERVAL 3 MONTH);** and press Enter.

■ This displays the current date plus three months.

2 Type **SELECT NOW() + INTERVAL 2 YEAR;** and press Enter.

■ This adds two years to the current date.

3 Type **USE testdb;** and press Enter.

4 Type **SELECT * FROM address WHERE** and press Enter.

5 Type **updatetime > (NOW() – INTERVAL 30 DAY);** and press Enter.

■ All rows updated within the last 30 days are displayed.

MISCELLANEOUS FUNCTIONS

A long with the functions described earlier in this chapter, MySQL includes a variety of other functions. These include functions to display information about the MySQL server, current user, and session; functions to encode and decode strings in various ways; and functions for working with binary numbers.

MYSQL INFORMATION FUNCTIONS

The functions described here return information about the current database, the current user, and the MySQL server itself. These are particularly useful from within an application.

DATABASE

The DATABASE function does not require any arguments. It returns the name of the currently selected database. Usually this is the database you selected with the USE statement.

Example:
```
SELECT DATABASE();
```

USER

The USER function displays the name of the current MySQL username. If you are using the MySQL monitor, this is the user you specified on the command line. The returned value includes the username and the hostname the user is connecting from, separated by the @ symbol. The SYSTEM_USER and SESSION_USER functions are synonyms for USER.

Example:
```
SELECT USER();
```

VERSION

The VERSION function returns the MySQL server's software version number as a string. This function does not require any arguments.

Example:
```
SELECT VERSION();
```

CONNECTION_ID

The CONNECTION_ID function returns the current connection ID. This is a number assigned when the client connects to the MySQL server and will be a unique number for each current client session.

Example:
```
SELECT CONNECTION_ID();
```

LAST_INSERT_ID

The LAST_INSERT_ID function returns the last value assigned to a column with the AUTO_INCREMENT attribute when a row was added using the INSERT statement within the current client session. If you have added a row to a table that includes an auto-increment column, you can use this function to obtain a unique identifier for the new row.

Example:
```
SELECT LAST_INSERT_ID();
```

MySQL includes a variety of functions that can encode or decode strings. These are useful when working with passwords and other sensitive information in a database.

PASSWORD

The PASSWORD function accepts a string and encrypts it. This function is used by MySQL itself to encrypt passwords for users. For security reasons, after you have an encrypted value, there is no way to calculate the original password; to check user passwords, MySQL encrypts the value entered by the user and compares it with the encrypted password stored in the database.

Example:
```
SELECT PASSWORD("zephyr");
```

ENCRYPT

The ENCRYPT function accepts a string as an argument and encrypts it. This function is available only on UNIX servers, as it uses the standard UNIX function crypt(). As with the PASSWORD function, this is a one-way encryption and cannot be reversed.

Depending on the operating system, the ENCRYPT function may work with only the first eight characters of the string. This is due to the fact that the underlying UNIX function is intended for encrypting short passwords.

Example:
```
SELECT ENCRYPT("zephyr");
```

ENCODE

The ENCODE function encodes a string using another string as a password. It uses the letters in the password to determine how to alter the original string. Unlike PASSWORD and ENCRYPT, the encoding is reversible.

The result of the ENCODE function is a binary string with the same length as the original string. Because it may contain nontext characters, this value cannot be stored in a text column, such as CHAR or TEXT. You can store it in a binary column type such as BLOB.

Example:
```
SELECT ENCODE("Hello there", "zephyr");
```

DECODE

The DECODE function accepts a string encoded with the ENCODE function and a password. It decodes the string using the password. If the password is the same one used when encoding the string, this should restore the original value of the string.

MD5

The MD5 function calculates an MD5 checksum for a string. A *checksum* is a value calculated from a string value using a formula. MD5 is a standard developed by RSA Data Security. It uses a complex formula to create an alphanumeric checksum based on the original string value. The checksum cannot be used to recreate the original string, but it can be compared with another string's checksum to determine whether the strings match.

Example:
```
SELECT MD5("Hello there");
```

MySQL includes several operators and functions that you can use to work with individual bits of binary data. These include logical AND and OR functions that work on the individual bits (binary digits) of a number and other operations. The following table describes the binary operators available in MySQL.

Along with these operations, MySQL includes a function, BIT_COUNT, which returns the number of bits used to store a number. This is useful for checking whether a number will fit in a particular numeric column type.

OPERATOR	DESCRIPTION
|	Logical bitwise OR
&	Logical bitwise AND
<<	Shift the bits of a number one space to the left
>	Shift the bits of a number one space to the right
~	Convert all 1 bits to 0 and all 0 bits to 1

IMPORT AND EXPORT TOOLS

MySQL includes a variety of tools for importing and exporting data. These are useful for transferring data to and from other database systems, spreadsheets, and other applications, and to back up and restore data in MySQL tables.

Export with SELECT

The INTO OUTFILE option can be used with any SELECT query to create a text file with the resulting row data. Each row of the table is written as a row in the text file. By default, the fields within each line are separated by tab characters. The file is saved on the MySQL server. The default location is the directory where the MySQL database itself is stored.

Example:
```
SELECT name, address, city
  INTO OUTFILE "mail.txt"
  FROM mail;
```

Text File Formats

The SELECT INTO OUTFILE and LOAD DATA INFILE commands support several options to control the structure of the output file. You can specify these options after the table name and before any list of column names with LOAD DATA, or after the name of the output file with SELECT INTO OUTFILE. The table below shows the available options.

The ENCLOSED BY option can also be used as OPTIONALLY ENCLOSED BY. If this is specified, text values are enclosed in the character, but numeric fields are not enclosed.

KEYWORDS	DESCRIPTION	DEFAULT
FIELDS TERMINATED BY	Separates fields	\t (tab)
FIELDS ENCLOSED BY	Encloses each field	none
FIELDS ESCAPED BY	Prefixes special characters	\ (backslash)
LINES TERMINATED BY	Ends each line	\n (newline)

Import with LOAD DATA

You can use the LOAD DATA INFILE command in MySQL to read a text file into a database table. This command can be used to import a text file created by the SELECT INTO OUTFILE command, or a file you have exported from another application. To use this command, use LOAD DATA INFILE and the filename to import. Specify the table to import to with the INTO TABLE keywords, and specify a list of column names if needed.

If you do not specify a list of column names, MySQL will expect all columns to appear in the file in the same order they are defined in the table's structure.

You can specify the LOW_PRIORITY keyword after LOAD DATA to wait until no clients are reading from the table before importing the data. The CONCURRENT option can be used to allow clients to read data while the import is in progress. The LOCAL option allows you to specify a file on the client machine instead of the MySQL server.

If a row in the text file contains the same value for a unique or key field as an existing row of the table, an error will occur, and the import operation will be aborted. You can optionally specify the REPLACE keyword after the filename to replace the existing rows with the rows from the text file, avoiding this error. Alternately, specify the IGNORE keyword to skip any duplicate rows and continue the import.

Example:
```
LOAD DATA INFILE 'address.txt'
  INTO TABLE address (name, address, city);
```

Back Up Data with mysqldump

The `mysqldump` utility dumps the contents of a table or an entire database to the screen, and you can redirect its output to a file. This command does not create a text file suitable for use with the `LOAD DATA` command. Instead, it creates a file of SQL commands, such as `CREATE TABLE` and `INSERT`, to re-create the table.

Because it can be used to re-create a table or an entire database easily, `mysqldump`'s output files are ideal backups for the MySQL server. You can use a utility like `cron` under UNIX or the Task Scheduler under Windows to schedule `mysqldump` to create regular daily backups.

To use `mysqldump`, specify a database and a list of tables on the command line. If you do not specify tables, the entire database is included in the dump. This utility also includes a number of options; some of the most useful are described in the table.

Example:
```
mysqldump -uuser -ppassword testdb address
>backup.sql
```

OPTION	DESCRIPTION
`-A` or `--all-databases`	Includes all databases on the server
`-C` or `--compress`	Attempts to compress data sent from the server to the client
`-B` or `--databases`	Backs up multiple databases listed after this option
`--help`	Displays a complete list of options
`-f` or `--force`	Ignores MySQL errors during the dump
`-h` or `--host`	Specifies the hostname for the MySQL server
`-u` or `--user`	Specifies the MySQL username
`-p` or `--password`	Specifies the password for the MySQL username
`-t` or `--no-create-info`	Writes data only, no table structure
`-d` or `--no-data`	Writes table structure only, no data
`-w` or `--where`	Adds a `WHERE` clause to select specific rows

Restore a Backup File

The backup file created by `mysqldump` contains MySQL commands. You can restore the data by executing those commands. You can do this with the `mysql` command or with the `SOURCE` command within the MySQL monitor.

Example:
```
mysql -uuser -ppassword -Dtestdb <backup.sql
```

Copy Data Between Tables

You can use several methods to copy data between tables. One of the simplest is to create a table with the same structure as the existing table, and then use the `SELECT` option with an `INSERT` query to copy the data from the old table to the new table.

Another method of copying a table is to create a backup of the table using `mysqldump`, and then edit the file to use a different table name or rename the original table on the database server. You can then restore the backup file to create the new table.

Example:
```
INSERT INTO address2 SELECT * FROM address;
```

EXPORT TO A TEXT FILE WITH SELECT

The SELECT query in MySQL includes an INTO OUTFILE option to save the results of the SELECT query to a file. You can use this to create a text file containing row and column values from a table. To use this option, specify INTO OUTFILE and the name of the file after the column names and before the FROM clause.

The following example saves all of the rows of the mail table into a text file:

```
SELECT name, address, city
   INTO OUTFILE "mail.txt"
   FROM mail;
```

The INTO OUTFILE option saves a file on the MySQL server, and the MySQL username you are using must have the correct permissions to be able to create a file. If you do not have access to write a file on the server or to read the file after it has been created, you can use client-side utilities

to create a similar file. These include the mysqldump utility, described in the section "Back Up Data from a Table," later in this chapter.

When you use this option, the created file is a simple text file, with one row per database row. The fields are separated with tab characters by default. You can use various options with the FIELDS and ROWS keywords to modify the format of the output file. These options are explained in the Extra section.

You can use INTO OUTFILE with any combination of SELECT query options. You can specify column names to export, use a WHERE clause to choose rows from the table, and use a LIMIT clause to limit the number of rows. You can test the SELECT query without the INTO OUTFILE clause and make sure the right data is displayed before creating the output file.

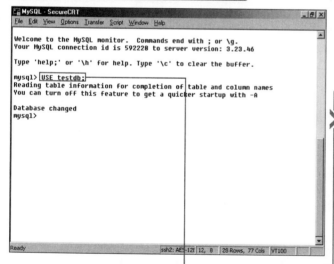

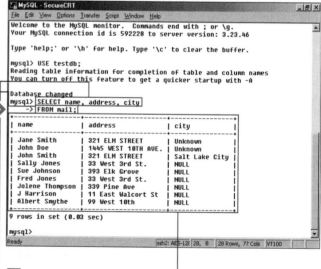

Note: This example uses the mail table in the testdb database, available on the CD-ROM.

1 From the MySQL monitor, type **USE testdb;** and press Enter.

■ The database is now selected.

2 Type **SELECT name, address, city** and press Enter.

3 Type **FROM mail;** and press Enter.

■ This displays the data that will be exported to the text file.

158

Extra

The INTO OUTFILE option allows several optional keywords to modify the format of the output file. These are divided into FIELDS and LINES options. The FIELDS keyword can be followed by one or more of the following options:

KEYWORDS	DESCRIPTION	DEFAULT
TERMINATED BY	Character used to separate fields	\t (tab)
ENCLOSED BY	Character surrounding each field	none
ESCAPED BY	Character used to escape special characters	\ (backslash)

The ESCAPED BY character is used to prefix special characters, such as commas or quotation marks, within the column data. The ESCAPED BY character itself is represented by a doubled character, such as \\ for a backslash.

The LINES keyword can include a single option, LINES TERMINATED BY. This specifies the character that ends each line in the output file. The default is \n, the newline character.

You can specify OPTIONALLY ENCLOSED BY instead of ENCLOSED BY. In this case, MySQL will only enclose strings with the character. Numeric fields will not be enclosed.

To use the FIELDS or LINES options, specify them after the export filename in the SELECT INTO OUTFILE query. If you specify multiple options, separate them with commas.

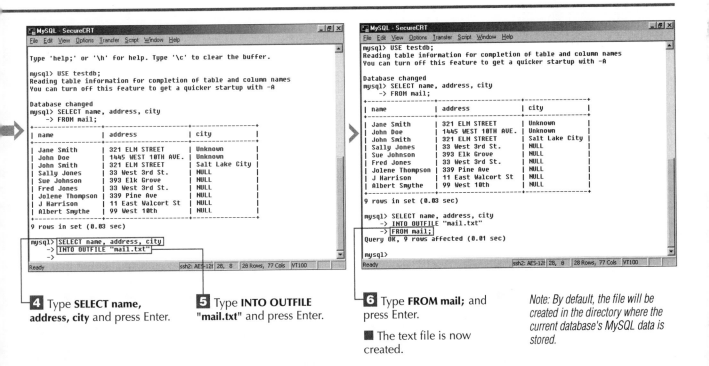

4 Type **SELECT name, address, city** and press Enter.

5 Type **INTO OUTFILE "mail.txt"** and press Enter.

6 Type **FROM mail;** and press Enter.

■ The text file is now created.

Note: By default, the file will be created in the directory where the current database's MySQL data is stored.

FORMAT AN IMPORT FILE

MySQL allows you to import data into a table from a text file. This is useful when you need to transfer data from another application into MySQL. Before you attempt to import a file, be sure it is formatted correctly.

To create an import file compatible with MySQL, start with a simple text file. You can create a text file in an editor or export one from an application. Be sure to use a text editor that saves as raw text. Common text editors include Notepad under Windows, and emacs, vi, and pico under UNIX. You can also use a word processor to create the file if you save it as a simple text file.

The file should include one line for each row of data to be added to the table. Each line should end with a newline character. The columns of data should be in the same order on each row. The particular order is not important as long as it is consistent.

Separate the columns with a tab character if possible. If not, consistently use another character, such as a comma, and MySQL can still recognize the file. The file will be easiest to import if the fields are not enclosed within quotation marks or other characters. If your application insists on quotation marks, you will need to specify a `FIELDS ENCLOSED BY` option when you import the data into MySQL.

Your text file should include only data for the table. There should not be any headers, column names, or other extraneous text at the beginning or end of the file. The file should not include any blank lines. If a column's value is blank, you can include a blank field in the file as long as you still include the correct number of tabs or separator characters.

FORMAT AN IMPORT FILE

Note: This example uses Notepad under Windows, but any text editor can be used.

1 From the text editor, start a new text file.

■ You can also open an existing file containing data and edit it into the correct format.

2 Type a row of data into the editor. Press the Tab key to separate fields of data.

Note: This example uses name, address, and city fields.

3 After you complete a row, press Enter to continue to the next row.

Extra

If you want to include special characters in the text file, you need to prefix them with an escape character. The default escape character is a backslash (\). The following are some typical character sequences that you can use to specify special characters:

SEQUENCE	CHARACTER
\t	Tab
\n	Newline
\\	Backslash
\"	Quotation marks
\'	Apostrophe
\N	Null value (must be the entire column value)

You can use the ESCAPED BY clause when you import the file to specify a character other than the backslash. If you will be using quotation marks to enclose the fields and specifying them in an ENCLOSED BY clause, you must also escape any quotation marks that appear within a field's value.

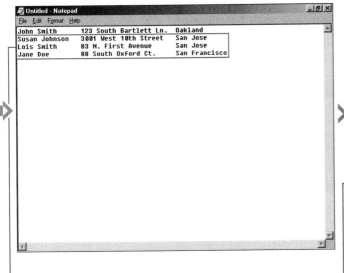

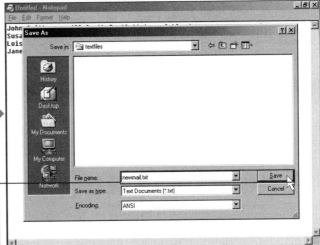

4 Continue typing rows until all of the desired data is included in the file.

Note: You will often start with a file saved from an application, rather than typing the data manually.

5 Click File ▷ Save As from the menu.

6 Specify a filename for the text file and click the Save button.

■ The text file is now saved.

Note: The save option will vary depending on the editor you are using.

IMPORT FROM A TEXT FILE

The LOAD DATA command in MySQL allows you to import a text file into a MySQL table. You can use this command to import a text file you created with a SELECT INTO OUTFILE command, or a file you created yourself or exported from another application.

The following is a simple example of a LOAD DATA statement. This loads the file mail.txt into the address table and looks for values for the name, address, and city columns.

```
LOAD DATA INFILE "mail.txt"
   INTO TABLE address (name, address, city);
```

The LOAD DATA statement supports several options. First, if you specify the LOW_PRIORITY keyword before INFILE, MySQL waits until no clients are reading from the table before importing the data. If you specify CONCURRENT instead, other clients are allowed to read data from the table while the LOAD DATA operation is working.

You specify the column names after INTO TABLE in parentheses, in the same order they appear in the import file. If you do not specify column names, MySQL will expect the file to contain values for every column in the table's definition, in the same order as they are defined in the table.

By default, MySQL expects column values to be separated with tab characters and lines to end with a newline character. You can change this behavior with the FIELDS TERMINATED BY and LINES TERMINATED BY options. You can also specify ENCLOSED BY and ESCAPED BY options, described in the section "Import and Export Tools" earlier in this chapter, if your file is not in the default format. Specify any of these options after the table name and before the list of columns.

If the text file contains an entry that would conflict with an existing table row, the import stops with an error. You can specify the IGNORE option to prevent this error and skip conflicting rows, or specify REPLACE and the data in the text file will override any conflicting data in the table.

IMPORT FROM A TEXT FILE

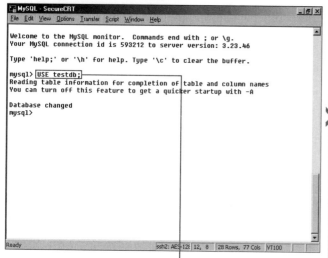

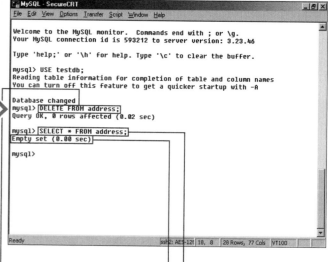

Note: This example uses the address table in the testdb database. It also requires the mail.txt file you created in the previous section.

1 From the MySQL monitor, type **USE testdb;** and press Enter.

■ The database is now selected.

2 Type **DELETE FROM address;** and press Enter.

■ This deletes the current contents of the table.

3 Type **SELECT * FROM address;** and press Enter.

■ Verify that the table is currently empty.

Extra

By default, the LOAD DATA statement looks for a file on the MySQL server. You can use the LOCAL option to load a file from the client machine instead. To use this option, specify LOCAL immediately after LOAD DATA.

Example:
```
LOAD DATA LOCAL INFILE "mail.txt"
  INTO TABLE address (name, address, city);
```

If you use the LOCAL option, the default location for the file will be the current directory on the client machine. You can optionally specify a full path to the file. Because this option transfers the file across the network from the client to the server, it takes longer than LOAD DATA without LOCAL. If you have access, you may find it faster to upload the file to the server and then use LOAD DATA.

If you have a text file on a different machine than the MySQL server or client, you can upload it to the client or server machine using FTP or a similar application. When you use FTP between Windows and UNIX hosts, text files are automatically converted from Windows-style line breaks to UNIX style. This may prevent errors when importing the file in MySQL.

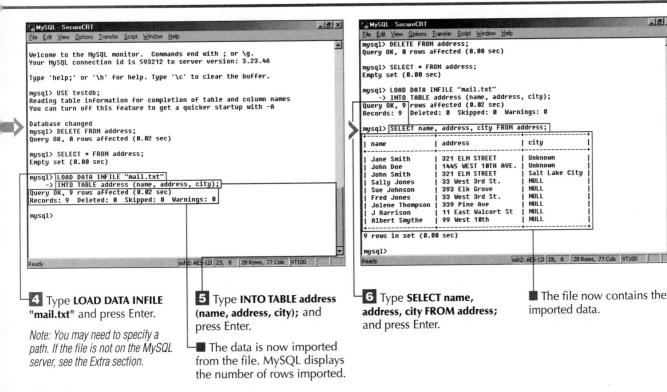

4 Type **LOAD DATA INFILE "mail.txt"** and press Enter.

Note: You may need to specify a path. If the file is not on the MySQL server, see the Extra section.

5 Type **INTO TABLE address (name, address, city);** and press Enter.

■ The data is now imported from the file. MySQL displays the number of rows imported.

6 Type **SELECT name, address, city FROM address;** and press Enter.

■ The file now contains the imported data.

163

EXPORT DATA FROM A SPREADSHEET

Because MySQL allows you to import a simple text file, you can move data into a MySQL table from any application that can export to a text file. One common application is a spreadsheet, such as Microsoft Excel. Because spreadsheets store data in columns and rows, their format can easily be adapted to a MySQL table.

When exporting data from any application, the ideal format is a text file with tabs separating columns and one line per row. This is the MySQL default format for the LOAD DATA statement. If this option is not available, columns separated by commas or other characters will work.

When you save a file in Excel, one of the available file types is Text (tab delimited). This format matches MySQL's default settings and makes it easy to export data for use with a MySQL table. If you are using a different spreadsheet, look

for a similar option. If a character other than a tab is used to separate fields, note it so you can specify it in the FIELDS SEPARATED BY clause of the LOAD DATA statement later.

Before exporting data, be sure your data is organized into a single worksheet with a consistent number of columns on each row. Remove any rows that contain header information, captions, or comments. Only rows of data should be included.

If you do not yet have a MySQL table prepared for the data, create it based on the fields in the spreadsheet. If you define the columns of the table in the same order as they are used in the spreadsheet, you will not need to specify column names in the LOAD DATA statement when you import the file into MySQL.

EXPORT DATA FROM A SPREADSHEET

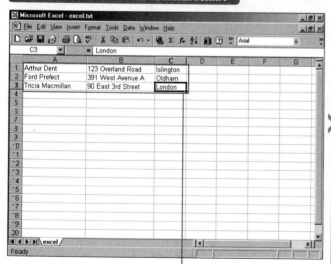

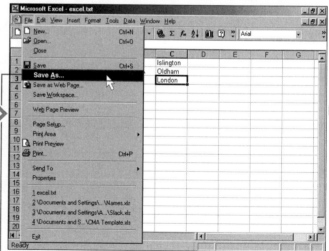

Note: This example creates a file containing name, address, and city fields, suitable for import into the mail or address tables described earlier in this book.

1 From Microsoft Excel, type the data you want to export or load an existing spreadsheet file.

Note: Be sure only rows of valid data for export are included in the spreadsheet.

2 Click File ⇨ Save As from the menu.

Extra

You can also import a text file you created with the SELECT INTO OUTFILE option in MySQL into a spreadsheet. Microsoft Excel, in particular, works well with files created in MySQL's default tab-delimited format.

To import a text file, select Open from the File menu and choose the file. After you click the Open button, Excel runs the Text Import Wizard to prompt you for information about the text file you will be importing. The first dialog box displayed by the wizard prompts you to choose between Delimited and Fixed width fields and to choose a starting row for the import. Data is imported starting with the first row by default.

The next dialog box prompts you for more detailed information. You can choose the delimiter character and the character that encloses fields. If you exported the file using MySQL's default settings, choose Tab as the delimiter and none as the enclosing character.

The final dialog box displayed by the wizard allows you to choose a format, such as numeric values or text, for each of the imported fields. This formats the spreadsheet cells after the import is completed.

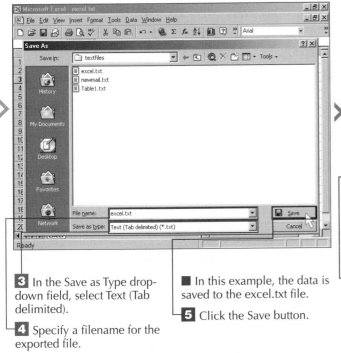

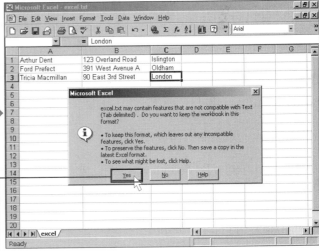

3 In the Save as Type drop-down field, select Text (Tab delimited).

4 Specify a filename for the exported file.

■ In this example, the data is saved to the excel.txt file.

5 Click the Save button.

6 Excel may show a warning that some data cannot be saved into a text file. Click Yes to save the file.

■ You are returned to the main Excel window. The data has now been exported and you can import the text file into MySQL.

EXPORT DATA FROM MICROSOFT ACCESS

Microsoft Access is the most popular desktop database application, and it is often used to store business data. Access includes a sophisticated Export option that can export a file in several different formats. You can use this feature to create a text file that you can import into a MySQL table using the LOAD DATA statement.

To export data from Access, open the table you want to export and select Export from the File menu. Select a filename and select Text Files as the file type. After you click the Save button, the Export Text Wizard prompts you for several options to control the formatting of the text file. You can select comma, tab, or another character to separate fields, and choose whether to enclose data in quotation marks or another character.

If you select the Tab delimited option from the wizard and select none for the Text Qualifier option rather than a

quotation mark, the file will be created in the default format for the LOAD DATA command in MySQL.

Like a MySQL database, an Access database can contain any number of tables. If you need to transfer multiple tables of data to MySQL, you must export each table separately to a text file.

To prepare a table for export, be sure it contains only rows of data you want to include in the MySQL table. The table should not include any comments or field names in the first rows, as this would result in invalid data being exported.

You can use a similar process to export data from most other database applications. If an application does not let you choose the characters to enclose and separate fields, you can use the FIELDS SEPARATED BY and ENCLOSED BY options in the LOAD DATA statement to make MySQL work with the format of the file.

EXPORT DATA FROM MICROSOFT ACCESS

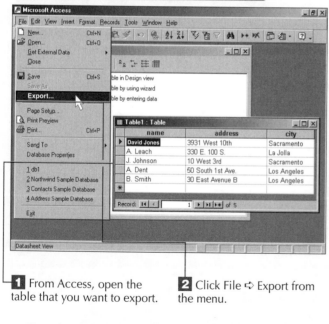

1 From Access, open the table that you want to export.

2 Click File ⇨ Export from the menu.

3 Choose a filename for the exported file.

Note: In this example, the filename is Table1.txt.

4 Select Text Files as the file type to export.

5 Click the Save All button.

Extra

You can also import a text file you created with the SELECT INTO OUTFILE option in MySQL into Microsoft Access. To import a text file, select Get External Data, and then Import from the File menu. From the file selection dialog box, select Text Files as the file type. Select the text file to import and click OK.

Access now starts the Import Text Wizard to prompt you for information about the text file. In the first dialog box, choose between Delimited and Fixed width fields. Choose Delimited for most MySQL export files. You can also choose a starting row for the import.

Click Next to display the next dialog box. Choose the character that delimits the fields, typically Tab for MySQL files. You can also choose Text Qualifier if your text file encloses fields in quotation marks. Click Next to continue.

In the next dialog box, choose whether to add the data to a new table or an existing table in the current database. Click Next to display another dialog box, which prompts you for the name and data type of each field. The next dialog box lets you choose a field to act as primary key. Finally, enter a table name and click Finish to complete the import.

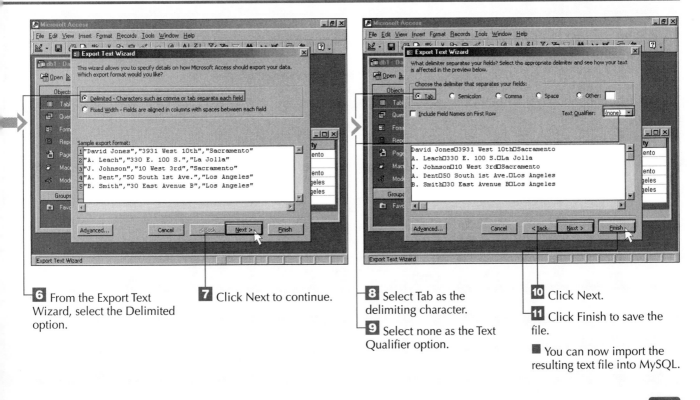

6 From the Export Text Wizard, select the Delimited option.

7 Click Next to continue.

8 Select Tab as the delimiting character.

9 Select none as the Text Qualifier option.

10 Click Next.

11 Click Finish to save the file.

■ You can now import the resulting text file into MySQL.

BACK UP DATA FROM A TABLE

While you can export data to a text file using SELECT and the INTO OUTFILE option, this process creates a simple text file. MySQL includes a separate utility, mysqldump, that you can use from the command line to back up a database to a text file. The output file includes SQL statements and can be used to rebuild the database or tables.

To use mysqldump, specify a database name and one or more table names. The following example dumps the mail and address tables from the testdb database:

```
mysqldump testdb mail address
```

If you do not specify table names, mysqldump will dump the entire database. You can also back up more than one database by specifying the -B option and a list of databases. In this case, you cannot specify particular table names. The following example backs up the db1 and db2 databases:

```
mysqldump -B db1 db2
```

The mysqldump utility always includes all of the columns of each table. You can specify the format of the text output using several options: --fields-terminated-by, --fields-enclosed-by, --fields escaped by, and --lines-terminated-by. These are the same as the options for the LOAD DATA command, described earlier in this chapter.

This utility supports the same -u and -p options as the mysql command. You will usually need to use these options to specify a username with access to the tables you are dumping and the correct password.

The mysqldump utility does not create a text file by itself — it normally dumps the text to the standard output at the shell prompt. You can use the > operator from the command line to save the output to a file instead.

BACK UP DATA FROM A TABLE

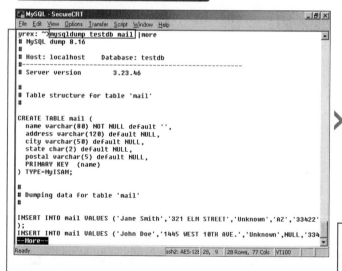

Note: This example uses the testdb database and the mail and address tables.

■1 From the command line, type **mysqldump testdb mail** and press Enter.

■ This dumps the contents of the mail table to the screen.

Note: You may need to specify the username and password with the −u and −p options.

Note: Under Windows, you may need to specify the full path to the command, for example, c:\mysql\bin\mysqldump.

■2 Type **mysqldump testdb mail address >tables.txt** and press Enter.

■ This backs up both tables to the tables.txt file.

■3 Type **mysqldump testdb >db.txt** and press Enter.

■ This backs up the entire database to the db.txt file.

Note: You may need to specify the username and password with the −u and −p options.

RESTORE A BACKUP FILE

When you have created a backup text file using `mysqldump`, you can use it to re-create the database or tables that were backed up. The text file includes SQL statements, such as `CREATE TABLE` and `INSERT`, to rebuild the backed up databases or tables. To use the file, you can simply route it through the `mysql` command to process the SQL statements.

The following example uses the `mysql` command to restore the database backed up in the db.txt file:

```
mysql testdb <db.txt
```

You can also use the `SOURCE` command within the MySQL monitor. This command reads SQL commands from a text file you specify.

As with the standard `mysql` command, you can use the `-u` option to specify a username and the `-p` option to specify a password. The username you specify must have permission

to create the database or table you are restoring. You may also need to use the `-h` option to specify a host name.

If you are restoring a database or table that has been corrupted or updated incorrectly, you should first use the `DROP TABLE` or `DROP DATABASE` commands to delete any existing data.

The file created by `mysqldump` is a standard text file. If you need to modify the SQL statements in the file before importing, you can use any text editor. If you have a backup file for an entire database and need to restore a single table, you can use a text editor to move the statements for that table to a different file.

Along with restoring a database that has been lost or corrupted, you can use the backup file to import the database and tables onto a different MySQL server. This is an efficient way to move data between servers.

RESTORE A BACKUP FILE

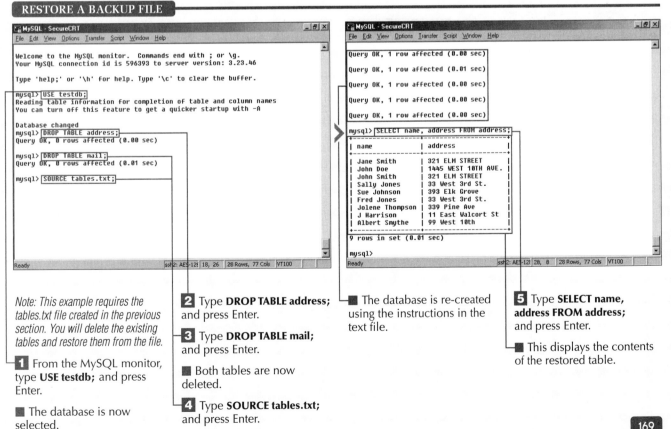

Note: This example requires the tables.txt file created in the previous section. You will delete the existing tables and restore them from the file.

1 From the MySQL monitor, type **USE testdb;** and press Enter.

■ The database is now selected.

2 Type **DROP TABLE address;** and press Enter.

3 Type **DROP TABLE mail;** and press Enter.

■ Both tables are now deleted.

4 Type **SOURCE tables.txt;** and press Enter.

■ The database is re-created using the instructions in the text file.

5 Type **SELECT name, address FROM address;** and press Enter.

■ This displays the contents of the restored table.

MANAGE AUTOMATED BACKUPS

You can use the `mysqldump` utility to create a backup of a table, a database, or multiple databases. You can use a scheduling utility, such as `cron`, under UNIX platforms to schedule regular backups using this utility.

To schedule backups, first test the `mysqldump` command you will use to back up the data. For example, the following command backs up the entire testdb database to the backup.txt file:

```
mysqldump -uuser -ppassword testdb
>backup.txt
```

Replace *user* and *password* with the username and password. After you have the correct `mysqldump` command, you can schedule backups. To use `cron`, type `crontab -e` to edit the crontab file. Each line in this file includes five options for scheduling the command and the command itself.

The first five options in the entry specify the minute, hour, day of month, month, and day of week to execute the command. You can use a number in each of these fields, or * to include all of the possible values. Separate the fields with spaces or tabs. For example, the following `cron` entry executes the `mysqldump` command every day at 3:30 AM:

```
30 3 * * * mysqldump -uuser -ppassword
testdb >backup.txt
```

If you are using a shared system, you may need to contact the system administrator to gain access to `cron` features. Each username has a separate `cron` table. The username you use to set up the scheduled backup should have access to the `mysqldump` command and permission to create a file.

When this command executes daily, it will usually override the existing file. You may need to rename files regularly or set up a more complex arrangement of `cron` events to use different filenames each day.

MANAGE AUTOMATED BACKUPS

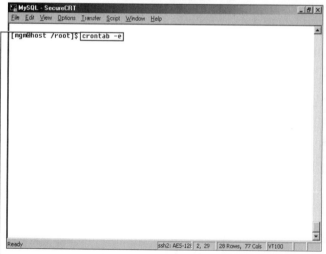

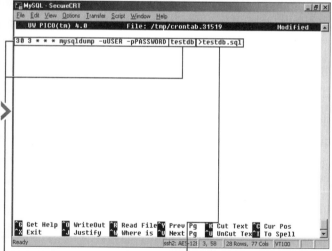

Note: This example uses the testdb database. You will need access to the `crontab` command.

1 From the UNIX command prompt, type **crontab -e** to edit the `cron` table.

■ This launches a text editor and loads the existing table, if any, into the editor.

Note: This example is for UNIX systems. For Windows, see the Extra section.

2 Type **30 3 * * * mysqldump** and add **–u** and **–p** options specifying the username and password for the MySQL database, if necessary.

3 Type the name of the database to back up.

4 Type **>** followed by the filename for the backup file.

Note: You may need to specify a path to the file.

Extra   You can also use `mysqldump` to make backups on a Windows-based MySQL server. Under Windows, the utility is `mysqldump.exe` in the c:\mysql\bin directory. Its options are the same as the UNIX version, and the Windows command prompt also supports the > operator to redirect the output of a command to a file.

To automate backups, you can use the `at` command from the command line under Windows NT, Windows 2000, or Windows XP. Type `at /?` at the command line to display a list of options for this program.

You can also use the Task Scheduler included with most versions of Windows to schedule a backup. To use Task Scheduler, select Scheduled Tasks from the Control Panel. Double-click the Add Scheduled Task entry to add a new task. A wizard prompts you for information about the program that should be run and the schedule it should follow.

As an alternative, you can use any standard Windows backup program to back up the MySQL data to tape or to a disk archive. The data is stored in the c:\mysql\data directory. Each database has a subdirectory under `data` where its data is stored. One backup utility, `ntbackup.exe`, is included with Windows NT and Windows 2000.

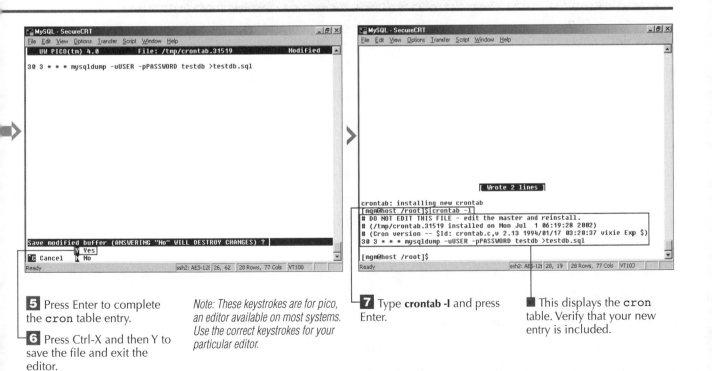

5 Press Enter to complete the `cron` table entry.

6 Press Ctrl-X and then Y to save the file and exit the editor.

Note: These keystrokes are for pico, an editor available on most systems. Use the correct keystrokes for your particular editor.

7 Type **crontab -l** and press Enter.

■ This displays the `cron` table. Verify that your new entry is included.

BACK UP TABLE STRUCTURE

The mysqldump utility includes an option, -d or --no-create-db, that dumps the structure of the table but not the data. You can use this option to create an empty table with the same structure as the existing table. This is useful if you need to store similar data in a different table. You can also use the resulting SQL statements as a starting point to create a different table.

For example, the following mysqldump command dumps only the structure of the address table in the testdb database to the table.txt file:

```
mysqldump -uuser -ppassword -d testdb
address >address.txt
```

After you have dumped the structure of the table to a file, you can edit the file in a text editor to change the name of the table and any other options within the CREATE TABLE

statements. You can then import the file using the mysql command. For example, the following command imports the table structure saved to address.txt in the testdb database:

```
mysql -uuser -ppassword testdb <address.txt
```

You can also use the source command within the MySQL monitor to import the saved table structure. If you attempt to import the file without changing the name of the table first, MySQL will display an error message because the table already exists.

Conversely, you can use the -t option with mysqldump to dump the data from the table, but not its structure — the resulting file will include the INSERT statements for the data of the table, but not the CREATE TABLE statement. This option is useful if you want to merge the data in the table into a different table rather than creating a new table.

BACK UP TABLE STRUCTURE

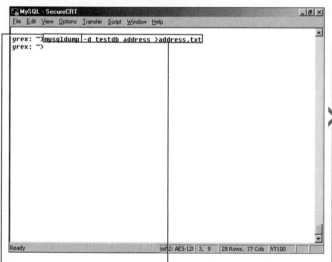

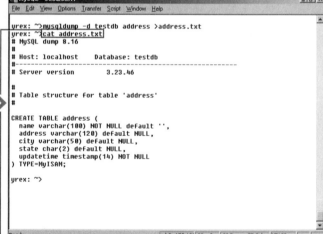

Note: This example uses the address table in the testdb database.

1 From the command prompt, type **mysqldump**.

■ If necessary, type **-u*user* -p*password***, replacing user and password with the correct options for your server.

Note: In Windows, you may need to specify the full path, for example, c:\mysql\bin\mysqldump.

2 Type **-d testdb address >address.txt** and press Enter.

■ The structure of the table is saved to the file you specified.

3 Type **cat address.txt** and press Enter.

■ This displays the contents of the file you have created.

Note: Under Windows systems, use the command more instead of cat.

CREATE A COPY OF A TABLE

I f you need to copy a table's structure or data to a different table, you can use several different methods. One simple way to copy a table is to first create the new table with the same structure, and then use an INSERT query with the SELECT option to copy the data from one table to the other.

For example, to copy the address table, you would first type DESCRIBE address; to view the structure of the table. Next, use a CREATE TABLE query using the same column types and other information to create the new table. After the table is created, you can use a single INSERT query to copy all of the rows of the table to the new table. The following query copies all of the data in the address table to the address2 table:

```
INSERT INTO address2 SELECT * FROM address;
```

This form of the INSERT command uses a standard SELECT statement to select the data to copy. You can optionally specify a list of columns to copy, and include a WHERE clause to select only certain rows to be copied into the new table.

An alternate method of copying the table may be easier for complex tables. Use mysqldump -d to create a backup of the table's structure, as described in the previous section. Next, edit the resulting file and change the table name in the CREATE TABLE command to the name of the new table. Use mysql to read the file and create the new table, and then use an INSERT query like the above to copy the data.

CREATE A COPY OF A TABLE

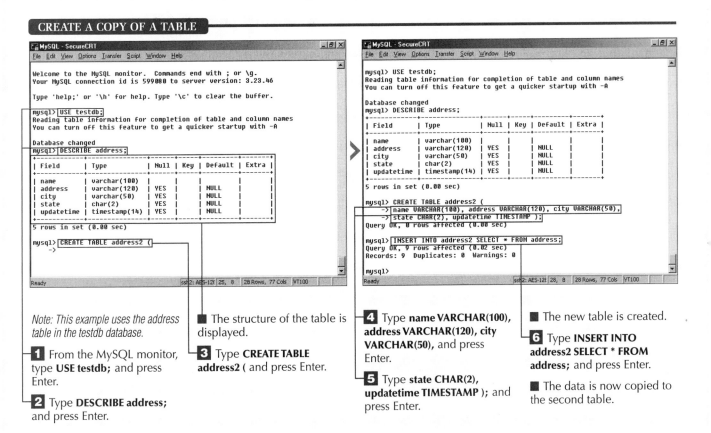

Note: This example uses the address table in the testdb database.

1 From the MySQL monitor, type **USE testdb;** and press Enter.

2 Type **DESCRIBE address;** and press Enter.

■ The structure of the table is displayed.

3 Type **CREATE TABLE address2 (** and press Enter.

4 Type **name VARCHAR(100), address VARCHAR(120), city VARCHAR(50),** and press Enter.

5 Type **state CHAR(2), updatetime TIMESTAMP);** and press Enter.

■ The new table is created.

6 Type **INSERT INTO address2 SELECT * FROM address;** and press Enter.

■ The data is now copied to the second table.

MYSQL ADMINISTRATION TOOLS

A fter you have installed a MySQL server, it runs continuously and requires little intervention. However, you may need to start and stop the server and perform other administrative tasks from time to time. MySQL includes a variety of tools for this purpose.

BASIC MYSQL ADMINISTRATION

All installations of the MySQL server and client include some basic command-line administration tools. The `mysqladmin` utility handles many of the administration tasks.

The mysqladmin Utility

The `mysqladmin` utility runs from a client machine and is installed with the MySQL client software. This utility supports a number of different commands for managing the MySQL server. To use this utility, type `mysqladmin` followed by the command name. You may also need to specify the `-u` and `-p` options with a valid username and password. The table below shows some of the most useful `mysqladmin` commands.

COMMAND	DESCRIPTION
create	Create a database
drop	Drop a database
ping	Check whether the server is running
status	Display basic status information
extended-status	Display a detailed status report
processlist	Show a list of the current MySQL server processes
kill	Stop one or more server processes
variables	List MySQL variables and their values
version	Display the MySQL server version number
shutdown	Shut down the MySQL server
password	Change the password for the current MySQL user

Examples:
```
mysqladmin create newdatabase
mysqladmin ping
mysqladmin shutdown
```

Start and Stop MySQL (UNIX)

On a UNIX system, you typically start the MySQL server with the `mysqld` or `safe_mysqld` programs. `mysqld` is the server program itself, and `safe_mysqld` is a wrapper that determines the correct settings and starts `mysqld`. These programs are stored in the MySQL binaries directory, typically /usr/local/mysql/bin.

To stop the MySQL server, you can use the `mysqladmin shutdown` command. This sends a signal to the server to shut it down.

Start and Stop MySQL (Windows)

On a Windows system, you can also use `mysqld` to start the server and `mysqladmin shutdown` to shut it down. These commands are typically located in the C:\mysql\bin directory and can be run from the command prompt.

On Windows NT, 2000, and XP systems, you can also use the operating system's service management features to start and stop the server. MySQL is listed on the Services control panel, and you can start or stop it or configure it to start automatically when the system starts. You can also use the `NET START` and `NET STOP` commands to start and stop the server.

Example:
```
NET START mysql
NET STOP mysql
```

The Windows installation of MySQL includes a utility called `WinMySQLadmin`. This utility allows you to display information about the server and perform many of the same functions as the `mysqladmin` utility. To run `WinMySQLadmin`, start the `c:\mysql\bin\winmysqladmin.exe` program.

When you start `WinMySQLadmin`, it briefly displays its window and then hides itself. It adds an icon resembling a traffic light to the system tray. To show the `WinMySQLadmin` window, right-click the tray icon and

select the Show Me option. The right-click menu also includes an option to start or stop the MySQL server.

Although this utility provides a graphical interface to many MySQL settings, you can also use the command-line `mysqladmin` utility under Windows.

The `WinMySQLadmin` window is divided into a number of tabbed sections. Select each tab to display the associated page. The pages available are described below.

Environment The Environment tab displays the host name, user name, operating system, IP address, and the amount of RAM available on the server machine. If you click the Extended Server Status button, detailed statistics for the server are displayed. These are the same values shown in the `mysqladmin status` command.	**Variables** The Variables tab displays a list of MySQL variables and their values. These are the same settings available in the my.ini file. Rather than show the contents of this file, this tab displays the server's current variable settings. This is the same information shown in the `mysqladmin variables` command.
Start Check `WinMySQLadmin` performs a basic check when it starts to determine whether the server is running correctly. The Start Check tab displays the results of this check and any error messages that were reported.	**Process** The Process tab displays a list of currently running *threads*, or processes, on the MySQL server. Each entry includes a process ID number, the username and host, the database in use, the command the thread is running, the thread's current status, and the amount of time it has spent processing. This list is the same produced by the `mysqladmin processlist` command.
Server The Server tab displays a list of MySQL server status variables and their values. These provide a detailed snapshot of the server's current performance. These values are the same as those listed by the `mysqladmin extended-status` command and are described in Chapter 11.	You can right-click a process and select Kill to stop the process. This feature is also available from the `mysqladmin kill` command.
my.ini Setup The Windows version of MySQL uses a file called my.ini to determine various settings for the server. The my.ini Setup tab in `WinMySQLadmin` displays the current contents of the my.ini file and allows you to edit the options and save any changes you have made. Be sure not to change values in this file unless you are sure what they will affect. The settings available in this file are described in Chapter 11.	**Databases** The Databases tab displays a current list of databases on the server. If you select a database from the list, the list of tables in the database is displayed. If you select a table from the list, detailed information about its available columns and indexes is displayed. The right-click menu allows you to create and drop databases.
Err File The MySQL server maintains a log file that includes any errors encountered by the server as well as basic status messages created when the server starts up or shuts down. The Err File tab displays the contents of this log file.	**Report** The Report tab creates and displays a detailed report of the MySQL server's configuration and status, including the information in several of the prior tabs. You can print the report or save it to a file.

CHECK SERVER STATUS

I f you or other users of the system are having trouble accessing the MySQL server, the first step is to determine whether the MySQL server is running at all. One simple way to check this is with the mysqladmin utility. This utility includes a variety of different options for working with the MySQL server and is installed as part of the MySQL client package.

To test the server, first try the ping option within mysqladmin. This option communicates with the server and displays a simple message indicating whether it is responding. The following is a simple example:

```
mysqladmin ping -uuser -ppassword
```

This command tests the default server on the local host. It displays the message "mysqld is alive" if the server responds. If there is no response from the server, it displays an error message that may help you resolve the problem.

As with other mysql client commands, you can specify the -h (host) option if necessary to refer to a different MySQL server. For a complete list of mysqladmin options, type mysqladmin with no options.

Sometimes, although the MySQL server is running, it may not be responding quickly or correctly. You can find out a bit more about the server's condition with the mysqladmin status command. This displays the amount of time the server has been running, the number of active threads, the number of queries since the server started, and other information.

You can use the information displayed by the status option, and the more detailed extended-status option from mysqladmin, to determine the server's current performance and learn how performance can be improved. See Chapter 10 for details about optimizing the MySQL server.

CHECK SERVER STATUS

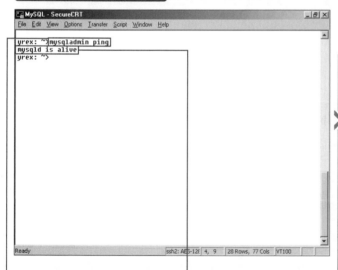

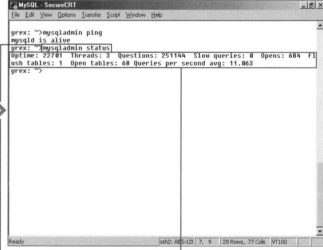

1 From the command line, type **mysqladmin ping** and press Enter.

Note: You may need to specify the -u and -p options with the correct username and password values for your server.

■ The message indicates whether the server is responding.

Note: Under Windows, you may need to include the path with the command, for example, c:\mysql\bin\mysqladmin.exe.

2 Type **mysqladmin status** and press Enter.

Note: You may need to specify a username and password.

■ A more detailed status report is displayed.

CHECK THE MYSQL SERVER VERSION

The mysqladmin utility also includes an option to display version information for the MySQL server. You can use this option to determine whether your server supports certain features or requires an upgrade. To check the server version, use the version command with mysqladmin, as shown in this example:

mysqladmin version -uuser -ppassword

This command displays the server version number, the protocol in use, and the amount of time the server has been running. It also displays information about threads, queries, and other statistics, similar to the output of the status command. The following is an example of how the server version information appears. This may vary depending on your specific system.

```
Server version     3.23.46
Protocol version   10
```

```
Connection         Localhost via UNIX socket
UNIX socket        /tmp/mysql.sock
Uptime:            17 min 24 sec
```

As with other mysqladmin commands, you must specify a correct username and password with the -u and -p options. You can also specify a hostname with the -h option and a socket file with the -S option, if necessary.

At this writing, the latest version of MySQL 3 is version 3.23. MySQL 4.0 is also available, although it is currently in alpha testing. Visit www.mysql.com to find out information about the current version and to download files for a new version if necessary.

When you start the MySQL monitor with the mysql command, a brief message is displayed indicating the version number of the server and the current connection.

CHECK THE MYSQL SERVER VERSION

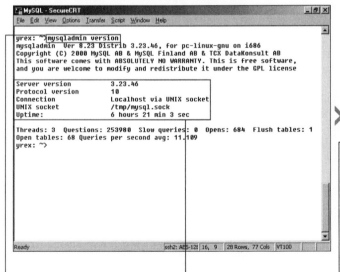

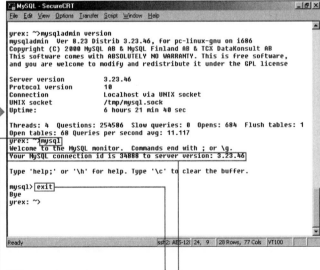

1 From the command prompt, type **mysqladmin version** and press Enter.

Note: You may need to specify the –u and –p options with the correct username and password values for your server.

■ The server's version information is displayed.

Note: Under Windows, you may need to specify the path with the command, for example, `c:\mysql\bin\mysqladmin.exe`.

2 Type **mysql** to start the MySQL monitor.

Note: You may need to specify a username and password.

■ Notice the version information displayed before the prompt.

3 Type **exit** and press Enter.

■ This exits the MySQL monitor.

START AND STOP THE MYSQL SERVER UNDER UNIX

I f the MySQL server is not currently running, you can restart it. You may also need to stop and restart the server if you have changed its configuration, or if it is not responding. On UNIX systems, you can start the MySQL server using the `safe_mysqld` command, which starts the `mysqld` server program.

The `mysqld` and `safe_mysqld` programs are located in the bin directory under the MySQL installation directory. On most systems, this directory is /usr/local/mysql/bin or /usr/local/bin. The exact directory depends on how the MySQL server was installed. The following example starts the MySQL server:

```
/usr/local/bin/safe_mysqld &
```

The `&` character indicates that the program should run in the background on most systems. After you have started the server, you can use `mysqladmin ping` or `mysqladmin status` to verify that it is running.

To shut down the MySQL server, use the `mysqladmin shutdown` command. The following command shuts down the MySQL server on the local host:

```
mysqladmin shutdown -uuser -ppassword
```

To use the `shutdown` command, the username you specify must have the correct permissions to shut down the server. On a default installation, only the root user can do this. See Chapter 11 for information on configuring MySQL users and passwords.

When you use the `shutdown` command, the server is immediately shut down. It does not complete any pending queries. While the server is down, clients who attempt to connect to it will receive an error message.

See Chapter 1 for information about setting up the MySQL server to start automatically when the system boots under UNIX and Windows systems.

START THE MYSQL SERVER

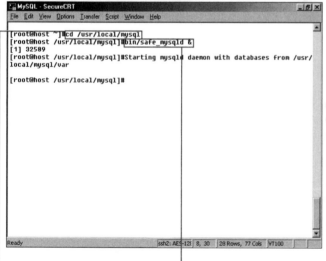

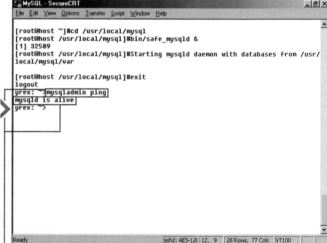

1 From the UNIX command prompt, type **cd** followed by the directory where the MySQL server is installed, typically /usr/local/mysql.

2 Type **bin/safe_mysqld &** and press Enter.

■ This starts the MySQL server.

3 Type **mysqladmin ping** and press Enter.

■ This indicates that the server is now running.

Note: If necessary, add the –u and –p options with the correct username and password.

Extra

If you encounter an error when starting the MySQL server, there are a number of potential causes. The first item to check is whether the MySQL server is currently running — you cannot run two copies of the MySQL server at the same time unless you have customized the port and socket settings. Type `mysqladmin ping` to check whether the server is already running. You can also type `ps` on a UNIX system to list running processes and check whether `mysqld` is included.

If the server fails to start, you may find some useful information about the error that occurred in the MySQL log files. These files are located in the MySQL data directory, typically /usr/local/var or /usr/local/mysql/data on UNIX systems. The files are hostname.log and hostname.err, with your server host name in place of hostname.

If an error message is displayed indicating that the TCP/IP port or socket is already in use, either MySQL is already running, or some other service is using the port you have selected for MySQL.

You need to have the correct permissions to start the MySQL server. If it did not start correctly, log in as root and attempt to start the MySQL server again.

STOP THE MYSQL SERVER

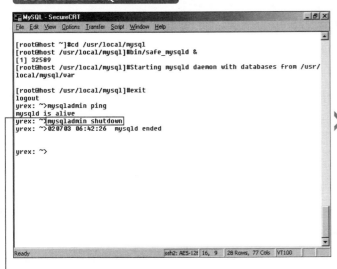

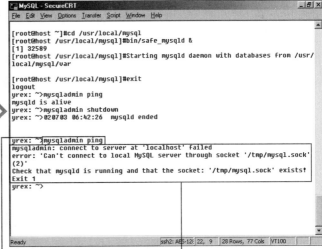

1 From the UNIX command prompt, type **mysqladmin shutdown** and press Enter.

■ This immediately shuts down the MySQL server.

Note: If necessary, add the –u and –p options with the correct username and password.

2 Type **mysqladmin ping** and press Enter. Add your username and password if needed.

■ This indicates that the server is no longer running.

Note: If other users require the MySQL server, be sure to restart it after you are finished.

START AND STOP THE MYSQL SERVER UNDER WINDOWS

If you are running the MySQL server on a Windows system, you can start and stop the server in a number of different ways. Under Windows 95, 98, and Me, you can use the `mysqld` command from the command prompt to start the server. This is typically located in the C:\mysql\bin directory. The following command starts the MySQL server on a typical system:

```
C:\mysql\bin\mysqld
```

You can shut down the MySQL server from the command prompt using the `mysqladmin` utility, located at `C:\mysql\bin\mysqladmin.exe`. The following example shuts down the MySQL server on the local machine:

```
C:\mysql\bin\mysqladmin shutdown -u root -p
password
```

On Windows NT, 2000, and XP systems, MySQL is usually set up to run as a service, and you can use the standard Windows methods to control it. The first of these is the Services control panel, located under Administrative Tools

in Windows 2000. Find MySQL in the list of services and use the toolbar buttons to start or stop the service. You can also use the Services control panel to set up MySQL to run automatically when the system starts.

An alternative way to control the MySQL service on Windows NT, 2000, and XP is to use the NET command from the command prompt. To start the MySQL server, use the NET START command. The following command starts the server:

```
NET START mysql
```

To shut down the MySQL server, use the `NET STOP` command at the command prompt. The following command shuts down the MySQL server:

```
NET STOP mysql
```

You can also use the `mysqladmin` utility to shut down MySQL when it is run as a service. Choose the most convenient method for your particular system.

START AND STOP MYSQL FROM THE COMMAND PROMPT

1 From the command prompt, type **NET START mysql** and press Enter.

■ This starts the MySQL server.

Note: Under Windows 95, 98, and Me, type the path to `mysqld.exe` *instead.*

2 Type **NET STOP mysql** and press Enter.

■ This shuts down the MySQL server.

Note: Under Windows 95, 98, and Me, type **mysqladmin shutdown** *instead.*

Extra

If you are unable to start the MySQL server under Windows, be sure your system has the necessary components installed. In particular, MySQL requires the TCP/IP protocol, which you can install using the Network control panel. MySQL also requires that your system support the Winsock 2 standard. This is included in Windows 98 and later; you may need to install an update from Microsoft for Windows 95 systems.

On Windows NT, 2000, and XP systems, most users do not have permission to start and stop services by default. If you are unable to start MySQL, log on as Administrator and try again. Although Windows uses the Administrator account, the default administrative user under MySQL is root, as on UNIX systems.

You cannot shut down the MySQL server using the Task Manager. If you attempt to shut down the MySQL server in this way, it may lock up your system or fail to shut down. Use the mysqladmin utility or one of the service control methods described in this section instead.

If the MySQL server does not start correctly, check the error log for information. This log is stored at c:\mysql\data using the filename mysql.err by default. The WinMySQLadmin utility, described in the section "Using WinMySQLadmin," later in this chapter, also includes an option to view the log file.

START AND STOP MYSQL FROM THE SERVICES CONTROL PANEL

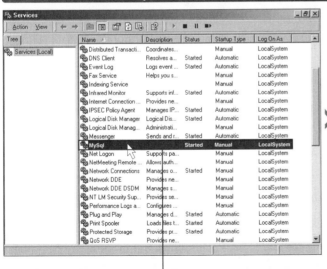

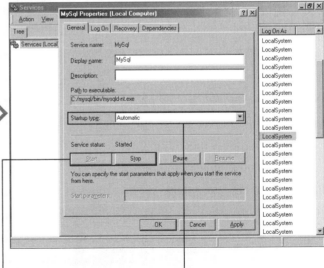

Note: These instructions are for Windows NT, 2000, and XP.

1 Start the Services control panel from the Control Panel or Administrative Tools window.

■ The display indicates the MySQL server's current status.

2 Double-click the MySQL entry.

■ The MySql Properties dialog box is displayed.

3 To start or stop the MySQL server, use the **Start** and **Stop** buttons.

4 You can set the Startup type option to Automatic, Manual, or Disabled. Use Automatic to start MySQL when the computer starts.

VIEW AND MANAGE RUNNING PROCESSES

You can use the `mysqladmin` utility with the `processlist` command to display a list of the processes currently running on the MySQL server. This list includes all of the queries currently running for clients as well as commands entered from the MySQL monitor. The following is an example of the `processlist` command:

```
mysqladmin processlist -uuser -ppassword
```

For each process currently running, this command lists its process ID number, the MySQL user ID that started it, the host the client connected from, the database used by the query, the command issued to the server, the amount of time the query has been in progress, the current status of the process, and the query or command that started the process.

Occasionally, a database query will take an excessive amount of time, slowing down the server, or an error will

cause a process to lock up and stop responding. When this happens, you can use `mysqladmin processlist` to display the list of processes and find the problematic one. You can then stop the process.

To stop a process, use the `kill` command with `mysqladmin`. To use this command, specify one or more process ID numbers. They will be immediately stopped, not completing their queries. The MySQL server will continue to run and process other requests. For example, the following command kills a process with the ID number 3037:

```
mysqladmin kill 3037
```

If you stop a process that is currently writing data to a table, it may leave partial or corrupt data in the table. Because of this, you should use the `kill` command only when you are certain the process will not complete on its own.

VIEW AND MANAGE RUNNING PROCESSES

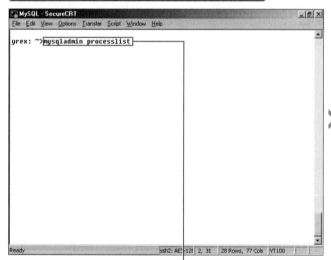

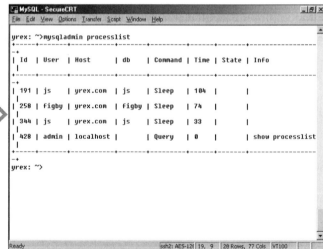

VIEW RUNNING PROCESSES

Note: This example assumes that the MySQL server is currently running on the local machine.

1 From the command prompt, type **mysqladmin processlist** and press Enter.

Note: You may need to add −u and −p options to specify a valid username and password.

■ The list of processes is displayed.

Extra

The MySQL server can have a number of *processes*, also known as *threads*, running concurrently. The number of threads that can run at the same time depends on the operating system and on the configuration of the MySQL server. Chapter 10 explains how you can configure the server for a maximum number of concurrent threads.

The status of threads in the process list may indicate Query if a query is in process or Sleep if the thread is currently inactive. The server keeps a number of threads in an inactive state so that it can use them for queries rather than starting a new thread each time.

You can use the ps command in most UNIX systems to display a list of processes currently running on the server and their ID numbers. While this will show all of the MySQL threads currently in use, the process numbers used by MySQL are not the same as the system's ID numbers.

You can also kill MySQL threads using the operating system's commands. However, using the mysqladmin utility to kill threads has less chance of corrupting data, and is easier because you can use the processlist command to determine the correct thread to kill.

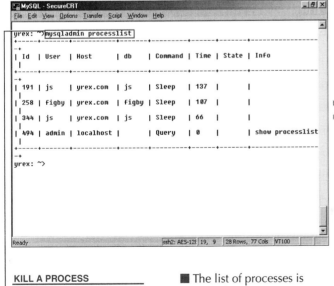

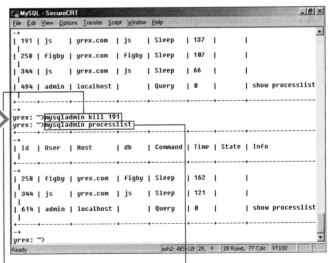

KILL A PROCESS

1 From the command prompt, type **mysqladmin processlist** and press Enter.

■ The list of processes is displayed.

2 Type **mysqladmin kill** followed by the number of the process to kill.

■ The process is immediately stopped.

3 Type **mysqladmin processlist** and press Enter.

■ The list of processes is displayed again. Note that the killed process is no longer listed.

USING WINMYSQLADMIN

The Windows version of the MySQL server includes the `WinMySQLadmin` utility. This is a graphical utility that allows you to manage settings and display statistics for the MySQL server from within Windows. To run this tool, start the `winmysqladmin.exe` program in the C:\mysql\bin directory.

When `WinMySQLadmin` is first run, it shows briefly and then hides itself. It remains resident, and an icon appears in the system tray. Right-click the icon and select the Show Me option to view the utility.

The `WinMySQLadmin` display is divided into a number of tabbed sections. The first, Environment, includes information about the computer MySQL is running on and a number of statistics for the server. These are the same values available from the `mysqladmin status` command.

The Start Check tab runs some tests to verify that the server is running correctly. The Server tab displays a list of statistics for the MySQL server. The my.ini Setup tab allows you to edit the my.ini file, which stores default settings for the server. The Err File tab displays the server error log. The Variables tab displays a list of MySQL variables and their current settings; these are explained in detail in Chapter 11.

The Process tab in `WinMySQLadmin` shows a list of processes and their ID numbers, similar to the output of the `mysqladmin processlist` command. You can right-click an entry in the list and select Kill Process to stop a process.

The Databases tab allows you to view information about the databases stored on the server, the tables within a database, and the columns of each table. This is similar to the `SHOW DATABASES` and `SHOW TABLES` commands from the MySQL monitor. The right-click menu includes options to create or drop databases and to refresh the current list.

USING WINMYSQLADMIN

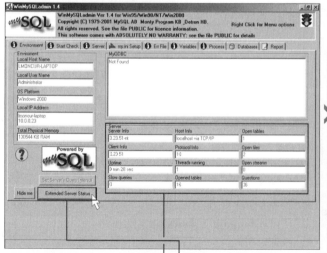

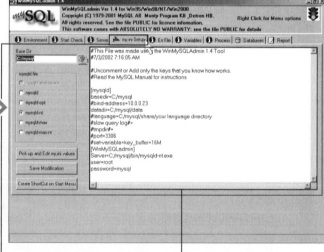

*Note: Type **c:\mysql\bin\ winmysqladmin** from the command prompt to start the utility. Right-click the tray icon and select Show Me to display the utility.*

1 From `WinMySQLadmin`'s Environment tab, click the Extended Server Status button.

■ This displays a detailed set of statistics for the MySQL server.

2 Click the my.ini Setup tab at the top of the `WinMySQLadmin` dialog box.

■ This displays the contents of the initialization file, which you can edit if needed.

Extra

The final tab of the `WinMySQLadmin` utility, Report, allows you to display a detailed report about the MySQL server. After you select the Report tab, click the Create the Report button to create the report.

The report includes information about the current installation of MySQL, how it was compiled, and the system it is running on. It also lists the contents of the my.ini file, the current status of the server as displayed in the Server tab, the list of variables as shown in the Variables tab, and the error log as listed in the Err File tab.

The report is displayed in a text window within the `WinMySQLadmin` interface. You can use the Print button to print a copy of the report or use the Save As button to save it as a text file. This tab also includes Cut, Copy, Paste, Delete, and Select All buttons that you can use to edit the report or copy it to another program.

All of the information in the `WinMySQLadmin` utility is also available from the command line using the MySQL monitor and the `mysqladmin` utility. You can use whichever tools you are most comfortable with to manage the server.

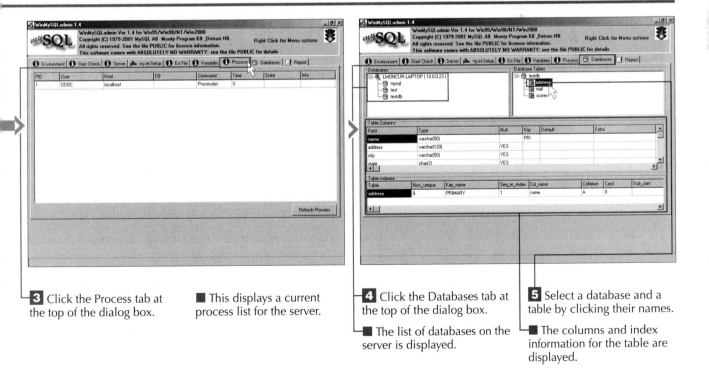

3 Click the Process tab at the top of the dialog box.

■ This displays a current process list for the server.

4 Click the Databases tab at the top of the dialog box.

■ The list of databases on the server is displayed.

5 Select a database and a table by clicking their names.

■ The columns and index information for the table are displayed.

185

MANAGE MYSQL WITH MYSQLGUI

The `MySQLGUI` utility provides another interface to the MySQL server, and includes a variety of useful administration functions. While most of these are also available from command-line utilities, `MySQLGUI` provides a user-friendly graphic interface. This utility provides some of the same features as `WinMySQLadmin`, described in the previous section, but is also available for non-Windows operating systems. See Chapter 1 for information on obtaining and installing `MySQLGUI`.

To manage the MySQL server using `MySQLGUI`, select Commands, Tables, and then Administration from the menu. The Administrator Panel option provides a central method of accessing various management functions. Some of these functions are also available directly from the Administration menu.

The Administrator Panel displays a summary of the server's status, similar to the output of the `mysqladmin status` command, and displays the current time from the MySQL server. The panel also includes buttons for administrative

functions. These include Ping to check on the server, Refresh to refresh the status display, and Shutdown to shut down the server.

The Show variables button displays MySQL's current variable settings. The Display status button displays a complete status report, similar to the output of the `mysqladmin extended-status` command. The Show processes button displays a list of current MySQL threads, similar to the `mysqladmin processlist` command.

The Flush tables button closes all open tables. The Flush hosts button clears the host cache. The Flush logs button closes and re-opens the log files. See Chapter 10 for more information about log files. The Flush status command clears the status variables.

In addition to these options, `MySQLGUI`s administration panel includes options to create and drop databases, and to change passwords and grant privileges to users. See Chapter 11 for more information about securing MySQL by setting up users and passwords.

MANAGE MYSQL WITH MYSQLGUI

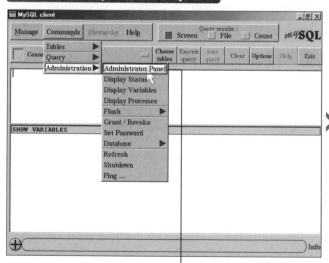

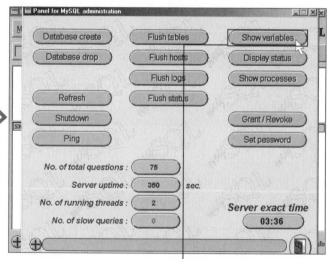

Note: See Chapter 1 for information on installing and starting `MySQLGUI`*.*

1 From the `MySQLGUI` menu, click Commands, Administration, and then Administrator Panel.

■ The administration panel is displayed.

2 Click the Show variables button to display the variable list.

Extra

You may have noticed that there is often more than one way to achieve the same result. For example, if you want to display a list of MySQL variables and their current values, you can use several commands: `show variables` from the MySQL monitor, `mysqladmin variables` from the command prompt, the Variables tab in `WinMySQLadmin`, or the Show variables button in `MySQLGUI`.

Each of these methods of MySQL administration has its advantages and disadvantages. The MySQL monitor and the `mysqladmin` utility are available on all operating systems and provide a consistent interface, while the `MySQLGUI` and `WinMySQLadmin` utilities provide a graphical interface with easy access to common options. You can use whichever commands are available to you, and whichever you find the most comfortable to work with.

In addition to the administrative features discussed here, you can use `MySQLGUI` to send queries to the MySQL server and display the results. Unlike the command-line MySQL monitor, `MySQLGUI` includes options to save query results to a file after you view them, and saves a list of the most recent queries for easy access.

While `MySQLGUI` looks simple, keep in mind that it is every bit as powerful as the command-line utilities. You can use it to delete an entire database or shut down the MySQL server. Be sure to select commands carefully.

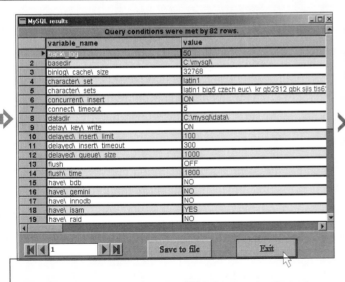

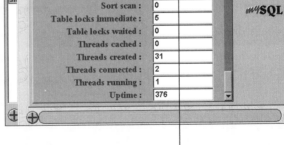

■ The variable list is displayed.

3 Click the Exit button to return to the administration panel.

4 Click the Display status button to display detailed server status.

■ The status information is displayed in a new window.

5 Click Exit to return to the administration panel.

OPTIMIZE MYSQL

W hile MySQL will work remarkably well using the default settings, you can change a variety of factors to improve performance. Some of the most important factors that affect MySQL server performance include the speed of the server hardware, the design of tables, and the performance of particular queries.

OPTIMIZE THE MYSQL SERVER

One aspect of MySQL that is relatively easy to optimize is the speed of the machine running the MySQL server. Upgrading disks, memory, or processor, or switching to a faster machine can dramatically improve performance.

Disk Access

Disk access is usually the largest bottleneck affecting a MySQL server. Because tables are stored on disk, virtually every MySQL operation involves disk access. MySQL will benefit from a fast disk drive. Additionally, you may want to consider using a separate drive for MySQL data so that other server functions do not slow down MySQL.

Processor Speed

While not as important as disk speed, the processor, or CPU, of the MySQL server comes into play when working with data that has been read from disk: A faster processor will handle MySQL queries faster. It is also beneficial to analyze the other applications on the server. If a Web server or other software is using the CPU intensively, MySQL would benefit from a faster processor or a dedicated MySQL server machine.

Memory

A busy MySQL server requires a large amount of memory. This is used to store data temporarily while it is sent to clients, and for temporary tables. Adding memory will often improve performance, especially if the disk drives and CPU are already reasonably fast.

OPTIMIZE TABLE DESIGN

The design of a table can also affect performance. By considering performance when you design and create a table under MySQL, you can ensure that queries on the table can be quickly handled by the server.

Using Fixed-Length Rows

When a table is frequently changed, MySQL performs better using fixed-length rows. To use fixed-length rows on a table, avoid using variable-length column types such as VARCHAR, TEXT, and BLOB. The disadvantage of fixed-length rows is that all rows take the same amount of space. Variable-length rows will make more efficient use of disk space if there is a large amount of variation in the sizes of data items.

Reduce Data Size

The less data MySQL has to work with, the faster it will be. Use the smallest column sizes possible for your data and eliminate unnecessary columns to improve the MySQL server's performance working with a table.

Multiple Tables and Relationships

Performance problems multiply when you are working with multiple tables. Because JOIN queries that retrieve data from multiple tables tend to be slow, do not divide data into more tables than necessary.

When you do use multiple tables that have a relationship, be sure the columns that form the relationship are the same type, length, and preferably have the same name. This will ensure that the MySQL server can perform a JOIN query efficiently.

Sort Table Data

You can use the ORDER BY keywords with an ALTER TABLE command to sort the data in the table. This can improve performance when the contents of the table are often read in the same order, and are not changed frequently.

Example:
```
ALTER TABLE address ORDER BY name;
```

OPTIMIZE SLOW QUERIES

Often, a particular query that is used frequently can slow down the MySQL server. By optimizing a query's syntax, you can often improve its performance.

The MySQL server keeps track of the number of slow queries, or queries that took more than a certain length of time, since the server started. You can display this value using the SHOW STATUS command in the MySQL monitor or the mysqladmin status command at the command prompt.

The MySQL server can optionally maintain a slow query log, which keeps a record of each slow query. This is particularly useful for determining which queries are slowing down the server. This log file is described in detail in "View MySQL Log Files," later in this chapter.

Using EXPLAIN

You can use the EXPLAIN command with a SELECT query to display information about how MySQL will handle the query. When you use EXPLAIN, the MySQL server does not actually process the SELECT query. Instead, it displays a chart of information about the query.

The information displayed by EXPLAIN includes the tables the query will use, the keys it can use to quickly find records, the number of rows the query will return, and any extra explanation the server can offer about the query.

The Extra column will indicate whether a file sort is necessary to process an ORDER BY clause. It will also indicate whether a temporary table will be needed to handle a GROUP BY clause. If either of these is present, it indicates a major bottleneck for the query. You may be able to eliminate the problem by adding an index or changing the query.

Example:
```
EXPLAIN SELECT * FROM quotes;
```

Improve Queries

After you have isolated a slow query, you can try changing its syntax. Eliminate any unnecessary ORDER BY clauses, as they can slow down the query. Add WHERE clauses to target specific records wherever possible, and use the LIMIT clause to limit the number of records returned. See Chapter 6 for details about the syntax of these SELECT query clauses.

Add Indexes

If you frequently search for values in a particular column, you may be able to improve performance by adding an index on that column. You can use the ALTER TABLE command to add an index at any time. This is explained further in "Improve Performance with Indexes," later in this chapter.

Lock Tables

MySQL normally handles table locking automatically. You may be able to improve the performance of a complex query or series of queries by locking the table first. You can use the LOCK TABLES and UNLOCK TABLES commands to control table locking. This is described in "Manage Table Locking," later in this chapter.

CHECK A TABLE FOR ERRORS

MySQL includes a utility called `myisamchk` that allows you to check tables for errors and repair any errors that occur. You can use this utility as a regular check to watch for errors, or when you suspect a problem with a table. This utility is for the default MyISAM table type. An older utility, `isamchk`, works for ISAM tables.

To check a table for errors, start in the directory where the database files are stored, typically /usr/local/mysql/data/ *database_name*. Type `myisamchk` followed by one or more table names. The check will be performed immediately, and may take several minutes on a large table. No clients can access the table while `myisamchk` is running, and `myisamchk` only works if no clients have a lock on the table. The following example checks the quotes table:

```
cd /usr/local/mysql/data/testdb
myisamchk quotes
```

The `myisamchk` utility displays a series of status messages during the table check. If any of these indicate an error in the table, you can attempt to repair the table. Use the `myisamchk -r` option to attempt to repair a corrupt table. The following example repairs the quotes table:

```
myisamchk -r quotes
```

If an error message is displayed, and `myisamchk` is unable to repair the table using this option, you can try the `-o` option. This performs a slower recovery process that may work when the standard process fails.

Unlike other MySQL utilities, the `myisamchk` utility does not require a MySQL username and password. It works directly with database files. For this reason, in the default installation, your UNIX username must have root access to run `myisamchk`. On Windows systems, this utility is available as `c:\mysql\bin\myisamchk.exe`.

CHECK A TABLE FOR ERRORS

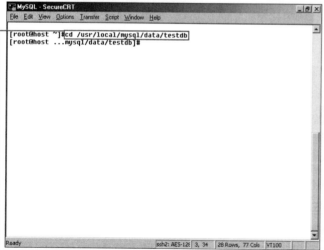

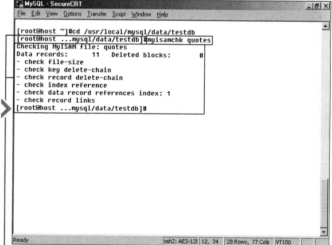

1 From the command prompt, type **cd /usr/local/ mysql/data/testdb** and press Enter.

■ This switches to the directory where the testdb database is stored.

Note: On Windows systems, the directory is usually c:\mysql\data\testdb.

2 Type **myisamchk quotes** and press Enter.

■ This checks the table for errors and displays a report.

Note: To check a different table, replace quotes with the name of the table.

Extra

The `myisamchk` utility includes a number of additional options to control the check and repair process. Type `myisamchk --help` for a complete list of options. The following table describes some of the most useful options:

OPTION	DESCRIPTION
-c	Check (default if no options are specified)
-e	Extended check — slow but more thorough
-m	Medium check — faster than extended
-F	Fast check — only checks improperly closed tables
-C	Checks only tables changed since the last check
-i	Displays information about the table while checking
-f	Automatically repairs the table if any errors are detected
-T	Does not mark table as checked
-r	Recover — attempts to repair table and recover data
-o	Safe recover — uses slower recovery method
-q	Quick recover — checks index files only
-v	Verbose — displays detailed information
-V	Displays the `myisamchk` version number
-w	Wait — waits until no clients are locking table before checking

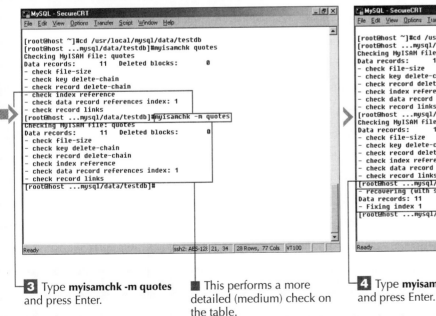

3 Type **myisamchk -m quotes** and press Enter.

■ This performs a more detailed (medium) check on the table.

4 Type **myisamchk -r quotes** and press Enter.

■ This attempts to recover the table data.

OPTIMIZE AND REPAIR TABLES

When you delete rows from a MySQL table, they are not actually deleted. Instead, MySQL marks the rows as deleted and re-uses the space later when rows are inserted. If you have deleted a large number of rows from a table, you should optimize the table to reclaim the space. Optimizing is also necessary when a table with variable-length rows has been changed many times.

To optimize a table, use the OPTIMIZE TABLE command within the MySQL monitor. To use this command, specify the table name. The following example optimizes the quotes table:

OPTIMIZE TABLE quotes;

Along with reclaiming space from deleted rows, the OPTIMIZE TABLE command also repairs minor errors in table rows, sorts the index files, and updates the table's statistics. You can use this command as often as you desire without damaging a table. However, the table is locked and cannot be used by clients during the optimization process.

From time to time, you may run into a situation where a MySQL table becomes corrupted. This usually happens when a power outage or hardware failure causes the server to go down unexpectedly while a table is being updated. In most cases, you can easily repair the table. You can use the myisamchk utility discussed earlier or the REPAIR TABLE command to repair a damaged table.

To use REPAIR TABLE, specify the table name. You can also specify the optional keyword QUICK for a quick repair or EXTENDED for an extended repair. If the regular repair does not work, the extended option may. The following command repairs the quotes table:

REPAIR TABLE quotes;

OPTIMIZE AND REPAIR TABLES

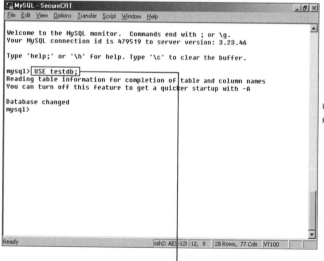

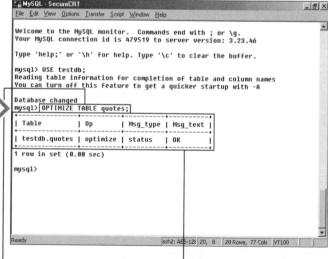

Note: This example uses the quotes table in the testdb database, but it would work with any table.

1 From the MySQL monitor, type **USE testdb;** and press Enter.

■ The database is now selected.

2 Type **OPTIMIZE TABLE quotes;** and press Enter.

■ The table is scanned and optimized, and a report is displayed.

Extra

Along with OPTIMIZE TABLE and REPAIR TABLE, MySQL includes a CHECK TABLE command. This command is equivalent to the myisamchk utility, but runs from the MySQL monitor or another client. To use CHECK TABLE, specify one or more table names. The following example checks the quotes table for errors:

Example:
CHECK TABLE quotes;

You can also use several optional keywords with CHECK TABLE after the table name. These are described in the table below.

KEYWORD	DESCRIPTION
QUICK	Quick check — does not scan all table rows
FAST	Fast check — only checks improperly closed tables
CHANGED	Checks only tables that have changed since the last check
MEDIUM	Medium check — checks each table row (default)
EXTENDED	Extended check — comprehensive but slow on large tables

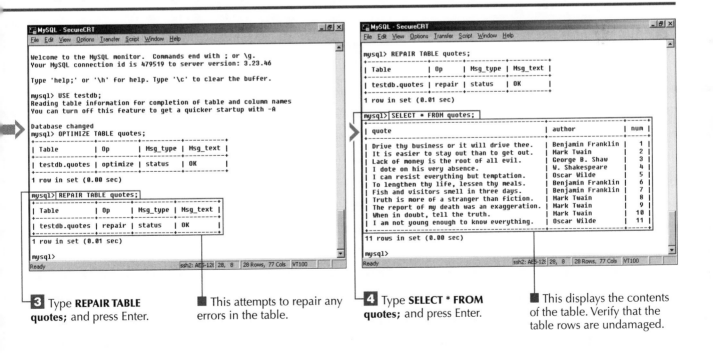

3 Type **REPAIR TABLE quotes;** and press Enter.

■ This attempts to repair any errors in the table.

4 Type **SELECT * FROM quotes;** and press Enter.

■ This displays the contents of the table. Verify that the table rows are undamaged.

MYSQL CONFIGURATION OPTIONS

The MySQL server is a complex system, and includes a number of parameters you can use to tune the server's performance. You can modify these values by editing configuration files or with command-line options.

Each configuration file is divided into sections for different MySQL components. For example, the line [mysqld] begins the section for the server, and [client] begins the section for clients. Within each section, each line can include an option from the program's command-line options or the set-variable command to set a system variable.

CONFIGURATION FILES

MySQL supports a variety of configuration files. Each can contain the same commands and settings, but the order in which they are read determines which files can override others.

The Global Configuration File

The global configuration file is read first. On UNIX systems, this file is /etc/my.cnf. On Windows systems, the two global files are supported: my.ini in the Windows system directory, and my.cnf in the root directory, typically C:\.

The User Configuration File

On UNIX systems, each user can have their own configuration file, .my.cnf, in their home directory. You can use this file to set values for each user, typically for MySQL client utilities.

The Server Configuration File

The server configuration file affects a particular copy of the MySQL server software, and is only needed when multiple servers are installed on the same machine. This file also has the filename my.cnf. On UNIX systems, it is stored in the data directory under the MySQL installation, typically /usr/local/mysql/data. On Windows systems, the file is usually under C:\mysql\data\. The values you specify in the server configuration file override the values in the global file.

CLIENT OPTIONS

The [client] section in the configuration file includes options that affect all of the MySQL client programs, including the MySQL monitor, mysql, the mysqladmin utility, myisamchk, and other client tools. This section is particularly useful in a .my.cnf file in a user's home directory. For example, the following file excerpt sets the password option for MySQL clients. If you include this in the .my.cnf file in your home directory, you do not need to specify a password when using MySQL client programs.

```
[client]
password=mypassword
```

The table below lists several options that may also be useful in the [client] section for a particular user.

VALUE	DESCRIPTION
host=name	Specifies a MySQL server to connect to
user=name	Username for the MySQL server, if different from UNIX username
password=value	Password for the MySQL server
database=value	Default database to select

MySQL includes a number of system variables that control the behavior of the server. While these variables have sensible default values, setting them to optimal values for your system can dramatically improve the server's performance. The table below describes key system variables for optimizing performance.

VARIABLE	DESCRIPTION
back_log	Maximum number of client requests waiting for threads
concurrent_inserts	Specifies ON to allow INSERT operations while clients are reading data
connect_timeout	Number of seconds the server waits for a connection before timing out
delayed_insert_limit	Number of rows of an INSERT DELAYED query to process at a time
delayed_insert_timeout	Time the server waits for additional INSERT DELAYED items
delayed_queue_size	Number of INSERT DELAYED rows to store
flush_time	Closes all tables after the specified number of seconds
interactive_timeout	Number of seconds of idle time before disconnecting interactive clients
join_buffer_size	Buffer size for full joins (queries from multiple tables)
key_buffer_size	Buffer size for index values
long_query_time	Amount of seconds before a query is considered slow
max_allowed_packet	Maximum size of a single packet of data
max_connections	Maximum number of simultaneous client connections allowed
max_connect_errors	Number of allowed errors before blocking connections from a host
max_delayed_threads	Maximum number of threads used for INSERT DELAYED queries
max_join_size	Maximum number of rows for JOIN queries
max_sort_length	The number of bytes of each BLOB or TEXT value to use when sorting
max_user_connections	Maximum number of connections for each username
net_buffer_length	Default size for the communication buffer
net_read_timeout	Number of seconds to wait before aborting when reading data
net_write_timeout	Number of seconds to wait before aborting when writing data
thread_cache_size	Number of threads kept standing by for use by clients
wait_timeout	Number of seconds of idle time before disconnecting a client

Set Variables

You can set MySQL system variables by including them in the [mysqld] section of a configuration file, using the set-variable command. The following example sets the max_allowed_packet variable:

```
[mysqld]
set-variable max_allowed_packet=1M
```

You can also set variables using the --set-variable option when mysqld is started.

Display Current Values

You can display the current values of all of the system variables using the SHOW VARIABLES command from the MySQL monitor or the mysqladmin variables command at the UNIX or Windows command prompt. This is useful if you are unsure whether the configuration files are being read correctly, and is the first thing you should do if a variable change has not produced the effect you expected.

You can also use the LIKE operator with SHOW VARIABLES to show a section of the list. The following example shows the values of all variables that include the characters "max" in their names:

```
SHOW VARIABLES LIKE '%max%';
```

DISPLAY SERVER PERFORMANCE INFORMATION

To optimize the performance of a MySQL server, the first step is to determine how it is currently performing. MySQL keeps a number of running status variables that you can examine to get a snapshot of the server's current performance. This will let you know how much traffic the server is handling, as well as early indications of performance problems.

To display the status variables, you can use the SHOW STATUS command in the MySQL monitor or the mysqladmin extended-status command at the command prompt. The output of either command is a table of variables and their values. You can use the LIKE operator with SHOW STATUS to show only certain values.

Most of the variables count the number of times something has happened since the server started. For example, the Opened_tables value is the number of table that have been opened, and the Questions value is the number of queries the server has received. The Uptime value gives

you the number of seconds the server has been running, so you can use this and the various variables to get an idea of how the server performs over time.

The Threads_connected value indicates how many client connections are currently open to the server, and the Max_used_connections value is the largest number of clients that are simultaneously connected. You can use these values to determine whether the server is busy and whether the max_concurrent_users system variable needs to be increased.

Slow_queries is another value you should watch carefully. This is the number of queries that have taken more than the expected amount of time. The time for a slow query is set using the long_query_time system variable. If many slow queries are being counted, this means the server is running slower than expected, or some particular queries in use are slowing down the server.

DISPLAY SERVER PERFORMANCE INFORMATION

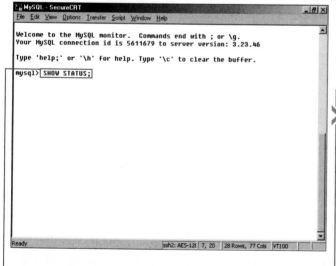

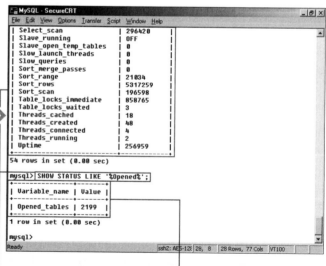

1 From the MySQL monitor, type **SHOW STATUS;** and press Enter.

■ The current values of the status variables are displayed.

2 Type **SHOW STATUS LIKE '%Opened%';** and press Enter.

■ The variables that match the string you specified are displayed.

Extra

The list of values returned by SHOW STATUS is quite long, but certain values are important to watch. The table below describes some of the most important status variables.

VARIABLE	DESCRIPTION
Aborted_clients	Number of client connections not closed properly
Aborted_connects	Number of failed connections to the server
Bytes_received	Total bytes of data received from clients
Bytes_sent	Total bytes of data sent to clients
Connections	Number of times clients have connected to the server
Open_tables	Number of tables currently in use
Open_files	Number of files currently in use
Opened_tables	Number of tables opened since the server started
Questions	Total number of queries received from clients
Slow_queries	Number of queries that have taken longer than a maximum amount of time
Threads_cached	Number of threads standing by for clients
Threads_created	Number of threads created since the server started
Threads_running	Current number of active threads
Uptime	Number of seconds since the server started

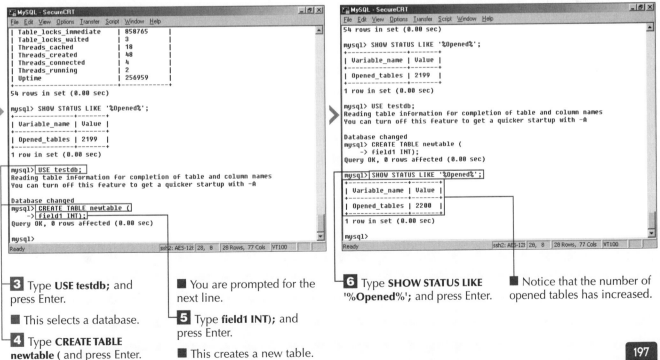

3 Type **USE testdb;** and press Enter.

■ This selects a database.

4 Type **CREATE TABLE newtable (** and press Enter.

■ You are prompted for the next line.

5 Type **field1 INT);** and press Enter.

■ This creates a new table.

6 Type **SHOW STATUS LIKE '%Opened%';** and press Enter.

■ Notice that the number of opened tables has increased.

EDIT THE CONFIGURATION FILE IN UNIX

I f you decide to change some of the MySQL options to improve the performance of the server, you can edit the configuration file to make the changes. As discussed earlier in this chapter, there may be several configuration files on a UNIX system. The main configuration file is usually /etc/my.cnf.

To edit the configuration file, load it into a text editor such as pico, vi, or emacs. One or more of these editors is included with most UNIX and Linux systems. Depending on your MySQL installation, the file may not yet exist. You can create it using the text editor. On most systems, only the root user can edit files in the /etc directory. The following example loads the /etc/my.cnf file into the pico editor:

```
pico /etc/my.cnf
```

When adding commands to the configuration file, the best strategy is to make one change at a time and test the server with the modified value before making other changes. This is especially important on a busy production server; changing variables incorrectly can reduce performance or even cripple the server.

After you make changes to the configuration file, save it and exit the editor. MySQL does not read the new configuration automatically. You will need to shut down the server using the mysqladmin shutdown command and restart it to read the modified configuration information. Chapter 9 includes information on stopping and restarting the MySQL server.

After you have changed system variable values in the configuration file, you can use the SHOW VARIABLES command from the MySQL monitor or the mysqladmin variables command from the command prompt to verify that the changes were read and implemented by the server.

EDIT THE CONFIGURATION FILE IN UNIX

1 From the command prompt, type **pico /etc/my.cnf** and press Enter.

■ This loads the configuration file into the editor.

Note: You may need to use a different editor name on your system.

2 From the editor, make the desired changes to the configuration file.

3 When you are finished, press Ctrl-X and then Y.

■ This saves the file and exits the editor.

Note: The command to save and exit may be different depending on the editor you are using.

EDIT THE CONFIGURATION FILE IN WINDOWS

The Windows version of MySQL supports three different configuration files. The first has the filename my.ini. This file is stored in the Windows system directory, typically C:\windows\system or C:\winnt\system32. You can also use a global options file with the filename my.cnf in the C:\ root directory, and a server options file called my.cnf in the C:\mysql\data directory.

When the MySQL server starts in Windows, it reads the my.ini file first, followed by the my.cnf file in the root directory, and finally the my.cnf file in the data directory. Values in a later file can override those set in an earlier file.

There are two ways to edit the configuration file in Windows. The first is to load the file into any text editor. The Notepad accessory included with Windows will work fine. Use the following command from the command prompt or the Run dialog box to edit the my.cnf file in Notepad:

```
notepad c:\mysql\my.cnf
```

The second method is to use the WinMySQLadmin utility, introduced in Chapter 9. This utility provides a graphical overview of the MySQL server's configuration, and the my.ini Setup tab allows you to create a configuration file using default values or edit the existing file.

By default, none of the MySQL configuration files exist after you install the MySQL server. You can create them using a text editor or the WinMySQLadmin utility. After you have created or modified a configuration file, you need to restart the server. See Chapter 9 for instructions to restart the server.

After you have changed system variable values in a configuration file, you can verify that the changes were read by using the SHOW VARIABLES command from the MySQL monitor, or the mysqladmin variables command from the command prompt.

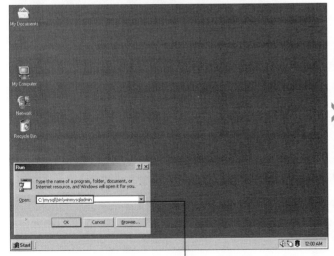

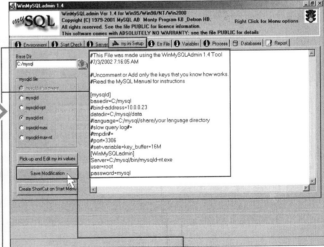

Note: Select Run from the Start menu to display the Run dialog box.

1 From the Run dialog box, type **C:\mysql\bin\winmysqladmin** and press Enter.

■ This starts the WinMySQLadmin utility.

2 Within MySQLadmin, click the my.ini Setup tab.

3 Make the desired changes to the file.

4 Click the Save Modification button to save the changes you have made.

VIEW MYSQL LOG FILES

MySQL supports a number of different log files. You can use these to analyze the performance of the server and to detect errors and potential problems when they occur. The log files are standard text files stored in the same directory as the database files, typically /usr/local/mysql/data.

The only log file created by default is the error log. This logs all errors encountered by the server and each time the server is started or stopped. The error log is named with the hostname of the server and the .err extension under UNIX, and is stored at c:\mysql\data\mysql.err on Windows systems.

MySQL can optionally create a general query log, which logs each query sent to the server. This log file is created if you specify the -1 or --log option when you start the mysqld server. Unless you specify a different name in the

command line, the filename for this log is the hostname of the server, and the extension .log is added.

If you specify the --log-update option when you start mysqld, an update log is created. This is similar to the query log, but includes only queries that have resulted in updates to a table. You can use the update log to reconstruct a table from a backup, using the logged queries to make any changes that were not backed up.

The final available log is the slow query log. This is a log of all queries that have exceeded the defined long_query_time value. This log is very useful in determining which queries are taking a large amount of time and potentially slowing down the server. To turn on the slow query log, use the --log-slow-queries option on the command line.

VIEW MYSQL LOG FILES

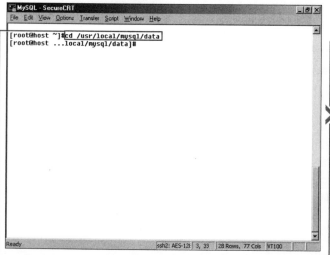

1 From the command prompt, type **cd /usr/local/mysql/data** and press Enter.

■ This switches to the location where logs are stored.

Note: The location may vary depending on your installation. Under Windows, the location is usually c:\mysql\data.

2 To view the error log, type **cat hostname.err**, replacing *hostname* with the name of your server, and press Enter.

■ The contents of the error log are displayed.

*Note: Under Windows, type **more hostname.err** instead.*

Note: If the log is large, you can use the tail command to view only the most recent entries on UNIX systems.

Extra

Newer versions of MySQL support a binary update log. This is similar to the update log, but stored in a binary rather than text format for greater efficiency. To use the binary log, specify the `--log-bin` option on the command line to `mysqld`. MySQL includes a utility, `mysqlbinlog`, to convert the binary log to a text format.

You can maintain the MySQL log files at any time by renaming or deleting them. After you have done this, use the `mysqladmin flush-logs` command to restart logging. When you do this, the update log is automatically recreated with a new sequence number; you can then move the old log to a backup location or delete it. The binary log is also rotated automatically. If you want to regularly rotate the query log or slow query log, you need to do so manually.

The `FLUSH LOGS` command within the MySQL monitor also refreshes the logs and rotates the update logs. The Redhat Linux version of the MySQL server includes a `mysql-log-rotate` script that rotates the logs. This is set up automatically if you install the RPM version of the MySQL server.

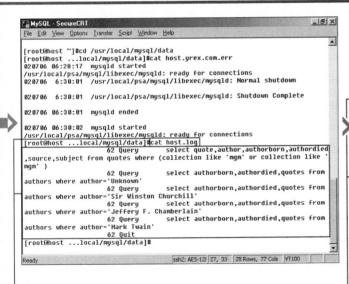

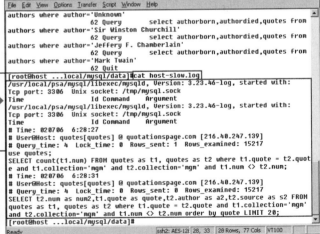

3 To view the query log, type **cat *hostname*.log**, replacing *hostname* with the server name, and press Enter.

■ The contents of the log are displayed.

*Note: Under Windows, use the command **more hostname.log** instead.*

Note: Depending on your configuration, the query log may not be created by default.

4 To view the slow query log, type **cat *hostname-slow*.log**, replacing *hostname* with the server name, and press Enter.

■ The contents of the log are displayed.

*Note: Under Windows, use the command **more hostname-slow.log** instead.*

Note: The slow query log is not created by default; you must explicitly enable it.

IMPROVE PERFORMANCE WITH INDEXES

A MySQL table can have one or more indexes associated with it. While at least one unique index is usually used as a primary key to uniquely identify each row of the table, you can add additional indexes, unique or not, to improve performance.

The MySQL status values shown by the `SHOW STATUS` command or the `mysqladmin extended-status` command can help you determine whether an index would improve performance. In particular, a high value for the `Handler_read_key` counter indicates that records are often being read by key and that indexing is working well.

The `Handler_read_rnd_next` value, on the other hand, indicates that sequential reads are being used often rather than direct access by key. This may mean that you are using inefficient queries, or that an additional index would improve performance. If you add an index, be sure to test

the performance of your queries afterward and remove the index if it has not improved performance.

To add an index, use the `ALTER TABLE` query with the `ADD_INDEX` keyword. Specify the index name, if desired, followed by a list of columns to index in parentheses. For example, the following query adds an index on the author field of the quotes table:

```
ALTER TABLE quotes
   ADD INDEX authorind (author);
```

The process of adding a unique index is similar, but uses the `ADD UNIQUE` keyword instead of `ADD INDEX`. To use a unique index, the column must have unique values for each row. However, if you specify multiple columns for the unique index, only the combination of the column values needs to be unique.

IMPROVE PERFORMANCE WITH INDEXES

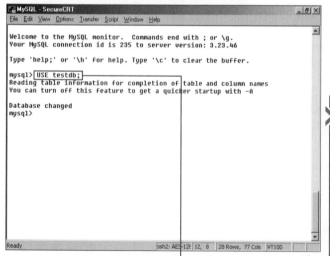

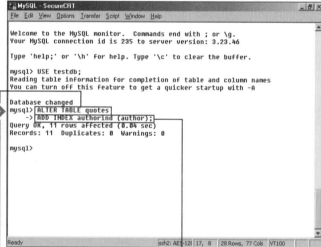

Note: This example uses the quotes table in the testdb database. You can import this table from the CD-ROM.

1 From the MySQL monitor, type **USE testdb;** and press Enter.

■ This selects the database.

2 Type **ALTER TABLE quotes** and press Enter.

■ You are prompted for the next line.

3 Type **ADD INDEX authorind (author);** and press Enter.

■ This adds an index to the table.

Extra

Sometimes an index does not improve performance. In particular, if you are not frequently searching for particular values of a column, indexing that column is not likely to help. In a table with few rows, often very little indexing is needed for optimal performance.

If an index is slowing down performance or is not an improvement, you can remove it from the table. To remove an index, use `DROP INDEX` with the `ALTER TABLE` command. The following command removes the index named authorind from the quotes table:

Example:
```
ALTER TABLE quotes DROP INDEX authorind;
```

When you use `DROP INDEX`, only the extra data stored in index files is deleted; no rows of the table are modified or deleted. However, if the index was a unique index or primary key, it may be the only way to refer to a single row of the table. In this case, removing the index can reduce the usefulness of the table.

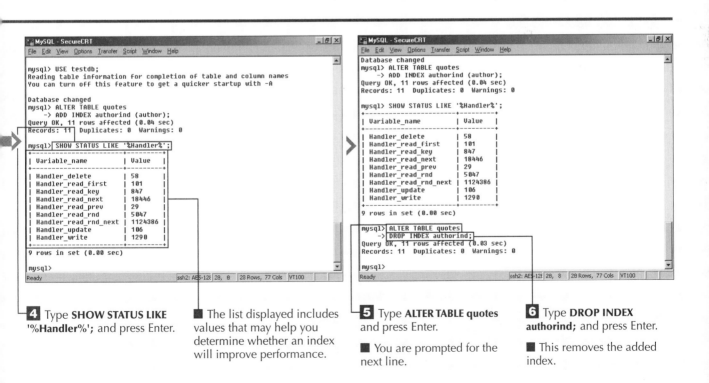

4 Type **SHOW STATUS LIKE '%Handler%';** and press Enter.

■ The list displayed includes values that may help you determine whether an index will improve performance.

5 Type **ALTER TABLE quotes** and press Enter.

■ You are prompted for the next line.

6 Type **DROP INDEX authorind;** and press Enter.

■ This removes the added index.

MANAGE TABLE LOCKING

MySQL uses a system of table locking to ensure that the various threads working with a table do not conflict. When a thread has a lock on a table, MySQL prevents other threads from performing conflicting operations on the table. While this is normally handled automatically, you can use the LOCK TABLES and UNLOCK TABLES commands to manually lock and unlock tables.

MySQL supports two basic types of table lock: READ locks and WRITE locks. When a thread obtains a READ lock for a table, other threads can still read the table, but no threads can write to the table. You can use this to ensure that the table is not changed during a SELECT query or other operation, and to improve the speed of a complex query.

When a thread obtains a WRITE lock for a table, no other threads are allowed to read from or write to the table. This ensures that other writes do not interfere with your updates to the table, and that no clients read a partially-updated version of the table during the update.

To lock one or more tables, use the LOCK TABLES command. Specify one or more tables and the keywords READ or WRITE to indicate the lock type. For example, the following command requests a READ lock for the address table:

LOCK TABLES address READ;

When you use LOCK TABLES, the client waits until the table is not locked by another thread and then locks it for your session. The lock ends automatically when you close your connection to the server or use another LOCK TABLES command. You can also use the UNLOCK TABLES command to end all current locks:

UNLOCK TABLES;

The MySQL server gives priority to WRITE locks. If you add the LOW_PRIORITY keyword before WRITE in a LOCK TABLES command, the server allows READ locks for other threads while it waits for exclusive access to the table.

MANAGE TABLE LOCKING

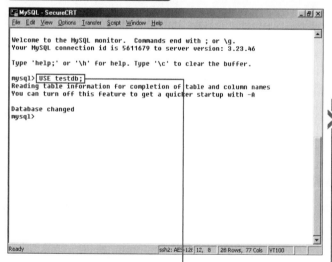

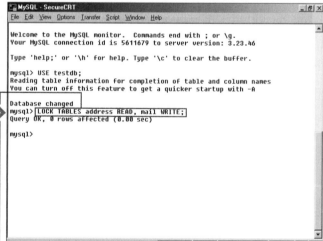

Note: This example uses the testdb database and the address and mail tables. If you have not created these, see the CD-ROM for instructions.

1 From the MySQL monitor, type **USE testdb;** and press Enter.

■ This selects the database.

2 Type **LOCK TABLES address READ, mail WRITE;** and press Enter.

■ This obtains a READ lock for the address table and a WRITE lock for the mail table.

Extra

There are two basic reasons to manually lock tables. The first is to ensure that a complex operation is not interfered with by other threads. This is not necessary with basic UPDATE queries, because MySQL uses locking automatically. You may need to use it when you are performing a series of UPDATE queries and do not want the table to be changed in between.

When you use a READ lock, you ensure that the table cannot be changed during a SELECT query. This allows the SELECT query to obtain an accurate snapshot of the current table data. If you keep the READ lock in place, you can be sure that multiple SELECT queries will be working with exactly the same data.

The second reason to lock tables is to improve performance. A complex SELECT query can run faster when no other clients can access the table, so a READ lock will improve performance. A complex UPDATE query will run much faster with a WRITE lock, giving it exclusive access to the table.

In general, you should only use table locking when you are sure you need it for data integrity, or when you have experienced performance problems without locking. Using locking unnecessarily can create performance problems for other clients.

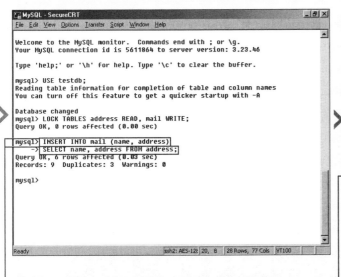

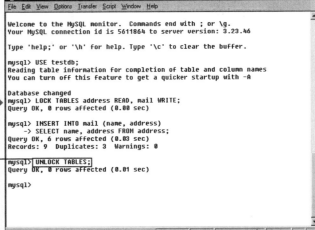

3 Type **INSERT INTO mail (name, address)** and press Enter.

4 Type **SELECT name, address FROM address;** and press Enter.

■ This copies data between the tables. On a busy system, it would execute faster because of the table locking.

5 Type **UNLOCK TABLES;** and press Enter.

■ This releases the locks on both tables.

THE IMPORTANCE OF SECURITY

Security is a growing concern among system administrators. Any system that stores data critical to a company or organization is vulnerable to security risks. A MySQL database may store thousands of tables of crucial data and can be a major vulnerability if it is not properly secured.

Database Security

Because databases are often used to store important data, MySQL does not rely on the security abilities of the underlying operating system. Instead, it includes its own security system. This allows you to control access to each database, each table, and even specific columns within a table individually.

Users should be given access only to the data they need to work with directly, and should be given the minimum amount of access to be able to do their jobs. MySQL includes a number of commands that allow you to create users and assign them specific privileges, or abilities.

System Security

Because the MySQL data files for each database are stored in the file system of the underlying operating system, a secure operating system is also important for a secure database server. Be sure that no users except trusted administrators have the ability to directly access the MySQL data files. Anyone who can access these files directly can completely circumvent MySQL's security system.

Physical Security

When you are planning the security of a database server, be sure not to forget the server hardware itself. Despite the most sophisticated security and encryption in MySQL and the operating system, the data is still stored on a hard disk and is vulnerable if there is physical access to the server machine. Client machines should also be kept physically secure if they have the ability to connect without specifying a password each time.

Network Security

Because a MySQL server is often accessed across a local or wide-area network, the security of the network is also important. Malicious users can scan network traffic and view data or passwords as they are transmitted between database clients and servers.

To prevent potential network security issues, MySQL encrypts passwords before sending them across the network. You can also use data compression between MySQL clients and servers, which prevents data from being sent as readable text.

The best network security is provided by a good firewall or proxy server. Because the MySQL server usually does not need to be accessed from everywhere in the world, you can keep it behind the firewall and allow connections only from trusted systems.

Password Guidelines

MySQL relies on passwords for security. While this provides a basic level of security in authenticating users, this system is only as secure as the passwords chosen. To keep the MySQL server secure, be sure to have a set of guidelines in place for assigning passwords.

You should never create users without passwords. Passwords should be as long as possible. MySQL allows passwords up to at least eight characters, depending on the operating system. Avoid passwords that contain names, words that appear in the dictionary, or common abbreviations, as they can be easily guessed.

Security Risks

While most people imagine data security as a battle against crackers and malicious vandals, the reality is that most security threats come from inside the company. Well-meaning users who have more access than they should have can accidentally delete or invalidate entire MySQL tables with a single command, and disgruntled employees are an even greater risk. For this reason, avoid giving users more than the minimum privileges they require.

MYSQL SECURITY BASICS

MySQL includes a sophisticated security system. You can use MySQL commands to create users and grant them privileges for a database or table.

The Grant Tables

Internally, the MySQL server stores its usernames, passwords, and privileges in several tables within the mysql database. This database is created when you install the MySQL server. The user table within this database stores a row for each user and a number of fields that define the basic privileges granted to the user.

The other tables in the mysql database include the host table, which stores privileges specific to particular hostnames, and the db table, which stores privileges granted to users for a specific database. The tables_priv table stores privileges granted for specific table names, and the columns_priv table stores privileges granted for only specific columns of a table.

Default Users

When you install the MySQL server, the root user is created by default. This user is granted all privileges for all databases and tables, and can create additional users. The root user does not have a password by default, and this is a major security hole. Be sure to change the root password before allowing users to access the MySQL server.

The installation also creates an anonymous user, which allows users on the local host to connect without specifying a username and password. This user is restricted to a database named test or with a name beginning with test_, so this does not represent a serious security risk.

MySQL Users and Privileges

You must specify a username when you use MySQL client programs, such as mysql or mysqladmin. If you are the administrator of the MySQL server, you can create usernames and control the privileges, or permissions, of each user.

You use the GRANT command in MySQL to grant one or more privileges to a user. If the username you specify does not exist, it is created. The REVOKE command is the opposite. This command removes one or more privileges from a user.

The Authentication Process

When you attempt to connect to a MySQL server, the client encrypts your password and sends a request including the username you specified to the server. The server checks whether the username is listed in the user table and whether the password matches the encrypted password stored in that table. If they match, you are allowed to connect.

After this initial authentication, the MySQL client authenticates each command the client sends to the server, and checks the user, db, and other tables to determine whether the username has the right privileges for the command being issued.

Security Commands

MySQL includes three basic commands for working with security. The first, GRANT, grants one or more privileges to a user for a database or table. If the user does not already exist, it is created.

The REVOKE command removes one or more privileges from a username. It can leave a user without privileges, but does not delete users from the user table.

The SHOW GRANTS command displays the privileges granted to a particular user. These are displayed as GRANT statements and can be used to recreate or duplicate the user's privileges.

A user in MySQL is actually the combination of a username and hostname. If a username is set up with a specific host, the user can only connect from that host. Users can also be configured to allow multiple hosts or all hosts.

The privileges you can grant to a user include most of the different things that can be done with SQL queries, including SELECT, INSERT, and DELETE. The complete list of privileges is included later in this chapter.

GRANT PRIVILEGES TO USERS

MySQL uses its own system of usernames and passwords, unrelated to the underlying operating system. You can use the GRANT command from MySQL to create a username and assign one or more privileges to the user. You can assign privileges for all databases, a single database, a table, or even a single column.

The basic syntax of the GRANT command specifies a privilege type, a table or database name, a username, and a password. The username can be an existing MySQL user. If it is a new user, the user is added. The following GRANT command grants all privileges to the user nancy for the testdb database:

```
GRANT ALL ON testdb.*
   TO nancy IDENTIFIED BY 'thepass';
```

Usernames on MySQL can be a simple name like the above, or a combination of a username, the @ symbol, and hostname. If you specify a hostname, the user can only access MySQL from that host. If you do not specify a hostname, the username will work from any host. You can use the wildcard character, %, as the hostname to explicitly indicate that the user can connect from any host.

You can specify a database name with the * symbol, meaning all tables under that database, a table name under the current database selected with the USE command, or the wildcard *.*, meaning all databases on the server. You can optionally specify a list of columns in parentheses before the ON keyword, and the user will have the privileges you specify for only those columns.

The IDENTIFIED BY clause in the GRANT statement allows you to specify a password for the user. The password will be encrypted and stored in the MySQL user table. If the user has already been created with a previous GRANT statement, you do not need to use the IDENTIFIED BY clause again.

In order to grant privileges to a user, you must be logged in as a user with those privileges and the ability to grant. If you specify WITH GRANT OPTION at the end of the GRANT command, the user will have the ability to grant any privileges they have to other users.

The REVOKE command allows you to revoke one or more privileges from a user. To use this command, specify REVOKE, the privilege type or ALL, the ON keyword, the table or database name, the FROM keyword, and the username.

GRANT PRIVILEGES TO USERS

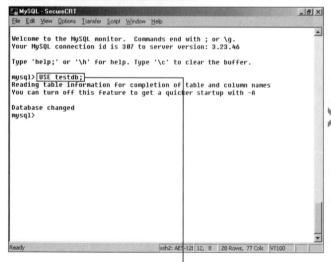

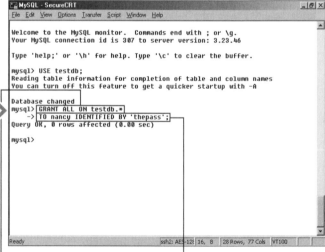

Note: This example uses the testdb database and the quotes table, which you can import from the CD-ROM.

1 From the MySQL monitor, type **USE testdb;** and press Enter.

■ The database is now selected.

2 Type **GRANT ALL ON testdb.*** and press Enter.

■ You are prompted for the next line.

3 Type **TO nancy IDENTIFIED BY 'thepass';** and press Enter.

■ The user is now created. This user has all privileges for the entire database.

Extra

Most of the examples here use the ALL keyword as the privilege type. This keyword assigns all available privileges. You can also assign the specific privileges listed in the table below.

PRIVILEGE	ALLOWS
ALTER	Use ALTER TABLE command
CREATE	Use CREATE TABLE command
DELETE	Use DELETE command
DROP	Use DROP TABLE command
FILE	Use SELECT INTO OUTFILE and LOAD DATA INFILE
INDEX	Use CREATE INDEX or DROP INDEX
INSERT	Use INSERT command
LOCK TABLES	Use LOCK TABLES command
PROCESS	Use SHOW PROCESSLIST and mysqladmin processlist
RELOAD	Use the FLUSH command
SELECT	Use SELECT queries
SHOW DATABASES	Show all databases
SHUTDOWN	Shut down the server with mysqladmin shutdown
SUPER	Various administrative privileges including mysqladmin kill
UPDATE	Use UPDATE queries

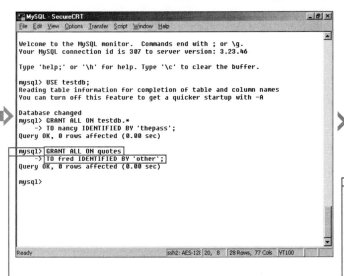

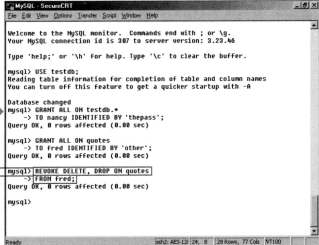

4 Type **GRANT ALL ON quotes** and press Enter.

5 Type **TO fred IDENTIFIED BY 'other';** and press Enter.

■ This creates another user. This one has access to the quotes table only.

6 Type **REVOKE DELETE, DROP ON quotes** and press Enter.

7 Type **FROM fred;** and press Enter.

■ This removes the DELETE and DROP privileges, leaving the user with the remaining privileges.

MODIFY USER PASSWORDS

After you have created a user and granted privileges with GRANT, you can change the user's password using the SET PASSWORD command within the MySQL monitor. For example, the following command changes the password for the user fred:

```
SET PASSWORD FOR fred = PASSWORD('newpass');
```

MySQL stores passwords in an encrypted form. When you change a password with the SET PASSWORD command, you must use the PASSWORD function to encrypt the new password. MySQL expects the new password to be in encrypted form.

In order to change a user's password, you must either be logged in as that user or as a user with the GRANT OPTION privilege. This allows you to change the password for any user. You can also assign passwords by using the IDENTIFIED BY clause when creating users or adding privileges using the GRANT command, as explained in the previous section.

You can also change a user's password using the mysqladmin password command at the command prompt. In this case, you do not need to use the PASSWORD function. For example, the following command changes the password for the current user:

```
mysqladmin password 'newpass'
```

If you specify the -u option with mysqladmin, you can set the password for the specified user. However, this option requires the user's current password. If you need to set a password and do not know the user's current password, use the SET PASSWORD command.

When MySQL is first installed, the root user may be set up with no password or a default password. To secure the MySQL server, you should immediately change the password for this user using SET PASSWORD or mysqladmin password.

MODIFY USER PASSWORDS

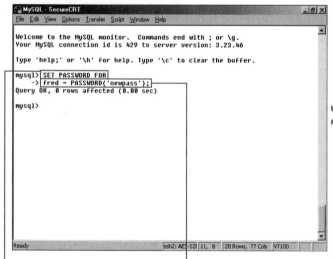

Note: This example uses the users you created in the previous section. You must be connected to MySQL as the root user or another user that can grant privileges.

1 From the MySQL monitor, type **SET PASSWORD FOR** and press Enter.

2 Type **fred = PASSWORD('newpass');** and press Enter.

■ This sets the user's password.

3 Type **SET PASSWORD = PASSWORD('newpass');** and press Enter.

■ This sets the password for the current user.

Note: If you change your password, be sure not to use the default value given here, and be sure to remember the password you have chosen.

Extra

MySQL uses its own system of usernames and passwords. Usernames in MySQL are limited to a length of 16 characters. There is no limit to password length in MySQL, but some systems limit the length to eight characters. While the username and password can be the same as a UNIX or Windows user account, they are separate and do not need to be the same.

When you choose a password, be sure to make it difficult to guess. Names and words that appear in the dictionary are bad choices for passwords. The ideal choice is a combination of random letters mixed with numbers, although truly random passwords are not easy for users to remember.

Because MySQL stores passwords encrypted using the PASSWORD function, knowing the encrypted password for a user is as good as knowing the real password. Do not allow users to view the grant tables, described later in this chapter, as the encrypted passwords would be displayed.

When users specify a password on the command line to mysql or other client programs, other users may be able to see the password in the system's process list. A better strategy is to store the password in a .my.cnf file in each user's home directory. This file is explained in Chapter 10.

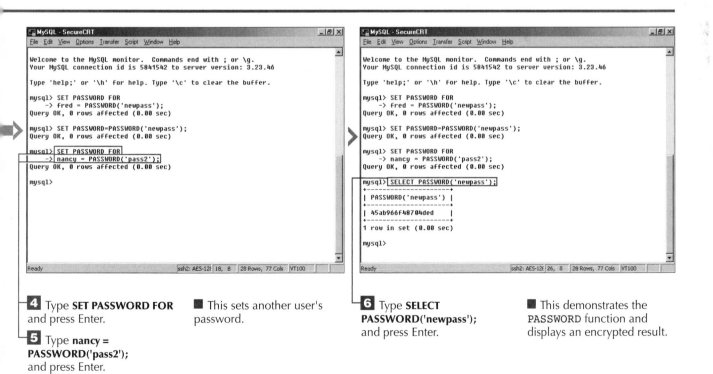

4 Type **SET PASSWORD FOR** and press Enter.

5 Type **nancy = PASSWORD('pass2');** and press Enter.

■ This sets another user's password.

6 Type **SELECT PASSWORD('newpass');** and press Enter.

■ This demonstrates the PASSWORD function and displays an encrypted result.

VIEW A USER'S PRIVILEGES

Y ou can use the VIEW GRANTS command from the MySQL monitor to find out what privileges have been granted to a particular user. This is useful if you need to check what abilities have been given to a user. For example, the following statement displays the privileges granted to the user fred:

SHOW GRANTS FOR fred;

The results for SHOW GRANTS are presented in the form of one or more GRANT statements. You can copy these statements and use them to restore the user's privileges in the event of data loss, or use them to create another user with the same privileges. The password in the GRANT statement is shown in encrypted form.

In some cases a user is configured in MySQL but does not have any privileges. This can happen if you create a user manually in the users table, or if you have revoked all of a

user's privileges. In this case, when you use SHOW GRANTS, the results show a GRANT USAGE statement. USAGE is a special privilege meaning "no privileges." In other words, the user can connect to the MySQL server but cannot access any databases or tables.

When using SHOW GRANTS, remember that MySQL stores users as a combination of username and hostname. If a username is configured with a specific host, you must specify the hostname to view their privileges. If you have created the user ted@localhost, for example, no privileges will be shown if you use this command:

SHOW GRANTS FOR ted;

Because no hostname is specified, this command looks for a user with access from all hosts, and no user is found. To show the privileges for the correct user, specify the hostname with the @ symbol.

VIEW A USER'S PRIVILEGES

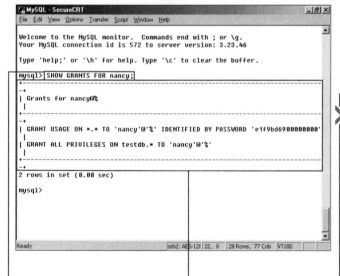

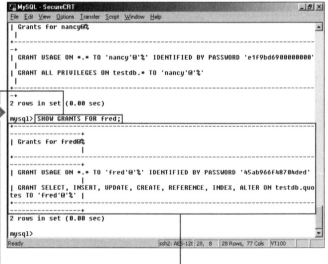

Note: The users referred to in this example were created in the section "Grant Privileges to Users."

1 From the MySQL monitor, type **SHOW GRANTS FOR nancy;** and press Enter.

■ The privileges for the user are displayed.

Note: You must be connected to MySQL as the root user or another user that can grant privileges to use this command.

2 Type **SHOW GRANTS FOR fred;** and press Enter.

■ This user's privileges are displayed.

Extra

In order to use SHOW GRANTS, your username must have the GRANT OPTION in its list of privileges. When you display the privileges for a user, the encrypted password is shown in the GRANT statements, and this could be used to gain access to the user's resources.

When you change a user's privileges using GRANT or REVOKE, the changes take effect immediately and are shown in subsequent SHOW GRANTS commands. The privileges are checked both when a user attempts to connect to the MySQL server and when they issue each command after connecting.

You cannot use wildcards with SHOW GRANTS to display the privileges of multiple users. To display a list of users or quickly view privileges for multiple users, you can access the grant tables directly, as described in the next section.

The GRANT statements shown when you use SHOW GRANTS are a summary of the user's privileges. While they can be used to recreate the user's privileges, they are not necessarily the same commands you used to assign the privileges and create the user.

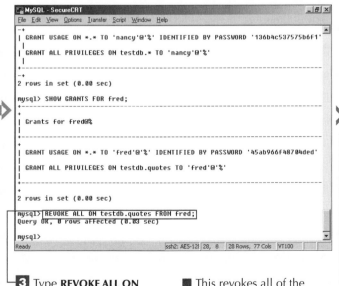

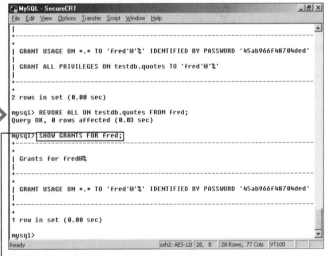

3 Type **REVOKE ALL ON testdb.quotes FROM fred;** and press Enter.

■ This revokes all of the user's privileges.

4 Type **SHOW GRANTS FOR fred;** and press Enter.

■ The user's privileges now include only the USAGE privilege, which allows access but no privileges.

VIEW SECURITY TABLES

MySQL stores the users and privileges you assign in a set of tables under the `mysql` database, which was created when you installed the server. You can view these tables directly to find out detailed information about a user or to view the complete lists of users and privileges.

The `mysql` database is accessible only to the root user by default. Because this database contains usernames, passwords, and privileges for all users, access to it effectively allows you to view or modify any user's privileges on the server.

The user table within the `mysql` database stores the list of usernames and their basic privileges. This table is used by the MySQL server to determine whether to allow access when a user attempts to connect. Various columns of this table store values of "Y" or "N" to indicate whether a privilege is granted. You can use the following command to view the complete list of users:

```
SELECT * FROM user;
```

Because the output of this command includes encrypted passwords, be sure not to let anyone other than an administrator view the list.

The db table stores a row for each user that has privileges for a specific database on the server. For each row, the username, hostname, and database name are stored along with flags indicating various privileges specific to the database for that user.

The host table stores information for specific hostnames, and is used when a user is given access from multiple hosts. The tables_priv and columns_priv tables are used to store any privileges that have been granted to users specific to a table or one or more columns of a table.

VIEW SECURITY TABLES

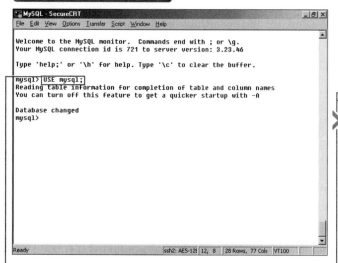

1 From the MySQL monitor, type **USE mysql;** and press Enter.

■ The database is now selected.

Note: Usually you must be logged in as the root user to access this database.

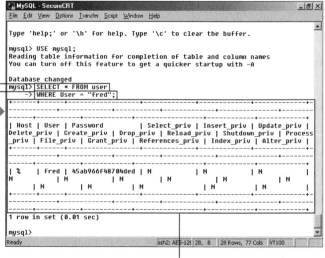

2 Type **SELECT * FROM user** and press Enter.

3 Type **WHERE User = "fred";** and press Enter.

■ The user's entry in the user table is displayed.

Extra

You can manipulate the tables in the `mysql` database directly. For example, you can use the following `UPDATE` query to change a user's password rather than using the `SET PASSWORD` command.

Example:
```
UPDATE user SET  Password=PASSWORD('newpass')
  WHERE user='fred';
```

You can also use `INSERT` queries to add users or `DELETE` queries to delete users from the user table. You can also modify the other tables to add or remove privileges. While this is rarely necessary, it gives you more complete access to the various settings stored in the tables and may be more practical than using `GRANT` and `REVOKE` in some cases.

When you have made changes to users or other tables in the `mysql` database, they are not automatically reloaded by the server. You can use the command `FLUSH PRIVILEGES` from the MySQL monitor, or `mysqladmin flush-privileges` from the command prompt, to force the tables to be reloaded. They will also be reloaded if you restart the MySQL server.

While modifying these tables directly is powerful, it can also be dangerous: You could easily delete the root username, for example, and lose root access to the server. Use these tables with caution, or use the `GRANT` and `REVOKE` commands instead. Also, be sure that you do not give any other users access to view or modify the tables in the `mysql` database.

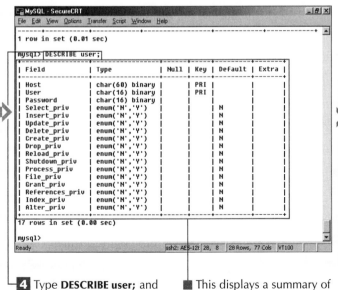

4 Type **DESCRIBE user;** and press Enter.

■ This displays a summary of the columns of the user table.

5 Type **DESCRIBE db;** and press Enter.

■ This displays the columns of the db table.

CONTROL NETWORK ACCESS

When you created users on the MySQL server earlier in this chapter, you did not specify a hostname in the GRANT command. This allows the user to connect to the MySQL server from any host on the network. While this is often what you need, when a user will only be connecting from the local host or a specific host, you can give them access only from certain hosts. This greatly reduces the possibility of the user account being used maliciously across the network.

To specify the hostname a user can connect from, use the @ symbol to combine the user name and hostname. For example, the following GRANT command creates a username, henry, that can be used to connect only from the machine running MySQL server:

```
GRANT ALL ON testdb.* TO henry@localhost
   IDENTIFIED BY 'password';
```

MySQL allows multiple users with the same name in the user table, as long as their hostnames are different. For this reason, limiting the user to the local host will only work if

you have not previously granted privileges to the same username without specifying a hostname. If you have done this, use REVOKE to remove the privileges for the original user before adding a user with a specified hostname.

You can specify a hostname or IP address that the user can connect from instead of using localhost. For example, the following GRANT command creates a username, sue, that can connect only from a host called example.com:

```
GRANT ALL ON testdb.* TO sue@example.com
   IDENTIFIED BY 'password';
```

If you need to allow access for a user from more than one host, simply repeat the GRANT command for each hostname. You can use the wildcard character % in the hostname to allow a set of host names or IP addresses. When you do this, you must enclose the username and hostname in quotation marks:

```
GRANT ALL ON testdb.* TO
'user1'@'192.168.%';
```

CONTROL NETWORK ACCESS

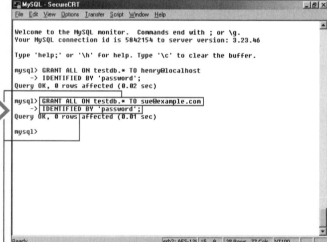

Note: This example uses the testdb database. You must be connected to MySQL as the root user or another user that can grant privileges.

1 From the MySQL monitor, type **GRANT ALL ON testdb.* TO henry@localhost** and press Enter.

2 Type **IDENTIFIED BY 'password';** and press Enter.

■ This creates a user that can access MySQL from the local host only.

Note: For security, choose your own password rather than using the one given here.

3 Type **GRANT ALL ON testdb.* TO sue@example.com** and press Enter.

4 Type **IDENTIFIED BY 'password';** and press Enter.

■ This creates a user that can connect to MySQL from the **example.com** host only.

Note: For security, choose a different password.

ADVANCED MYSQL SECURITY

MySQL includes a number of more advanced security options. You can use various startup options when you start the MySQL server to control specific aspects of security. You can also use the secure SSL protocol when connecting clients to a MySQL server.

SSL AND MYSQL

When you connect to a MySQL server using a client, the traffic between the two is not encrypted. This means that a machine on the network may be able to scan network traffic and discover passwords or data being transferred to and from the MySQL server.

To prevent this type of network vulnerability, MySQL supports the SSL (Secure Sockets Library) protocol, the same system used by Web servers to provide encrypted access to clients. Setting up SSL on MySQL requires re-compiling the server, if it was not initially set up with this option. For details on using SSL with MySQL, see the MySQL documentation at www.mysql.com.

USING STARTUP OPTIONS

The program that handles the MySQL server, `mysqld`, includes a variety of startup options. This section describes several options that you can use to manage the security of the MySQL server. To use these options, add one or more of them to the command line when you start the MySQL server. See Chapter 1 for information on starting the server.

--local-infile

This option should be followed by the = symbol and a value of zero or one. If the value is zero, the `LOAD DATA LOCAL INFILE` command is not permitted. This command may be a security risk because it allows files on the local system to be read and sent to the MySQL server. See Chapter 8 for details on using the `LOAD DATA` command.

Example:
```
mysqld -local-infile=0
```

--safe-show-database

Normally, any MySQL user can use the `SHOW DATABASES` command to display a complete list of databases on the server. If you use the `--safe-show-database` option, users are only shown the databases for which they have been granted one or more privileges.

--safe-user-create

If this option is included, users are not allowed to use `GRANT` to create a new user unless they have been explicitly granted the `INSERT` privilege for the user table in the `mysql` database. Users who have the `GRANT OPTION` privilege can still grant any privileges they have to any existing user.

--skip-show-database

If this option is used, the `SHOW DATABASES` command is not allowed at all, except for users who have been explicitly given the `SHOW DATABASES` privilege.

--skip-grant-tables

If this option is specified, the grant tables are not used at all — in other words, MySQL is running with no security at all. You should never use this option unless you have a special situation that requires MySQL security to be turned off.

One use for this command is for recovering access to the server when you have accidentally changed or deleted the root user. You can start the server with the `--skip-grant-tables` option, use `GRANT` to restore the root user, and then restart the server to turn security back on.

--skip-name-resolve

If this option is used, MySQL will not use DNS (domain name system) to convert hostnames to IP addresses. This effectively means that you cannot use a hostname when granting privileges to users, and you must explicitly use an IP address instead. This can increase security if your DNS server is not secure.

--skip-networking

If this option is specified, MySQL does not allow TCP/IP connections to the server across the network. Connections can only use UNIX sockets, which means that the local host is usually the only machine that can connect. This option will increase security if you do not require access to the server from other machines.

INTRODUCING PHP

PHP is one of the most popular Web scripting languages, and one of the most popular languages for creating applications to work with MySQL. PHP is a scripting language that is interpreted by Web servers. In particular, the popular open source Apache server can support PHP as a module, which allows for efficient execution of scripts.

This is only a brief introduction to PHP. PHP is a project of the Apache Software Foundation, and you can find out more or download software from the PHP Web site: www.php.net.

PHP and HTML

To use PHP, you embed a script within an HTML document and save the document with the `.php` or `.php3` extension. The Web server looks for PHP scripts in files with these extensions and interprets them before sending the document to the Web browser. Thus, the browser does not have access to the PHP script — only to the output of the script and the surrounding HTML.

You begin and end a PHP script with the `<?php` and `?>` tags. Anything between these two tags is interpreted as PHP rather than HTML. Anything outside these tags should be valid HTML.

Create Output

PHP supports a number of commands. One basic example is the `echo` command, which sends output to the Web browser as part of the HTML document. Each statement within the PHP script should end with a semicolon. The following example displays a message using PHP:

```php
<?php
echo "This is a test.";
?>
```

Using Variables

PHP supports *variables*, containers that can store numbers, text strings, or other data. PHP variables do not need to be defined before you use them, and they can store any type of data. The following example assigns a string value and a numeric value to two variables:

```php
<?php
$num=39;
$string="This is a test.";
?>
```

PHP also supports *arrays*, or variables with indexes. An array is basically a number of variables with a common name. The indexes for an array can be either numbers or string values. The following example assigns a value to an array element:

```php
<?php
$array[1]="number one";
?>
```

PHP variables can be included in string values. This is useful when you need to combine a variable's value with some text. The following example displays the value of the $num variable within a string:

```php
<?php
echo "The number is $num.";
?>
```

PHP and MySQL

PHP includes support for MySQL with a number of functions, described throughout this chapter. These allow you to connect to a MySQL server, submit a query to the server and retrieve the results, and perform other MySQL tasks. Virtually anything you can do with the MySQL monitor can also be done from a PHP script.

Using Functions

You can combine several statements into a group with a *function* in PHP. To define a function, you use the `function` keyword and surround the statements with braces. The following example defines a function called `print_bold`:

```php
<?php
function print_bold($text) {
   echo "<b>$text</b>";
}
?>
```

The values in parentheses are the *arguments*, or parameters, of the function. To call a function, you specify its name and the arguments in parentheses. The following statement calls the `print_bold` function:

```php
print_bold("This is a test.");
```

Functions can also return a value using the `return` keyword. When you call such a function, you can store its result in a variable.

Loops

PHP supports *loops* to perform a statement or a block of statements multiple times. The `while` statement defines a simple type of loop that repeats as long as a condition is true. The following is an example of a `while` loop:

```php
while ($num < 30) {
    $num = $num + 1;
    echo "The number is $num.";
}
```

PHP also supports `for` loops. This type of loop starts with a `for` statement specifying a beginning value, a condition, and an increment expression for a variable. The following `for` loop is equivalent to the previous `while` example:

```php
for ($num=0; $num<30; $num = $num + 1)
{
    echo "The number is $num.";
}
```

Operators

PHP supports a number of standard operators for working with numbers and strings. You can use these in any expression to work with constants or variables. The operators available in PHP are similar to those of MySQL. The following table summarizes some of the basic PHP operators:

OPERATOR	MEANING
+	Addition
–	Subtraction
*	Multiplication
/	Division
%	Modulo (remainder)
.	Concatenation (combines strings)

Conditional Statements

You can use the `if` statement in PHP to perform one or more statements conditionally. This statement uses a conditional expression followed by a single PHP statement, or a block of statements enclosed in braces. For example, this `if` statement displays a message if the `$num` variable has a value greater than 30:

```php
if ($num > 30) echo "It's bigger than
30.";
```

The condition in an `if` statement can use one or more conditional operators. These are similar to the conditional operators in MySQL, and are summarized in the table below.

OPERATOR	MEANING
==	Is equal to
!=	Is not equal to
>	Is greater than
<	Is less than
>=	Is greater than or equal to
<=	Is less than or equal to
&&	Logical AND
||	Logical OR

TEST THE PHP INSTALLATION

I f you are running your own Web server and are not already running PHP, you can install PHP on the server. Depending on your system, this can be a simple or complicated process. Most Linux distributions include PHP, so you may not need to do anything.

If you are using a shared hosting provider, there is a good chance it supports PHP. In particular, most installations using the Apache Web server are set up to run PHP. Consult your host's instructions to find out how to use PHP on the server.

To test whether your server already supports PHP, create a file with a .php extension and include the following text in the file:

```
<?php
  phpinfo();
?>
```

The `phpinfo` command displays a detailed list of information about the current PHP installation. If this information is displayed when you load the .php file you

created into a Web browser, then PHP is installed. Next, check the Configure Command entry for the `with-mysql` option. If this is present, your PHP installation is set up to work with MySQL.

If PHP does not work or is not configured to work with MySQL, you may need to install PHP. If you are running Linux, first check with the vendor of your Linux distribution to see if they have a prepackaged binary version of PHP available. This provides an easy way to install PHP. If a binary version is not available, you will need to install PHP from source code.

You can download the PHP source code from the PHP Web site at www.php.net. This site also provides detailed instructions for installing PHP on a wide variety of systems. The download will be in the form of a .tar.gz archive. You can use the `tar zxf` command to expand the files from the archive. After the files are extracted, you will need to use a `configure` command to choose how PHP will be configured, and then compile PHP following the instructions.

TEST THE PHP INSTALLATION

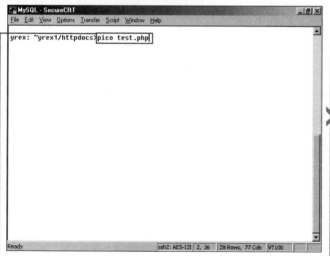

1 From the UNIX command prompt, type **pico test.php** and press Enter.

■ This opens a text file for editing.

Note: Use the appropriate command to open a file on your system. On Windows, you can use Notepad to create the file. With earlier versions of PHP, you will need to use the .php3 extension.

2 Type **<?php** to begin the test PHP script and press Enter.

3 Type the **phpinfo();** command to display PHP information, and press Enter.

Extra

For Windows servers, a binary version of PHP is available from the PHP Web site at www.php.net. PHP for Windows is available in two packages: one as a .zip archive, and a second as an .exe file that automatically begins the installation. Both packages include built-in support for MySQL, so you do not need to change the configuration to support MySQL.

If you are using Microsoft's IIS (Internet Information Server) or PWS (Personal Web Server), included with some versions of Windows, the .exe version of the PHP binary will automatically configure your server to work with PHP.

If you are using the Apache Web server under Windows, download the .zip version of the PHP package. This includes everything you need to support PHP as an Apache module. At this writing, this feature only works reliably with PHP 1.x, and does not yet support the new PHP 2.x versions.

The www.php.net site includes links to external sites where you can find binary versions of PHP for Mac OS X, Novell NetWare, and a variety of other systems.

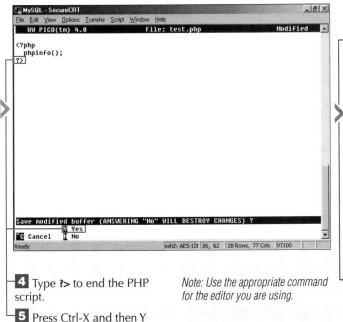

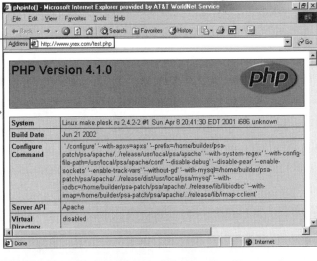

4 Type ?> to end the PHP script.

5 Press Ctrl-X and then Y to save the file and exit the editor.

Note: Use the appropriate command for the editor you are using.

6 Type the URL for the test file into a Web browser.

■ If the PHP information is displayed, PHP is working on your server.

INSTALL AND TEST PHPMYADMIN

PhpMyAdmin is a free, open source application that gives you a user-friendly interface to a MySQL database or an entire MySQL server. While this program is written in PHP and requires PHP, you can use it to manage your databases and tables even if you do not know how to program in PHP. This utility allows you to create databases and tables, browse through data, and perform most MySQL queries from a Web interface.

To use phpMyAdmin, you must first download and install it. Because it is written in PHP, it should work on most Web servers that support PHP. You can download the phpMyAdmin installation files from the project's Web page at www.phpmyadmin.net.

The installation files are available in two formats, with the PHP or PHP3 extension. You can use whichever version will best work on your server. In most cases, the version with PHP extensions will work best. Downloads are available in various archive formats, including .tar.gz, typically used on UNIX systems, and .zip, usually used under Windows.

To install phpMyAdmin, you can simply install the files from the archive in a directory on your Web server. After the files are in place, you will need to edit the config.inc.php file and specify a username, password, and hostname for the MySQL server.

After you install phpMyAdmin, you can use it to perform most of the same functions as the MySQL monitor from any Web browser. This is very useful for beginners to MySQL and even for experienced users who want a more convenient interface to the database.

INSTALL AND TEST PHPMYADMIN

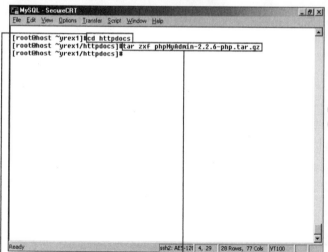

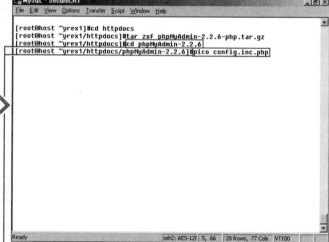

1 Type **cd** followed by the name of a directory on your Web server and press Enter.

Note: This assumes you have downloaded the phpMyAdmin installation file to the same directory.

2 Type **tar zxf** *filename*, replacing *filename* with the name of the .tar.gz file, and press Enter.

■ The files are extracted into a new directory.

3 Type **cd phpmyadmin-** *version*, replacing *version* with the version you downloaded, and press Enter.

4 Type **pico config.inc.php** and press Enter.

Note: Use the appropriate editor command on your system. The file may end in .php3, depending on the version you downloaded.

Extra

You can use phpMyAdmin to perform virtually any task on the MySQL server, including dangerous tasks like dropping a database or running a DELETE query. Because you have specified a MySQL username and password in phpMyAdmin's configuration, anyone who can access the Web page can access the database.

Because of this, you should secure the directory where you have installed phpMyAdmin in some way. Most Web servers allow you to create an .htaccess file that requires a username and password. You can secure the page in this way, or place it on a private Web server or a secure directory you have already configured.

In addition to securing the Web location where phpMyAdmin is installed, you should also use a username and password in the configuration file that allow only a minimum of access. You can create a special user in MySQL that has access to only a certain database, and this way other databases are inaccessible from the phpMyAdmin utility.

See Chapter 11 for information on creating users in MySQL and assigning privileges. The phpMyAdmin Web page at www.phpmyadmin.net/ has more information on security and authentication.

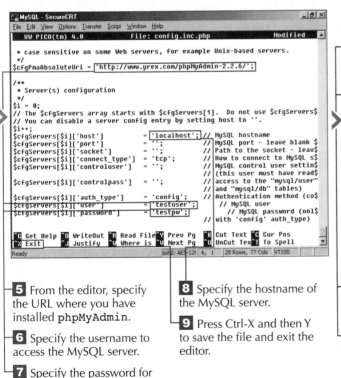

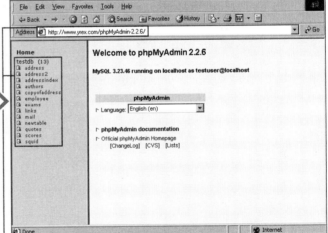

5 From the editor, specify the URL where you have installed **phpMyAdmin**.

6 Specify the username to access the MySQL server.

7 Specify the password for the MySQL user.

8 Specify the hostname of the MySQL server.

9 Press Ctrl-X and then Y to save the file and exit the editor.

10 Type the URL where you installed **phpMyAdmin** into a Web browser.

■ You can now access the databases and tables permitted for the username you specified.

Note: See the security notes in the Extra section.

Note: You may want to create a user specifically for running phpMyAdmin. See Chapter 11 for details.

MANAGE DATA WITH PHPMYADMIN

After you have installed phpMyAdmin, you can use it as an alternative to the MySQL monitor and general-purpose MySQL client. The phpMyAdmin screen is divided into two frames. The left frame displays a list of the databases you have access to and can list the tables within each database. The right frame displays the data with which you are currently working.

To work with a table in phpMyAdmin, click its entry in the left frame. The right frame displays a summary of the table's structure and several additional options. After you have selected a table, you can select several options.

The Browse option displays the data from the table in pages, using a series of SELECT queries. An Edit link is displayed to the left of each row of data. You can click this to edit the row in a Web form. The Delete link displays a confirmation prompt and allows you to delete a row from the table.

The SQL option for a table allows you to enter your own MySQL queries. A default SELECT query is displayed, and you can edit the query and click the Go button. The results of the query, if any, are displayed on the next screen.

The Select option for the table displays a friendly interface that allows you to create a SELECT query. You can enter a WHERE clause, select a value for the LIMIT clause, and enter text values with wildcards.

The Insert option for a table allows you to add a row to the table using a Web form. Fields are displayed for each of the columns of the table, and you can enter a value for a column or select a function such as ENCRYPT to encrypt a string or NOW for the current date.

MANAGE DATA WITH PHPMYADMIN

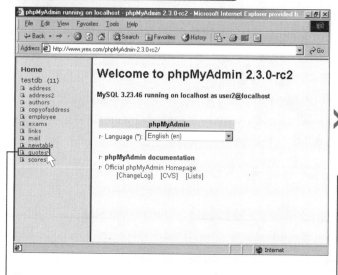

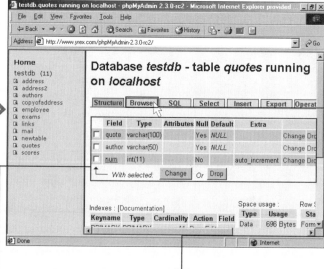

1 From the main phpMyAdmin screen, select the table with which to work on the left side of the screen.

Note: This example shows the quotes table in the testdb database.

■ The structure of the selected table is displayed.

2 Click the Browse link to display the contents of the table.

Extra

The `phpMyAdmin` utility includes several other options for working with tables. The Export page allows you to export data from the table. You can choose to export the table data, the table structure, or both. An option is included to format the data in a CSV format that can be imported into Microsoft Excel, or you can customize the formatting. You can also choose to limit the number of rows of data that will be included in the exported file.

The Operations page includes an interface to several MySQL options, including options to sort the table data by a particular column value, rename the table, move it to a different database or table, or copy it to another table. There are also options to optimize or repair the table.

The Options page allows you to modify the table options. This includes the table type, the comment associated with the table, and a number of other options.

Two final options are included for tables: Empty deletes all of the rows of a table, and Drop deletes the table completely. Both of these prompt you for confirmation before deleting anything.

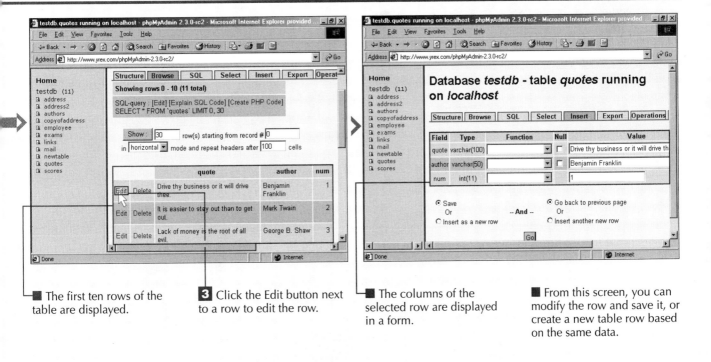

■ The first ten rows of the table are displayed.

3 Click the Edit button next to a row to edit the row.

■ The columns of the selected row are displayed in a form.

■ From this screen, you can modify the row and save it, or create a new table row based on the same data.

MANAGE THE MYSQL SERVER WITH PHPMYADMIN

I n addition to working with data in MySQL tables, you can use `phpMyAdmin` to manage various aspects of the MySQL server. This allows you to display information about the server's current status, manage users, and create and drop databases.

In order to use these features, you must specify a user with root access in the config.inc.php file. If the user has access, `phpMyAdmin` includes a number of extra features on the main page. The first of these are interfaces to various `SHOW` commands in MySQL.

The Show MySQL runtime information option displays status information, similar to `SHOW STATUS`. The Show MySQL system variables option is equivalent to `SHOW VARIABLES`. The Show processes option displays a list of current threads, the same as the `SHOW PROCESSLIST` command.

The Reload MySQL option executes a `FLUSH` command to reload the security tables and configuration files. The Users

option opens the user table in the `mysql` database, and allows you to manage users.

The Database Statistics option displays a summary of the size of each database, and the total amount of disk storage used by all tables. This is useful to keep track of which tables are using the most space.

Finally, the Create new database option allows you to create a new database, assuming your username has the correct privileges. You can also delete a database using `phpMyAdmin`. To drop a database, first select it from the list in the left column, and then click the Drop link at the top of the page. You will be asked to confirm this action.

Because using a user with root access for `phpMyAdmin` allows it to perform some powerful and potentially dangerous functions, be sure you are running it on a secure Web server or behind a firewall. Otherwise it represents a serious security risk.

MANAGE THE MYSQL SERVER WITH PHPMYADMIN

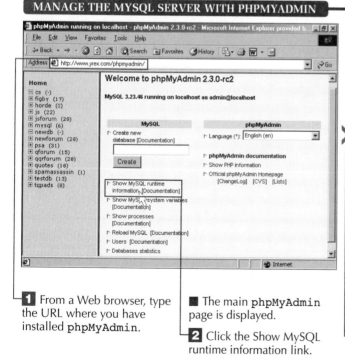

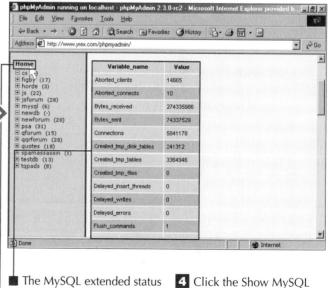

1 From a Web browser, type the URL where you have installed `phpMyAdmin`.

■ The main `phpMyAdmin` page is displayed.

2 Click the Show MySQL runtime information link.

■ The MySQL extended status values are displayed.

3 Click the Home link to return to the main `phpMyAdmin` page.

4 Click the Show MySQL system variables link.

Extra

When you select the Users option, the user table in the mysql database is opened, and the list of current users is displayed. The Edit link next to each username allows you to change the user's hostname and assign privileges. The Delete link deletes a user. The Grants link displays the current list of privileges granted to a user, and allows you to delete or modify the privileges.

The Users page also includes a form that allows you to create a new user. You can specify the hostname the user is allowed to connect from, a password, and the privileges the user should be assigned for a particular database.

You can also open the mysql database directly in phpMyAdmin to work with the various security tables. Keep in mind that this feature is potentially dangerous; if you mistakenly delete the root user, for example, you can lose access to the server. See Chapter 11 for more information about managing MySQL security.

For details on using phpMyAdmin to manage a MySQL server, see the official documentation. The complete phpMyAdmin documentation is usually installed when you set up this utility. To access your local copy of the documentation, follow the phpMyAdmin documentation link on the main page.

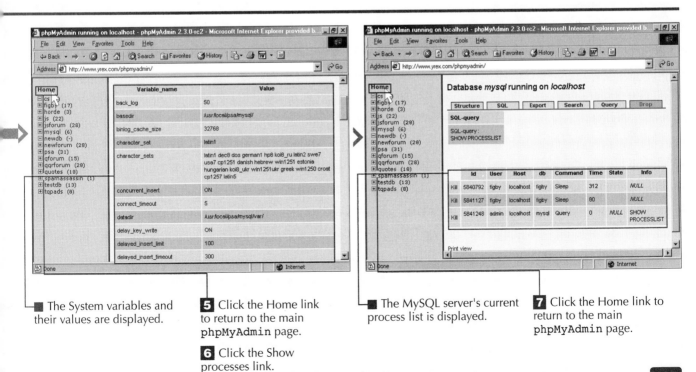

■ The System variables and their values are displayed.

5 Click the Home link to return to the main phpMyAdmin page.

6 Click the Show processes link.

■ The MySQL server's current process list is displayed.

7 Click the Home link to return to the main phpMyAdmin page.

CONNECT TO A MYSQL SERVER

Before you can use any MySQL functions in PHP, you must first open a connection to the MySQL server. You can do this using the `mysql_connect` function. To use this function, specify a hostname, username, and password for the MySQL server:

```
$link=mysql_connect("localhost", "testuser",
"testpw");
```

This command opens a connection to the MySQL server and returns a link identifier that can be used to perform operations on the server. In this example, the identifier is stored in the `$link` variable. If the connection to the server is not opened successfully, the boolean value `false` is returned, and an error message is displayed.

If you do not specify one or more of the parameters for the `mysql_connect` command, PHP assumes default values. It attempts to use `localhost` as the server hostname, the

username the Web server uses for PHP, and no password. If these values do not work on your MySQL server, an error will be returned unless you specify a valid hostname, username, and password.

After you have opened a connection to the MySQL server, you can use the connection throughout the PHP script. If you only have a single connection to a single server open, you can use it without needing the link identifier.

The connection to the MySQL server stays open until your PHP script ends, or until you explicitly close the connection. To close a connection, use the `mysql_close` command and specify the link identifier returned when you opened the connection. This command closes the link opened by the previous example:

```
mysql_close($link);
```

CONNECT TO A MYSQL SERVER

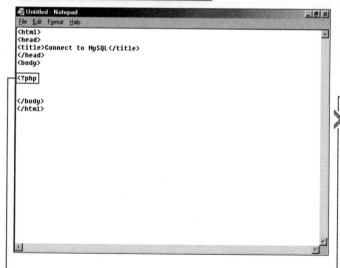

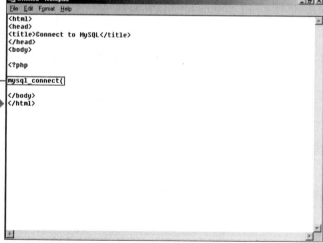

1 Type **<?php** to start the PHP script.

Note: You will usually want to include basic HTML tags, as shown here.

2 Type **mysql_connect(** to begin the command.

Extra

MySQL also supports *persistent connections*. This is a special type of connection that stays open even after the PHP script ends. If the same user attempts to connect to the server a second time, PHP finds the existing connection and returns its identifier rather than returning a new connection.

To use persistent connections, use `mysql_pconnect()` to open the connection. The arguments for this function are the same as for the standard `mysql_connect()` function. You cannot close a persistent connection manually; instead, the server will keep the connection open until MySQL's `wait_timeout` period expires. See Chapter 10 for information on setting this timeout value on a MySQL server.

Example:
```
$link=mysql_pconnect("localhost", "testuser", "testpw");
// Add statements that use the database server here
```

Persistent connections can be more efficient in an application where the same user will make many queries on different PHP scripts. In a simple application, they are less efficient because connections are left open and not used further, and MySQL may run out of connections for future clients.

Persistent connections only work if PHP is running as a module on an Apache Web server. They are not currently supported when PHP is run as a CGI program or on other Web servers.

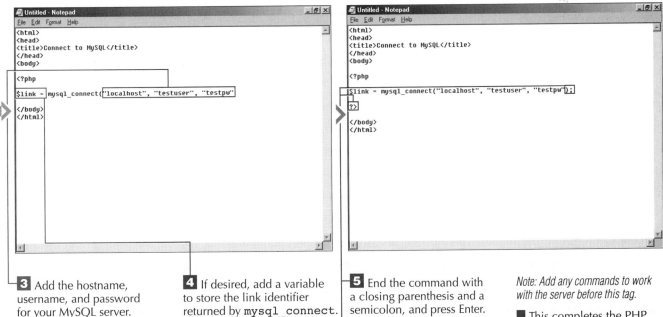

3 Add the hostname, username, and password for your MySQL server.

Note: See Chapter 11 for information on creating a username and password.

4 If desired, add a variable to store the link identifier returned by `mysql_connect`.

5 End the command with a closing parenthesis and a semicolon, and press Enter.

6 Type **?>** to end the script.

Note: Add any commands to work with the server before this tag.

■ This completes the PHP script to connect to MySQL.

DISPLAY QUERY RESULTS

After you have connected to the MySQL server from a PHP script, you can run one or more MySQL queries. Often, you will want to send a SELECT query to the server and display the resulting data. PHP includes a number of ways to receive data from the SQL server.

As with the MySQL monitor, before you can make a query, you must select a database. To do this, use the mysql_select_db function. To use this function, specify the database name as a string:

```
mysql_select_db("testdb");
```

After you have selected a database, you can send an SQL query to the server using the mysql_query function. To use this function, specify the query as a string. The following example sends a simple SELECT query to the server:

```
$result=mysql_query("SELECT quote, author
FROM quotes");
```

If the query is successful, the mysql_query function returns a result identifier. In this example, the $result variable stores the result identifier. You can use this identifier later in the script to display the query results.

While the result identifier indicates that the query was successful, this only means that MySQL understood the query — it does not mean there are definitely one or more rows of data in the result. If the query is unsuccessful, the mysql_query function returns a FALSE value instead. Some queries, such as INSERT and DELETE, do not return data from the server. In this case, mysql_query simply returns TRUE if the query was successful.

To display query results, you can use the mysql_fetch_row function. This function accepts a result identifier, and returns the next row of the result as an array. The array includes all of the columns of the result in order. You can repeat the function to retrieve all of the result rows. The following example uses a while loop to retrieve all of the rows:

```
while(list($quote, $author) =
mysql_fetch_row($result)) {
    echo "<p>$quote --$author</p>";   }
```

This example retrieves each row into the $quote and $author variables. These are used with an echo statement to display each row as an HTML paragraph. The list function allows the array returned by mysql_fetch_row to be stored in two regular variables instead of an array, and is a convenient way to handle simple queries.

DISPLAY QUERY RESULTS

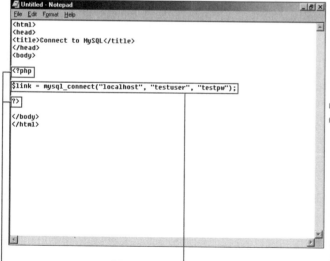

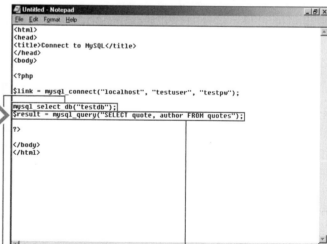

Note: Start with a basic HTML document.

1 Type **<?php** and **?>** to begin and end the PHP script.

2 Type **mysql_connect** to begin the statement that connects to the database, and add the details for the server, username, and password.

3 Type **mysql_select_db** followed by the database name to select the database for future queries.

4 Type **mysql_query** to begin the function that sends the query to the MySQL server, and add the query and a variable to store the result identifier.

Extra

You can optionally specify a link identifier from `mysql_connect` as a second parameter to the `mysql_select_db` and `mysql_query` functions. However, these and most other MySQL functions in PHP default to using the last connection you opened, so this is usually not necessary.

You can use the `mysql_db_query` function to avoid selecting a database first. This function is similar to `mysql_query`, but accepts a database name as its first parameter.

To use this script or any PHP script you create, you must first save the edited file, and then upload it to your Web server that supports PHP. If you are using PHP version 3, save the file with the .php3 extension. For PHP version 4, save the file with the .php extension.

After the file is saved, you will need to upload it to the correct directory of the Web server. You can do this using the same program you use to upload HTML documents. Typically this is done using the FTP protocol.

After the file is uploaded to the server, you can use a Web browser to display the result. PHP does not require a particular browser because it creates HTML output. PHP pages display just like HTML pages.

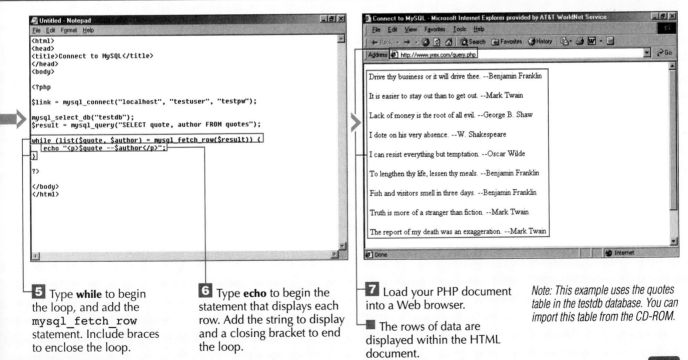

5 Type **while** to begin the loop, and add the `mysql_fetch_row` statement. Include braces to enclose the loop.

6 Type **echo** to begin the statement that displays each row. Add the string to display and a closing bracket to end the loop.

7 Load your PHP document into a Web browser.

■ The rows of data are displayed within the HTML document.

Note: This example uses the quotes table in the testdb database. You can import this table from the CD-ROM.

STORE QUERY RESULTS AS OBJECTS

When you use the `mysql_fetch_row` function to retrieve rows from a query, you must specify the column names in the query and retrieve them in the same order. If you are trying to use a query that returns all columns of a table, and are unsure of the order the columns will be returned in, you can use `mysql_fetch_object` instead.

For example, suppose you have made the following query to the MySQL server. This query retrieves all columns and all rows from the quotes table.

```
$result=mysql_query("SELECT * FROM quotes");
```

To retrieve the data, you can use `mysql_fetch_object`. This returns an object whose properties are the column values for the row. Thus, you can refer directly to the MySQL column names rather than assigning your own variable names to each column. The following `while` loop uses the `mysql_fetch_object` function to retrieve and display each row:

```
while($row = mysql_fetch_object($result)) {
    echo "<p>$row->quote --$row->author</p>";
}
```

In this example, the `$row` variable stores each row. You can use the `->` operator to refer to each MySQL column name as a property of the object. Thus, you can refer to the quote column as `$row->quote` and the author column as `$row->author`. Because the MySQL query specified the wildcard `*` rather than specific column names, all columns of the table are available from the object.

You can use whichever function you are most comfortable with to return data from a MySQL query. The data returned is the same; only the method you use to access it changes. PHP includes several other `fetch` commands that return the results in different formats, such as `mysql_fetch_assoc` to store the data in an associative array. This type of array uses column names to index the results rather than numeric indexes.

STORE QUERY RESULTS AS OBJECTS

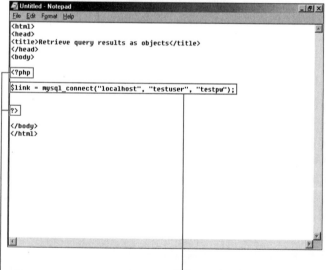

Note: Start with a basic HTML document.

1 Type **<?php** and **?>** to begin and end the PHP script.

2 Type **mysql_connect** followed by the correct user, password, and hostname to connect to the database.

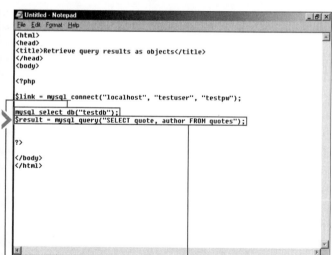

3 Type **mysql_select_db** followed by the database name to select the database for future queries.

4 Type **$result = mysql_query** to begin the function that sends the query to the MySQL server, and add the query in quotation marks.

Note: This example uses the quotes table in the testdb database. You can import this table from the CD-ROM.

Extra

If you are running into MySQL errors while attempting to use a database from PHP, it is useful to display the results within your PHP script. The following PHP script adds `if` statements to check whether each MySQL command succeeded. It displays an appropriate error message if any command fails.

Example:
```
<?php
$link = mysql_connect("localhost", "testuser", "testpw");
if (!$link) echo "Failed to connect to MySQL server!";
$status=mysql_select_db("testdb");
if (!$status) echo "Failed to select database!";
$result=mysql_query("SELECT * FROM quotes");
if (!$result) echo "The MySQL query failed!";
while($row = mysql_fetch_object($result)) {
    echo "<p>$row->quote --$row->author</p>";   }
?>
```

This example checks the results of the `mysql_connect`, `mysql_select_db`, `mysql_query`, and `mysql_fetch_object` commands. All of these return a `FALSE` value if they fail. The one condition that these do not account for is if the query succeeds but returns a zero-row result. If this happens, the `while` loop will end immediately without displaying any data.

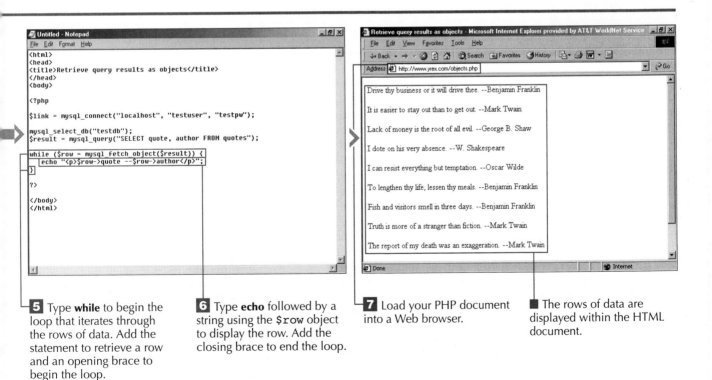

5 Type **while** to begin the loop that iterates through the rows of data. Add the statement to retrieve a row and an opening brace to begin the loop.

6 Type **echo** followed by a string using the **$row** object to display the row. Add the closing brace to end the loop.

7 Load your PHP document into a Web browser.

■ The rows of data are displayed within the HTML document.

INSERT A RECORD FROM PHP

Y ou can use the `mysql_query` command in PHP to send an INSERT query to the MySQL server. When you do this, a result identifier is not returned because an INSERT query does not return any data from the MySQL server. Instead, the result returned from `mysql_query` is a simple `true` or `false` value that indicates whether the query was successful.

For example, the following PHP statements add a record to the scores table and display a message indicating success or failure:

```
$query="INSERT INTO scores (name, score)
VALUES ('Fred', 92)";
$success = mysql_query($query);
if ($success) echo "The INSERT query was
successful.";
    else echo "Error: INSERT query failed.";
```

This example stores the query in the `$query` variable, and then uses the `mysql_query` function to send the query to

the MySQL server. The result of the query is stored in the `$success` variable. The `if` statement checks this variable and displays a success message, and the `else` statement displays an error message if the insert was unsuccessful. Unlike SELECT queries, an INSERT query does not return a result identifier. The result stored in the `$success` variable will be a simple TRUE or FALSE value.

As with other MySQL queries, you must first connect to the MySQL server using the `mysql_connect` function, and then select a database with `mysql_select_db` before attempting to insert a row. You must be connected using a MySQL username that has the INSERT privilege for the table you are using in the INSERT command.

Because double quotation marks are used to define the `$query` string, you cannot use double quotes inside the query. You can substitute single quotation marks within the query. Only values to be stored in text columns need to be quoted. You can use a PHP variable within the INSERT query by including its name in the `$query` string.

INSERT A RECORD FROM PHP

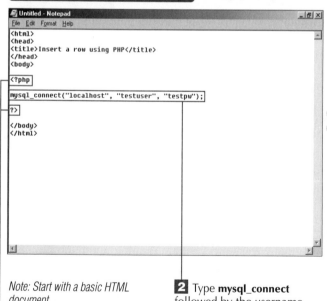

Note: Start with a basic HTML document.

1 Type **<?php** and **?>** to begin and end the PHP script.

2 Type **mysql_connect** followed by the username, host, and password to connect to the MySQL server.

3 Type **mysql_select_db** followed by the database name to select the database.

Note: This example uses the testdb database and the scores table. You can import this table from the CD-ROM.

4 Type **$query=** followed by the MySQL query in quotation marks.

5 Type **$success = mysql_query ($query);** to create the statement that sends the query to the server.

Apply It

If a table includes an auto-increment column, it will automatically be updated with a new unique value each time you insert a record. After you have inserted a row into a table from PHP, you can use the `mysql_insert_id` function to find out what number was assigned to the auto-increment field in the `INSERT` query.

This technique is useful because you now have a value that you can use to find the inserted row in a subsequent query. Without this feature, you would have to use a separate query to find the newest row, and even that may find a row inserted by a different user.

For example, the following PHP code inserts a row into the quotes table and then displays the ID assigned to the auto-increment field.

Example:
```
$link=mysql_connect("localhost", "testuser", "testpw");
mysql_select_db("testdb");
$query = "INSERT INTO quotes (quote, author) VALUES ";
$query .= "('Union gives strength.', 'Aesop')";
$success = mysql_query($query);
if ($success) {
    echo "The INSERT query was successful.";
    echo "The record number is: " + mysql_insert_id();
} else echo "Error: INSERT query failed.";
```

You can optionally specify a link identifier from `mysql_connect` with the `mysql_insert_id` function. If you do not use an identifier, the most recent connection used is assumed.

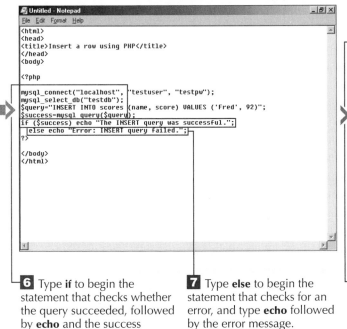

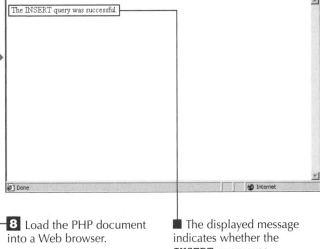

6 Type **if** to begin the statement that checks whether the query succeeded, followed by **echo** and the success message in quotation marks.

7 Type **else** to begin the statement that checks for an error, and type **echo** followed by the error message.

8 Load the PHP document into a Web browser.

■ The displayed message indicates whether the `INSERT` query was successful.

DELETE RECORDS USING PHP

You can also use PHP to send a DELETE query to the MySQL server. As with an INSERT query, when you use the mysql_query function with a DELETE query, a simple true or false result is returned that indicates whether the delete was successful.

To delete one or more rows of a table, you usually will need to specify a WHERE clause. Without this clause, all records of the table would be deleted. The following PHP statements send a DELETE query to the MySQL server:

```
$query="DELETE FROM scores WHERE name =
'fred'";
$success=mysql_query($query);
if ($success) echo "The DELETE query was
successful.";
   else echo "Error: DELETE query failed.";
```

These statements store the query in the $query variable and send it to the MySQL server using the mysql_query function. The if statement displays a message if the DELETE query succeeded, and the else statement displays a message if the query failed.

Note that a failed query is not the same as a nonmatching WHERE clause. If the WHERE clause does not match any records, the mysql_query function will still succeed. The query will only fail if the server cannot be reached, or if there is a syntax error in the query.

You can find out how many rows were affected by the DELETE query with the mysql_affected_rows function. This function returns the number of rows affected by the most recent DELETE, INSERT, or UPDATE query. You can use this to determine how many rows the WHERE clause matched.

DELETE RECORDS USING PHP

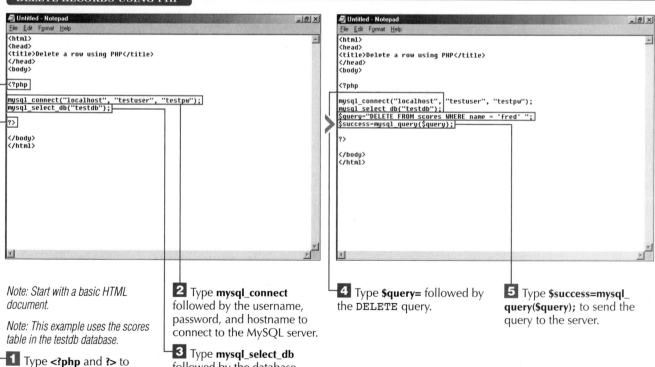

Note: Start with a basic HTML document.

Note: This example uses the scores table in the testdb database.

1 Type **<?php** and **?>** to begin and end the PHP script.

2 Type **mysql_connect** followed by the username, password, and hostname to connect to the MySQL server.

3 Type **mysql_select_db** followed by the database name to select the database.

4 Type **$query=** followed by the DELETE query.

5 Type **$success=mysql_query($query);** to send the query to the server.

Apply It

You can also use the `mysql_query` function in PHP to send an UPDATE query to the MySQL server to modify one or more rows of a table. As with an INSERT or DELETE query, the result of an UPDATE query is a TRUE or FALSE value indicating whether the query was successful. You can use the `mysql_affected_rows` function to determine how many rows were affected by the UPDATE query.

The following example updates the quotes table. It uses the MySQL function UPPER to convert the quote field of each row to uppercase, and then displays the number of affected rows.

Example:
```php
<?php
mysql_connect("localhost", "testuser", "testpw");
mysql_select_db("testdb");
$query="UPDATE quotes SET quote = UPPER(quote)";
$result = mysql_query($query);
$numrows = mysql_affected_rows();
if ($result) echo "Rows updated: $numrows";
    else echo "Error: UPDATE query failed.";
?>
```

As with other MySQL queries, the `mysql_query` function will return a TRUE value indicating success even if no rows were modified by the query. This can happen if you have used a WHERE clause that did not match any rows of the table. Your script can check the `mysql_affected_rows` function to make sure the correct number of rows has been updated.

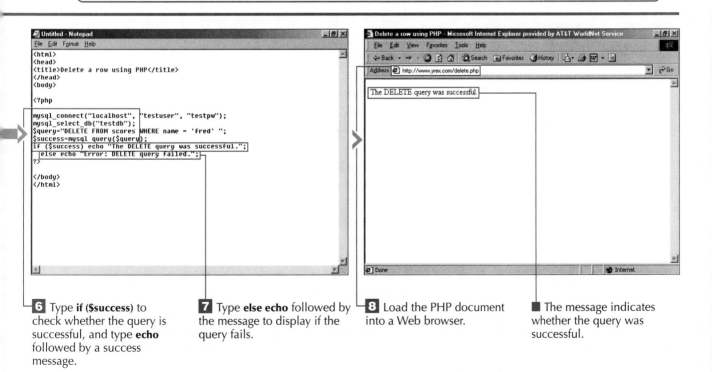

6 Type **if ($success)** to check whether the query is successful, and type **echo** followed by a success message.

7 Type **else echo** followed by the message to display if the query fails.

8 Load the PHP document into a Web browser.

■ The message indicates whether the query was successful.

CREATE A FORM TO ADD RECORDS

One of the strengths of PHP is its ability to work directly in an HTML document. You can create an HTML form and use a PHP script in the same document to write the data entered into the form to a MySQL database. As an example, you can create an HTML form and PHP script that allow you to add a row to the quotes table.

The <form> tag in HTML starts an HTML form. You can use the action attribute of the <form> tag to specify the CGI or PHP program that handles the results of the form. In the case of PHP, you can specify the same file that contains the form itself. The following HTML defines a form that calls the add.php script:

```
<form method="get" action="add.php">
Quote: <input type="text" name="quote"><br>
Author: <input type="text"
name="author"><br>
<input type="submit" name="add"
value="Submit">
</form>
```

After you have defined the form, you can create the PHP script to handle the form results. PHP automatically stores the form values as variables. In this case, the $quote and $author variables store the entered data. You can make these variables part of an INSERT query and send it to the MySQL server with the mysql_query function. The following PHP code adds a record from the form:

```
if ($add) {
    mysql_connect("localhost", "testuser",
"testpw");
    mysql_select_db("testdb");
$query="INSERT INTO quotes(quote, author)";
$query .=" VALUES( '$quote','$author')";
$result=mysql_query($query);
    if ($result) echo "<b>Added one row
successfully.</b>";
}
```

The if statement checks the $add variable, which is set when the Submit button has been clicked. The rest of the script creates a query and sends it to the MySQL server.

CREATE A FORM TO ADD RECORDS

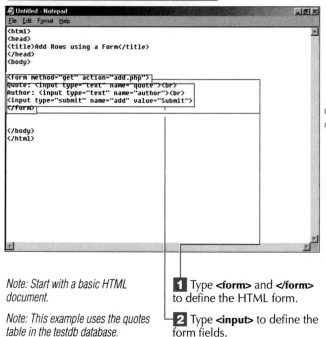

Note: Start with a basic HTML document.

Note: This example uses the quotes table in the testdb database.

1 Type **<form>** and **</form>** to define the HTML form.

2 Type **<input>** to define the form fields.

3 Type **<?php** and **?>** to begin and end the PHP script.

4 Type **if ($add)** to begin a statement that checks whether the form has already been submitted.

5 Type **mysql_connect** followed by the username, password, and hostname to connect to the MySQL server.

6 Type **mysql_select_db** followed by the database name to select the database.

The form in this example uses the `<form>` HTML tag to begin a form. Within the `<form>` and `</form>` tags, you can use various HTML tags to define form elements for different input types. This example uses two different input types.

The `<input type="text">` tag defines a text input field. The `name` attribute assigns a name to the field. This name is used as the PHP variable name to store the data entered into the field.

The `<input type="submit">` tag is also used in this example. This tag defines a Submit button. When you click this button, the form data is submitted to the script specified in the `action` attribute of the `<form>` tag. This tag has a `name` attribute to name the button, and a `value` attribute to define the text displayed on the button.

The Submit button in this example has the name `add` and the value "Submit". As with other form fields, this name is used as a PHP variable name when you submit the form to a PHP script. The `if` statement within the PHP script checks for the `$add` variable to see whether the form has already been submitted.

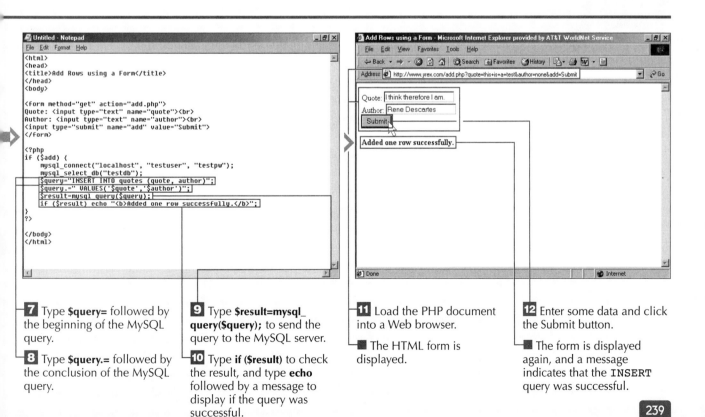

7 Type **$query=** followed by the beginning of the MySQL query.

8 Type **$query.=** followed by the conclusion of the MySQL query.

9 Type **$result=mysql_query($query);** to send the query to the MySQL server.

10 Type **if ($result)** to check the result, and type **echo** followed by a message to display if the query was successful.

11 Load the PHP document into a Web browser.

■ The HTML form is displayed.

12 Enter some data and click the Submit button.

■ The form is displayed again, and a message indicates that the INSERT query was successful.

239

CREATE A DATABASE SEARCH FORM

Another common application of PHP is to create a search engine for a database. You can use an HTML form and a short PHP script to search a table. The PHP script runs a SELECT query using the value entered into the form and displays the results.

As an example, you can create a form to search the quotes table. The following HTML tags define the form:

```
<form method="get" action="search.php">
Search for: <input type="text"
name="search">
<input type="submit" name="submit"
value="Search">
</form>
```

This defines a form that sends data to search.php, the filename of the current page. There is one text field named search to specify a search term, and a Submit button named submit. The PHP script can check for the submit button, and if it has been clicked, display the results of a search. The following section of PHP handles the search:

```
if ($submit) {
   echo "Searching for: <b>$search</b><br>";
   mysql_connect("localhost", "testuser",
"testpw");
   mysql_select_db("testdb");
   $query="SELECT * FROM quotes WHERE quote
LIKE '%$search%' ";
   $result=mysql_query($query);
   while ($row = mysql_fetch_object($result)) {
     echo "Found: $row->quote --$row->author<br>";
   }
}
```

This code creates a SELECT query, placing the $search value from the form into a WHERE clause. It then uses mysql_query to submit the query to MySQL, and a while loop with the mysql_fetch_object function to display the results.

CREATE A DATABASE SEARCH FORM

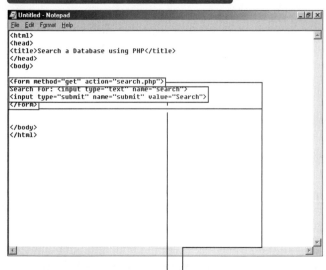

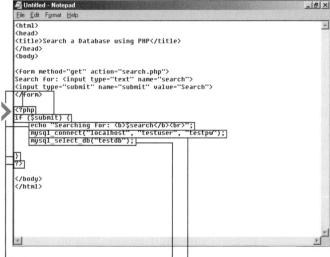

Note: Start with a basic HTML document.

Note: This example uses the quotes table in the testdb database. You can import this table from the CD-ROM.

1 Type **<form>** and **</form>** to define the HTML form.

2 Type **<input>** to define the form fields.

3 Type **<?php** and **?>** to begin and end the PHP script.

4 Type **if ($submit)** to begin the statement that checks whether the Submit button has been clicked.

5 Type **echo** followed by text to display at the beginning of the search results.

6 Type **mysql_connect** followed by the username, password, and hostname to connect to the MySQL server.

7 Type **mysql_select_db ("testdb");** to select the database.

Apply It

You can use a separate SELECT query using the COUNT(*) keyword to count the number of results that will be returned from the query. This is useful in a large table, because displaying all of the rows and counting them would be slow. It is also useful if your script needs to display data in multiple pages. You can use the count to determine a LIMIT clause to use for each page of data.

The following PHP code could be added to the example to display a count before the search results.

Example:
```
$q="SELECT COUNT(*) FROM quotes AS c WHERE quote LIKE '%$search%' ";
$cr=mysql_query($q);
$r = mysql_fetch_object($cr);
echo "Number of quotes found: $r->c";
```

This example uses the $q variable to store the count query, and the $cr variable for the result of the query. It retrieves a row of the result using mysql_fetch_object into the $r variable. Only a single row is returned, and the $r->c field is the number of records found.

PHP also includes the mysql_num_rows function. This function accepts a result identifier as a parameter, and returns the number of rows in the result. You can use this to find out how many rows a SELECT query returned without using COUNT. However, this technique is very inefficient because it requires the MySQL server to process the entire SELECT. It is better to use COUNT unless you will be retrieving all of the rows from the SELECT query.

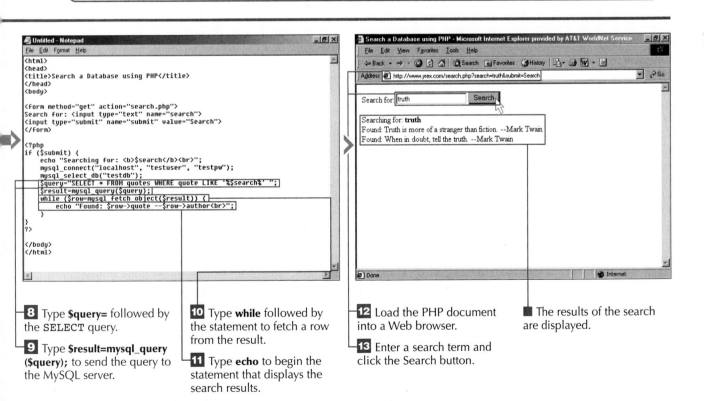

8 Type **$query=** followed by the SELECT query.

9 Type **$result=mysql_query ($query);** to send the query to the MySQL server.

10 Type **while** followed by the statement to fetch a row from the result.

11 Type **echo** to begin the statement that displays the search results.

12 Load the PHP document into a Web browser.

13 Enter a search term and click the Search button.

■ The results of the search are displayed.

INTRODUCING PERL

Perl, originally an acronym for Practical Extraction and Report Language, is a sophisticated and powerful language included on most UNIX systems. Perl is one of the most popular languages for use with dynamic Web pages, and includes everything you need to create powerful applications that connect with MySQL databases.

This is only a brief introduction to Perl. For complete documentation as well as downloadable versions of Perl and other packages, visit the Perl web page: www.perl.com/.

The Perl Interpreter

After Perl is installed, the Perl interpreter, `perl`, is available. This program reads Perl scripts and outputs their results. The Perl interpreter is included on many Linux and UNIX systems and can be installed on Windows.

Perl can also be handled by the `mod_perl` module of the Apache Web server. This allows Perl scripts to be handled efficiently by the Web server itself.

Basic Syntax

Perl files usually begin with a shell header that tells the system where the Perl interpreter is located. The following is a typical example:

```
#!/usr/local/bin/perl
```

After this line, the script can contain one or more Perl statements. Each statement ends with a semicolon.

Create Output

The `print` command is the most common way to create output in Perl. You can follow this command with an expression in quotation marks. Perl also includes a variety of other quoting methods to allow you to efficiently specify text to be printed.

Example:
```
print "This is a test.";
```

Operators

Perl supports a number of standard operators. You can use these within any Perl statement to work with numbers or strings. Some of the most common operators are described in the table.

Using Variables

Like most languages, Perl supports *variables*, or containers that can store a value such as a number or text string. Perl variables begin with the $ symbol, as in `$text` and `$score`. You do not need to declare variables before using them, and a variable can store any type of data.

Perl variables can be included in a text string if it uses double quotes. Strings defined with single quotes are not evaluated for variables. The following example defines a variable called `$text` and then prints it with a message:

Example:
```
$text = "Hello there.";
print "Here is the text: $text";
```

Using Arrays

An *array* is a special type of variable that can store multiple values, indexed with numbers or text strings. Perl uses @ followed by the variable name to refer to an array as a whole, and $ followed by the name and an index in square brackets to refer to an element of the array. The following example assigns values to two elements of the score array:

Example:
```
$score[0]=59;
$score[1]=95;
```

OPERATOR	MEANING
+	Addition
–	Subtraction
*	Multiplication
/	Division
%	Modulo (remainder)
.	Concatenation (combines strings)

Regular Expressions

One of Perl's most powerful features is the ability to work with *regular expressions*. These are patterns consisting of text and special characters to search strings of text. The following are some of the most useful special characters within regular expressions:

CHARACTER	DESCRIPTION
.	Matches any character
^	Matches the beginning of a string
$	Matches the end of a string
*	Repeats the previous character zero or more times
+	Repeats the previous character one or more times
?	Repeats the previous expression zero or one time

You can search using a regular expression with the `=~` operator. The following example searches the `$text` string for the text `search` followed by any number of characters:

```
$text =~ /search.*/;
```

Conditional Statements

You can use the `if` statement in Perl to perform one or more statements conditionally. This statement uses a conditional expression followed by a block of Perl statements enclosed in braces. For example, this `if` statement displays a message if the `$num` variable has a value greater than 30:

```
if ($num > 30) {print "It's bigger than
30.";}
```

The condition in an `if` statement can use a variety of conditional operators. The table describes some of the most common conditional operators.

Loops

Perl supports *loops*, or blocks of statements that can be repeated a number of times. The simplest of these is the `while` loop, which checks a condition and repeats the block of statements as long as the condition is true.

Example:
```
while ($num < 30) {
    $num = $num + 1;
    print "The number is $num.";
}
```

Packages

One of Perl's most powerful features is the ability to add *packages*, or modules, that support additional functions. For example, a package is available to work with databases such as MySQL. To use a package in a Perl script, add the `use` statement and the package name at the beginning of the script.

Example:
```
use DBI;
```

Perl and MySQL

The DBI package adds numerous functions to Perl for working with databases, tables, queries, and results. The process of installing this package is explained in "Install the Perl DBI," later in this chapter. Using the functions provided by this package, you can do anything from Perl that you can do from the MySQL monitor or other clients.

OPERATOR	MEANING
==	Is equal to (numeric)
eq	Is equal to (string)
!=	Is not equal to (numeric)
ne	Is not equal to (string)
>	Is greater than (numeric)
<	Is less than (numeric)
>=	Is greater than or equal to
<=	Is less than or equal to
&&	Logical AND
||	Logical OR

INSTALL PERL UNDER UNIX

Perl is included with most Linux distributions. If you are using an operating system that does not include Perl, or need to upgrade to the latest version, it is easy to install from source code. Binary distributions are also available for most systems. To test whether Perl is already installed on your system, try the following command at the command prompt:

```
perl -v
```

This command displays version information for the current Perl installation, if any. If the command fails, either Perl is not installed or your path is not configured correctly for the `perl` command.

To install or upgrade Perl, download the latest source distribution. This is available from the Perl Web page at www.perl.com/. The download is in the form of a compressed .tar.gz archive.

After you have expanded the files from this archive, run the Configure script. This is an automated script that tests

various aspects of your system configuration and sets up options to compile the source code. After the Configure script is finished, you can use the following commands to compile and install the Perl distribution:

```
make
make test
make install
```

You can also install Perl from a binary RPM package under many Linux distributions, and a wide variety of other packages are available. See the Downloads section at www.perl.com for details. To install Perl on a Windows system, see the section "Install Perl under Windows," later in this chapter.

Perl can be expanded with modules that add support for additional features, including the MySQL modules described later in this chapter. Most of these are available from CPAN, the Comprehensive Perl Archive Network, along with a great deal of documentation for Perl. You can reach CPAN at this URL: www.perl.com/CPAN/index.html.

INSTALL PERL UNDER UNIX

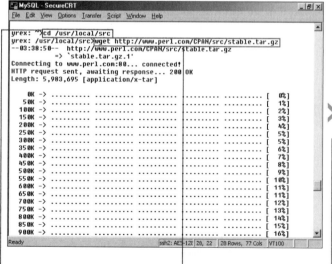

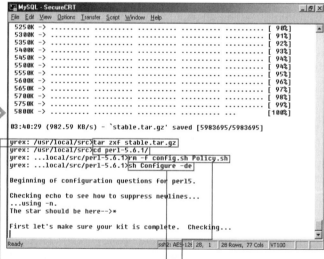

1 From the UNIX command prompt, type **cd** followed by a directory name where the source code will be stored and press Enter.

2 Type **wget** followed by the URL for the source distribution and press Enter.

■ The file is now downloaded.

3 Type **tar zxf stable.tar.gz** and press Enter to extract the Perl source files into their own directory.

4 Type **cd perl-*version*** and press Enter, replacing *version* with the current Perl version.

5 Type **rm -f config.sh Policy.sh** and press Enter to remove unneeded files.

6 Type **sh Configure -de** and press Enter.

■ The Configure program scans your system.

Extra

Perl is included with many Linux distributions, and binary packages are available for others. Most of these are available in a package format such as RPM, which can be installed using a simple command, and do not require you to configure or compile Perl yourself.

After you have installed the Perl interpreter, you can use Perl scripts on the Web using the CGI interface with most Web servers. If you are using the Apache Web server, you can also install the mod_perl module. This module allows you to use Apache modules written in Perl, and also interprets Perl scripts directly within the Web server, while making more efficient use of system resources. This module is available from the following URL: http://perl.apache.org/.

The Apache Web server software itself is included with many Linux distributions. You will need this or another Web server to use Perl for Web applications. Apache is open source software and is available from the Apache Software Foundation at the following URL: www.apache.org/.

Perl can connect to many database systems, including MySQL, with installable modules. The process of installing these modules for MySQL support on most systems is explained in "Install the Perl DBI" and "Install the MySQL DBD," later in this chapter.

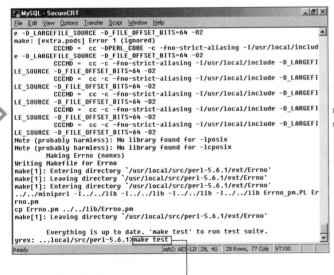

7 After Configure finishes, type **make** and press Enter.

■ This compiles the source code. This may take several minutes.

8 Type **make test** and press Enter.

■ This tests the Perl binaries before installing them.

9 Type **make install** and press Enter.

■ The Perl files are now installed.

INSTALL PERL UNDER WINDOWS

I f you are using MySQL on a Windows-based server, Perl is also available in a Windows distribution. The most popular Windows version of Perl is ActivePerl, developed by ActiveState. The distribution for ActivePerl is available from the following URL: www.activestate.com/ActivePerl/.

ActivePerl requires approximately 55MB of free disk space. It also requires Internet Explorer 5.0 or later and Service Pack 5 or later for Windows NT 4.0 systems. It should install on most Windows 2000 and Windows XP systems without additional software. The other system requirements are listed on the download page.

ActivePerl is distributed as an .msi file. This is a format used by Microsoft's Windows Installer utility. The installer is included with Windows 2000 and Windows XP. For Windows 95, 98, or ME systems, you can download the installer from Microsoft and install it before installing ActivePerl. A package that uses an alternate installer is also available.

After you have downloaded ActivePerl, double-click the .msi file to begin the installation. The Setup Wizard first displays an introductory screen, and then displays the ActivePerl license agreement. After you accept the license agreement and click Next, you can choose which components to install and the location for the installed files.

The final screen of the Setup Wizard asks whether to add Perl to your PATH setting and whether to associate .pl files with the Perl interpreter. Click Next from this screen, and then click Install to complete the installation.

After the installation is complete, switch to the new PERL directory from a command prompt window. Within this directory you will find an example Perl script, `example.pl`. Type `perl example.pl` to test this script. If it displays a brief Hello message and no error messages, ActivePerl is working on your system.

INSTALL PERL UNDER WINDOWS

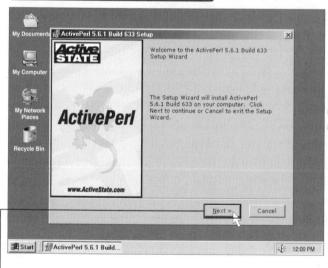

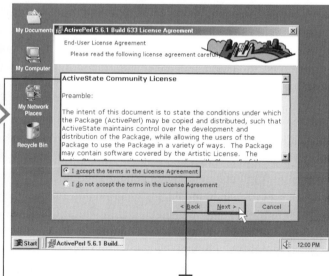

1 After you start the installer, a Welcome message is displayed. Click the Next button to begin the installation.

■ The license agreement is displayed.

2 Accept the license agreement and click Next to continue.

Extra

ActivePerl includes optional modules to work with Microsoft's IIS Web server, included with Windows 2000 Server and Windows XP Server. You can choose to install these modules within the Setup Wizard when you are installing ActivePerl. For more information about IIS, see Microsoft's Web site: www.microsoft.com/iis/.

The Apache Web server is also available for Windows systems. If you do not have a Web server already, Apache is a good choice and is available at no charge. The 32-bit Windows version of Apache is provided as an .msi file for Microsoft's Windows Installer utility and as an .exe file that includes the Window Installer. You can download Apache for Windows from the Apache Software Foundation's Web site: www.apache.org/.

Apache 2.0, the most recent stable release, is tested and reliable on Windows systems, and a good alternative to Microsoft's IIS for many users. As with the UNIX version of Apache, you can install the mod_perl module to directly support Perl scripts from within the Web server.

To use MySQL with ActivePerl, you will need to install the DBD and DBI modules for MySQL support. The process of installing these modules is described later in this chapter.

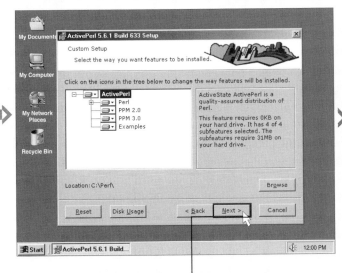

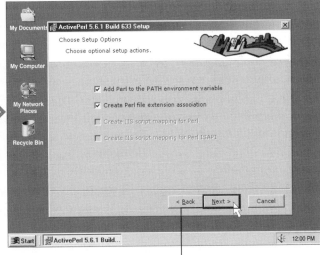

■ The next screen allows you to choose components and the install location.

3 Make any changes desired and click Next to continue.

■ The final options screen is displayed.

4 Click Next, and then click Install on the following screen to complete the installation.

INSTALL THE PERL DBI

The DBI package for Perl supports a number of different database systems. Because it uses the same syntax for all database servers, you can use it to write portable Perl applications that work with any supported database server. Along with the DBI, you will need to install a separate database driver, or DBD, for each database server your applications will be working with.

The DBI for Perl is available from the MySQL Web page, www.mysql.com/, in the Downloads section. For UNIX systems, this is distributed as a .tar.gz archive. You can expand this archive and use the following commands to compile and install the DBI:

```
perl Makefile.PL
make
make test
make install
```

The first command sets up the compilation options for your system. The make command compiles the programs for the DBI. The make test command runs some tests to make sure

the files work correctly, and make install installs the DBI in your Perl libraries. If the final command does not display any error messages, the DBI should work on your server.

If you run into trouble with installation, there is some documentation on the Perl DBI within the MySQL documentation, available from the MySQL Web site. After the installation, you will need to install the DBD for MySQL.

Under Windows systems, you can use the Perl Package Manager (PPM) included with ActiveState's Perl distribution to automatically install the DBI. To use this, start the c:\perl\bin\ppm.pl program from a command prompt window, and then type the following command:

```
install DBI
```

MySQL also provides a downloadable Perl distribution for Windows that includes the DBI and DBD modules required for your scripts to connect to a MySQL server. See the Downloads page at the MySQL Web site for a link to this distribution.

INSTALL THE PERL DBI

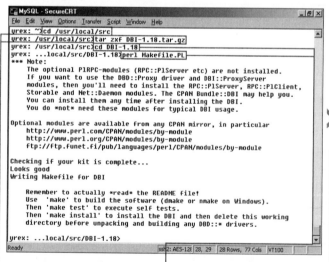

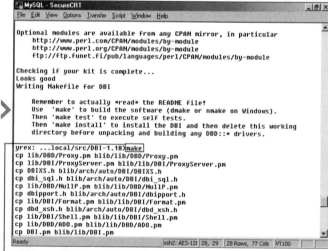

1 Type **cd** followed by the directory name where the .tar.gz file was downloaded and press Enter.

2 Type **tar zxf** followed by the name of the downloaded file and press Enter.

■ The files are expanded into a new directory.

3 Type **cd** followed by the new directory name and press Enter.

4 Type **perl Makefile.PL** and press Enter.

5 Type **make** and press Enter.

■ This compiles the files.

6 Type **make test** and press Enter.

■ The compiled files are now tested.

7 Type **make install** and press Enter.

■ The DBI files are now installed.

INSTALL THE MYSQL DBD

The DBI package cannot access a MySQL database, or any database, by itself. It requires a *DBD*, or database driver, module for each database server. The MySQL DBD actually supports both MySQL servers and mSQL servers in the same module. You can download the DBD from the Downloads section of the MySQL Web page, www.mysql.com/.

The DBD distribution file is in the .tar.gz format and usually has a filename such as Msql-Mysql-modules-1.2216.tar.gz. After you have downloaded this file, you use the same sequence of commands used for the DBI module to install the package:

```
perl Makefile.PL
make
make test
make install
```

The make test command runs some tests on the compiled files, and the make install command installs

the files on your system. If these commands do not display any error messages, the DBD is successfully installed. If you run into trouble with the installation, consult the documentation at the MySQL Web site.

After the DBI and DBD modules are installed, you can begin to use Perl scripts to connect to a MySQL server and make queries. If you are writing a Perl application that will use MySQL, you need to include a use command at the beginning of the script to load the DBI package. A separate command for the DBD module is not required. The following command loads the DBI package in Perl:

```
use DBI;
```

After this module is loaded, you can use the various methods, or built-in functions, to work with MySQL. For example, the DBI->connect method connects to a MySQL server, as described in the next section. Complete documentation for the various DBI functions is included as part of the MySQL documentation, available from the MySQL Web site at www.mysql.com/.

INSTALL THE MYSQL DBD

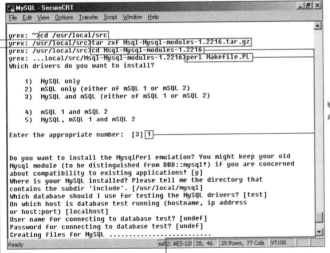

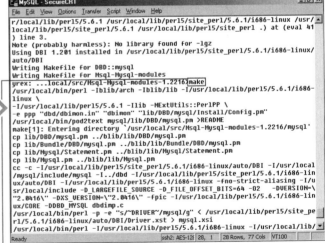

■ **1** Type **cd** followed by the directory name where the .tar.gz file was downloaded and press Enter.

■ **2** Type **tar zxf** followed by the name of the downloaded file and press Enter to expand the files into a new directory.

■ **3** Type **cd** followed by the new directory name and press Enter.

■ **4** Type **perl Makefile.PL** and press Enter.

■ **5** Type **1** to choose MySQL support and press Enter.

■ The Perl files are configured for your system.

■ **6** Type **make** and press Enter.

■ This compiles the files.

■ **7** Type **make test** and press Enter.

■ The compiled files are now tested.

■ **8** Type **make install** and press Enter.

■ The DBD files are now installed.

CONNECT TO A MYSQL SERVER

After you have loaded the DBI package within a Perl script, you can use the methods built into the DBI to access MySQL. To connect to a MySQL server, you use the DBI->connect method. To use this method, first create a single string that includes the database type, mysql, the database name, and the hostname. For example, use DBI:mysql:testdb:localhost to connect to the testdb database on the local host.

To connect to the database, specify the string you created, the username for the MySQL server, and the password. If you do not specify a username or password, the DBI uses the default values defined by the DBI_USER and DBI_PASS environmental variables. The following example connects to the server at the local host and selects the testdb database:

```
use DBI;

$dbh = DBI->connect(
    "DBI:mysql:testdb:localhost",
    "testuser", "testpw");
```

The connect method returns a database handle object, here stored in the $dbh variable. You can use the methods of this object to send queries to the MySQL server and retrieve the results. If the connection to the MySQL server is unsuccessful, the connect method returns a false value instead. You can test this variable to determine whether the connection was successful. The following if statement checks the database handler and prints a message if the connection was successful:

```
if ($dbh) {print "Connected to MySQL
successfully.";}

else {print "Error: can't connect to
MySQL.";}
```

When you are finished using the connection to MySQL, you can use the disconnect method to end the connection. You use this method with the database handle. The following example disconnects from the MySQL server:

```
$dbh->disconnect;
```

CONNECT TO A MYSQL SERVER

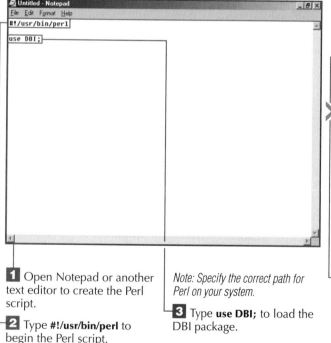

1 Open Notepad or another text editor to create the Perl script.

2 Type **#!/usr/bin/perl** to begin the Perl script.

Note: Specify the correct path for Perl on your system.

3 Type **use DBI;** to load the DBI package.

4 Type **print** to begin the command to output the CGI header, and add the Content-type header.

5 Type **print** to begin the commands that begin and end the HTML document, and add the appropriate HTML tags.

Note: See the Extra section for further information about CGI.

250

Extra

When you use a Perl script as a CGI script on a Web server, you need to send the output in HTML as it will be interpreted by the Web browser. Before any output, your Perl script should first send a `Content-type` header to indicate that the rest of the page is interpreted as HTML. The following section of the example code uses a `print` statement to send this header and then prints the basic tags to begin the HTML document:

Example:
```
print "Content-type:text/html\n\n";
print "<html><head><title>Connecting to MySQL";
print "</title></head><body>";
```

When you send output within a CGI program, be sure to use HTML tags to format it correctly. For example, you cannot end a line using the standard `\n` code, as it will be ignored by the browser. You can send a line break tag, `<br>`, or format the text into paragraphs using `<p>` and `</p>` tags instead.

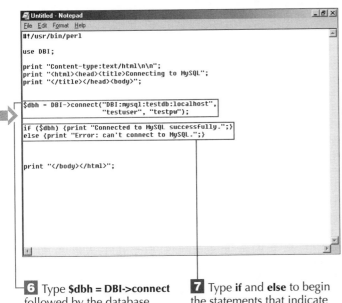

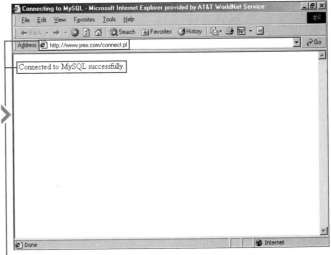

━ **6** Type **$dbh = DBI->connect** followed by the database name, hostname, username, and password to connect to the MySQL server.

Note: Be sure to specify the correct hostname, username, and password for your server.

7 Type **if** and **else** to begin the statements that indicate whether the connection was successful, and add the print commands.

8 Load the Perl document into a Web browser.

■ The displayed message indicates whether the connection was made.

Note: You will need to upload the Perl file to a Web server before you can use it.

DISPLAY QUERY RESULTS

After you have made a connection to a MySQL server from a Perl script, you can send a MySQL query to the server. One way to do this is to use the `prepare` method of the database handler. This accepts a query as a parameter, and prepares a statement handler object to execute the query. The query is not yet sent to the server. The following example prepares a query:

```
$query = "SELECT quote, author FROM quotes";

$sth = $dbh->prepare($query);
```

This method returns a statement handler object, stored in the `$sth` variable here. After you have prepared the query, you can use the `execute` method on the statement handler to send the query to the MySQL server. The following example executes the query in the `$sth` object:

```
$result = $sth->execute;
```

This executes queries that do not return a result, such as `INSERT` or `DELETE`, immediately. For a `SELECT` query, the query is started. You can then use one of the `fetch` methods to retrieve each row of the result. One such method is `fetchrow_array`, which fetches a row from the MySQL server and stores its fields in an array. The following example uses a `while` loop to print each row of the query result:

```
while(@row = $sth->fetchrow_array) {
        print "<p>$row[0] —$row[1]</p>";    }
```

The columns of the result are returned in order, starting with zero. Thus, in this example, `$row[0]` represents the quote column, and `$row[1]` represents the author column. The `print` statement prints each row, formatted as an HTML paragraph.

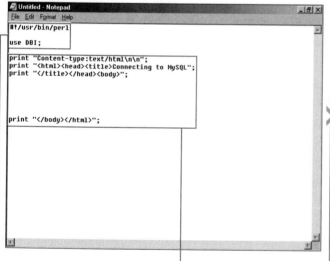

Note: Open the Perl script in a text editor.

1 Type the Perl header and **use DBI;** to load the DBI package.

2 Type **print** to begin the statements that send a CGI header and start and end the HTML document, and add the header and HTML tags.

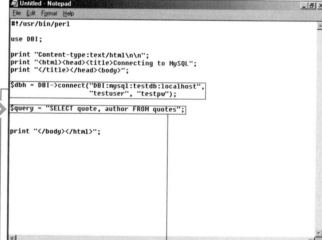

3 Type **$dbh = DBI->connect** and add the correct database name, hostname, username, and password to connect to the MySQL server.

Note: Be sure to use the correct hostname, username, and password for your system.

4 Type **$query =** followed by the MySQL query to store the query in a variable.

Apply It

The DBI includes a number of different `fetch` methods, and you can use any of them to retrieve the results of a `SELECT` query. For example, the `fetchrow_hashref` returns each row as a reference to a hash table containing each column name and its corresponding value. This is not as efficient as the `fetchrow_array` method, but allows you to refer to result columns by their MySQL column name rather than by number.

For example, the following Perl code sends a `SELECT` query to the MySQL server, and then uses a `while` loop with the `fetchrow_hashref` method to display the results of the `SELECT` query.

Example:
```
use DBI;
$dbh = DBI->connect("DBI:mysql:testdb:localhost",
    "testuser", "testpw");
$query = "SELECT quote, author FROM quotes";
$sth = $dbh->prepare($query);
$result = $sth->execute;
while($hash = $sth->fetchrow_hashref) {
        print "<p>$hash->{quote}  --$hash->{author}</p>";   }
```

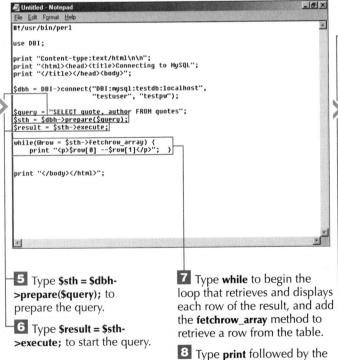

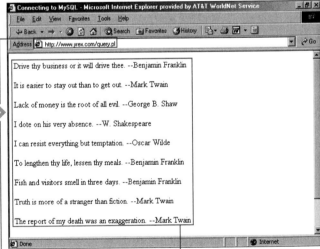

5 Type **$sth = $dbh->prepare($query);** to prepare the query.

6 Type **$result = $sth->execute;** to start the query.

7 Type **while** to begin the loop that retrieves and displays each row of the result, and add the **fetchrow_array** method to retrieve a row from the table.

8 Type **print** followed by the text that will be displayed with each row, including the variable values.

Note: Save the document and upload it to a Web server.

9 Load the Perl document into a Web browser.

■ The results of the query are displayed.

INSERT A RECORD FROM PERL

You can use Perl to perform an INSERT query on the MySQL server to add a record to a table. Because an INSERT query is simple and does not return a result, you do not need to use the prepare method. Instead, you can use the do method of the database handler. This function accepts a MySQL query and executes it immediately.

As with other DBI methods, you must first use the connect method to open a connection to a MySQL server and select a database. To use the do method, specify the database handler that was returned by the connect method and specify a MySQL query. The following statements store an INSERT query in the $query variable and use the do method to execute the query:

```
$query = "INSERT INTO scores (name, score)
VALUES ('Fred', 92)";

$rows = $dbh->do($query);
```

The do method returns the number of rows affected by the query. Because a single record should have been added by the INSERT query, the $rows variable will be nonzero if the insert succeeded. You can use an if statement to check the number of rows and print a message indicating whether the row was successfully inserted:

```
if ($rows > 0) {print "Inserted record
successfully.";}

else {print "Error: INSERT query failed.";}
```

Because the do method does not return a statement handler, you cannot use it to process a SELECT query. However, it works well for queries that return the number of rows affected rather than returning rows of data, such as INSERT, UPDATE, and DELETE.

INSERT A RECORD FROM PERL

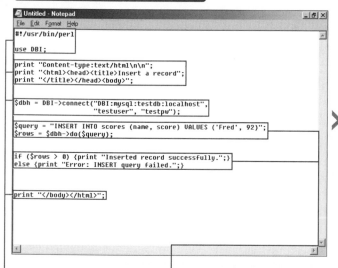

■1 Type the Perl header and **use DBI;** to load the DBI package.

■2 Type **print** followed by the CGI header.

■3 Type **print** followed by the HTML tags to format the output.

■4 Type **$dbh = DBI->connect** followed by the database name, hostname, username, and password to connect to the MySQL server.

■5 Type **$query =** followed by the MySQL query.

■6 Type **$rows = $dbh->do($query);** to execute the query.

■7 Type **if** and **else** and add the statements to print the result.

■8 Load the Perl document into a Web browser.

■ The displayed message indicates that the record was successfully inserted.

DELETE RECORDS USING PERL

You can also use Perl to send a DELETE query to the MySQL server to delete one or more records. As with the INSERT query, you can use the do method to execute the query and return the number of rows that were deleted.

To delete one or more rows of a table, create a DELETE query that includes a WHERE clause. The WHERE clause will determine the rows to be deleted. Without this clause, the entire contents of the table would be deleted. The following statements store a DELETE query in the $query variable and execute the query using the do method:

```
$query = "DELETE FROM scores WHERE name = 'fred'";

$rows = $dbh->do($query);
```

As with the INSERT query, you can check the returned result in the $rows variable to determine that the rows were deleted successfully. The following statements check the result and display a message:

```
if ($rows > 0) {print "Deleted record successfully.";}

else {print "Error: DELETE query failed.";}
```

Note that a failed query is not the same as a query that did not match any rows. If the query was invalid or caused a MySQL error, the do method returns zero. If the query simply matches no rows, it returns the special value "0E0". Perl treats this value as true, but numerically it is evaluated to zero. If you use an if statement like the following, it will print a success message if the query succeeded, regardless of whether it affected any rows:

```
if ($rows) {print "DELETE query was successful.";}
```

DELETE RECORDS USING PERL

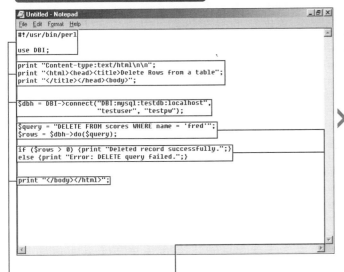

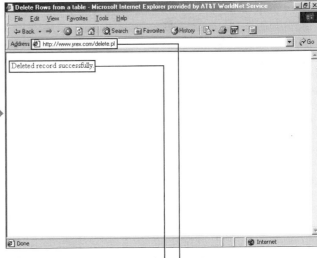

1 Type the Perl header and **use DBI;** to load the DBI package.

2 Type **print** followed by the CGI header.

3 Type **print** followed by the HTML tags to format the document.

4 Type **$dbh = DBI->connect** followed by the correct database name, hostname, username, and password to connect to the MySQL server.

5 Type **$query=** followed by the MySQL query.

6 Type **$rows = $dbh->do($query);** to execute the query.

7 Type **if** and **else** followed by the statements to print the result.

8 Load the Perl document into a Web browser.

■ The displayed message indicates that the DELETE query was successful.

WORK WITH WEB FORMS

Y ou can use Perl to send the results of an HTML form to a MySQL query. For example, you can create a search form to search the quotes table. To output the form, you can use a special Perl syntax that allows you to include several rows of content to output. The following Perl code displays the form:

```
print <<EOF;

<form method="get" action="search.pl">

Search for: <input type="text"
name="search">

<input type="submit" name="submit"
value="Search">

</form>

EOF
```

The print << syntax means that everything starting on the next line and ending with the text EOF should be output. This allows you to include HTML directly within the Perl script. When the user clicks the Search button, the form data is sent to the Perl script in the QUERY_STRING environmental variable. The following if statement checks this variable:

```
if ($ENV{'QUERY_STRING'} =~ /search=(.*)&/)
{
```

This statement uses a regular expression to look for the field name search in the query string. It uses the (.*) expression to capture the value of the search field. Perl stores this value in the $1 variable, and it can then be used to create a MySQL query.

After you have created the MySQL query in the $query variable, you can use the prepare method to prepare the query and the execute method to send it to the server.

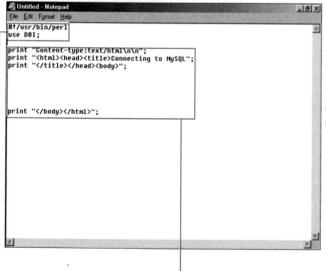

1 Type the Perl header and **use DBI;** to load the DBI package.

2 Type **print** followed by the CGI header.

3 Type **print** followed by the HTML tags to format the output.

4 Type **print <<EOF;** followed by the HTML tags for the search form.

5 Type **if** to begin the statement that detects when the form is submitted.

6 Type **$dbh = DBI->connect** followed by the database name, hostname, username, and password to connect to the MySQL server.

Extra

You can simplify the use of HTML forms and their results using CGI.pm, a popular Perl package. You can download this package and view its documentation at this URL: http://stein.cshl.org/WWW/CGI/.

The following example shows the search form example rewritten to use this package.

Example:

```
use DBI;
use CGI qw(:standard);
print header, start_html("Search Form"), start_form, "Search for: ",
    textfield('search'), submit, end_form;
if (param()) {
  $s=param('search');
  print "<p>Searching for: <b>$search</b></p>";
  $dbh = DBI->connect("DBI:mysql:testdb", "testuser", "testpw");
  $query = "SELECT quote,author FROM quotes WHERE QUOTE LIKE '%$s%' ";
  $sth = $dbh->prepare($query);
  $result = $sth->execute;
  while(@row = $sth->fetchrow_array) {
      print "<p>$row[0] --$row[1]</p>";   }
}
print end_html;
```

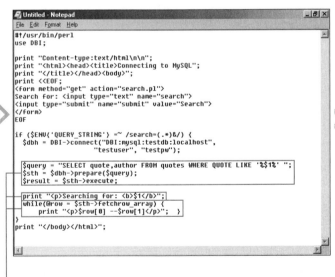

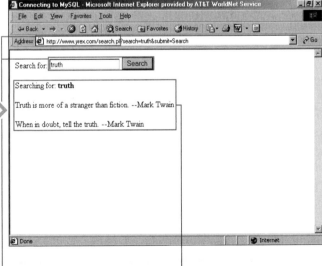

-7 Type **$query=** followed by the MySQL query.

-8 Type **$sth = $dbh->prepare($query);** to prepare the query.

-9 Type **$result = $sth->execute;** to execute the query.

-10 Type **print** to begin the statement that prints a heading for the search results.

-11 Type **while** to begin the loop that displays each row of the search results.

-12 Load the Perl document into a Web browser.

-13 Type a search term and click the Search button.

■ The results of the search are displayed below the form.

GLOSSARY

ALTER

To modify the definition of a database table. MySQL supports the `ALTER TABLE` command for this purpose.

BIT

The smallest unit of storage in computer memory. A bit can store an on or off value and represents the numbers zero or one.

BYTE

The standard unit of storage in computer memory. A byte is comprised of 8 bits, and can represent numbers from 0 to 255. Multiple bytes can be combined to store larger numbers.

CLIENT

An application or interface that accesses an application on a server, such as a MySQL database server. The MySQL monitor is a command-line client for MySQL.

COLUMN

An item of data that can be stored in a database table. Each column stores a specific type of data, and stores one value for each row of data. Columns are sometimes known as *fields*.

CONDITION

An expression that can be evaluated to a true or false value. Conditions can be used in a `WHERE` clause to select rows of data from a table.

DATABASE

A combination of one or more tables stored in a single directory. A MySQL server can store any number of databases.

DATABASE MANAGEMENT SYSTEM (DBMS)

A software application that stores data in files and organizes it into columns, rows, and tables. MySQL is a database management system.

DEFAULT

The value that is stored in a column when no value is explicitly assigned. If you do not specify a default value for a table column, MySQL uses zero or the `NULL` value, depending on the column type.

DROP

To delete a column, table, or database. This action is accomplished with MySQL commands such as `DROP TABLE` and `DROP DATABASE`.

FIELD

See *column*.

FLOATING POINT

A type of numeric data that can be stored in a database. Floating point numbers support fractional values and exponents, and can have any number of decimal places. MySQL data types such as `FLOAT` and `DOUBLE` support floating point numbers.

GRANT

To allow a user one or more privileges for a database or table. MySQL privileges are assigned with the `GRANT` command.

HEAP

A type of MySQL table that stores data in RAM memory rather than on disk, most often used for temporary tables.

INDEX

A file that stores pointers to rows in a table for a particular column or columns. An index can be assigned to any column in a MySQL table. Indexed columns are known as keys.

INDEXED SEQUENTIAL ACCESS METHOD (ISAM)

A method for storing data in files that can be accessed sequentially as well as through one or more indexes, or keys. MySQL supports ISAM as a table type. The default table type, MyISAM, is an improved version of this system.

INSERT

To add one or more rows to an existing table in a database. MySQL supports the `INSERT` command for this purpose.

INTEGER

A number with no decimal portion. MySQL includes several column types devoted to storing integers, such as `INT` and `TINYINT`.

JOIN

To retrieve data from two or more tables using a relationship defined by two or more columns that match between the tables. This is accomplished with the `SELECT` command in MySQL, either specifying multiple tables or using the `JOIN` keyword explicitly.

KEY

A column in a database table that has been indexed. Values for a key column can be used to quickly access a row of data without having to search sequentially through the table.

MYSQL

A database management system (DBMS) that runs on UNIX, Windows, and a variety of other systems. MySQL supports the SQL query language.

MYSQL MONITOR

A command-line interface, or client, for MySQL. This utility allows you to enter MySQL queries. It sends each query to a MySQL server and displays the results. The `mysql` command starts the monitor on most systems.

MYSQL SERVER

A computer running the MySQL server software. This software takes requests, or queries, from clients, and acts on them to manage one or more databases.

NULL

A special value meaning that no value has been explicitly assigned to a column. In MySQL, a column with the `NULL` attribute is allowed to store `NULL` values.

PERL

An open source language widely used for text processing and Web programming. Perl modules are available for use with MySQL databases.

PHP

An open source server-side language that runs on Web servers and integrates with HTML files. PHP includes features for working with MySQL databases.

PRIMARY KEY

A column that contains a unique value for each row of a table, and can be used to refer to a single row.

PRIVILEGE

An action that a user or group is allowed to perform on a table or database, such as creating a table or deleting records. MySQL's security system allows combinations of privileges to be assigned to users to control access.

QUERY

A command in the SQL language to request data or perform another action on a database server. Queries are sent from the client to the server, and the server returns the results.

RECORD

See *row*.

REVOKE

To take away one or more access privileges from a user in MySQL's security system. The `REVOKE` command in MySQL is used for this purpose.

ROW

An element of a database table. A table can store any number of rows. Each row contains a value for each of the table's defined columns. Rows are sometimes known as *records*.

SECURE SOCKETS LAYER (SSL)

A standard for secure, encrypted communication between clients and servers. SSL is used for secure Web services and is also supported by MySQL clients and servers.

SELECT

A type of SQL query that uses the `SELECT` command to request one or more rows of data from a table to be returned to the client. `SELECT` supports a variety of clauses to control the amount and type of data returned.

SERVER

A hardware or software service that accepts requests from clients and acts on them. The MySQL software acts as a database server.

STRING

A text value that can be stored in a database column. MySQL includes a number of column types and functions for working with strings.

STRUCTURED QUERY LANGUAGE (SQL)

A standardized language for retrieving data from database tables, inserting data, creating and modifying tables, and performing other database management functions. MySQL's query language is based on the SQL standard.

TABLE

The basic element of data storage in a MySQL database. Each table is defined to store one or more columns, each assigned a specific type of data. The table can store a number of rows, each of which includes a value for each defined column.

TIMESTAMP

A numeric value that represents a specific date and time, often used for time logging of events. MySQL includes a `TIMESTAMP` column type to store these values. Timestamp columns are automatically updated with the current date and time when a row is added or modified.

UNIQUE INDEX

A type of index that requires a unique value in each row of the table for the column or columns being indexed. A primary key is a special type of unique index.

UPDATE

To modify one or more existing rows of a table. MySQL supports `UPDATE` queries for this purpose.

CREATE AND DELETE TABLES AND DATABASES

M ySQL includes `CREATE` and `DROP` commands for creating and deleting databases and tables. These commands are described in the following sections.

CREATE TABLE

This command creates a new table within the current database. To use this command, specify the table name, one or more column definitions, and any table options. You can also specify the `IF NOT EXISTS` keywords before the table name to suppress an error message if the specified table already exists.

Example:
```
CREATE TABLE inventory (
    itemno INTEGER UNSIGNED NOT NULL PRIMARY KEY,
    description VARCHAR(200),
    price DECIMAL (9,2),
    count TINYINT ) TYPE=ISAM;
```

Specify Columns

The `CREATE TABLE` command requires that you specify one or more columns for the new table. To define a column, specify a column name, column type, and any options. Separate the column definitions with commas and enclose the entire column list in parentheses.

Along with the specific column options listed in the table, all columns can have the `NULL` or `NOT NULL` attributes. This indicates whether the column can store a `NULL` value. You can also specify `DEFAULT` followed by a default value for the column, and `AUTO_INCREMENT` to create an auto-increment column.

COLUMN TYPE	DATA DESCRIPTION	POSSIBLE OPTIONS
INT or INTEGER	Integer	UNSIGNED, ZEROFILL
TINYINT	Integer (0-255)	UNSIGNED, ZEROFILL
SMALLINT	Integer	UNSIGNED, ZEROFILL
MEDIUMINT	Integer	UNSIGNED, ZEROFILL
BIGINT	Integer	UNSIGNED, ZEROFILL
REAL	Floating-point	UNSIGNED, ZEROFILL
DOUBLE	Floating-point	UNSIGNED, ZEROFILL
FLOAT	Floating-point	UNSIGNED, ZEROFILL
DECIMAL	Decimal	UNSIGNED, ZEROFILL
CHAR	Text (fixed)	BINARY
VARCHAR	Text (variable)	BINARY
TEXT	Text (variable)	
TINYTEXT	Text (variable)	

COLUMN TYPE	DATA DESCRIPTION	POSSIBLE OPTIONS
MEDIUMTEXT	Text (variable)	
LONGTEXT	Text (variable)	
BLOB	Binary (variable)	
TINYBLOB	Binary (variable)	
MEDIUMBLOB	Binary (variable)	
LONGBLOB	Binary (variable)	
ENUM	Enumerated data (single)	
SET	Enumerated data (multiple)	
DATE	Date	
TIME	Time	
DATETIME	Date and Time	
TIMESTAMP	Date and Time (automatic)	

Indexes and Keys

You can include the `PRIMARY KEY` keyword within a `CREATE TABLE` command to specify a primary key. Specify one or more column names for the primary key in parentheses. Specify the `INDEX` keyword to create an index on one or more columns, or `UNIQUE` for a unique index. Specify an index name followed by one or more column names in parentheses.

TABLE OPTIONS

At the end of the `CREATE TABLE` command, you can specify one or more table options. To use options, specify the option name followed by an equal sign and its value. Separate multiple options with commas.

TYPE Specify the column type. The default type, MyISAM, is adequate for most purposes. Alternate types include BDB, InnoDB, Heap, ISAM, and MERGE.	**COMMENT** Specify an optional comment in quotation marks as a description of the table. The comment can be up to 60 characters in length.
AUTO_INCREMENT Use this option to specify the next index number for an auto-increment column. The column values will start at one if this option is not specified.	**MAX_ROWS** Specify the maximum number of rows the table will store.
AVG_ROW_LENGTH For tables with variable-length rows, specify an approximate row length. This helps MySQL to optimize data storage.	**MIN_ROWS** Specify the approximate minimum number of rows the table will store.
CHECKSUM If this option is set to one, MySQL maintains a checksum value for each row. This makes it easier to detect errors, but decreases performance.	**ROW_FORMAT** Specify `DYNAMIC` or `FIXED` to determine whether the table will use fixed or variable-length rows.

COPY FROM ANOTHER TABLE

You can optionally specify a `SELECT` statement at the end of the `CREATE TABLE` command. This retrieves column names from an existing table and creates corresponding columns in the new table.

DROP TABLE

This command deletes an existing table. This command does not prompt you for confirmation and should be used with caution. You can optionally specify the `IF EXISTS` keywords before the table name to suppress an error message if the table does not exist.

Example:
```
DROP TABLE IF EXISTS inventory;
```

CREATE DATABASE

This command creates a new database. This is a fast operation as the database does not yet contain any data. You can optionally specify the `IF NOT EXISTS` keywords before the database name to suppress an error message if the database already exists.

Example:
```
CREATE DATABASE newdb;
```

DROP DATABASE

This command deletes an existing database, including all tables and all of the data they contain. This command does not prompt you for confirmation, so use it with caution. You can optionally specify the `IF EXISTS` keywords before the database name to suppress an error message if the specified database does not exist.

Example:
```
DROP DATABASE newdb;
```

MODIFY TABLES WITH ALTER TABLE

The ALTER TABLE command in MySQL modifies the definition of an existing table. To use ALTER TABLE, specify one or more of the following commands. You can separate multiple commands with commas.

ADD COLUMN

This command adds a column to an existing table. You can specify a list of multiple columns, separated by commas and enclosed in parentheses.

Example:
```
ALTER TABLE address ADD COLUMN newcol INT;
```

ADD INDEX and ADD UNIQUE

The ADD INDEX command adds an index to the table. Specify a name for the index followed by one or more column names to index in parentheses. Use ADD UNIQUE to add a unique index.

Example:
```
ALTER TABLE address ADD INDEX newindex (name,
address);
```

ADD PRIMARY KEY

This command adds a primary key to an existing table. It can only be used if the table does not already have a defined primary key. Specify the column or columns for the primary key in parentheses.

Example:
```
ALTER TABLE address ADD PRIMARY KEY (name);
```

CHANGE COLUMN

This command changes the definition of an existing column and can also rename the column. To use this command, specify the current column name, the new name, and the new definition of the column. MySQL will attempt to convert existing data to the new format.

Example:
```
ALTER TABLE address CHANGE COLUMN name name
VARCHAR(50);
```

ORDER BY

This command sorts the existing data in the table by the column name you specify.

MODIFY COLUMN

This command changes the definition of an existing column. Specify the column name followed by the new column definition.

Example:
```
ALTER TABLE address MODIFY COLUMN name
VARCHAR(100);
```

DROP COLUMN

This command deletes a specified column from an existing table. This deletes all data currently stored in the column

Example:
```
ALTER TABLE address DROP COLUMN newcol;
```

DROP INDEX

This command deletes an index or unique index. Specify the index name. This command does not delete any data.

DROP PRIMARY KEY

This command deletes the table's primary key, if one is defined. You do not need to specify a column name. This command does not delete any existing data.

RENAME TO

This command renames the table. Specify RENAME TO followed by the new table name. The TO keyword is optional.

Example:
```
ALTER TABLE address RENAME TO mailings;
```

Using Table Options

You can specify table options, such as TYPE for the table type or COMMENT for a comment about the table, within the ALTER TABLE command.

Example:
```
ALTER TABLE address TYPE=ISAM;
```

ADD AND DELETE DATA

MySQL includes the INSERT command to add one or more rows to a table and the DELETE command to delete one or more rows. These are described in the following sections.

INSERT

This command adds a row, or multiple rows, to an existing table. To use INSERT, specify the table name, column names, and values.

Example:
```
INSERT INTO address (name, address)
   VALUES ("John Smith", "181 West 7th");
```

Insert Options

If you specify the LOW_PRIORITY option before the INTO keyword in an INSERT command, MySQL does not add the data until no other clients are using the table. The DELAYED keyword is similar, but the data is held on the server for later insertion and the client does not wait for the operation to complete.

Specify the IGNORE keyword to ignore any conflicts with existing data and continue without inserting that row.

INTO

The INTO keyword is followed by the name of the table to add data into. You can optionally specify a list of column names in parentheses.

VALUES

The VALUES keyword is followed by the values for each column of the new row. If you specified a list of columns, specify the values in the same order. If you did not specify a list of columns, a value must be specified for each column in the table's definition.

SELECT

You can optionally specify a SELECT statement at the end of the INSERT command. This retrieves data from one or more columns of an existing table and copies it to the specified table.

DELETE

The DELETE command deletes one or more rows of a table. This command does not prompt you for confirmation; use it with caution. To use this command to delete all of a table's data, specify the FROM keyword and the table name.

Example:
```
DELETE FROM address;
```

Delete Options

You can specify one of two optional keywords after the DELETE command and before the FROM keyword. If the LOW_PRIORITY keyword is specified, MySQL waits until no other clients are using the table before deleting data. If the QUICK option is specified, indexes are not updated during the delete, which may speed up the process.

WHERE

Specify a WHERE clause and one or more conditions to choose one or more rows to be deleted. If this clause is not included, all rows of the table will be deleted.

Example:
```
DELETE FROM address WHERE name="John Smith";
```

ORDER BY

In MySQL 4.0 and later, you can optionally specify the ORDER BY keyword followed by a list of column names to delete rows in a specified order.

LIMIT

Specify a number after the LIMIT keyword to limit the number of rows that can be deleted

Example:
```
DELETE FROM address WHERE name > "A" LIMIT 10;
```

MODIFY EXISTING DATA WITH UPDATE

The UPDATE command in MySQL makes changes to existing rows of a table. To use this command, specify the table name followed by the SET keyword and one or more pairs of column names and values.

Example:
```
UPDATE address
   SET name="John Smith"
   WHERE name="J. Smith";
```

UPDATE Options

You can specify two optional keywords with the UPDATE query. If you specify the LOW_PRIORITY keyword, the MySQL server waits until no other clients are using the table before updating the data.

Example:
```
UPDATE LOW_PRIORITY address
   SET name = UPPER(name);
```

The UPDATE command can make a change that results in a conflict between two rows in a primary key or unique index column. If this will occur, MySQL displays an error message and stops the update. If you specify the IGNORE keyword, MySQL skips any conflicting rows and continues the update.

WHERE

Specify the WHERE clause with one or more conditions to control which rows of the table will be updated. If this clause is not specified, all rows of the table are updated.

Example:
```
UPDATE address
   SET address="830 West Terrace"
   WHERE name = "John Smith";
```

LIMIT

If you specify the LIMIT keyword followed by a number, only the specified maximum number of rows can be updated.

Example:
```
UPDATE address
   SET name = UPPER(name) LIMIT 10;
```

Multiple Updates

If you include more than one column name and value after the SET keyword, all of the columns are updated at once. This allows for complex updates in a single command. This can also be combined with the WHERE or LIMIT clauses as needed.

Example:
```
UPDATE address
   SET address="392 East 10th",
   city = "Salt Lake City", state="UT"
   WHERE name = "Jane Smith";
```

RETRIEVE DATA WITH SELECT

The SELECT command returns the values of the columns you specify for one or more rows of a table in a MySQL database. This command supports a variety of options.

Basic SELECT Syntax

Specify one or more column names after the SELECT command, separated by commas. You can also specify the wildcard character * to return values for all columns in the order defined when the table was created.

Example:
```
SELECT name, address, city, state
   FROM address;
```

WHERE

Specify the WHERE keyword followed by one or more conditions to choose one or more rows from the table. If this clause is omitted, all rows are returned. This clause should be specified immediately after the table name.

Example:
```
SELECT * FROM address
   WHERE name = "John Smith";
```

ORDER BY

The ORDER BY clause determines the order of the rows returned from a SELECT query. Specify one or more column names, separated by commas. For each column, you can specify the ASC (ascending) or DESC (descending) keywords. ASC is the default. You can also order by a MySQL function or formula. The RAND() function is useful for returning rows in random order.

Example:
```
SELECT * FROM address
   ORDER BY state ASC, city ASC;
```

GROUP BY

If you specify the GROUP BY clause, MySQL groups the returned rows into single rows for each value of the specified columns. As with ORDER BY, separate the column names with commas and optionally use the ASC or DESC keywords.

Example:
```
SELECT * FROM address
   GROUP BY city;
```

LIMIT

Specify the LIMIT keyword followed by a number to return, at maximum, the specified number of rows. You can optionally specify two numbers, separated by commas, in the LIMIT clause. In this case, the first number is the first row of the result to return and the second is the maximum number of rows.

Example:
```
SELECT * FROM address LIMIT 10;
```

Multiple Tables

You can specify two or more table names separated by commas. This joins data from multiple tables, and requires a WHERE condition that matches rows between the tables. Specify the table name for each column name, with a period separating table and column names.

Example:
```
SELECT quotes.quote, quotes.author,
   authors.born, authors.died
   FROM quotes, authors
   WHERE quotes.author = authors.author;
```

DISPLAY STATUS INFORMATION

MySQL includes a variety of SHOW commands that display information about databases, tables, and the server itself. These are described in the following sections.

SHOW DATABASES

This command lists all of the databases on the current server. Depending on security settings, it may only list the databases you have access to.

Example:
```
SHOW DATABASES;
```

SHOW TABLES

This command lists all of the tables stored in the current database. You can also specify the FROM keyword and a database name to list the tables in another database.

SHOW OPEN TABLES

This command is similar to SHOW TABLES, but only lists the tables that are currently in use or have a cached connection. Information about the number of users is displayed.

SHOW COLUMNS

This command displays a detailed list of columns for a table. Specify the FROM keyword followed by a table name. DESCRIBE is equivalent to SHOW COLUMNS FROM.

Example:
```
SHOW COLUMNS FROM address;
```

SHOW TABLE STATUS

This command displays a detailed list of information for each table in the current database, including the table type, row format, and table options.

SHOW CREATE TABLE

This command displays a CREATE TABLE command to create the table specified. This is useful if you need to recreate the table in another database or on another server.

Example:
```
SHOW CREATE TABLE address;
```

SHOW INDEX

This command lists the indexes or keys defined for the table you specify with the FROM keyword. The detailed information listed for each index includes the columns to which it applies.

Example:
```
SHOW INDEX FROM address;
```

SHOW STATUS

This command displays a detailed list of status information for the MySQL server. This information is useful for determining the server's current use and optimizing performance.

SHOW VARIABLES

This command lists all of the MySQL system variables. These are usually defined in the configuration file or on the command line when the MySQL server is started. This listing is useful for checking the server's configuration.

SHOW PROCESSLIST

This command displays a list of processes, or threads, currently running on the MySQL server. The results include the username, hostname, current command, and an ID number for each process.

Example:
```
SHOW PROCESSLIST;
```

SHOW GRANTS

The SHOW GRANTS command displays the privileges granted to a MySQL user. Specify the FOR keyword followed by the username.

Example:
```
SHOW GRANTS FOR testuser;
```

ADMINISTRATIVE COMMANDS

 ySQL includes a variety of administrative commands for managing tables, processes, users, and various server components.

OPTIMIZE TABLE

The `OPTIMIZE TABLE` command sorts a table's index files and reclaims any space used by deleted rows. To use this command, specify the table name.

Example:
```
OPTIMIZE TABLE address;
```

CHECK TABLE

The `CHECK TABLE` command checks a table for errors. Specify a table name and optionally one or more of the keywords `QUICK`, `FAST`, `CHANGED`, `MEDIUM`, or `EXTENDED`.

Example:
```
CHECK TABLE address;
```

REPAIR TABLE

The `REPAIR TABLE` command attempts to repair a damaged table. You can optionally specify the keywords `QUICK` for a fast scan or `EXTENDED` for a more thorough scan.

ANALYZE TABLE

The `ANALYZE TABLE` command analyzes a table's content and configures its keys for use in future queries. To use this command, specify the table name.

FLUSH HOSTS

The `FLUSH HOSTS` command clears the host cache tables MySQL uses to manage access by users from remote hosts. This allows access by users who were previously blocked due to connection errors.

FLUSH LOGS

This command closes and reopens the MySQL log files. It is useful if you have changed logging settings or if you are backing up or deleting old data in the log files.

FLUSH PRIVILEGES

This command reloads the MySQL grant tables, used to control access by users. This is useful if you have made changes to the tables manually.

FLUSH QUERY CACHE

This command arranges MySQL's cache of queries in memory to conserve memory. Use the command `RESET QUERY CACHE` to clear this cache completely.

FLUSH TABLES

This command closes and reopens all MySQL tables, and clears the query cache.

FLUSH STATUS

This command resets most of the status variables that are shown with the `SHOW STATUS` command. These variables are also cleared each time you start the MySQL server.

KILL

This command stops a thread on the MySQL server. Specify the process ID number, available from the output of `SHOW PROCESSLIST`.

Example:
```
KILL 3931;
```

GRANT

The `GRANT` command grants one or more privileges to a user of the MySQL server. If the user does not already exist, it is created. Specify the privileges to grant, the database and table names, the `TO` keyword followed by the username, and the `IDENTIFIED BY` keywords followed by a password.

Example:
```
GRANT ALL ON testdb.quotes
   TO fred IDENTIFIED BY 'password';
```

REVOKE

The `REVOKE` command takes away one or more privileges from a user of the MySQL server. Specify the privileges to revoke, the `FROM` keyword, and the username.

Example:
```
REVOKE ALL ON testdb.quotes FROM fred;
```

APPENDIX
COMMAND-LINE UTILITIES

MySQL includes a number of utilities that can be used from the command prompt on a UNIX or Windows system. These are described in the following sections.

MYSQL

This command starts the MySQL monitor, a command-line interface that enables you to enter MySQL commands and view their results.

COMMAND	DESCRIPTION
-?	Display a complete list of options
-D	Select a database to use
-h	Specify the host (server name or IP address)
-p	Specify the password to access the server
-P	Specify the TCP/IP port number for the server
-u	Specify a username for the server
-V	Display server version number

After you are in the MySQL monitor, you can type any MySQL command. The monitor also supports a number of special commands:

COMMAND	DESCRIPTION
\c	Clears the current command
\e	Edits the command in a text editor
\g	Executes the current command
\G	Executes the current command and displays a vertical result
\h	Displays a list of commands and their descriptions
\p	Displays the current command
\q	Exits the MySQL monitor
\r	Attempts to reconnect to the server
\s	Displays MySQL status information
\	Executes MySQL commands from a specified file

MYSQLADMIN

The `mysqladmin` utility runs from a client machine and supports a number of different commands for managing the MySQL server. Type `mysqladmin` followed by the command name.

Example:
`mysqladmin extended-status`

COMMAND	DESCRIPTION
create	Create a database
drop	Drop a database
ping	Check whether the server is running
status	Display basic status information
extended-status	Display a detailed status report
processlist	Show a list of the current MySQL server processes

COMMAND	DESCRIPTION
kill	Stop one or more server processes
variables	List MySQL variables and their values
version	Display the MySQL server version number
shutdown	Shut down the MySQL server
password	Change the password for the current MySQL user

MYSQLDUMP

The `mysqldump` utility dumps the contents of a table or an entire database to the screen, and you can redirect its output to a file. This command creates a file of SQL commands to re-create the table.

OPTION	DESCRIPTION
-A or --all-databases	Includes all databases on the server
-C or --compress	Attempts to compress data
-B or --databases	Backs up multiple databases
—help	Displays a complete list of options
-f or --force	Ignores MySQL errors

OPTION	DESCRIPTION
-h or --host	Specifies the server hostname for the MySQL server
-u or --user	Specifies the MySQL username
-p or --password	Specifies the password
-t or --no-create-info	Writes data only, no table structure

To use `mysqldump`, specify a database and a list of tables on the command line. If you do not specify tables, the entire database is included in the dump.

Example:
```
mysqldump -uuser -ppassword testdb address
>backup.sql
```

MYISAMCHK

The `myisamchk` utility checks MyISAM tables for errors and optionally attempts to repair any problems found. This utility works directly on the MySQL data files, and should be used while the server is not running or no users are accessing the tables being checked.

Example:
```
myisamchk -r /var/mysql/data/testdb/address
```

The following table describes some of the most useful command-line options for the `myisamchk` utility.

OPTION	DESCRIPTION
-e	Extended check: slow but more thorough
-m	Medium check: faster than extended
-F	Fast check: only checks improperly closed tables
-C	Checks only tables changed since the last check
-i	Displays information about the table while checking
-f	Automatically repairs the table if any errors are detected
-r	Recover: attempts to repair table and recover data
-o	Safe recover: uses a slower and safer recovery method
-q	Quick recover: checks index files only
-w	Waits until no clients are locking the table before checking

WHAT'S ON THE CD-ROM

The CD-ROM included in this book contains many useful files and programs. Before installing any of the programs on the disc, make sure that you do not already have a newer version of the program already installed on your computer. For information on installing different versions of the same program, contact the program's manufacturer. For the latest and greatest information, please refer to the ReadMe file located at the root level of the CD-ROM.

SYSTEM REQUIREMENTS

To use the contents of the CD-ROM, your computer must have the following hardware and software:

- A PC with a Pentium or faster processor
- Microsoft Windows 95, 98, ME, NT, 2000, or XP; or Linux or UNIX. MySQL can also be compiled on other systems, such as Mac OSX.
- At least 128MB of physical RAM installed on your computer
- A double-speed (8x) or faster CD-ROM drive
- A monitor capable of displaying at least 256 colors or grayscale
- A network card

AUTHOR'S SOURCE CODE

These files include SQL files you can use to create the example tables used throughout the book as well as the sample PHP and Perl code from Chapters 12 and 13. You can browse the files directly from the CD-ROM, or you can copy them to your hard drive and use them as the basis for your own projects. To find the files on the CD-ROM, open the \Samples folder on the CD-ROM drive.

To import an SQL file, use the MySQL monitor from the command line and specify the database:

```
mysql testdb <file.sql
```

You must create the testdb database, as described in Chapter 1, before importing any files. Chapter 1 also includes more information about the MySQL monitor. See Chapter 8 for more information about importing and exporting files.

ACROBAT VERSION

The CD-ROM contains an e-version of this book that you can view and search using Adobe Acrobat Reader. You can also use the hyperlinks provided in the text to access all the Web pages and Internet references in the book. You cannot print the pages or copy text from the Acrobat files. The CD-ROM includes a freeware version of Adobe Acrobat Reader.

INSTALLING AND USING THE SOFTWARE

For your convenience, the software titles appearing on the CD-ROM are listed alphabetically.

Acrobat Reader
For Windows 95/98/NT/2000 and Linux. Freeware.

Adobe Acrobat Reader allows you to view the online version of this book. For more information on using Acrobat Reader, see the section "Using the E-Version of this Book" in this appendix. For more information about Acrobat Reader and Adobe Systems, see www.adobe.com.

Apache
For Windows and UNIX. Open source.

Apache is a Web server from the Apache Software Foundation. It is used throughout the world on a large number of Web sites. It supports PHP and Perl as modules and integrates well with MySQL.

You can download the latest version of Apache as well as view information, such as troubleshooting tips and FAQs, at the www.apache.org Web site.

MySQL
For Windows and UNIX. GNU version.

MySQL is a fast and reliable database management system. It includes powerful features that allow you to add, access, and process information stored in databases. The latest version of MySQL also features full-text searching and indexing capabilities.

MySQL is free for non-commercial use. For more information about MySQL or to download server or client software, visit the www.mysql.com Web site.

Perl
For Windows and UNIX. Open source.

Perl is a powerful scripting language with features that make it ideal for text processing and as a language for dynamic Web pages. Perl is a popular language for creating database applications and database-driven Web sites with MySQL.

Perl is open source software. For more information about Perl or to download source code or binary distributions, visit the www.perl.org Web site.

Perl DBI and DBD: MySQL
For Windows and UNIX. GNU version.

The DBI is a programmatic interface that allows the Perl language to connect to a variety of database management systems, including MySQL. It supports DBDs, or database drivers, for each database system. The MySQL DBD is also included on the CD-ROM.

The DBI and the MySQL DBD are open source software. For more information on the DBI or to download the latest version, visit the Web site at http://dbi.perl.org.

PHP
For Windows and UNIX. Open source.

PHP is a powerful server-side scripting language that integrates with HTML. You must have PHP installed on your Web server in order to create and view PHP Web pages.

PHP is free, open source software. For more information about PHP or to download the latest version, visit the www.php.net Web site.

phpMyAdmin
For Windows and UNIX. GNU version.

phpMyAdmin administers the MySQL database management system on the Web. It allows you to create and edit databases and tables, execute SQL statements, and administer multiple databases and servers.

TROUBLESHOOTING
The programs on the CD-ROM should work on computers with the minimum of system requirements. However, some programs may not work properly.

The two most likely problems for the programs not working properly include not having enough memory (RAM) for the programs you want to use, or having other programs running that affect the installation or running of a program. If you receive error messages such as Not enough memory or Setup cannot continue, try one or more of the methods below and then try using the software again:

- Turn off any anti-virus software
- Close all running programs
- In Windows, close the CD-ROM interface and run demos or installations directly from Windows Explorer
- Have your local computer store add more RAM to your computer

If you still have trouble installing the items from the CD-ROM, call the Wiley Customer Service phone number: 800-762-2974 (outside the U.S.: 317-572-3994). You can also contact Wiley Customer Service by e-mail at techsupdum@wiley.com.

USING THE E-VERSION OF THIS BOOK

You can view *MySQL: Your visual blueprint to open source database management* on your screen using the CD-ROM included at the back of this book. The CD-ROM allows you to search the contents of each chapter of the book for a specific word or phrase. The CD-ROM also provides a convenient way of keeping the book handy while traveling.

You must install Adobe Acrobat Reader on your computer before you can view the book on the CD-ROM. The CD-ROM includes this program for your convenience. Acrobat Reader allows you to view Portable Document Format (PDF) files, which can display books and magazines on your screen exactly as they appear in printed form.

Acrobat Reader is a popular and useful program. There are many files available on the Web that are designed to be viewed using Acrobat Reader. Look for files with the .pdf extension. For more information about Acrobat Reader, visit the Web site at www.adobe.com/products/acrobat/reader.html.

To view the contents of the book using Acrobat Reader, display the main menu on the CD-ROM. Click the eBook link, select the section of the book you want to view, and then click Install.

USING THE E-VERSION OF THIS BOOK

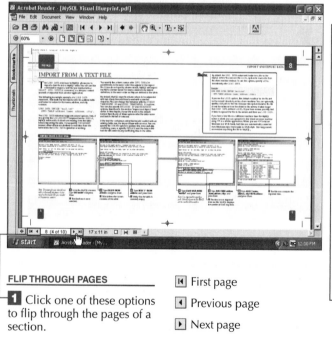

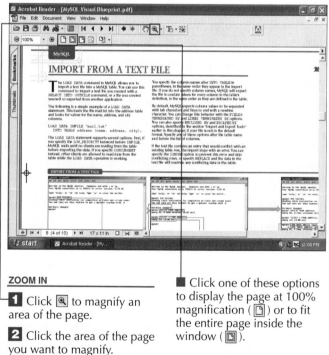

FLIP THROUGH PAGES

1 Click one of these options to flip through the pages of a section.

|◄| First page

|◄| Previous page

|►| Next page

|►| Last page

ZOOM IN

1 Click 🔍 to magnify an area of the page.

2 Click the area of the page you want to magnify.

■ Click one of these options to display the page at 100% magnification (🔲) or to fit the entire page inside the window (🔲).

Extra

To install Acrobat Reader, insert the CD-ROM into a drive. In the screen that appears, click Software. Click Acrobat Reader and then follow the instructions on your screen to install the program.

You can make searching the book more convenient by copying the PDF files to your computer. To do this, display the contents of the CD-ROM and then copy the Book folder from the CD-ROM to your hard drive. This allows you to easily access the contents of the book at any time.

When you search for text, the text that Acrobat Reader highlights may be difficult to read. To make highlighted text easier to read, turn off the font smoothing capabilities of Acrobat Reader. In the Acrobat Reader window, click Edit ➪ Preferences. Click Display at the left side of the Preferences dialog box. In the Smoothing area, click Smooth Text (☐ changes to ✔), and then click OK.

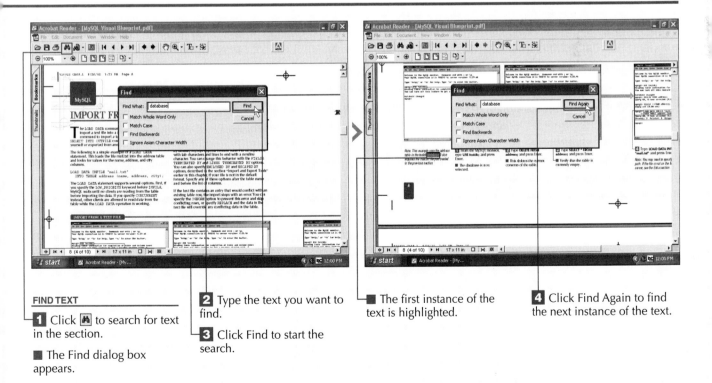

FIND TEXT

1 Click 🔍 to search for text in the section.

■ The Find dialog box appears.

2 Type the text you want to find.

3 Click Find to start the search.

■ The first instance of the text is highlighted.

4 Click Find Again to find the next instance of the text.

APPENDIX

WILEY PUBLISHING, INC.
END-USER LICENSE AGREEMENT

READ THIS. You should carefully read these terms and conditions before opening the software packet(s) included with *MySQL: Your visual blueprint to open source database management* ("Book"). This is a license agreement ("Agreement") between you and Wiley Publishing, Inc. ("WPI"). By opening the accompanying software packet(s), you acknowledge that you have read and accept the following terms and conditions. If you do not agree and do not want to be bound by such terms and conditions, promptly return the Book and the unopened software packet(s) to the place you obtained them for a full refund.

1.   License Grant.

WPI grants to you (either an individual or entity) a nonexclusive license to use one copy of the enclosed software program(s) (collectively, the "Software") solely for your own personal or business purposes on a single computer (whether a standard computer or a workstation component of a multi-user network). The Software is in use on a computer when it is loaded into temporary memory (RAM) or installed into permanent memory (hard disk, CD-ROM, or other storage device). WPI reserves all rights not expressly granted herein.

2.   Ownership.

WPI is the owner of all right, title, and interest, including copyright, in and to the compilation of the Software recorded on the disk(s) or CD-ROM "Software Media." Copyright to the individual programs recorded on the Software Media is owned by the author or other authorized copyright owner of each program. Ownership of the Software and all proprietary rights relating thereto remain with WPI and its licensers.

3.   Restrictions On Use and Transfer.

(a)   You may only (i) make one copy of the Software for backup or archival purposes, or (ii) transfer the Software to a single hard disk, provided that you keep the original for backup or archival purposes. You may not (i) rent or lease the Software, (ii) copy or reproduce the Software through a LAN or other network system or through any computer subscriber system or bulletin-board system, or (iii) modify, adapt, or create derivative works based on the Software.

(b)   You may not reverse engineer, decompile, or disassemble the Software. You may transfer the Software and user documentation on a permanent basis, provided that the transferee agrees to accept the terms and conditions of this Agreement and you retain no copies. If the Software is an update or has been updated, any transfer must include the most recent update and all prior versions.

4.   Restrictions on Use of Individual Programs.

You must follow the individual requirements and restrictions detailed for each individual program in Appendix C of this Book. These limitations are also contained in the individual license agreements recorded on the Software Media. These limitations may include a requirement that after using the program for a specified period of time, the user must pay a registration fee or discontinue use. By opening the Software packet(s), you will be agreeing to abide by the licenses and restrictions for these individual programs that are detailed in Appendix C and on the Software Media. None of the material on this Software Media or listed in this Book may ever be redistributed, in original or modified form, for commercial purposes.

5.   Limited Warranty.

(a)   WPI warrants that the Software and Software Media are free from defects in materials and workmanship under normal use for a period of sixty (60) days from the date of purchase of this Book. If WPI receives notification within the warranty period of defects in materials or workmanship, WPI will replace the defective Software Media.

(b) WPI AND THE AUTHOR OF THE BOOK DISCLAIM ALL OTHER WARRANTIES, EXPRESS OR IMPLIED, INCLUDING WITHOUT LIMITATION IMPLIED WARRANTIES OF MERCHANTABILITY AND FITNESS FOR A PARTICULAR PURPOSE, WITH RESPECT TO THE SOFTWARE, THE PROGRAMS, THE SOURCE CODE CONTAINED THEREIN, AND/OR THE TECHNIQUES DESCRIBED IN THIS BOOK. WPI DOES NOT WARRANT THAT THE FUNCTIONS CONTAINED IN THE SOFTWARE WILL MEET YOUR REQUIREMENTS OR THAT THE OPERATION OF THE SOFTWARE WILL BE ERROR FREE.

(c) This limited warranty gives you specific legal rights, and you may have other rights that vary from jurisdiction to jurisdiction.

6. Remedies.

(a) WPI's entire liability and your exclusive remedy for defects in materials and workmanship shall be limited to replacement of the Software Media, which may be returned to WPI with a copy of your receipt at the following address: Software Media Fulfillment Department, Attn.: *MySQL: Your visual blueprint to open source database management*, Wiley Publishing, Inc., 10475 Crosspoint Blvd., Indianapolis, IN 46256, or call 1-800-762-2974. Please allow four to six weeks for delivery. This Limited Warranty is void if failure of the Software Media has resulted from accident, abuse, or misapplication. Any replacement Software Media will be warranted for the remainder of the original warranty period or thirty (30) days, whichever is longer.

(b) In no event shall WPI or the author be liable for any damages whatsoever (including without limitation damages for loss of business profits, business interruption, loss of business information, or any other pecuniary loss) arising from the use of or inability to use the Book or the Software, even if WPI has been advised of the possibility of such damages.

(c) Because some jurisdictions do not allow the exclusion or limitation of liability for consequential or incidental damages, the above limitation or exclusion may not apply to you.

7. U.S. Government Restricted Rights.

Use, duplication, or disclosure of the Software for or on behalf of the United States of America, its agencies and/or instrumentalities "U.S. Government" is subject to restrictions as stated in paragraph (c)(1)(ii) of the Rights in Technical Data and Computer Software clause of DFARS 252.227-7013, or subparagraphs (c) (1) and (2) of the Commercial Computer Software - Restricted Rights clause at FAR 52.227-19, and in similar clauses in the NASA FAR supplement, as applicable.

8. General.

This Agreement constitutes the entire understanding of the parties and revokes and supersedes all prior agreements, oral or written, between them and may not be modified or amended except in a writing signed by both parties hereto that specifically refers to this Agreement. This Agreement shall take precedence over any other documents that may be in conflict herewith. If any one or more provisions contained in this Agreement are held by any court or tribunal to be invalid, illegal, or otherwise unenforceable, each and every other provision shall remain in full force and effect.

GNU GENERAL PUBLIC LICENSE

Version 2, June 1991

Copyright © 1989, 1991 Free Software Foundation, Inc.

59 Temple Place - Suite 330, Boston, MA 02111-1307, USA

Everyone is permitted to copy and distribute verbatim copies of this license document, but changing it is not allowed.

PREAMBLE

The licenses for most software are designed to take away your freedom to share and change it. By contrast, the GNU General Public License is intended to guarantee your freedom to share and change free software—to make sure the software is free for all its users. This General Public License applies to most of the Free Software Foundation's software and to any other program whose authors commit to using it. (Some other Free Software Foundation software is covered by the GNU Library General Public License instead.) You can apply it to your programs, too.

When we speak of free software, we are referring to freedom, not price. Our General Public Licenses are designed to make sure that you have the freedom to distribute copies of free software (and charge for this service if you wish), that you receive source code or can get it if you want it, that you can change the software or use pieces of it in new free programs; and that you know you can do these things.

To protect your rights, we need to make restrictions that forbid anyone to deny you these rights or to ask you to surrender the rights. These restrictions translate to certain responsibilities for you if you distribute copies of the software, or if you modify it.

For example, if you distribute copies of such a program, whether gratis or for a fee, you must give the recipients all the rights that you have. You must make sure that they, too, receive or can get the source code. And you must show them these terms so they know their rights.

We protect your rights with two steps: (1) copyright the software, and (2) offer you this license which gives you legal permission to copy, distribute and/or modify the software.

Also, for each author's protection and ours, we want to make certain that everyone understands that there is no warranty for this free software. If the software is modified by someone else and passed on, we want its recipients to know that what they have is not the original, so that any problems introduced by others will not reflect on the original authors' reputations.

Finally, any free program is threatened constantly by software patents. We wish to avoid the danger that redistributors of a free program will individually obtain patent licenses, in effect making the program proprietary. To prevent this, we have made it clear that any patent must be licensed for everyone's free use or not licensed at all.

The precise terms and conditions for copying, distribution, and modification follow.

TERMS AND CONDITIONS FOR COPYING, DISTRIBUTION AND MODIFICATION

0. This License applies to any program or other work which contains a notice placed by the copyright holder saying it may be distributed under the terms of this General Public License. The "Program", below, refers to any such program or work, and a "work based on the Program" means either the Program or any derivative work under copyright law: that is to say, a work containing the Program or a portion of it, either verbatim or with modifications and/or translated into another language. (Hereinafter, translation is included without limitation in the term "modification".) Each licensee is addressed as "you".

    Activities other than copying, distribution and modification are not covered by this License; they are outside its scope. The act of running the Program is not restricted, and the output from the Program is covered only if its contents constitute a work based on the Program (independent of having been made by running the Program). Whether that is true depends on what the Program does.

1. You may copy and distribute verbatim copies of the Program's source code as you receive it, in any medium, provided that you conspicuously and appropriately publish on each copy an appropriate copyright notice and disclaimer of warranty; keep intact all the notices that refer to this License and to the absence of any warranty; and give any other recipients of the Program a copy of this License along with the Program.

    You may charge a fee for the physical act of transferring a copy, and you may at your option offer warranty protection in exchange for a fee.

2. You may modify your copy or copies of the Program or any portion of it, thus forming a work based on the Program, and copy and distribute such modifications or work under the terms of Section 1 above, provided that you also meet all of these conditions:

    a) You must cause the modified files to carry prominent notices stating that you changed the files and the date of any change.

    b) You must cause any work that you distribute or publish, that in whole or in part contains or is derived from the Program or any part thereof, to be licensed as a whole at no charge to all third parties under the terms of this License.

    c) If the modified program normally reads commands interactively when run, you must cause it, when started running for such interactive use in the most ordinary way, to print or display an announcement including an appropriate copyright notice and a notice that there is no warranty (or else, saying that you provide a warranty) and that users may redistribute the program under these conditions, and telling the user how to view a copy of this License. (Exception: if the Program itself is interactive but does not normally print such an announcement, your work based on the Program is not required to print an announcement.)

    These requirements apply to the modified work as a whole. If identifiable sections of that work are not derived from the Program, and can be reasonably considered independent and separate works in themselves, then this License, and its terms, do not apply to those sections when you distribute them as separate works. But when you distribute the same sections as part of a whole which is a work based on the Program, the distribution of the whole must be on the terms of this License, whose permissions for other licensees extend to the entire whole, and thus to each and every part regardless of who wrote it.

    Thus, it is not the intent of this section to claim rights or contest your rights to work written entirely by you; rather, the intent is to exercise the right to control the distribution of derivative or collective works based on the Program.

    In addition, mere aggregation of another work not based on the Program with the Program (or with a work based on the Program) on a volume of a storage or distribution medium does not bring the other work under the scope of this License.

3. You may copy and distribute the Program (or a work based on it, under Section 2) in object code or executable form under the terms of Sections 1 and 2 above provided that you also do one of the following:

    a) Accompany it with the complete corresponding machine-readable source code, which must be distributed under the terms of Sections 1 and 2 above on a medium customarily used for software interchange; or,

    b) Accompany it with a written offer, valid for at least three years, to give any third party, for a charge no more than your cost of physically performing source distribution, a complete machine-readable copy of the corresponding source code, to be distributed under the terms of Sections 1 and 2 above on a medium customarily used for software interchange; or,

    c) Accompany it with the information you received as to the offer to distribute corresponding source code. (This alternative is allowed only for noncommercial distribution and only if you received the program in object code or executable form with such an offer, in accord with Subsection b above.)

    The source code for a work means the preferred form of the work for making modifications to it. For an executable work, complete source code means all the source code for all modules it contains, plus any associated interface definition files, plus the scripts used to control compilation and installation of the executable. However, as a special exception, the source code distributed need not include anything that is normally distributed (in either source or binary form) with the major components (compiler, kernel, and so on) of the operating system on which the executable runs, unless that component itself accompanies the executable.

    If distribution of executable or object code is made by offering access to copy from a designated place, then offering equivalent access to copy the source code from the same place counts as distribution of the source code, even though third parties are not compelled to copy the source along with the object code.

4. You may not copy, modify, sublicense, or distribute the Program except as expressly provided under this License. Any attempt otherwise to copy, modify, sublicense or distribute the Program is void, and will automatically terminate your rights under this License. However, parties who have received copies, or rights, from you under this License will not have their licenses terminated so long as such parties remain in full compliance.

5. You are not required to accept this License, since you have not signed it. However, nothing else grants you permission to modify or distribute the Program or its derivative works. These actions are prohibited by law if you do not accept this License. Therefore, by modifying or distributing the Program (or any work based on the Program), you indicate your acceptance of this License to do so, and all its terms and conditions for copying, distributing or modifying the Program or works based on it.

6. Each time you redistribute the Program (or any work based on the Program), the recipient automatically receives a license from the original licensor to copy, distribute or modify the Program subject to these terms and conditions. You may not impose any further restrictions on the recipients' exercise of the rights granted herein. You are not responsible for enforcing compliance by third parties to this License.

7. If, as a consequence of a court judgment or allegation of patent infringement or for any other reason (not limited to patent issues), conditions are imposed on you (whether by court order, agreement or otherwise) that contradict the conditions of this License, they do not excuse you from the conditions of this License. If you cannot distribute so as to satisfy simultaneously your obligations under this License and any other pertinent obligations, then as a consequence you may not distribute the Program at all. For example, if a patent license would not permit royalty-free redistribution of the Program by all those who receive copies directly or indirectly through you, then the only way you could satisfy both it and this License would be to refrain entirely from distribution of the Program.

If any portion of this section is held invalid or unenforceable under any particular circumstance, the balance of the section is intended to apply and the section as a whole is intended to apply in other circumstances.

It is not the purpose of this section to induce you to infringe any patents or other property right claims or to contest validity of any such claims; this section has the sole purpose of protecting the integrity of the free software distribution system, which is implemented by public license practices. Many people have made generous contributions to the wide range of software distributed through that system in reliance on consistent application of that system; it is up to the author/donor to decide if he or she is willing to distribute software through any other system and a licensee cannot impose that choice.

This section is intended to make thoroughly clear what is believed to be a consequence of the rest of this License.

8. If the distribution and/or use of the Program is restricted in certain countries either by patents or by copyrighted interfaces, the original copyright holder who places the Program under this License may add an explicit geographical distribution limitation excluding those countries, so that distribution is permitted only in or among countries not thus excluded. In such case, this License incorporates the limitation as if written in the body of this License.

9. The Free Software Foundation may publish revised and/or new versions of the General Public License from time to time. Such new versions will be similar in spirit to the present version, but may differ in detail to address new problems or concerns.

Each version is given a distinguishing version number. If the Program specifies a version number of this License which applies to it and "any later version", you have the option of following the terms and conditions either of that version or of any later version published by the Free Software Foundation. If the Program does not specify a version number of this License, you may choose any version ever published by the Free Software Foundation.

10. If you wish to incorporate parts of the Program into other free programs whose distribution conditions are different, write to the author to ask for permission. For software which is copyrighted by the Free Software Foundation, write to the Free Software Foundation; we sometimes make exceptions for this. Our decision will be guided by the two goals of preserving the free status of all derivatives of our free software and of promoting the sharing and reuse of software generally.

NO WARRANTY

11. BECAUSE THE PROGRAM IS LICENSED FREE OF CHARGE, THERE IS NO WARRANTY FOR THE PROGRAM, TO THE EXTENT PERMITTED BY APPLICABLE LAW. EXCEPT WHEN OTHERWISE STATED IN WRITING THE COPYRIGHT HOLDERS AND/OR OTHER PARTIES PROVIDE THE PROGRAM "AS IS" WITHOUT WARRANTY OF ANY KIND, EITHER EXPRESSED OR IMPLIED, INCLUDING, BUT NOT LIMITED TO, THE IMPLIED WARRANTIES OF MERCHANTABILITY AND FITNESS FOR A PARTICULAR PURPOSE. THE ENTIRE RISK AS TO THE QUALITY AND PERFORMANCE OF THE PROGRAM IS WITH YOU. SHOULD THE PROGRAM PROVE DEFECTIVE, YOU ASSUME THE COST OF ALL NECESSARY SERVICING, REPAIR OR CORRECTION.

12. IN NO EVENT UNLESS REQUIRED BY APPLICABLE LAW OR AGREED TO IN WRITING WILL ANY COPYRIGHT HOLDER, OR ANY OTHER PARTY WHO MAY MODIFY AND/OR REDISTRIBUTE THE PROGRAM AS PERMITTED ABOVE, BE LIABLE TO YOU FOR DAMAGES, INCLUDING ANY GENERAL, SPECIAL, INCIDENTAL OR CONSEQUENTIAL DAMAGES ARISING OUT OF THE USE OR INABILITY TO USE THE PROGRAM (INCLUDING BUT NOT LIMITED TO LOSS OF DATA OR DATA BEING RENDERED INACCURATE OR LOSSES SUSTAINED BY YOU OR THIRD PARTIES OR A FAILURE OF THE PROGRAM TO OPERATE WITH ANY OTHER PROGRAMS), EVEN IF SUCH HOLDER OR OTHER PARTY HAS BEEN ADVISED OF THE POSSIBILITY OF SUCH DAMAGES.

END OF TERMS AND CONDITIONS

INDEX

Symbols

A

B

C

MYSQL:
Your visual blueprint to open
source database management

MYSQL:
Your visual blueprint to open
source database management

INDEX

MYSQL:
Your visual blueprint to open
source database management

MYSQL:
Your visual blueprint to open
source database management

INDEX

MYSQL:
Your visual blueprint to open
source database management

INDEX